St. Petersburg
and Moscow

St. Petersburg and Moscow

Tsarist and Soviet Foreign Policy, 1814-1974

Barbara Jelavich

Indiana University Press

BLOOMINGTON   LONDON

Published in Canada by Fitzhenry & Whiteside Limited, Don Mills, Ontario

Manufactured in the United States of America

Library of Congress Cataloging in Publication Data
Jelavich, Barbara (Brightfield)
   St. Petersburg and Moscow: tsarist and Soviet foreign policy, 1814-1974.

   Bibliography: p. 458
   1. Russia—Foreign relations—History. I. Title.
DK66.J4   327.47   73-16537
ISBN 0-253-35050-6
ISBN 0-253-35051-4 (pbk.)

For Charles

Contents

vii

Part II: The Soviet Union

꒞꒞꒞꒞꒞

Maps

ᒋᒋᒋᒋᒋᒋ

Preface

This book presents a survey of tsarist and Soviet foreign policy from the Congress of Vienna, 1814, to 1974. The first section, covering the years through the First World War, was originally issued under the title of *A Century of Russian Foreign Policy, 1814–1914* (J. B. Lippincott Co., 1964). The second part, on the Soviet period, has not been published previously.

In the transcription of Russian names the spelling most familiar in the west has, in general, been adopted. In most cases this form is equivalent to a simple transliteration of the Cyrillic according to the Library of Congress system. First names for all nationalities have in general been anglicized. Although in the nineteenth century the Russian calendar (the Julian) ran twelve days behind that of the west, only the Gregorian, or new style, form will be given for the tsarist period. In the twentieth century the difference increases to thirteen. In January, 1918 the Bolshevik government adopted the Gregorian calendar.

The name of the tsarist capital, St. Petersburg, was changed to Petrograd in 1914 and to Leningrad in 1924. Moscow replaced this city as the capital in 1918. Other changes of place names have been indicated in the text.

The author wishes to express her great appreciation for the assistance which she has received from friends and colleagues in the preparation of this manuscript. The first part, on tsarist Russia, was read by Professors Robert F. Byrnes and John M. Thompson of Indiana University, Professor Peter Scheibert of the University of Marburg and Professor Richard A. Pierce of Queens College, who checked the material on Central Asia. The Soviet section was commented upon by Professor Donald W. Treadgold, University of Washington, Professor Adam B. Ulam, Harvard University, Professor Teddy J. Uldricks, University of California at Riverside; and by Professors Robert W. Ferrell and Alexander Rabinowitch, and by Sara Tucker, Michael Shaw, and Jean and Paul Michelson, all of Indiana University. Professor Ssu Yu Teng of Indiana University read the Far Eastern sections for both the tsarist and Soviet periods; Professor Fritz T. Epstein, Indiana University, made most helpful comments on the entire manuscript. The excellent maps on the Soviet section were prepared by John M. Hollingsworth, Indiana University staff cartographer.

As in the case of previous publications, this study is in fact the product of joint research and writing which the author has done with her husband, Charles Jelavich, to whom this book is dedicated. The preparation of the manuscript was also immensely aided by the assistance of Mark and Peter Jelavich, who have also read and commented upon both sections.

St. Petersburg
and Moscow

Part I

Tsarist Russia

ALEXANDER I

NICHOLAS I

ALEXANDER II

ALEXANDER III

NICHOLAS II

I

The Eighteenth Century Background

Although most of the first part of this study is devoted to the politics of the nineteenth century, a brief account of the developments of the previous period is necessary, chiefly because the major task of Russian diplomacy after 1815 was the protection of the empire whose construction was completed during the earlier years. With the conclusion of the Vienna treaties the Russian boundaries reached their maximum extension in the west, the culmination of three centuries of almost constant expansion. The eighteenth century was also of particular significance since it brought Russia into the European state system and thereafter linked her history primarily with that of the west. During that century the design for much of Russian policy for the succeeding decades was set, and diplomatic patterns were formed that were to remain constant until the outbreak of the First World War.

At the end of the seventeenth century, Europe, organized into a system of independent states usually under the rule of an absolute monarch, had as its guiding principle in international relations the idea of the balance of power, a concept designed to prevent one nation from dominating the continent. After the Thirty Years' War, which wrought great devastation in central Europe, France was clearly the strongest power and the state that threatened to achieve continental hegemony. In 1643 one of the most remarkable of European monarchs, Louis XIV, came to the throne of France and adopted a frankly expansionist program, aiming at the acquisition of France's "natural frontiers." The diplomatic pattern for western Europe was thereafter largely determined by the moves of the French king and the efforts made to block them. All of the other major powers of the age, Britain, Spain, the Habsburg Empire, the Ottoman Empire, Poland, Sweden, and Holland, were influenced by French activity.

The first area under attack from France was that of the Spanish Netherlands. Spain under the rule of a weak and mentally deficient monarch held but a shadow of her former glory. Although in possession of a great empire in America and of lands in Italy that gave her domination over that peninsula, the nation as a whole was in a process of economic and political decay. In contrast, Holland, the second state under pressure from France, presented a glowing picture of wealth and prosperity. This former Spanish possession had raised itself to a height of mercantile and commercial achievement despite the obvious fact that the country itself was too weak to be able to withstand the attack of a major power. Across the channel, Britain, the major beneficiary of the balance of power principle, like Holland, had built its position on sea power as well as on widespread commercial and colonial ventures. At first primarily concerned with Dutch competition, Britain entered the ranks against France when the victories of Louis XIV threatened to result in a tremendous increase in French power.

In central Europe the traditional rival of the French Bourbon kings, the Habsburg Empire, found itself in a difficult strategic position, which, when combined with its internal divisions, limited its power. Pressed on the one side by France and by problems arising from the Habsburg position in Italy, Spain, and the Germanies, this state was also threatened on its other front by the Ottoman Empire. After 1355, when the first conquests on the European continent were made, this Moslem power had successfully extended its control over the Balkans and threatened to expand into central Europe. The end of the seventeenth century brought the last great attack; in 1683 the Ottoman armies again approached the gates of Vienna. With their failure to capture this city, the force of Turkish power thereafter waned. In 1699, in the Treaty of Karlowitz, the Habsburg Monarchy made the first victorious peace with Turkey and the menace to Europe was ended. Thereafter the situation reversed itself; the Christian powers now turned to the conquest of Turkish territories.

Despite its successes against the Turks, the Habsburg state as a power complex was not equivalent to France. By 1720 Austria had also gained the former Spanish territories of Naples, Sicily, and Milan and thereby the control of Italy. The addition of new lands did not, however, contribute to Habsburg strength. The basic problem of the empire remained what it was to be until its collapse in 1918—that of how to organize and administer as an effective unit lands of varying national composition, historical development, and past tradition. Success in foreign relations in the next two centuries was to lie more in the hands of those with strong national centers, such as France, Britain, and even Russia, and to be denied to loosely organized empires such as Austria and Turkey.

Habsburg influence also remained strong in Germany, although this land was little more than a geographic expression. Economically devastated by the Thirty Years' War and politically fragmented into over 300 competitive entities, this area could play no part as a unit in international politics. Certain individual states, nevertheless, such as Prussia, Saxony, and Bavaria, did compete for great power status and for a stronger position in relation to their other German rivals.

To the ranks of the major powers two other states, Poland and Sweden, must also be added. The fate of the first, Poland, who held an area the size of France, will be discussed in detail in the following pages. Sweden, whose conflict with Russia in the Great Northern War dominated the reign of Peter the Great, had, under the leadership of the able house of Vasa, expanded in the Baltic region until it in fact controlled that sea. Swedish domination was naturally contested by the powers with Baltic interests—the independent kingdom of Denmark (at this time united with Norway), Prussia, and Russia, who were naturally interested in limiting or breaking Swedish power.

The diplomatic pattern confronting Russia at the accession of Peter the Great was, therefore, one dominated by France and Louis XIV. It must also be noted that France traditionally had followed the policy of the eastern barrier in central Europe. In an effort to outflank the Habsburgs she had maintained close relationships with Sweden, Poland, and Turkey. This combination was also to prove useful against Russia. Because her attention was focused primarily upon these states, Russia thus usually found herself in the opposite camp to France. She did not, however, directly participate in the great allied campaigns against Louis XIV that ended in his defeat and in the settlement of Utrecht of 1713.

PETER THE GREAT

The diplomatic history of Russia as a European great power commences with the reign of Peter the Great in 1682. Prior to that date the Russian rulers had devoted their energies to the great task of re-assembling the Russian lands after the Mongol conquest, establishing a state that could protect itself against renewed foreign invasion, and extending their dominion across Siberia to the Pacific. Peter the Great not only brought Russia into the politics of western Europe, in the manner to be discussed on the following pages, but he also laid the lines of Russian foreign policy

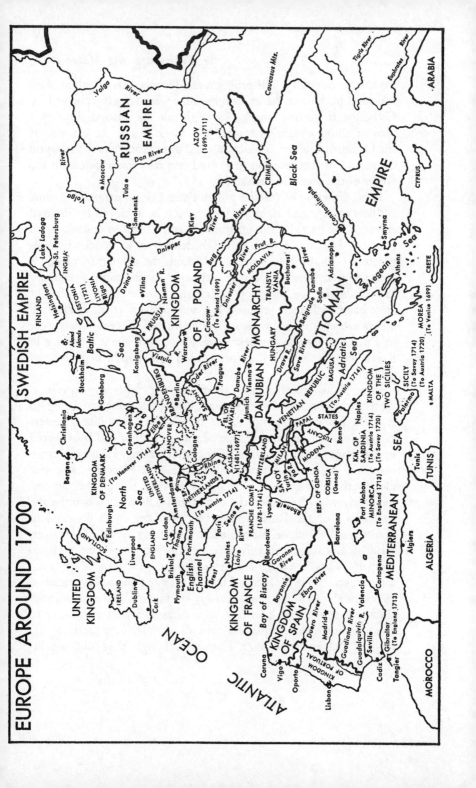

EUROPE AROUND 1700

for the next century. His program and his methods of action were followed by his successors, and his aims were largely achieved by Catherine II by the 1790's. His reign saw the inauguration of a plan of active expansion toward the Black Sea at the expense of the Ottoman Empire, of conquest and annexation along the Baltic coast, and of intervention in Poland and to a lesser extent in the affairs of the small German states.

In his direction of foreign policy Peter I demonstrated the same ruthless energy and ambition with which he achieved his internal reforms. He had also the imagination and daring to embark upon courses of action which, although dangerous in conception, ultimately brought great rewards. Without the driving force of his leadership, it is probable that although Russia might inevitably have followed the direction which she now took, it would not have been with such precipitation and, perhaps as far as external affairs are concerned, with such a degree of success. The career of Peter I is perhaps the best demonstration of the importance in Russia of the tsar in the formulation and conduct of foreign policy.

Peter I inaugurated his career in 1695 with an expedition directed against the khan of the Crimea, his intention being to take the Black Sea port of Azov. In this, his first military undertaking, he took personal charge of the operations and thus shared in the blame for the failure of the undertaking. However, from his initial defeat he learned valuable lessons. Since he now saw clearly the necessity of developing Russian sea power, he immediately embarked upon the construction of what was to be the forerunner of the Russian navy. A year later, with his crudely constructed ships, he succeeded in capturing Azov. Thereafter, with his attention primarily directed toward the seizing of lands from the Ottoman Empire, he devoted a great deal of personal attention to naval problems. He sent many of his subjects abroad to study shipbuilding, and in 1697 he himself visited European shipyards and docks. There he worked as a carpenter in order to become thoroughly acquainted with the details of the craft.

Peter's journeys through Europe, although they did not include France, the leading nation of western Europe, brought the tsar into close contact with the civilization of the west. What fascinated him in his travels was not so much the culture and refinements of European life as its technological superiority. Therefore he sought first to bring into Russia those aspects of western life that would contribute to the ultimate power of his state. The manners and customs, the frills and decorations of aristocratic life were also admired and desired, but the concentration remained on the elements that would eventually contribute to Russian military power.

Since his chief interest at this time lay in expansion southward, Peter I used his European trip to lay the groundwork for a campaign against the Turks in which he proposed to join with the two nations with similar interests, Austria and Venice. Although the alliance concluded with Austria in 1697 marks the beginning of Russo-Austrian collaboration in the Balkans against the Ottoman Empire, the Habsburg Monarchy at this time was not ready for ambitious undertakings. In 1698, at the Congress of Karlowitz, Russia joined with Austria, Poland, and Venice in negotiations with Turkey. This assembly gave Austria a great victory; Russia, who received only a two-year armistice, felt betrayed by her ally. In 1700 Peter I was able to conclude a further treaty with the Porte, providing for a thirty-year truce, the possession of the port of Azov, the right to keep a resident minister at Constantinople, and permission for the Orthodox to make pilgrimages to the Holy Places, which were under Ottoman control. Despite the fact that this agreement was not long kept, its provisions had a tremendous significance for the relations of the two countries, and they set a pattern for future treaties. The settlement with Turkey now permitted Peter to turn his attention northward toward the Baltic.

The Great Northern War, which commenced for Russia in 1700, dominated the entire period of Peter's reign and lasted for twenty-one years. None of the major participants, Russia, Saxony, or Denmark, anticipated such a protracted struggle when in 1698 they determined to attack Sweden. In fact, on the surface the situation appeared ideal for a joint assault. Although Sweden at the time ranked among the great powers and dominated the Baltic Sea, her position was steadily deteriorating. Moreover, she was ruled by a new king, Charles XII, who ascended the throne at the age of fifteen. In 1699 an alliance was concluded between the three Swedish opponents under the sponsorship and on the initiative of the Saxon ruler, Augustus II, who was also King of Poland. Since Peter I was still involved in hostilities with the Porte, Saxony and Denmark commenced the war alone. To the immense surprise of the allies, it soon became apparent that in the person of her king Sweden had a military genius of the first order. Even before Peter I had made peace with the Porte, Denmark had been defeated and forced to leave the war. The first Russian major engagement resulted in one of the most crushing defeats in Russian military history—that of the battle of Narva in November, 1700. Here a force of about 8,000 Swedish soldiers completely routed 35,000 Russians. The battle clearly showed Peter the poor quality of his army.

The disaster at Narva, however, forced Peter I to inaugurate a thoroughgoing program of military reform. He immediately embarked upon a complete reorganization of the army, and he sought in particular to improve the training methods and discipline of the soldiers and the quality of the armaments. He clearly recognized the danger that threatened Russia from a probable Swedish invasion; the question was whether his opponent would allow him time to prepare. Fortunately for the tsar, the rout of the Russian army at Narva had left Charles XII with little more than contempt for Russian power. Instead of following up his victory against Russia, he turned instead toward Saxony and for six years campaigned in Poland. Peter I thus won the necessary time to recover his strength and reorganize his armies. By 1701 he was able to begin action against the Swedish forces in the Baltic provinces. In 1703 he took the mouth of the Neva river where he began the construction of the city of St. Petersburg.

The chief field of battle in the meantime remained Poland. Here Augustus II was unable to withstand his brilliant opponent. In 1704 Charles XII chose a puppet ruler, Stanislaw Leszczynski, for the Polish throne. Although Peter despatched an army to his aid in 1705, the Saxon king was forced in the next year to make peace with Sweden, thereby renouncing both the Polish crown and the Russian alliance. With the status of Poland, Saxony, and Denmark now settled in his favor, Charles XII could turn to Russia. Peter I, without allies and still unprepared for a major war, sought to make peace by every means possible. Charles XII, however, in January, 1708 with a well-equipped and experienced army of around 46,000 crossed the Russian border and began to march toward Moscow.

To meet this attack by the technically superior Swedish forces, Peter I adopted the tactics that were to be repeated in 1812 and 1941 when once again Russia faced invasion by stronger armies —the scorched earth policy. Peter I withdrew his forces toward the interior of the country and avoided any direct encounter with the Swedish army that could result in the annihilation of his forces. He simultaneously destroyed along his line of retreat all supplies that could be used by the enemy. The Swedish armies had first embarked upon a direct route to Moscow; in September it was decided that they should march southward where supplies were believed more plentiful and that then they should attack Moscow from the southwest rather than from the west. Charles XII was hopeful of receiving aid from malcontent Ukrainian groups, particularly because he was assured of the support of the hetman, Mazeppa. The Swedish hopes were not fulfilled; the winter proved severe and sufficient supplies could not be procured from the hostile countryside. Charles XII also did not receive reinforcements from outside, and no great Ukrainian uprising assisted the Swedish invasion. The Ukrainians feared that a Swedish victory would bring not national freedom, but renewed Polish domination.

The ravages of a bitter winter, the failure to obtain sufficient provisions, and an ever-decreasing army provided the background for the Swedish defeat at the battle of Poltava in July, 1709. Even though the Russian victory was gained over an exhausted and greatly weakened opponent, Russia had nevertheless successfully met an invasion by one of the most formidable military powers of the day. Charles XII, accompanied by Mazeppa, fled to Turkish territory. Once in Constantinople and supported by the French diplomats stationed there, the Swedish king worked assiduously to involve the Porte in renewed hostilities against Russia.

In 1710 the Swedish endeavors met with success and the Ottoman Empire declared war on Russia. To meet this new threat Peter determined upon a campaign in the Balkans where he hoped to enlist the support of the governors (*hospodars*) of the Turkish-controlled principalities of Moldavia and Wallachia. The Russian government also issued an appeal to the subject Christians of the Ottoman Empire to rise and fight with Russia to throw off Moslem rule. Although these initial efforts met with no response, the issue of Russian interest in and Russian responsibility toward the Orthodox Balkan peoples had been raised. Russia had also found a weapon that could be used most effectively as a threat against the Porte, but one that inevitably aroused the suspicion and hostility of the other powers.

The failure of Peter to win the co-operation of the Wallachian *hospodar* despite the fact that his counterpart in Moldavia, Cantemir, did render assistance, contributed to the Russian defeat. In July, 1711 on the Prut river Peter I suffered the most crushing personal defeat of his career. His forces were surrounded, and he was forced to seek peace. In this seemingly desperate situation Peter was prepared to make great sacrifices, including even the abandonment of his Baltic conquests. The Porte, however, perhaps as a result of a judicious distribution of bribes, demanded only the surrender of Azov and the destruction of the Russian Black Sea fleet. Although these terms signified that Peter I abandoned all of the gains which he had made in his wars with Tur-

ACQUISITIONS OF PETER THE GREAT

key, they were nevertheless moderate under the circumstances.

The victory of Poltava had not only freed Russia from the Swedish threat, but it had also allowed the Russian allies, Denmark and Saxony, to re-enter the conflict. They were later joined by Prussia and Hanover. Augustus II was able to take back the Polish throne, and operations were launched against the Swedish positions in the Baltic. In 1714, after quarreling with his Turkish hosts, Charles XII returned to Sweden. Despite the relative weakness of the Swedish forces, the war continued, largely because a lack of co-operation between the allies precluded any decisive victories. In 1718 Charles XII was killed on the field of battle, and with the loss of her greatest military leader Sweden gave up any hope of regaining her former domination of the Baltic.

The long war between Sweden and Russia was ended with the Peace of Nystadt, which was signed in August, 1721. In this agreement Russia received extensive gains on the Baltic coast: Livonia, including Riga, Ingria and a part of Karelia. The new lands not only gave Russia ports on the Baltic Sea, providing far better communications with western Europe, but they also brought into the state a population that was to play a most significant role in the future history of Russia, particularly in the administration of foreign policy and in the army. The Baltic lands Russia now acquired were inhabited by a Lettish and Estonian population ruled over by a predominantly German nobility. The Baltic Germans, who came from an area more highly developed than Russia proper, entered in large numbers into state service and in the course of the next century they came to dominate the highest positions in the army, navy, and civil administration. The use made by the tsars of this element of their population, which was in general diligent and talented in administrative work, was a great advantage to the Russian autocracy. Russia had no great middle class from which to draw state servants and bureaucrats. The fact that the Baltic nobility was non-Russian made them more reliable servants of the monarch and mitigated the danger that they would join with their Russian counterparts to form a strong center of opposition to the central power.

FROM PETER TO CATHERINE

Between the death of Peter the Great in 1725 and the beginning of the reign of his true successor, Catherine the Great, Russia was ruled by six sovereigns of widely varying abilities. Although, as could be expected, Russian foreign relations in this period did not show the great successes of the years of Peter's rule, it is to be noted that Russia suffered no major losses despite the comparative weakness of her government. Following in the path set by Peter I the Russian government continued to remain intensely concerned with the international balance in Europe, and an active policy was pursued in regard to Swedish, Polish, and Turkish affairs. The Russian position in these years was most deeply and permanently influenced by the chief diplomatic event of the mid-century—the emergence of Prussia under Frederick the Great as a great power. The other major struggle of the time, the colonial rivalry between Britain and France, affected Russia only indirectly in that it could be assumed that these two powers would always be on opposite sides in any diplomatic or military conflict. Policy could thus not be based on alliance or co-operation with both at once. As a result of the French policy of the eastern barrier, that is of the diplomatic support of Sweden, Poland, and the Ottoman Empire, Russia was usually hostile to France and, because of increasing commercial ties, friendly to Britain. Poland, Sweden, and the Ottoman Empire remained the centers of Russian diplomatic activity.

Because of her unique internal conditions, Poland after the death of Peter became and remained little more than a pawn in the power conflict of her stronger neighbors, Russia and Austria against France. Well before the death of Augustus II in 1733 the rival states prepared for the event. France supported the candidacy of Stanislaw Leszczynski, who was a relative of the French monarch, Louis XV. When Leszczynski was elected by a majority of the Polish diet, a pro-Russian minority of the Polish nobility appealed to Russia, who replied by sending troops to assist her friends. Although France was thus deeply engaged in Polish affairs, she gave her partisans only token support in the form of men and money. The War of Polish Succession of 1733, in which Russia and Austria were allied against France, Spain, and Sardinia, was concluded in 1735 with an Austro-French armistice. Subsequently under the rule of the Austro-Russian candidate, Augustus III, Poland was under the practical domination of Russia.

The Russian expansionist policy toward the Ottoman Empire was continued by the launching of another campaign in 1736. Austria joined in 1737, but the entire undertaking was not successful. When this ally withdrew, Russia was forced to conclude the Peace of Belgrade in 1739. Here Russia received Azov, but on the condition that the fortifications be destroyed. Russian commercial shipping also continued to be excluded from the Black Sea. Shortly after the conclusion of this agreement, Russia became involved in another war with Sweden, who had never accepted as final the terms of the Treaty of Nystadt. Russian military victories forced Sweden in 1743 to accept a peace that gave the victor some Finnish territories and brought the Russian candidate, Adolphus Frederick of Holstein, to the Swedish throne. The Russo-Swedish War had meanwhile merged with the far more significant War of Austrian Succession.

In 1740 Frederick II of Prussia, in agreement with France and other German states, used the occasion of the succession of Maria Theresa to seize the Austrian province of Silesia. The acquisition of this territory was to enable Prussia henceforth to play a major diplomatic role in European history. Although in theory Russia was allied to Austria and Britain in this conflict, her participation in the actual hostilities remained limited. The first part of the duel over Silesia between Austria and Prussia was ended in 1748 by the Treaty of Aix-la-Chapelle, which confirmed the Prussian conquest. It was however to be only the prelude to a major diplomatic realignment of the great powers.

Until the middle of the century, as we have seen, the major Russian opponent had been France, who in turn had supported Sweden, Poland, and the Ottoman Empire against their eastern neighbor. Despite disagreements over Balkan policy, Russia had been in alliance with Austria and had also worked with Britain and Prussia. In general, Russia, Austria, and Prussia had together opposed France, the strongest single power on the continent. The increase in Prussian strength under Frederick II introduced a change in the European balance. Once this state was raised out of the category of the German states of second rank, such as Saxony and Bavaria, the question of her potential danger to Russia arose. The signing of the Treaty of Westminster in 1756 between Prussia and Britain also increased Russian apprehensions since it appeared to be in contradiction to the existing Russo-British agreements.

Meanwhile, in a complete reversal of their previous policies, Austria and France now patched up their quarrels and formed an alliance against Prussia. This diplomatic revolution was accomplished chiefly through the activities of the Austrian minister, Prince Kaunitz. Fearing the gathering coalition, Frederick in August, 1756 attacked Saxony and thereby precipitated the Seven Years' War. In December Russia joined Austria and France and sent her armies into central Europe. Although Frederick II, like Charles XII, was a military commander of the highest caliber, the Prussian state, like the Swedish, did not have the manpower or resources to support a war of indefinite duration against a coalition. Aid from Britain came chiefly in the form of subsidies, which, although valuable, could not overcome the great disadvantages under which Prussia fought. Although Frederick was assisted by the divisions among his allies, his final victory came largely from a stroke of luck. In 1762 Empress Elizabeth, who had favored strongly Russian participation in the war against Prussia, died and was succeeded by her nephew Peter III, who had a deep admiration for Frederick. He not only immediately ended the war against Prussia, but he also formed a military alliance with the former enemy. Russian troops now marched to the aid of Prussia, and Elizabeth's policy was nullified.

Despite the fears of the empress, the Prussian state that now emerged as a major power proved an element of strength and not a threat to Russia. Henceforth, until the breaking of the Reinsurance Treaty in 1890, Prussia (united Germany after 1871) became the most enduring and reliable of Russia's allies. Joined by dynastic ties in the succeeding years and with similar interests in Europe, Russia and Prussia co-operated closely in international affairs, in most instances to the advantage of both powers.

CATHERINE THE GREAT

The true heir to the tradition of Peter the Great was the wife of Peter III, who came to the throne in 1762 after the assassination of her husband. A German princess from the minor principality of Anhalt-Zerbst, Catherine II identified herself with the interests of her adopted country and extended the Russian boundaries as had few other rulers in Russian history. Like Peter I she favored a policy of close participation in the life and politics of western Europe. The first question she faced was that of the liquidation of the war with Prussia. Although she did not return to the policy of Elizabeth, she did recall the troops which had been sent to the aid of Frederick II. Subsequently, the two belligerents, Prussia and Austria, now both without effective allies, came to terms, and the Prussian conquest of Silesia was again confirmed.

With the conclusion of the Seven Years' War the situation in Europe was favorable for the commencement of an expansionist policy by Russia. France and Britain had been and were to be preoccupied with colonial problems. Austria, exhausted by the past years of warfare, had little desire to contribute to the aggrandizement of Russian power, but she could be tempted into territorial divisions. Prussia was about to become a Russian ally.

Catherine could thus without the fear of the formation of a hostile coalition turn her attention to the Polish and Turkish problems.

By the 1770's the internal political conditions in Poland had rendered that enormous state virtually helpless before her neighbors. The third largest in territory and the fourth in population among the nations of Europe, she had fallen into a state of internal anarchy and could no longer defend her independence against foreign intrusions. The power in the government lay in the hands of the landowning aristocracy, which formed about 8 per cent of the population. In a series of measures introduced over the preceding years this group had rendered the central organs of the administration powerless. In the Diet of Lublin in 1569 they succeeded in making the kingship elective; through the institution of the Liberum Veto, by which one vote could negate all action, the Polish diet was prevented from becoming an effective and constructive instrument of government. Because of the right of the nobility to form confederations, or armed associations, civil war and civil turmoil were legalized. Although these measures in theory guaranteed the liberties of one class, they in fact made the Polish state a free field for foreign intrigue and intervention.

Poland, as has been mentioned, was part of the French eastern barrier, which had as its objective, first, the confinement of the Habsburg Empire and, second, the walling off of Russia from Europe. French interests, therefore, called for the maintenance of a militarily strong Poland in alliance with France. Certainly, strong natural connections existed between the two states apart from their common interests in international relations. Both were predominantly Catholic and the high level of French civilization exerted a strong attraction over the Polish gentry. In contrast to France, Russia had no interest in the existence of a strong Poland, particularly in alliance with France, Sweden, or the Ottoman Empire. The entire area was vital for Russian defense. In the hands of a hostile power it could be, and had been, the launching point for an invasion. Moreover, the religious conflict in the state, particularly in the areas where a Catholic Polish nobility ruled over an Orthodox Russian peasantry, was continually a source of irritation and discord. Thus in her national interest and in her position as the defender of Orthodoxy, Russia had convincing reasons for her intervention in Polish internal affairs. Throughout the eighteenth century the Russian government kept a strict watch on events in Poland and tried at first to control the state without actual annexation.

Prussia and Austria had similar interests in the fate of Poland. Prussia desired to annex the Polish territories that separated her East Prussian territories and prevented the consolidation of her lands. Austria, although with less at stake than her neighbors, had seen Poland used against her by her Bourbon enemies. However, perhaps the greatest concern of the two German powers was that Russia would simply annex the territory she in fact controlled already and that she would do this without compensating Berlin or Vienna. This disturbance of the balance of power in eastern Europe would have been dangerous for both powers.

The death of Augustus III in 1763 again reopened the question of the Polish kingship. Catherine II at once produced a candidate in the person of her former lover, Stanislas Poniatowski, a Polish nobleman. The support of Prussia for the Russian choice was assured through the alliance of 1764. In this treaty, both powers agreed to aid Poniatowski, to guarantee the religious rights of the non-Catholic people of Poland, and to assist each other in case of attack. The agreement, which remained in effect until 1780, joined the two powers together in a common front in international affairs. Thereafter Catherine II embarked on a policy in Poland that led to far more active interference in the internal affairs of the country than had hitherto been the case. In 1767 Russian troops entered the country, and the diet was forced to pass measures in the interest of the Lutheran and Orthodox elements of the population. Russian intervention led to the formation of the Confederation of Bar in 1768 and to four years of guerilla warfare. Both France and Austria, in an attempt to prevent absolute Russian domination, sent the rebels arms, men, and money. The Russian troops, however, were led by one of the greatest of all Russian generals, Alexander Suvorov.

Meanwhile, the Polish revolt merged with a renewed Russo-Turkish conflict. French diplomats worked actively in Constantinople to gain the support of the Porte for the Polish Confederation. In October, 1768 a border incident led to a Turkish declaration of war on Russia. Thereafter the principal attention of the Russian government once again shifted southward toward the Black Sea and the Balkans. With great energy and resourcefulness Catherine II and her advisors began the campaign against Turkey. An army was despatched along the now familiar route to the Danube. Of greater interest, however, was the Russian naval expedition that was sent to the Mediterranean from the Baltic. The aim of this move was to challenge the Turkish navy in its home waters and, if possible, to raise in revolt the Christian populations of the empire. In this endeavor Russia received encouragement and naval supplies from Britain, who at this time considered France the principal threat to her commercial and imperial supremacy. Britain thus welcomed Russian victories over the French allies—Sweden, Poland, and the Ottoman Empire.

Once in the Mediterranean the Russian fleet, although in poor fighting condition and without experience, defeated an even weaker Turkish navy off the island of Chios in July, 1770. The subsequent destruction of Turkish naval power opened the possibility of an attack on Constantinople. The Russian commander, Orlov, was reluctant to take the risk, and, certainly, the Russian forces available were not adequate for grand military manoeuvres. Moreover, the Christian populations had not risen to support the Russian attack. The Greeks, who had expected large-scale Russian aid, were reluctant to move when only token assistance arrived. The minor rebellion that did occur was easily crushed by the Ottoman forces.

The Russian naval victories and the success of the armies operating in the Danubian Principalities had an alarming effect upon the other powers, particularly Prussia. Frederick II recognized that no advantages could be gained for his state from the collapse of the Ottoman Empire since this was an area in which he could not claim compensation. He also saw that the situation in the east could in the end lead to an Austro-Russian conflict, which he feared in view of his alliance with St. Petersburg. He, therefore, approached both powers with the suggestion of a partition of Poland with the understanding that Russia would make a moderate peace with Turkey. On August 5, 1772 the three powers signed the first of the partition treaties. Here Poland lost a third of her territory and almost half of her population. Russia received as her share a large part of White Russia; Austria took Galicia and southern Podolia; and Prussia annexed Polish Prussia.

The war with Turkey continued two more years, but, finally on July 21, 1774, the most important treaty in the entire history of Russo-Turkish relations, that of Kuchuk Kainardji, was signed. In this agreement Russia gained an increase of territory in the Black Sea region and the port of Azov; the Khanate of the Crimea was recognized as an independent state. The Principalities of Moldavia and Wallachia, which had been occupied by Russian troops, were returned to the control of the Porte on condition that religious freedom and good government be maintained. Russia reserved the right to intervene and speak in behalf of the Christian population. Wide commercial privileges in the Ottoman territories were also gained. Russia was allowed to appoint consuls in the principal cities of the empire; her subjects were permitted to trade and navigate in the Black Sea and the Danube. She also was to receive most friendly nation privileges in her trade with Turkey.

Although these gains were certainly considerable, the section of the treaty bearing most significantly on the future was that which concerned the position of the Orthodox in the Ottoman Empire. Russia was to be allowed to construct a church in Constantinople and to have jurisdiction over it. Even more important, however, was the clause: "The Sublime Porte promises to protect constantly the Christian religion and its churches, and it also allows the Ministers of the Imperial Court of Russia to make upon all oc-

casions representations as well in favor of the new church . . . ,"
to which "due consideration" was promised. The exact meaning
of this statement was never clarified. Later, Russian representatives were to use it as a justification of a policy of interference in
the internal affairs of the empire. Quite obviously the sentence
permitted Russia to complain officially of any measures Turkey
might take to the detriment of her subject Christian populations,
but it was not clear whether the Ottoman government was obligated to listen to or to accept Russian advice. The interpretation
to be given this clause remained a point of dispute until after the
Crimean War, when Russia was forced to abandon her claim to
the sole protectorship of the Balkan Christians.

The Treaty of Kuchuk Kainardji was thus a notable defeat for
the Ottoman Empire. It lost its attempt to maintain control over
the Black Sea; the Russian right of intervention in the Principalities obtained official recognition. Russia also gained certain ill-
defined rights to speak in behalf of the Balkan Orthodox. If the
terms of the treaty were to be interpreted in the sense most
favorable to Russia and if they were backed by predominant
military power in the Balkan Peninsula, Russian control could be
established over the Ottoman Empire.

The division of Poland and the peace with Turkey raised
Russian prestige to a new height. In 1778 Catherine II mediated
a dispute between Prussia and Austria concerning Bavaria. In 1780
she organized the League of Armed Neutrality between Denmark, Sweden, Prussia, and other states in protest against the
British treatment of neutral shipping in the American War of
Independence. The chief concern of Russian policy, nevertheless,
remained the fate of Poland and the Ottoman Empire. Despite the
great gains of Kuchuk Kainardji, Catherine, with the collaboration of her advisor, Gregory Potemkin, drew up further plans for
even greater conquests in the east.

The death of Maria Theresa in 1780 and the removal of her
restraining hand opened the way for closer co-operation between
Austria and Russia. Joseph II, who like Catherine II was a student
of the Enlightenment, had long been in correspondence with the

Russian empress. Although with less enthusiasm, Joseph II was won over to Catherine's wide plans for the destruction of the Ottoman Empire. In 1780 the Prusso-Russian pact lapsed; Austria and Russia then joined in the next year in a defensive alliance whose main aim was the ultimate partition of Turkey. Catherine II now proposed that in the division of Ottoman lands Russia should receive the western Caucasus, the Crimea, and territory to the Dniester river. Moldavia and Wallachia were to be joined to form the independent state of Dacia. Joseph II, for his share, was to have parts of Wallachia, Serbia, Bosnia, Hercegovina, Istria, and Dalmatia. What was left of Turkey-in-Europe, the Bulgarian and Greek lands, was to be formed into a new Greek Empire, with Constantinople as the capital and with Catherine's second grandson, Constantine, as emperor. The provision was also made that the new state should never become a part of Russia proper.

Conflict with Turkey was provoked through Russian interference in the affairs of the theoretically independent Khanate of the Crimea. Since it could obtain the support of no other state, the Porte was forced to accept the Russian annexation in 1783. Thereafter under the able direction of Potemkin, a policy of the rapid development of the newly acquired lands was undertaken. Nikolaev and Sebastopol were established as strong naval bases that could directly threaten Constantinople, now two and a half sailing days distant. At the same time Russian agents continued to agitate among the Christian populations of Turkey. The Russian activities in the areas bordering on the Ottoman territories in the Balkan peninsula and Georgia caused the deepest apprehension among the great powers, Britain and Prussia in particular. Open warfare finally broke out between Russia and Turkey in August, 1787 when the sultan demanded the evacuation of the Crimea and Georgia.

Although Austria also entered on the side of Russia in this conflict, the allies were unable to achieve decisive military successes. The British government, aware of the great danger to its own interests in Russian southward expansion, sought to find

ACQUISITIONS OF CATHERINE THE GREAT

SWEDEN

- Nystadt

- St. Petersburg
- Narva

Volga River

Baltic Sea

- Moscow

Oka River

Niemen River

Vistula

Bug River

Dnieper River

Warsaw

Don River

RUSSIA

- Kiev

AUSTRIAN EMPIRE

Dniester

Prut

River

Danube

- Azov

River

- Kuchuk Kainarji

Black Sea

OTTOMAN

EMPIRE

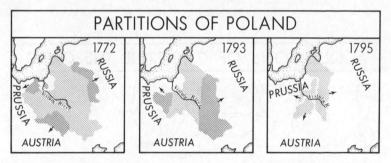

counterweights to the growth of Russian power. It first encouraged Sweden to declare war on Russia. This dispute was settled in 1790 on a *status quo ante* basis, but the Russian fleet in the Baltic was confined during the hostilities to the northern waters and could not be used in the Mediterranean. Austrian participation was also brought to an end by Joseph's successor, Leopold II. In 1791 he signed the Peace of Sistova with Turkey and terminated the alliance with Russia. Catherine II, again without an ally, made peace with the Ottoman Empire, but with significant additions of territory. The Treaty of Jassy in 1792 recognized the Russian annexation of the Crimea and of lands between the Bug and Dniester. Russia, not the Ottoman Empire, was henceforth to be the dominating power on the Black Sea.

Meanwhile, the Polish situation had again deteriorated. During the period after the first partition to 1793 when the state was under the political control of Russia, a strong reform movement had developed which was directed against Russian authority. The final partitions occurred under the shadow of the great event of the close of the century—the French revolution. The second partition of Poland in 1793 was again initiated by Prussia, who feared that Russia would seize the entire territory without compensating her neighbors. In this division Prussia took Danzig and Thorn; Russia received Lithuania and western Ukrainian lands. This action, in which Austria did not participate, touched off a final revolt. Prussia and Russia sent troops into the country, quelled the rebellion, and set the stage for the final destruction of the Polish state. In 1795 Austria joined Russia and Prussia in the third partition. The disappearance of Poland from the map of Europe in no way settled the Polish problem for Russia. The consequences of the policy of partition and the acquisition of a large hostile Polish population became, thereafter, one of the determining factors in Russian foreign policy.

THE FRENCH REVOLUTION AND NAPOLEON

Although the outbreak of the revolution in France in 1789 awakened enthusiasm in some elements of Russian society, Catherine was disturbed by the situation. At war at the time with both Sweden and Turkey, she wished no more complications on the international scene. In the following years, however, the events in western Europe served as a cover and a distraction for the division of Poland among the three eastern powers. Despite the fact that the execution of Louis XVI in 1793 was made the occasion of court mourning, Russia herself did not join the allies in the first coalition.

Catherine's successor, her son Paul, who came to the throne in 1796, showed early in his reign signs of great emotional instability. Like his father, Peter III, he was determined to reverse the policy of a hated predecessor. He particularly attacked the major achievement of his mother's reign—the imperial policies she had pursued. He announced that Russia would henceforth not follow a path of foreign conquest and expansion, and he denounced the partitions of Poland as a crime. Despite his aversion to the previous reign, he had to face the realities of the diplomatic situation. The victorious French armies not only threatened to upset the European balance of power, but, since they carried with them the ideas of the revolution, they also constituted a danger to the autocratic regimes.

Paul's attitude toward France and the revolution was determined finally by a relatively minor issue—the fate of the island of Malta, which was under the control of the Catholic religious order of the Knights of St. John. Under severe financial pressure because of the sequestration of its lands in France by the revolutionary government, the order sought funds in Russia and even welcomed the protectorship of the Orthodox tsar. Paul himself appears to have conceived the idea of forming an international organization, which, like the old crusading orders, would fight the menace of revolution. He was thus particularly aroused when Napoleon, while on his way to Egypt in June, 1798, occupied Malta.

Because of the French action and the real danger to Russian interests of the French victories, Russia joined with England, Austria, and Turkey in the Second Coalition. In 1799 a Russo-Turkish expedition took the Ionian Islands. The war on the continent, in contrast to that on the sea, did not proceed well, principally because of the quarrels between the allied powers. Finally, angered by apparent British and Austrian failures to fulfill their obligations to him, Paul withdrew from the Second Coalition in October, 1799.

Napoleon's seizure of power after his return from Egypt and his establishment of what was in fact a military dictatorship made possible a shift in Russo-French relations. The situation had also changed in Malta. In September, 1800 the British occupied the island to the great annoyance of Paul, who had been elected Grand Master of the Catholic order. Enraged by the British action, the tsar attempted in reprisal to form an alliance of Sweden, Prussia, and Denmark to block British interference with neutral shipping. Napoleon used the opportunity to assure Paul that he was willing to cede Malta (which was no longer his) to Russia, and he released with honor Russian prisoners he was holding. Paul was now even willing to co-operate with France in the foolhardy plan of an attack on India. The tsar's assassination in 1801 brought an end to this undertaking, and the Russian troops that had already been despatched were recalled. The death of Paul was greeted with joy in England, but Napoleon correctly saw it as a major defeat.

* * * * *

The accession of Alexander I, the son of Paul, at the beginning of the new century in effect brought to a close a century of Russian expansion in which war and war alliances had been the rule. Although Russia was to acquire Finland in 1809 and Bessarabia in 1812, the age of Russian territorial conquest in the west had in effect come to an end. Russian policy thereafter in the next century was largely devoted to the preservation of boundaries already established. The eighteenth century had thus witnessed the firm establishment of Russia as one of the European great powers. It had also brought about the weakening or destruction of the three powers bordering upon Russia—Sweden, Poland, and the Ottoman Empire. Russia now had ports on two seas, the Baltic and the Black, and she had built up a navy. The rise of Prussia to great power status, seen at first as a threat to Russian security, on the contrary provided a reliable ally for the next hundred years. The basic Russian alliance system, the union of the three northern courts of Vienna, Berlin, and St. Petersburg, was firmly founded at this time and further strengthened by the partitions of Poland. The policy of interference in the affairs of the Ottoman Empire and the use of the appeal to the subject Christians of the empire were also inaugurated in the eighteenth century, and the principles of the Treaty of Kuchuk Kainarji were to determine the future course of Russo-Turkish relations. Russian foreign policy after 1815 can thus only be fully understood against the background of the conquests of the previous century and the lines of development laid down at that time.

II

〰〰〰〰〰

Alexander I

Alexander I came to the throne in 1801 without adequate training or preparation for the decisive role that he was now called upon to fill in European and Russian affairs. His childhood had been made difficult by the estrangement between his grandmother, Catherine II, and his father. He had been forced to divide his time between two courts organized on differing principles and hostile to each other. He had also been given full knowledge of the conspiracy that had ended in the assassination of Paul. His education, which had been under Catherine's direction, was limited and superficial. He did, however, become acquainted with the ideas of the Enlightenment through the influence of his Swiss tutor, César de La Harpe. Although thereafter general principles and lofty ideas always had a compelling fascination for him, he lacked the ability or even the firm conviction necessary to translate any of his ideals into a successful course of action. At the beginning of his reign it seemed that he would inaugurate a period of reform in Russia. He first allied himself with men such as Prince Adam Czartoryski, Count Paul Stroganov, and Nicholas Novosiltsev, who wished to remodel the Russian government along more progressive lines. These early liberal inclinations of his thought soon changed, particularly after the invasion of 1812, to be replaced by a growing mystical and highly conservative turn of mind. Thus, despite the hopes that were first placed on him, Alexander's reign witnessed no improvement in the internal order of Russia.

In contrast to his relative lack of achievement at home, Alexander I throughout his career played a brilliant role on the international scene. He was able to repel an invasion launched by the foremost military power of the time, to take the lead in the organization of the peace, and thereafter to maintain the position of his country as the strongest single power on the continent. In foreign relations his propensity to base practical decisions on moral principles and general concepts was always apparent, but these considerations usually contributed in the end to the strengthening of the power of Russia abroad. Alexander's foreign policy, although often highly ideological in direction and presentation, thus also served Russian national interests.

ALEXANDER I AND NAPOLEON

At the beginning of his reign Alexander I drew back from Paul's policy of co-operation with Napoleon and sought to maintain a position of neutrality. He explained his attitude with one of those resplendent declarations that were to characterize his reign and so clearly show his mode of thought: "If I ever raise arms," he declared in 1801, "it will be exclusively in defense against aggression, for the protection of my peoples or of the victims of ambitions that endanger the peace of Europe . . . I shall never participate in the internal dissensions of foreign states." [1]

The Russian desire for a respite was shared by the other powers. In March, 1802 France and Britain signed the Peace of Amiens. This truce held scarcely a year, and in May, 1803 the conflict was resumed. In 1805 Russia joined with Britain in the Third Coalition, to which Austria later adhered. Once again the allied armies proved unable to withstand Napoleon's forces. Austria went down to defeat at the battle of Austerlitz. In July, 1806 Prussia belatedly entered the conflict only to lose the disastrous battles of Jena and Auerstädt. At the battle of Friedland in June, 1807 the Russian forces were so decimated that the commander, General Bennigsen, advised that Russia could not continue in the war. The French victories, the impotence of the Russian allies, and the entrance of the Ottoman Empire on the side of France influenced Alexander's decision at this time not only to make peace, but to join with France as an ally. Napoleon, who now also desired an end to the continental fighting so that he could concentrate on the reduction of Britain, wisely allowed Alexander a means of radically changing his policies without a loss of prestige.

Meeting with Alexander on a raft in the river Niemen, Napoleon sketched out a grandiose plan of the division of Europe: France was to rule in the west, Russia in the east. The Treaty of Tilsit, signed on July 7, 1807, provided for the joint solution of the outstanding European problems and brought Russia into the alignment against Britain by associating her in the so-called Continental System with the stringent French measures directed against Britain's extensive shipping and trade. France, in return, agreed to attempt to mediate between Turkey and Russia. If this failed, the two powers were to arrange for the partition of European Turkey. The Polish question was settled by the creation by Napoleon of the Duchy of Warsaw from the Prussian territories of Poland. Although it appears that Alexander I was well satisfied

1. Michael T. Florinsky, *Russia* (New York: Macmillan, 1960), II, p. 651.

with these arrangements, the treaty was not in the Russian interest. It was not a true division of Europe, since not only was French military power greater, but the French-controlled territories far outweighed in strength and importance those held by Russia. It also created on the Russian borders a satellite Polish state that could easily be turned into a weapon directed against Russia. The Russian entrance into the commercial war against Britain also interrupted a very beneficial economic relationship and was most heartily disliked at home. In fact, the entire idea of an alliance with France was extremely unpopular with the Russian aristocracy, particularly since it coincided with the period of the attempted reforms of Michael Speransky, who was a firm supporter of the French alignment. Land reform, co-operation with the French Revolution as embodied in the person of Napoleon, and the military and diplomatic support of France, the former national enemy, were all policies that could find little sympathy among influential circles in St. Petersburg.

The union of Tilsit, moreover, never functioned smoothly, principally because neither partner was sincere in his intentions; the treaty had been designed on both sides to win time. Napoleon, in order to offer Russia some immediate concrete advantage from the pact, encouraged her to go to war with Sweden in February, 1808. A year later Finland and the Aland Islands were added to the Russian Empire. The war with the Ottoman Empire, however, continued. In 1808 when the two emperors met at Erfurt, the tension between them was already apparent.

From 1808 to 1812 an uneasy truce was nevertheless maintained. Napoleon went to war again with Austria and added Galicia to the Duchy of Warsaw. In 1810 in an effort to close the holes in the blockade against Britain, he annexed Oldenburg, Bremen, Hamburg, and Lübeck. Since the tsar's favorite sister, Catherine, was married to the heir-apparent of the Duchy of Oldenburg, this move caused a severe reaction in the Russian court, but Napoleon did not even bother to answer the Russian note of protest. The continued presence of French troops in Prussia also caused apprehension. By 1811 both sides had begun to prepare for open conflict. Napoleon had been unable to subdue Britain by commercial warfare and the Continental System, nor had he quelled the revolt that had broken out against French rule in Spain. The temptation was now great to strike against the last unconquered continental state in order that thereafter he would be free to concentrate on the reduction of Britain.

The Russians had ample warning of the French intentions, although they were not eager for a test of strength at this time. To prepare for the coming conflict they made an agreement with Sweden in April, 1812 in which they promised to support Swedish claims to Norway to compensate for the loss of Finland. In the next month the Treaty of Bucharest was signed with Turkey, and the province of Bessarabia was taken from Moldavia. On his side Napoleon forced Austria and Prussia to make treaties with him, but both of these unwilling allies subsequently secretly assured Alexander of the practical worthlessness of these pacts. Both Russia and France had therefore set the stage for the conflict, but neither had gained the real support of another power. Spain and Britain ultimately joined Russia, but only after the outbreak of hostilities, and they could offer no concrete assistance during the invasion. France's allies hoped for Napoleon's defeat.

On June 24, 1812 Napoleon crossed the river Niemen at the head of an enormous army of 400,000, composed of soldiers of many nationalities; scarcely half were French. Opposed to him were three Russian armies whose combined strength totaled around 200,000 men. This second great invasion of Russia was met by tactics similar to those adopted by Peter to meet the attack of Charles XII, but on a larger scale. Under heavy criticism from large sections of the Russian aristocracy, who wished to fight the French troops on the periphery of their nation, the Russian commander, General Michael Barclay de Tolly, adopted a system of calculated retreat. Once again the scorched earth policy resulted in the destruction of all stores of food and munitions and in the burning of villages and forests. The effect on the French communications lines was immediate and catastrophic. Without sufficient fodder the horses perished and the military supplies and provisions could not be transported in sufficient quantities to care adequately for the rapidly advancing French armies. The ravished countryside offered no relief.

Although these methods of meeting an invasion were wise under the circumstances, since the Russian armies were not strong enough to defeat the French in open battle, the Russians themselves reacted bitterly against the surrender of so much territory. The failure of Barclay to engage the French in combat finally forced Alexander I to replace him with the popular hero, Michael Kutusov. Under heavy pressure, the new commander against his better judgment made a stand at the village of Borodino. There, on September 7, the Russian forces were able to inflict equal losses on their opponents although the battle was a technical French victory, which in fact opened the doors of Moscow to them. The march into the ancient Russian capital, however, proved to be anything but a triumph. Shortly before the French arrived the Russian government ordered the evacuation of the city, including the removal of firefighting equipment. The great fire which broke out and subsequently consumed the city after Napoleon's occupation thus left the French with a deserted, gutted city without supplies or adequate shelter for the winter. Despite his failure to engage the Russian armies in a decisive battle, Napoleon expected Alexander I to sue for peace. In this vain hope he delayed five weeks in Moscow. Finally, in October the French forces, now severely reduced by war losses, disease and desertion, started the long march back to Poland. The disaster of the French retreat, in bitter winter weather for which they were not prepared, harassed by guerilla forces and by units of the Russian army paralleling their march, has long been recounted as one of the great catastrophes of warfare. Of the 600,000 troops who took part in the campaign, barely 30,000 recrossed the Niemen on December 14.

The destruction of the French armies forced the Russian government to make a major decision. Throughout the retreat Kutusov had tried to spare his own tired forces, who had also suffered from the conditions of the campaign, and to avoid an open battle. He wished to see the foreign armies expelled from Russian soil with the least possible loss to his own troops. However, once the French armies left Russia, the question arose as to whether they should be pursued through foreign territory. Despite strong opposition at home, Alexander I chose to continue, and in January the Russian army crossed the Niemen. Joining with Austria and Prussia, Russia was able to defeat the hastily assembled French forces. The Battle of the Nations at Leipzig in October, 1813 marked the freeing of Europe from the long period of French domination. On March 31, 1814 Alexander I, accompanied by Frederick William III of Prussia, rode into Paris at the head of the victorious allied armies.

The entrance of Alexander I into the French capital marked the culmination of a line of development that had commenced during the reign of Peter the Great. In March, 1814 Russia emerged from the period of the revolutionary wars as the strongest European power. Thus Russia, who had entered into the politics of Europe only at the beginning of the eighteenth century, now had risen to a position of military predominance.

THE CONGRESS OF VIENNA

Because of the preponderant weight of Russian military power in 1814, the views of Alexander I toward the peace were of first significance. His attitude toward the future treaty was determined by three principal considerations: first, the influence of his education and his early companions, particularly of his first foreign minister, Prince Adam Czartoryski, second, the increasing influence that religion began to exert upon his outlook on international problems, and, third, the interests of Russia as a power. Although the effect of Alexander's education, particularly of the role of La Harpe, in the formation of his later ideas, is much debated, certainly the tsar acquired during this period a tendency to look upon political questions as moral problems. His endeavor at this time to construct an international system upon principles of right remained a constant goal of his policy throughout his reign, although his judgment on what constituted the fundamental bases of such an order altered with time. Prince Adam Czartoryski in his memoirs wrote: "I would have wished Alexander to become a sort of arbitor of peace for the civilized world, to be the protector of the weak and the oppressed, and that his reign should inaugurate a new era of justice and right in European politics." [2] This aim, to be the "arbitor of peace for the civilized world" exactly corresponded with the tsar's convictions of his own destiny, a conception that was reinforced after 1812 by his religious conversion.

His inclination to broad views and general settlements was shown as early as 1804 in instructions which he drew up for Novosiltsev, who was sent to negotiate with the British government. Here the principles that states should receive institutions of their own choice and fitting their internal development, that disputes between nations should be submitted to international arbitration, and that boundaries should be drawn to coincide with the geographic, economic, and national organization of the area in question were elaborated. The tsar's belief, which he held until at least 1820, that each people should have the government best suited to it and that all should be joined together in some sort of general union to protect the security of each member, was, of course, open to widely varying practical interpretations. The principles could, and were, applicable to differing situations and could be used to justify highly liberal or strongly reactionary courses of action.

To Alexander's conception of the existence of a basic European solidarity and the need for a morally justifiable peace settlement was added a growing religious fervor, whose direction was profoundly influenced by his experiences during the French invasion. He later related: "The burning of Moscow enlightened my soul, and the judgment of God on the fields of ice filled my heart with a faith which I had never so deeply before experienced. . . .

2. *Memoirs of Prince Adam Czartoryski*, edited by Adam Gielgud, (London: Remington & Co., 1888), II, p. 8.

I was filled with the deep and mature conviction to devote myself and my government only to Him and to the furtherance of His honor. Since that time I have been another man; to the salvation of Europe from destruction I thank my salvation and liberty." [3] His feelings were also expressed in his attitude toward the defeated enemy. To his troops he declared: "God does not love inhumanity and cruelty for he is compassionate. Forget all of the evil that the enemy has done to us." [4] Alexander's emphasis on the redeeming and forgiving aspects of Christianity were also clear in his treatment of France and in the conduct of the Russian armies during the period of their occupation of French territory.

The intensity of the faith of the tsar, which resulted in manifestations of a mystical and often hysterical nature, was chiefly affected by elements outside of and often inimical to the established Orthodox Church and its authorities. Alexander's experiences came in time to result in the conviction that he, and often he alone, was acting under divine inspiration and that he was God's chosen instrument. In 1821 he wrote: ". . . I feel that I am the depository of a sacred holy mission."

Fortunately for Russia, there was no basic contradiction between Alexander's ideals and Russian national interests in Europe. In a very practical sense Russia had gained a great deal through the Napoleonic Wars. First, the reduction of the strongest power had greatly enhanced her own, and, second, additional territory was brought into the Russian Empire. The annexation of Finland in 1809 and Bessarabia in 1812 must certainly be added to the balance sheet of the Congress of Vienna. Russian power in 1814 was clearly shown in the fact that Alexander, virtually alone, made the first settlements with France and determined the form of government that country should have after the defeat of Napoleon.

After his arrival in Paris in March, 1814 with Frederick Wil-

3. Karl Stählin, *Geschichte Russlands* (Graz: Akademische Druck, 1961), III, pp. 238, 239.
4. Valentin Gitermann, *Geschichte Russlands* (Frankfurt, n.d.), II, p. 369.

liam III, Alexander I henceforth conducted the negotiations in the name of the allies. Although he personally did not favor the return of the Bourbons and would have accepted a long list of alternatives, including Napoleon's son, the King of Rome, he finally decided upon a restoration, largely because of the influence of the brilliant French diplomat Talleyrand. An agreement which was signed in April, 1814 provided for Napoleon's abdication and his withdrawal to Elba. Thereafter the newly established provisional government of France proceeded to draw up a constitution, the Charter, and Louis XVIII was formally declared king of France. The first Peace of Paris was largely formulated under the tsar's direction. Prussia wished a far harsher treaty and British support for the first terms was only lukewarm. The provisions, reflecting Alexander's feelings toward the defeated country, were most generous in view of the devastation that had been inflicted by French armies since 1791. There were no annexations of French territory and no indemnities. The French boundaries became those of 1792, which meant that some of the former acquisitions were kept. The moderation of the terms also served to make the return of Bourbon rule more palatable to the French people.

With the signing of this agreement, Russian ability to influence and direct the course of the European settlement reached the limit of its extent. In the next months before the opening of the Congress of Vienna in September, 1814, the other allies, Britain and Austria, in particular, came to realize the danger to their own position in Russian predominance in Europe. Because of this division in the allied camp, Talleyrand was able to play the powers against each other to the ultimate benefit of France. The emergence of Russia to continental hegemony in place of defeated France was for Britain and Austria the replacement of one evil with another. Moreover, the statesmen were more than sceptical about Alexander's motives and his lofty declarations; they regarded him as eccentric, if not outright insane. Although they listened to his fine words, they also kept their eyes on the map of Europe. Alexander I now proposed that the peace should include the establishment of a Kingdom of Poland to be constituted out of the former Napoleonic Duchy of Warsaw. The state was to be autonomous in administration and organization, but the crown of Poland would be worn by the tsar of Russia. Prussia in compensation for her lost Polish lands was to be given Saxony, who had remained too long a faithful French ally. To the Austrian and British representatives, this proposal amounted to nothing less than the absorption of all of Poland into Russia and would signify a deep disarrangement of the balance of power, particularly in view of the fact that Prussia was largely under Russian influence. Metternich, whose views dominated Austrian policy until 1848, also was concerned about the increase of territory which the Saxon annexation would have on the position of Prussia in relation to the other German states.

Because of the conflict on the Polish and Saxon questions, the congress thus became an instrument to prevent further Russian encroachment in Europe, rather than a conference solely devoted to securing the redrawing of the European boundaries and providing for the containment of revolutionary France. Before the Russo-Prussian front, the three western powers, Britain, Austria, and France, on January 3, 1815 signed what was in effect a war alliance. Hanover, Bavaria, Württemberg, and Hesse later adhered. Conflict was, however, avoided when Alexander I accepted a compromise in which Prussia received back some of her Polish land, two-fifths of Saxony, and territory on the Rhine. Alexander I contented himself with the greater part of the Duchy of Warsaw.

No sooner had this major agreement been reached than the powers received the news that Napoleon had left Elba and had again landed in France. In this last phase of the campaign Russian troops played little part. This time the British and Prussian armies marched first into Paris and dictated the second and stronger Peace of Paris. France was now limited to her boundaries of 1790, an indemnity was levied, and an army of occupation was to remain in France until the debt was paid. Napoleon was banished to the remote island of St. Helena.

The Vienna settlement ranks with the treaties of Westphalia of 1648 and Versailles of 1919 in general European history. It created political and power relationships that remained stable until the middle of the century and provided a framework for international affairs that for a century enabled Europe to avoid a major, catastrophic war. The diplomats of the victorious powers, in making the peace, were concerned first with limiting and controlling France. The indemnity and the occupation would prevent further moves in the immediate future. For a more permanent control the allies surrounded France with a cordon of barrier states who were to check renewed French expansion. To help protect this strategic area, the Kingdom of the Netherlands was formed by combining the Austrian Netherlands with the Republic of Holland. In Italy the Kingdom of Piedmont-Sardinia was assigned a similar role. The extension of the Prussian territories on the Rhine was to enable that state to serve better as a guard against France. Prussia was also strengthened through the addition of Swedish Pomerania, Sweden being indemnified with Norway.

With the containment of France geographically secured, the victorious powers then divided among themselves the remaining territories in question. The Habsburg Monarchy acquired again dominance in Italy with the annexation of Lombardy and Venetia. The smaller kingdoms went back to their old rulers, who were closely tied to Vienna. The Pope regained his power in the Papal States, and the highly reactionary Bourbon ruler, Ferdinand I, received the crown of the Kingdom of the Two Sicilies. In addition to preponderance in the Italian peninsula, Austria received Dalmatia, the Tyrol, and Salzburg. Her position in the Germanies was reasserted through the organization of the Germanic Confederation, of which she was president. Although no attempt was made to undo the reforms of Napoleon, who had reduced the number of separate German political entities from over 300 to 38, little more was done to promote the closer political unification of the land. The Germanic Confederation was thus only a loose organization. Its diet, which met at Frankfurt,

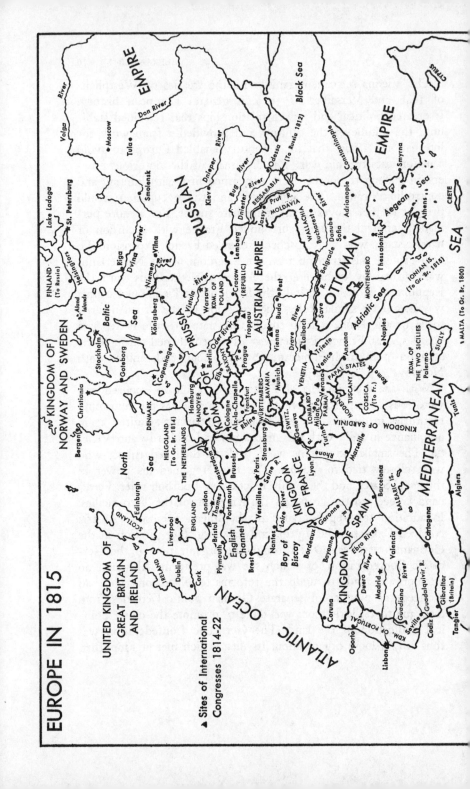

was attended by the instructed delegates of the rulers of the member states. The question of German unity and the rivalry of Austria and Prussia in this matter remained to be settled.

With the defeat of France, Britain had achieved her major aim —the preservation of the balance of power. It has already been mentioned how she recognized that Russia might replace France as a danger to the European equilibrium and how she had endeavored to prevent it. With the conclusion of the peace Britain remained in a most favorable position. She was the major colonial and commercial power; she stood at the beginning of that great epoch of her history marked by the industrial revolution. In the treaties she concentrated on the acquisition of strategic points that would be of value to her trade and her lines of communication with her colonies, as for example, Malta, Capetown, and the Ionian Islands, over which she assumed a protectorate. No attempt was made to acquire large pieces of territory overseas.

The peace treaties strongly emphasized, as we have seen, the principle of legitimacy. Wherever possible the former rulers were returned to their thrones, and the changes brought about by the Napoleonic occupations were annulled. In Spain and Portugal, as well as in the small states of Germany and Italy, the structure of the old regime was again introduced. This condition reflected the reaction felt in all states against the type of political experimentation embodied in the French Revolution and the universal desire for a period of stability. The international arrangements set up after the peace and the subsequent meetings of the powers therefore dealt not only with territorial questions, but also with the problem of the preservation of the political *status quo*. Although this development was to the chief benefit of Austria, it had the initial support of all of the powers.

Of the two major agreements made after Vienna, the Holy Alliance and the Quadruple Alliance, it was the first that owed its origin to the efforts of Alexander I. The Holy Alliance, which was the concrete expression of the tsar's ideas of the correct principles to be applied to international politics, was accepted with reluctance by the other powers despite the fact

that it was little more than a solemn statement that the signatories would "both in the administration of their respective states
and in their political relations with each other" base their actions
on "the precepts of religion, namely, the rules of Justice, Christian Charity and Peace." Although all of the European powers
except England, Turkey, and the Vatican adhered to this pact,
none of the contracting parties, with, of course, the exception
of Alexander I, took it seriously. Metternich entitled it a "loud-
sounding nothing"; the British minister Castlereagh called it a
combination of "mysticism and nonsense."

Although the Holy Alliance was generally regarded with
some derision, the congress renewed on November 20, 1815 the
Quadruple Alliance of 1814, which had been concluded among
the allies against Napoleon. In this pact the four great powers,
Russia, Austria, Prussia, and Britain now agreed "to renew their
meetings at fixed periods . . . for the purpose of consulting upon
their common interests, and for the consideration of measures
which at each of these periods shall be considered most salutary
for the repose and prosperity of the nations and for the maintenance of the peace of Europe." This stipulation became the basis
for the congress system that functioned between 1815 and 1823
and resulted in the holding of four great international gatherings
for the solution of specific problems. Although the agreement was
originally established to prevent a recurrence of French aggression on the continent, the adherence of France to the Quadruple,
now the Quintuple, Alliance in 1818 changed its direction. The
specific system established in 1815 lapsed with the defection of
Britain in the 1820's, but the principle that the great powers
should meet in congress to solve by arbitration and mediation
their common conflicts and disagreements remained accepted in
European international relations throughout the century.

The completion of the Vienna settlement left Russia in a most
advantageous diplomatic position and at a height of political
power that she did not achieve again until 1945. She was
recognized as the strongest military power on the continent; the
acquisition of control in Poland placed her armies within striking

distance of Vienna and Berlin. Her chief opponent, France, had been at least temporarily eliminated as a threat. The tripartite division of central Europe into Prussia, the Austrian Empire, and the "third Germany" of the small states gave her a great measure of protection on her sensitive western border. She could thereafter play the three political elements against each other. Her relations with Austria and Prussia were also to her great advantage. Prussia, until the unification of Germany in 1870, remained bound by strategic necessity and by dynastic ties to Russia. Austria, because of her insecure position in Italy, her rivalry with Prussia in Germany, and the ever present problem of France, could not afford to alienate Russia over questions in central Europe. Russia's neighbors, therefore, because of their need for Russian support, were valuable allies rather than rivals. Although Austria and Russia did not co-operate in the eastern question, which will be discussed in detail later, Prussia did remain a close collaborator through most of the nineteenth century.

With the attainment of a position of maximum advantage in 1815, the Russian government was thereafter satisfied with its western boundaries. From the Congress of Vienna until 1917 the primary problem for Russia was that of defending the enormous territory that had been conquered in the previous centuries. Because of the backward conditions prevailing in Russia in comparison to those in the lands of her European neighbors, the attention of her statesmen should now have turned to internal affairs. The Congress of Vienna settlement offered in the succeeding years a period of peace in which Russia was at no time faced with dangerous outside pressure and in which she therefore had ample opportunities for reform. The great military and political defeat that she was to suffer in 1856 was a result of her failure to utilize this period in modernizing and tightening her entire internal structure. The disaster of the Crimean War was thus primarily the result of a failure of Russian domestic policies and not of international relations.

Despite the scepticism of the powers, Alexander I personally was no doubt sincere in his desire to establish a truly autonomous Poland under Russian protection. His feelings, however, were not shared by significant groups in either Russia or Poland. Although the tsar wished Poles and Russians to live together as brothers under his paternal rule, the Poles continued to prefer complete independence, and the Russians disliked the special position allowed the new government. The Poles thus carried on their struggle for full freedom; the Russians looked back to the days immediately following the partition of Poland.

According to the terms of the Vienna Treaty Poland was to be established as a constitutional kingdom under the Russian tsar. A committee composed of Polish and Russian representatives prepared a constitution, which was liberal in character for its time. A diet of two chambers was established, with the upper house appointed by the crown and the lower elected by the nobility and the middle class. Although this body was supposed to meet every two years, only four sessions were actually held between 1815 and 1830. The diet could not legislate; it could only request that the tsar accept its recommendations. The autonomous kingdom was also allowed its own army, and the administration of the country was Polish in personnel and in language. Contrary to expectation General Joseph Zaionczek, and not Alexander's former close associate Czartoryski, became the tsar's viceroy. The real control in Warsaw, however, came to rest in the hands of Grand Duke Constantine, the tsar's brother, who was given command of the army.

The special constitutional arrangements enjoyed by Poland were not unusual in the Russian Empire. Finland, the Baltic provinces, and Bessarabia all retained their unique local organizations even after their incorporation with Russia. Although this disparity in systems was generally not favorably received in Russia, Alexander I after the Congress of Vienna was sympathetic with and supported the free institutions of Poland. In a speech in March, 1818 he raised the hopes of those in Russia who wished reform when he praised the Polish constitutional system and declared that he would extend the benefits of "free institutions" to other sections of his domains.

THE CONGRESS SYSTEM

In the years immediately following the peace, Russian relations with France were particularly good despite the tsar's personal dislike of Louis XVIII and his anger with Talleyrand over the treaty of January, 1815. This favorable condition was largely a result of the activities of the Russian ambassador in Paris, Count Pozzo di Borgo, and the French foreign minister, the Duke of Richelieu, who replaced Talleyrand. Richelieu had in fact played previously a larger role in Russian administration than in the affairs of his own country. His career in Russia had commenced in 1790 and had culminated after 1800 in his appointment as military governor of Odessa and governor-general of Novorossiia. Under his able guidance the Black Sea lands had flourished and the port of Odessa had risen in size and wealth. As foreign minister for Louis XVIII he kept in close touch with the Russian government and followed policies that won its approval. Like Alexander I he opposed the extreme groups among the royalists and former émigrés who wished to restore intact the pre-revolutionary conditions. In foreign affairs he sought first to obtain the removal of the allied army of occupation from French soil and a final settlement of the war debts.

In accordance with the provisions of the Quadruple Alliance, a congress was called to meet at Aix-la-Chapelle in September, 1818. Although the other powers wished to limit the discussion to the settlement of the French problem, Alexander sought to introduce questions pertaining to Europe in general. The tsar at this time was assisted by two statesmen, who jointly held the position of foreign minister, John Capodistrias and K. R. Nesselrode. Of the two, Capodistrias was the more brilliant and the more controversial. Born in Corfu, he retained his attachment to the Greek cause and was later forced to leave office as a result of the

Greek revolution. Nesselrode, who remained to serve under Nicholas I, was of a Protestant, German Rhineland family, and his father had also been in the Russian administration. His sober, industrious and modest character made him an excellent second to two impulsive sovereigns, both of whom were determined to conduct their own foreign affairs. Conservative and moderate in outlook, he exerted a restraining influence, but he did not direct the formulation or the conduct of the main lines of Russian policy.

The principal business of the Congress of Aix-la-Chapelle was quickly settled. The occupation armies were withdrawn from France and her financial obligations were settled. Thereafter France joined the four other powers on equal terms. The major controversy of the conference occurred when Alexander I, in an attempt to extend and strengthen the Holy Alliance, proposed the signature of another pact in which the powers would guarantee one another's territorial possessions and political systems as they existed at the time. This agreement would have established a tight organization of Europe and would have permitted a virtually unlimited right of intervention by the powers in each other's internal affairs. Alexander also wished to set up an international army with the Russian forces as the center. This proposal, so idealistic in appearance, would have served Russian interests in that it would have secured more strongly the status quo in Europe, which was to the benefit of Russia.

Austria and Britain, the two states that principally opposed the plan, again represented as at Vienna by Metternich and Castlereagh, did not object to the conservative aspects of the program, but they did shrink from the vision of Russian armies marching all over Europe to suppress revolutions. The Congress of Aix-la-Chapelle brought out clearly the fundamental differences in outlook on foreign affairs held by Britain and Russia. Alexander remained firm in his desire to form some kind of European order that would guarantee the continued existence of the political and territorial conditions of 1815. The British government, in contrast, would not go further than the terms of the Quadruple

Alliance, which it maintained was nothing more than an instrument to prevent the recurrence of French aggression and not the basis of a European super-government. The British attitude was best expressed in the State Paper of May 5, 1820, which was drafted by Castlereagh and issued by Canning in 1823. In contrast to Alexander's principle of intervention and co-operation, this statement of policy declared that the European alliance ". . . never was, however, intended as an union for the government of the world or for the superintendence of the internal affairs of other states."[5]

Russian relations with Austria also cooled after the Congress of Vienna. In the peace settlement the Austrian monarchy had achieved a position of dominance in the Italian peninsula and had won a measure of superiority over Prussia in the organization of the Germanic Confederation. Russian interests in central Europe from all points of view lay in the maintenance of the system established in 1815 and in the preservation of the balance among Prussia, Austria, and the states of the second order. Tied by dynastic links with the royal houses of the small monarchies, the Russian court was anxious to protect the independence of these governments from Austrian encroachments. It soon became apparent that Austria would attempt to use the apparent threat of revolutionary conspiracies in the area as a means of widening and deepening her influence.

The national and liberal fervor that had been awakened in central Europe, particularly during the wars of liberation against Napoleon, continued into the next years, chiefly among the students and intellectuals. Their activities centered in the organization of societies for the propagation of their ideals, and the movement culminated in a meeting held at the Wartburg in 1817. Political changes, occasioned by liberal agitation, also occurred in the smaller German states. In March, 1816 the Duke of Saxe-Weimar granted a constitution; his actions were duplicated in the following year in Württemberg and Baden. All three of these courts had

5. R. W. Seton-Watson, *Britain in Europe, 1789-1914* (Cambridge: Cambridge University Press, 1955), p. 73.

close relations with Russia, and Alexander had been consulted about the new measures. Metternich regarded the tsar's actions here and in Italy with deep suspicion. In his correspondence with Nesselrode and Capodistrias and in the letters that Emperor Francis sent to Alexander I, the dangers of revolution were strongly emphasized.

As could be expected, the Austrian government took the lead in the organization of joint measures in Germany to deal with the revolutionary agitation. In co-operation with Prussia, Austria was able to obtain the sanction of the other German states for the Karlsbad Decrees of 1819. The small governments also agreed to censor their publications, to control their universities, and to aid each other in the suppression of the new political movements. A central committee was established at Mainz to investigate revolutionary activities. Having instituted these measures with the co-operation of the German states, Metternich next turned to Britain and Russia for their sanction. Although Castlereagh personally supported strong action against revolutionary movements, he could not officially approve the provisions that called for interference in the internal affairs of other states. He therefore replied with the vague phrase: "We are always glad to see evil germs destroyed without the power to give our approval openly."

Alexander I, in contrast, did not hesitate to express his opposition to the Austrian actions. He had been shaken by the assassination in March, 1819 of the dramatist August von Kotzebue, who at the time was an agent of the tsar, particularly when it was reported that the murderer, Karl Sand, was acting on the instructions of a secret society. However, he had no desire to see Austria establish a firmer control over central Europe on the excuse of suppressing revolutionary dangers. Although he had himself proposed at Aix-la-Chapelle that a general alliance be established to guarantee the political *status quo* with rights of intervention, he was not prepared to grant this privilege to Austria in regard to German affairs. Moreover, Alexander I still held the belief that liberal institutions were acceptable if granted by a monarch and not extorted by revolutionary agitation. "Liberty," he stated, "is and has to be circumscribed in proper limits . . . and those limits are the principles of order." [6] He preferred that each German state adopt the measures necessary to ensure its own internal tranquillity.

Alexander's convictions were expressed in the Russian circular despatch of January 27, 1820 in which it was stated that the German states should be left free in their relations with each other, and that no league to defend absolutism should be set up. In this note the Russian government went so far as to say that it would welcome the formation of a unitary state to replace the Germanic Confederation. The Russian backing of the small states against Austria was also shown in the support that Alexander I gave his brother-in-law, the King of Württemberg, in his desire to maintain the constitution which he had granted. In the fall of 1819 the tsar massed troops in Poland as a threat to Vienna. These Russian actions were blamed by Metternich on the influence of Capodistrias. Hereafter the Austrian minister became the bitter opponent of the Russian statesman.

In the period between the Congress of Vienna and 1820 Alexander I was thus in no sense a blind reactionary in foreign politics. He accepted liberal reform in other lands when it was introduced by the legitimate ruler of the state; he opposed it when it was brought in by revolution or was based on the doctrine of the sovereignty of the people. He also sought to achieve general acceptance of the principle that the European powers acting in concert should protect reigning monarchs threatened by rebellion. He had, however, acted to prevent Austria from gaining a free hand in Germany through the use of this doctrine. Although he did not allow Austria to interfere freely in German affairs, he did after 1820 support the Austrian policy of intervention in Italy, which assured the monarchy's supremacy in that peninsula until 1860. Russian support of Austrian policies reflected the tsar's

6. F. F. Martens, *Recueil des traités et conventions conclus par la Russie avec les puissances étrangères* (St. Petersburg: A. Böhnke, 1874-1909), IV, p. 269-270.

increasing aversion to political reform and liberal ideas, which he now equated with Jacobinism and the revolution. The highly conservative emphasis that characterized Russian policies hereafter naturally led to increasing co-operation with Vienna. Austria also needed Russian assistance because of the virtual withdrawal of Britain from continental entanglements of any kind in the 1820's. The revolutions of 1820 were the occasion, therefore, of the reformation of the conservative coalition of Austria, Prussia, and Russia. Alexander I himself at this time fell more under the influence of Metternich and showed little of his old originality and spirit in the conduct of Russian policy. Vienna became again the European diplomatic center.

Although revolutions also broke out in Spain and Portugal in 1820, Austria was most concerned with the Italian revolts, since they involved her hegemony in that country. The Congress of Troppau, summoned in October, 1820, was convened chiefly to discuss the question of Austrian intervention in the Kingdom of the Two Sicilies to put down the revolutionary government. Because of their attitude toward intervention in this instance, Britain and France sent only "observers," and they did not sign the final declaration of the conference. The three conservative powers, however, co-operated well. Alexander at this time commented to Metternich: "You do not understand why I am no longer the same, I am going to tell you. Seven years have passed between 1813 and 1820, and these seven years appear to me a century. I would at no price do in 1820 what I did in 1813. You have not changed but I have. You have nothing to regret; I cannot say that of myself." [7]

The Preliminary Protocol of the Congress of Troppau, signed by the three powers in November, stressed the dangers of revolution and reaffirmed the principle of intervention. Austria was instructed to re-establish order in Italy in the name of the signatory powers. King Ferdinand I of the Kingdom of the Two Sicilies was invited to attend a second congress, which was to be held at Laibach. In this agreement Austria thus accepted and supported

7. Clemens von Metternich-Winneburg, *Mémoires laissés par le Prince de Metternich* (Paris: E. Plon, 1881), III, p. 374.

the doctrine of intervention which she had opposed at Aix-la-Chapelle and used it to protect her own interests. Britain and France did not agree to the Austrian action, not because they supported the revolutionary movements, but because they disliked the principle and feared its application under other circumstances.

Alexander's conservatism in foreign affairs increased after the outbreak of a mutiny in the Semenovsky Regiment in St. Petersburg. Although this revolt was no more than a protest against the conditions under which the troops served, the tsar preferred to regard it as part of the great revolutionary conspiracy which he saw at work everywhere in Europe. At the Congress of Laibach, which opened in January, 1821, Metternich had no difficulty in convincing Alexander I, who now firmly believed in the real existence of an international revolutionary committee "which gives the signal for the revolutions in countries which have been carefully prepared by intrigues and agitations." [8] Emperor Francis and Alexander I were now close friends, and the Austro-Russian co-operation rested on the firm ground of political compatibility.

The issue that was eventually to break the combination of the conservative powers arose at this time, although its effects were apparent only much later. In March, 1821, when the tsar was at Laibach, he received word of the outbreak in Moldavia of a revolution aimed at securing the liberation of the Greeks from Ottoman rule. Since the Greek revolution played such a great role in the European diplomacy of the 1820's, it will be treated in detail in a separate section. Suffice it to say that the revolt forced the tsar to face the contradiction in principle between his position as the protector of eastern Orthodoxy and his support of conservative regimes and legitimate monarchs. Under strong pressure from Metternich, he at this time denounced the revolution and dismissed his Greek foreign minister, Capodistrias, a strong supporter of the movement. Austria thus also gained her wishes in this first round of the reopened eastern question.

In March, 1821 a rebellion also broke out in Piedmont. The

8. A. A. Lobanov-Rostovsky, *Russia and Europe, 1789-1825* (Durham, N.C.: Duke University Press, 1947), p. 387.

Austrian troops, with Russian blessing, were thus able to deal with two Italian revolts at once. Northern Italy was subdued, Ferdinand I regained his throne, and Austrian pre-eminence in Italy was restored. With the Italian question settled, the powers now turned their attention to Spain. Here the chief governments with interests at stake were France and Britain rather than Austria.

Despite their geographical separation, Russia and Spain had maintained close relations after the end of the Napoleonic Wars. During the period of the French occupation of Spanish territory, the Spanish colonies had taken the occasion to revolt, and, with peace once restored, the Spanish government naturally sought for aid to secure their restoration. The Russian government, favoring the effort, even sent some old ships to assist in the endeavor. When Ferdinand VII was made prisoner in a revolutionary movement in 1820, Alexander naturally supported intervention by the powers to aid him. France, the tsar believed, was the logical power to carry out such an action. At the Congress of Verona in 1822 the four continental states agreed upon this policy, and in April, 1823 a French army placed Ferdinand VII back on his throne. The king immediately requested assistance from his allies in the winning back of his Central and South American colonies. Here, however, the British attitude would prove decisive since she controlled the seas. No new armada could be launched against America if she opposed it. The British position had from the outset been, as we have seen, that of strong disapproval of the doctrine of intervention. Moreover, she had developed a rich trade with the rebellious colonies, which would be interrupted if they were reconquered by Spain. She therefore had every interest in blocking the action of the continental powers.

The British position was also that most favorable to the interests of the United States. In 1823 President Monroe issued a statement to the effect that the United States would regard as an unfriendly act the interference of any European power in the affairs of an American republic. The Monroe Doctrine was directed not only against the European coalition but also against British moves in the Caribbean and Russian expansion along the Pacific coast of

North America. Without adequate sea power and without British and American support, Spain could not hope to regain her colonies.

The doctrine of intervention, supported enthusiastically by Alexander I, thus resulted in the restoration of the former governments in Spain, Portugal, Piedmont, and the Kingdom of the Two Sicilies. Revolutionary movements succeeded at this time only in South America. The co-operation of Austria, France, Russia, and Prussia had thus brought about a restoration of the general conditions of the Vienna settlement. One question, nevertheless, remained unsettled—that of the fate of the Greek revolutionary movement. This issue, which reopened the entire eastern question, which had been in abeyance since the Treaty of Bucharest of 1812, was to test the collaboration that had been established between Russia and Austria. Although bound by common ties in European affairs, the two powers faced a fundamental separation of interests in the Near East.

The Eastern Question

Throughout the nineteenth century the chief center of European diplomatic activity was the Near East; and the Turkish Straits, more than any other single geographical point, held the attention of the powers. The evident fatal weakness of the Ottoman Empire by the end of the eighteenth century made it apparent that the disposition of its ill-managed territories would soon be brought into question. Throughout the eighteenth century the internal conditions in the provinces had become increasingly chaotic; the central government was unable to control the activities of its governors in the outlying lands. The Janissaries, an elite infantry corps that was the principal military support of the state, had become a national danger through their lawlessness and rebellious temper. Almost useless against a foreign foe, they plundered the countryside and menaced the government itself. The attempt of Sultan Selim in 1793 to improve his military es-

THE OTTOMAN EMPIRE IN 1815

tablishment shattered on their opposition. By the end of the eighteenth century it was clear to foreigners and even to some Turks that either the entire structure of the empire would have to be reformed or it would surely fall apart. In the bad conditions under which they lived, Christian and Moslem suffered alike.

Unfortunately for the interests of the Porte, the Ottoman Empire was in a very real sense the crossroads of the world. The great religions, Christian, Jewish, and Moslem alike, had their holy centers here. Moreover, all the powers had vital interests and historical traditions that made the fate of the territories of the Porte of grave concern to them. In the nineteenth century the chief antagonists were Britain and Russia. After Britain's loss of the North American colonies, India played the predominant role in the British imperial system. The eastern Mediterranean as a route to India and as a commercial highway to the Far East was threatened chiefly by Russia, who also appeared to menace the wealthy colony through the back door of Afghanistan and Persia. Britain was thus always particularly sensitive about the buildup of Russian sea power in the Black Sea and the status of the Turkish Straits. She wished no regime set up in this area that would allow Russian warships to move freely into the Mediterranean to endanger her shipping and would at the same time prevent British fleets from entering the Black Sea. Her greatest fear was that the entire Ottoman Empire, because of its military weakness and the claims that St. Petersburg had on the Orthodox Christians, would simply fall into the hands of Russia. Because of this extreme anxiety, British opinion tended to hold that Russian policy was in all circumstances directed toward this goal and it saw aggressive intentions in Russian actions even when these did not exist.

Certainly, Russian interests and aims in the Near East were in the nineteenth century never so extensive as attributed to her by her British opponents. As we shall see, the Russian government throughout this period was extremely aware of the problems connected with its diplomatic position. Although quite willing to make small gains at Ottoman expense, it recognized that the conquest of the entire empire, were it possible, would not be an element of strength for the Russian state. The administration and defense of the existing boundaries taxed the resources of Russia enough without the addition of further territories. Moreover, the Russian statesmen always recognized the extreme danger of the formation of a hostile coalition directed against them, which could be brought into existence by the eastern question. Since the international situation in the nineteenth century did not allow them to achieve the ideal solution from their point of view, i.e., the opening of the waterway to their fleets, but its closure to the ships of other powers, they strove, in general, for the establishment of a regime at the Straits that would prevent all warships from entering and leaving the Black Sea. Since they did not have predominant sea power, they could only lose under any system that allowed British, or British combined with French, fleets to enter the Black Sea at will. In the question of the fate of Turkey, they favored in general its maintenance; if this were not possible, they preferred its partition, but in agreement with Britain and Austria.

Austria and France, as well as Britain and Russia, also had important interests in the area, although French influence declined relatively. However, France conquered Algeria in 1830, and she also played a major role in the modernization and development of Egypt under Mohammed Ali. She usually co-operated with Britain and was in opposition to Russia, but this diplomatic pattern underwent frequent modifications in the course of the century. Austria, although an ally in central European affairs, found herself generally in disagreement with Russia in the question of the Ottoman Empire. First and foremost, the Habsburg Empire from purely military and strategic considerations could not afford to allow a major extension of Russian power on her southern flank. In addition, with her own large population of Slavic peoples, she had no wish to see the inauguration of a great emancipation movement in the neighboring empire because of the influence it might have on her own subjects. She was thus bound to oppose any significant extension of Russian control or any attempts to raise in revolt the Balkan Christians under the banner of national liberation. The Austrian position was unusually complicated because of her need for Russian support to maintain her influence in Italy and Germany. She did not wish to be forced to bargain for aid in central Europe by concessions in the Balkans. The support of the *status quo* and the emphasis on legitimacy was therefore usually the Austrian program.

The Russian government in its dealings with the Porte was thus faced with two realities: first, that the Ottoman Empire was on the verge of collapse and, second, that somehow the European balance of power must be maintained should it fall. She also had to meet a diplomatic situation in which the other major powers considered that the principal danger in the situation was that Russia would simply grab the entire Ottoman inheritance. The problem of what to do with Turkey was never adequately settled before World War I. Three major alternatives were offered for the consideration of the powers, and all were used at one time or another. A fourth possibility, the conquest and control of the entire territory by one power, presumably Russia, was not a serious consideration in this period. It is difficult to imagine a situation in which the attempt by Russia to annex Turkey would not have brought about an immediate coalition of France, Britain, and Austria. Russia was never in a condition to meet such a military threat, and her statesmen were well aware of this fact.

The first and simplest solution for all concerned was the maintenance of the empire and its strengthening through internal reform. Britain, in particular, through most of the century clung to the hope that the entire structure might be so modernized that life would be made endurable for the Christians. The fear that any other alternative plan would mean the control of the area by Russia strengthened the British conviction that such a plan was feasible, although it is difficult to conceive a program that would have made the Christians happy subjects of the sultan.

The second alternative, the partition of the empire among the great powers in a manner that the balance would be preserved, was also discussed throughout the century. Although many different schemes of partition were offered, all of them followed certain general lines: Russia would take the Principalities and perhaps the Bulgarian lands; Austria would obtain territory in the western Balkans, possibly including Serbia; Britain would receive Egypt and Crete, and France lands in Asia Minor. These ideas, although fine on paper, were very hard to put into practical effect, because, in fact, the lines of interest of the powers so crossed that a settlement satisfactory to all was impossible to achieve. For example, the Russians were not enthusiastic about an Austrian occupation of Serbia, while the Austrians did not want Russia in control of the lower Danube. The single issue of who should hold the Turkish Straits always proved impossible to settle. The entire question of partition in the end also ran against the fact that any scheme that could be devised inevitably granted Russia a disproportionate increase of power because of her geographic position and her ties with the peoples of the Balkans.

The third possibility, the establishment of independent states among the subject populations, was greeted with suspicion until the latter part of the nineteenth century by the western states, particularly Britain, because no one believed that such nations would not indeed be Russian puppets. The Russians themselves were not enthusiastic, because of the ideological implications of the national liberation movements. The achievement of independence by the Greeks in the 1820's and of autonomy by the Serbs was a result of the actions of the peoples themselves and did not come about because the powers were attempting to free the subject Christians. It was only after the Crimean War, when the idea of national unification also caused a redrawing of the map of central Europe, that the establishment of independent states was accepted as the best solution. At that time it also became apparent that independent states, far from being Russian satellites, could also be used to form a bulwark against Russian southward expansion.

Because of the innate powerlessness of the Ottoman government, Constantinople became in the nineteenth century the scene of a constant duel between representatives of the powers, particularly between Russia and Britain, although the Russian-Austrian, the British-French, and the Russian-French antagonisms also played a role. Of great interest was the attempt made by both the Russian and British governments to dominate the decisions of the Porte through intrigue, intimidation, or bribery of officials. In general, when Russian influence was paramount at the Porte, the Russian government stood for the maintenance of the empire. When, on the contrary, another power held primary control, Russia supported the whole or partial partitioning of the territory.

The Ottoman Empire was not only an area where great power interests clashed, but also where the major European religions and political ideologies were involved in the international conflicts. Of greatest importance to Russian policy before 1856 was undoubtedly the religious question. Russia at this time used freely the appeal her Orthodox faith held for the Balkan peoples, who were indeed oppressed by Moslem overlords. This policy brought her into close association with the Greeks, Rumanians, Bulgarians, Serbians, and Montenegrins, all of whom were Orthodox. The religious issue had the advantage for Russia that it was part of the conservative tradition and one of the foundations of autocracy. The appeal to the faith of the people, moreover, did not bring into play the unfavorable elements associated with the idea of freedom, the second great consideration.

Undoubtedly for its time the Ottoman Empire was the most oppressive despotic power having European possessions. Although their situation was not as bleak as it is often pictured, the Christians certainly enjoyed none of the political privileges and rights dear to the heart of the liberal west. At the time of the French revolution and Napoleon the ideas of the European revolutionary movements came into the Balkans and thereafter provided the political ideology for Balkan revolt. Thus the Balkan uprisings became strongly influenced by French ideals and French thought at the same time that the rulers of Russia came to regard France as the center of political movements of deadly danger to their own form of government. Russia, in addition, had nothing to offer of her own to combat French influence. Tsarism did not offer a political pattern applicable to Balkan conditions. It was inevitable that once free, the Balkan peoples would set up some form of government adopted from western models. Thus if the Russian government supported the freedom of the Orthodox from Moslem subjection, the danger existed that the new states would form centers of subversion against Russia itself.

The third issue, racial and national, that of Slavic brotherhood with its emphasis on the conflict between Slav and German in the larger sense, was not invoked until after the Crimean War.

As long as the Holy Alliance maintained itself, Russia could not support a policy involving outright hostility with her German allies. Although perhaps the most effective bond between Russia and the Balkan peoples, this alternative proved possible only when the entire central European area became potentially a threat to the Russian state. The policy also had the disadvantage that although it could be used to influence the Bulgars, Serbs, and Montenegrins it excluded the Greeks, Albanians, and Rumanians. As a doctrine it was better designed to secure the downfall of the Habsburg Empire, rather than the control of Ottoman, or former Ottoman, lands in Europe.

Until 1856, because of these contradictions in the courses of action open to it, the Russian government favored usually a policy of the maintenance of the empire intact but the domination of the government at Constantinople. In its relations with the Balkan peoples, the common Orthodox religion was stressed. The recognition of Russia as the protector of the Christians, in accordance with the policy established in the Treaty of Kuchuk Kainardji, thus became a major goal of Russian diplomacy, because it could be used as a means of controlling the Porte. The continued existence of the Ottoman Empire but as a weak buffer state and, if possible, as a Russian satellite was the aim of Russian policy at Constantinople before 1856. This condition was in accord with Russian general policies in Europe as the defender of the political and territorial *status quo* and, if it could have been maintained, was certainly the alternative most advantageous to Russian practical interests as a great power.

Despite this desire and the dislike of revolutionary activity shown by both Alexander I and Nicholas I, the Russian government in the fifteen years following the Congress of Vienna aided in the establishment of independent or autonomous regimes in Serbia, Greece, and the Danubian Principalities and thus, in fact, launched the Balkan liberation movements. Nationalism in the Balkans as well as in the rest of Europe was strongly influenced by the events of the French revolution and the wars of Napoleon.

At the beginning of the century the entire peninsula with the exception of one small area was under the control of Constantinople and under varying degrees of subservience. Only in the mountain kingdom of Montenegro had a Balkan people been able to maintain their freedom from Ottoman rule although the empire did claim a dominance that it was never able to enforce.

Despite the fact that Montenegro will play no important part in the following narrative, because its size precluded it from a major role in international affairs, mention must be made of the particular and close relationship of this state to Russia. As the single Slavic, Orthodox people who had successfully resisted Moslem rule and who throughout their history had waged a constant struggle for their freedom, the Montenegrins naturally appealed to the Russians in the romantic and imaginative sense. In addition, the strategic position of Montenegro made it a valuable point from which Russia could conduct policy against other powers, as was shown in the events of 1875-1878 and in the Balkan Wars of 1912-1913. This extremely primitive land with a population of less than half a million maintained close, cordial ties with Russia and with the Russian court throughout the century under discussion. The relationship was well illustrated by Alexander III's remark in 1888 that Montenegro's ruler was his "only sincere friend"; later Prince Nikola made the proud declaration: "We and the Russians are 100,000,000 strong."

THE REVOLT OF SERBIA

Although intense diplomatic activity characterized the eastern scene during the Napoleonic period, the Russian attitude toward events in the Ottoman Empire remained determined by her relations with France. At this time Russia did, however, succeed in considerably strengthening her position in the Principalities. In 1802 she protested over conditions in the area on the basis of her rights under the Treaty of Kuchuk Kainardji and succeeded in having her candidates appointed as hospodars. In 1806 in a renewed quarrel over the area, Russia went to war with Turkey. The hostilities were interrupted by the Treaty of Tilsit, which brought about an armistice and two years of negotiations. In a secret clause in this latter agreement, Napoleon and Alexander I agreed upon the partition of Turkey, but they were never able to settle the ultimate disposition of the Straits. In 1809 the war was resumed until 1812, when Russia, faced by a possible invasion by France, was forced in the Treaty of Bucharest to give back to Turkey lands that her armies had occupied. The Porte thus won again control in the Principalities and Serbia and over certain Russian conquests in Asia. Russia retained Bessarabia and the Danube delta. This treaty thus marks the beginning of the Bessarabian problem, which was to poison the future relations of Russia and Rumania. The Treaty of Bucharest, however, freed the Russian armies to march northward to meet the Napoleonic invasion.

The period of the wars of Napoleon also witnessed the first successful uprising of a Christian people against the Porte. The Serbian revolution of 1804 began not as a full-scale revolution against Turkish rule, but as a mutiny against the local administration and the atrocities of the Janissaries. Later the movement turned into a real rebellion with the aim of achieving complete independence. At the beginning of the century Serbia occupied a definite position in Russian policies in the Balkans but was subordinate to the Principalities and Greece. Moreover, there was no possibility that the Russian government would compromise its wider European interests to aid a Balkan revolt. Thus, when in September, 1804 a request for aid was received from Serbia, it met with little success. Alexander I, who at the time was more concerned with the extension of French influence in Dalmatia than with events on the Danube, did not wish to see the entire issue of the position of the Christians in the empire opened again. He, therefore, advised caution, but he did agree to send arms and officers and promised diplomatic support at Constantinople.

At first the Serbian insurgents were able to win real victories.

In 1806 Belgrade was captured by the rebels, who next gained control of northern Serbia. However, the entire movement soon fell victim to the changing diplomatic conditions in Europe. In 1806 Selim joined with Napoleon; and, in an attempt to end the fighting, the Sultan offered autonomy to the Serbs. The revolutionary leader, Karageorge, preferred instead to join Russia. In July, 1807 an alliance was concluded, and a real war for independence was launched. The agreement with Russia, signed three days after the Treaty of Tilsit, was never honored. Instead of supporting the Serbs, the Russian government concluded an armistice with the Ottoman Empire. Free from the threat of Russian arms, the Turks could concentrate on the reduction of Serbia. Although in the Treaty of Bucharest Russia gained from Turkey the assurance that the Serbian rebels would receive full amnesty and that the country would be autonomous, the Porte failed to carry out these terms. With Russia engaged with France, Turkish troops were concentrated in Serbia, and Karageorge was compelled to flee. By 1813 the Ottoman forces had reoccupied Belgrade and were in effective control of the country.

The second stage of the Serbian revolution was carried out under the leadership of Miloš Obrenović, who at first adopted a policy of co-operation with the Turks. The retaliatory measures taken by the Ottoman officials and the Janissaries upon reoccupying the country were so violent that a second rebellion broke out in 1815. Faced with the possibility of renewed Russian intervention after the defeat of Napoleon, the Porte in December, 1815 recognized Miloš as Prince of the Pashalik of Belgrade and allowed the Serbs a large degree of autonomy. They were granted the right to retain their weapons and to have their own national assembly, but the usual taxes and tribute would be levied and Turkish troops would remain in occupation. Thus with indirect Russian help, Serbia won a measure of freedom from Ottoman control. The next stage in the winning of Serbian independence was closely connected with the Greek revolution of the 1820's.

THE GREEK REVOLUTION

Although the great powers were not drawn directly into the events leading to the achievement of Serbian autonomy, the Greek revolution was, in contrast, an event of general European importance and one that dominated the diplomatic history of its decade. Of the Christian inhabitants of the Ottoman Empire, the Greeks enjoyed a distinct and privileged position and, as such, were best qualified to lead a revolt against the dominating power. In the eighteenth century they had achieved a certain amount of control in the administrative and commercial system of the empire. Greeks from the Phanar district of Constantinople were regularly employed as secretaries and interpreters by Ottoman officials. Three important posts, that of grand dragoman (chief interpreter) of the Porte and the two hospodarships of the Danubian Principalities were traditionally held by Greeks. Because of the responsible offices which they occupied, Greek nationals came to have close relationships with Russia, particularly after the Russian conquest of the northern coast of the Black Sea. Many of them, as, for example, Capodistrias and K. K. Radofinikin, rose to high positions in the Russian state service.

The Greek domination of the Orthodox ecclesiastic organization of the empire and their commercial supremacy in the Black Sea and the eastern Mediterranean also resulted in frequent meetings with their Russian counterparts. The great Orthodox ecclesiastical centers, such as the monasteries of Mt. Athos and the Holy Places of Palestine, were largely administered by Greek clerics. Greek merchants throughout the eighteenth century, but particularly during the wars of the French revolution, were able to extend their commercial ventures over the entire area. The carrying trade of the Ottoman-controlled seas was in Greek hands. Over the years Greek and Russian worked well together, and the Greeks regarded Russia as their protector against Ottoman tyranny.

Because of Greek commercial interests in the Black Sea and their relations with Russia, it was natural that the port city of Odessa should become a center of conspiracy against the Ottoman Empire. There in 1814 the society Philike Hetairia (the Society of Friends) was founded with the aim of achieving Greek freedom. In view of the Russian past policy in the Balkans and the patronage offered Balkan Christianity, the organizers of the Hetairia expected to secure Russian aid. They were able to obtain financial support for their ventures from the wealthy Greek Black Sea merchants, and Greeks in Russian or Ottoman service in the Balkans were drawn into their plans. Revolts were organized both in Greece proper and in the Principalities, which were in the hands of Greek administrators. The headship of the revolution was first offered to Capodistrias, who, although refusing the titular leadership, did what he could to bring Russia behind the Greek cause. Thereafter Alexander Ypsilanti, a major-general in the Russian army and an aide-de-camp of the emperor, led the movement. On March 6, 1821 he invaded Moldavia, and he promptly sent an appeal to the tsar for assistance. Simultaneously, a Rumanian national revolt under the leadership of Tudor Vladimirescu broke out. Although both Greek and Rumanian shared a common interest in achieving freedom from Ottoman rule, the two groups soon came into conflict and Vladimirescu was executed on Greek authority.

Though the Greek rebellion received some support, principally from the hospodar Michael Sturdza, the uprising in the Principalities soon met with complete disaster. First, Alexander I was at the time at the Congress of Laibach, where, as we have seen, he had succumbed to the influence of Metternich's arguments. The Austrian chancellor, fearing the opening of the eastern question, convinced him that this revolt was just another manifestation of the revolutionary spirit in Europe. Capodistrias, who remained the champion of Russian intervention, was dismissed. Russian troops were therefore not sent across the Prut in aid of the Greeks as they had hoped. Second, the hatred of the Rumanian for the Greek-dominated administration of the Principalities soon became apparent. The Rumanians had no desire to change from Turkish to Greek rule; they sought an end also to Phanariote control. Without strong Russian aid, the Greek rebellion in the Principalities could only have succeeded if it had won the adherence of all of the Christian subject peoples, Rumanian, Serbian, and Bulgarian alike, and had joined them in a common uprising. Despite efforts by the Greek leaders, this endeavor proved impossible.

The suppression of the revolt in the Principalities, however, in no way marked the end of the Greek revolution. A rebellion that had broken out in the Morea proved more difficult to crush. Greek geography, with its wealth of islands, peninsulas, and high mountains, was well adapted to guerilla warfare and continued resistance. Throughout the Greek revolution the Turks never solved the problem of how to defeat decisively rebel groups who could always retreat to places inaccessible to the regular Ottoman troops. The Greeks, although divided among themselves, were thus able to prolong their resistance and create a condition in the Balkans that eventually forced the great powers to intervene.

The issue of the Greek revolution was complicated for the European governments by the hold that the idea of Greece had on the imagination of the educated public of Europe. In the west the close identification of classical Greece with the Greece of 1820 and the general association of that land with the idea of human liberty resulted in the great movement of Philhellenism. In Russia, sympathy for the Greek cause was based on the common Orthodox and Byzantine heritage of both peoples, a far more valid association. As a result of this wave of sympathy and ardent support, every power was faced with public pressure to act in the Greek interest. The Greek forces were swelled with men who came from all over Europe to fight for Greek freedom.

Despite the fact that Alexander I refused to send troops to the Principalities, he too was moved by opposing influences. Although he feared the spread of revolutionary movements, he could not allow a massacre of Balkan Christians. The defense of Orthodoxy was part of his conservative system; Russian prestige was deeply involved. The Treaty of Kuchuk Kainardji appeared to impose upon Russia the obligation as well as the right to protect threatened Balkan Christians. Russian economic interests were tied to the fate of the Greek merchant community; the sympathies of the Russian public were openly with their co-religionists. The action of the Russian government in the crisis was thus bound to depend upon the reaction of the Porte and the speed with which the rebellion could be crushed.

The first reaction of the Turks to the revolution was a direct challenge to the Russian position in regard to the protection of Balkan Christians. On Easter night Patriarch Gregory along with some of his bishops was seized by a group of Janissaries and hanged in front of his own church. This atrocity was followed by a general massacre of the Greeks of Constantinople. The violence of the Turkish reprisals and the choice of the target, the head of the Orthodox church, forced Russian action. In a strong note the Russian government warned the Porte not to use the occasion of the suppression of a political rebellion to open a religious war against its Christian subjects. Although the Turkish actions brought about a real Russo-Turkish crisis, culminating in the withdrawal of the Russian ambassador in June, Alexander I did not resort to war. Under the influence of Metternich, who saw the danger to Austria in a Russo-Turkish conflict, the tsar preferred to regard the revolution as the revolt of a people against their legitimate ruler rather than as a quarrel between Christians and Moslems. Moreover, the new situation in the Near East brought up for Russia, as for all of the powers, the question of the fate of the Ottoman Empire.

Thereafter the Greek question, which was not finally settled until 1832, became enmeshed in the far greater issue. Each power in the ensuing negotiations considered the revolt from the aspect of the effect that the weakening of the Porte would have on the balance of power and on its own position. Seen in this light, none of the great powers favored Greek independence. Britain and Austria continued to fear that Russia would use the situation to go to war with Turkey; Prussia with little to gain from a Near Eastern war wished to prevent a crisis. Russia, as we have seen, had sought to avoid a conflict. Moreover, the Greek constitution of 1822 was firmly based on western political principles; a free Greece would clearly be a liberal Greece. Neither Russian interests nor tsarist ideology would thus be benefited by Greek success.

The Greeks gained no aid from the Russian government, but they did obtain assistance from official and unofficial sources in Britain. In 1822 George Canning succeeded Castlereagh as foreign secretary. In no sense a partisan of Greece, he was nevertheless faced by the pressure of British opinion, particularly after the massacre of Chios when Turkish troops killed or sold into slavery all but 2,000 of a population of around 45,000 on the island. In 1823 the British government recognized the Greek rebels as belligerents; in 1824 they received the first of a series of British loans, which, in effect, made the City of London the financier of the revolution. British interests, public opinion, and fear of what Russia might do finally forced the government to seek an agreement with Russia for joint action.

Meanwhile the sultan had been unable to make headway against the Greek rebellion. Finally, in desperation he called upon the Pasha of Egypt, Mohammed Ali, for assistance. He promised his vassal the gift of the island of Crete for his son Ibrahim. Egyptian troops first took Crete and then landed in the Morea in 1825. Their early successes and the devastation they caused brought about a strong reaction among those sympathetic to the Greeks. British interests were also endangered by the increase of Egyptian power in the area. At this crucial point Alexander I suddenly died, leaving to his successor the solution of the Greek problem. Before his death, however, the possibility of British-Russian co-operation had already been discussed. Nicholas I thus continued a policy that had been inaugurated under his predecessor, but, as shall be shown, he carried it to its conclusion with a new strength and directness.

*   *   *   *   *

Although in internal affairs Russia advanced but little during the reign of Alexander I, in international affairs she had, as we have seen, won a position of continental superiority. As for all of the allied states, the period of the Napoleonic wars had been for her a time of trial and danger. Revolutionary France threatened Europe both as a military aggressor and as the carrier of an idea that could have subverted the regimes in power in the other states. At the Congress of Vienna Alexander I, like the other statesmen, made peace with the intention of ensuring that the upheaval of 1791-1814 would never be repeated. Far from being an uncritical reactionary, he wished not to enforce the acceptance of autocratic regimes everywhere, but to see that all received political forms corresponding to their historical development and general background. Having little feeling for political evolution, he then wished to solidify the system through an international organization that would, in effect, guarantee the *status quo*.

Despite the fact that the tsar's ideas were often presented in a form that made others doubt his emotional stability, they were in fact an example of wise statesmanship. The years after 1815 are known as the "era of Metternich," but Russia as much as Austria benefited from the system then established. The protection of the territorial settlement of Vienna and the defense of the principle of legitimacy gave the Russian government a lever for interference in any continental crisis. The ultimate dependence of both Austria and Prussia, in both a strategic and political sense, assured Russia that, where continental affairs alone were in question, she would have dependable allies. Austrian adherence was made more necessary by the British withdrawal from continental entanglements, particularly after 1820. The great danger to Russian policy lay in the eastern question where "traditional" and "legitimate" interests might in fact involve the support of revolutionary movements against the Ottoman Empire. There also any Russian advances met with Austrian and British opposition and carried the threat of the formation of a continental coalition. Thus, although Alexander I bequeathed to his successor an enviable inheritance in foreign affairs, the basic contradiction, which Nicholas could never resolve, was already apparent. Alexander died during one eastern crisis; Nicholas on his assumption of power was thus immediately faced with the general problem that was in the end to bring Russia a bitter defeat in the 1850's.

III

Nicholas I

Although in many ways profoundly different from his brother, Nicholas I, during his reign, made no fundamental alterations in Russian foreign policy. However, his character and temperament made it inevitable that his methods of dealing with situations would alter. In contrast to Alexander I, with his complex emotional structure, the new tsar was direct, blunt and stubborn. With none of Alexander's inclination to high idealism or religious mysticism, Nicholas I clung to a few principles with strong tenacity. His ideal was that of the perfect military order, where everything had its place and all functioned on a chain of command. Like Alexander I, Nicholas I also felt convinced that he held his power directly from God and that his decisions had thus divine sanction. He, therefore, preferred collaborators who would serve him as secretaries and not criticize or oppose his plans; Nesselrode was an ideal subordinate. Nicholas' political ideas had much in common with those of Alexander in his last years. Hereditary monarchy remained for him the only legitimate form of government; regimes based on revolutionary action or on doctrines of popular sovereignty could, in his eyes, never have real validity. The circumstances of his assumption of the throne reinforced his natural inclinations. During the reign of Alexander I the presumed heir to the throne was not Nicholas, but his elder brother Constantine. Since his marriage was morganatic and his children could not succeed him, Constantine preferred not to become tsar. Although Alexander I did indeed name Nicholas, this decision was kept secret from those directly concerned. As a result, when Alexander I died, Nicholas recognized Constantine, but at the same time the latter proclaimed Nicholas tsar. For a period of approximately three weeks political life in Russia was in a turmoil. This confusion gave the opportunity for a political disturbance, organized primarily in the guards regiments. Although this event, the Decembrist revolt, was in no sense a great national uprising, Nicholas I felt that he had crushed a real revolution and also that he had done this with the aid of God. His subsequent attitude toward European revolutionary movements was deeply influenced by this early experience, which he profoundly misinterpreted.

In addition to the questions connected with the internal rebellion, Nicholas I also inherited the unresolved Greek revolt and the problem of Russo-Turkish relations based on past treaties. In this field he acted with more vigor and decision than Alexander I. In fact, it is to be noted that throughout his reign Nicholas I showed more flexibility in eastern affairs than in his dealings with the continent itself. However, as has been emphasized, the interests of unreformed Russia demanded the maintenance of the *status quo* in central Europe. Nicholas' policies directed toward the suppression of liberal and national movements in that area, while motivated chiefly by ideological concerns, were to his country's advantage as long as the internal conditions in Russia remained in a state of stagnation and repression. The Near East, in contrast, offered a freer field of activity.

THE RUSSO-TURKISH WAR OF 1828

The principal international questions with which Nicholas I had to deal in the first years of his reign were those concerned with the Greek revolution and the events in the Balkans connected with it. Continuing the policy inaugurated by Alexander I, Nicholas I laid particular emphasis on the past agreements that Russia had made with the Ottoman Empire. These pacts, although not referring to Greece directly, covered, as we have seen, certain general Russian claims to the protection of the Balkan Christians and also specific rights in regard to the Principalities and Serbia. In the next years in his negotiations with the powers on the Greek question, Nicholas I made a clear separation in his policy in the east. Russian interests, he believed, were directly involved in questions of dispute between St. Petersburg and Constantinople, as, for example, the problem of the Principalities, Serbia, and Russian commercial rights in Turkish territories. In contrast, the Greek revolution was not treated as the primary issue. In fact, Nicholas shared Alexander's tendency to treat the Greeks as rebels against the authority of a legitimate ruler, although this feeling appears not to have influenced Russian decisions after 1825. In matters affecting the direct relations of Russia and Turkey, Nicholas I always negotiated with the Porte unilaterally and without reference to other governments. In the Greek affair, on the other hand, he accepted a wide measure of co-operation, particularly with Britain, and he acted in concert with his allies.

Agreement with Britain was made possible by the simultaneous desire of that government to settle the Greek question by mediation and joint action with Russia. The British prime minister, Canning, hoped that by working with Russia he could moderate and direct her actions and thus prevent a Russo-Turkish war. Moreover, neither Russia nor Britain had an interest in the increase of Egyptian power that would result should Mohammed Ali achieve a real triumph in Greece. In March, 1826, therefore, the Duke of Wellington was sent to St. Petersburg to greet the new monarch. There in April the Protocol of St. Petersburg was signed—a document in which Russia and Britain agreed upon a policy of mutual co-operation in the Greek revolution. Britain, with Russian support, was to attempt to act as mediator with the aim of securing the establishment of an autonomous Greek state under the sovereignty of the sultan. Should the British efforts fail, the two powers were to act in concert to set up an independent Greece.

Russia was thus obligated to act together with her British partner in the Greek question, but no such limitations hindered her activities in the other matters in dispute with the Porte. In April, 1826, in a virtual ultimatum, Nicholas called upon the Ottoman Empire to restore the conditions of 1821 in the Principalities and to carry out the provisions of the Treaty of Bucharest in regard to Serbia. After the rebellion of Ypsilanti, Turkish troops had occupied the Principalities and had failed to leave; the situation in Serbia was equally unsatisfactory. Caught in a moment of domestic weakness occasioned by his abolition of the Janissary corps, Sultan Mahmud was without the means to defend himself. In the Convention of Akkerman, signed on October 7, 1826, Russia gained not only the recognition of her demands for special privileges for Serbia and the Principalities, but also disputed territory in the Caucasus and the right of navigation in Turkish domestic waters.

With the chief Russian objectives secured in this pact, the Russian government was less anxious to hasten the implementation of the Protocol of St. Petersburg. On July 6, 1827 France joined Britain and Russia in the Treaty of London, which, like the previous agreement, called for the establishment of an autonomous tributary Greece. The powers, in addition, agreed to try within a month to induce both the rebels and the Porte to conclude an armistice. This agreement, which was not signed by Austria or

Prussia, marked a break of the Holy Alliance. Metternich throughout the crisis stood strongly against action in favor of the Greek revolution. He failed, nevertheless, to exert the same restraining influence on Nicholas I as he had on Alexander I.

Meanwhile, in an attempt to force an armistice on the Ottoman Empire through a blockade of the Morea, the combined French, British, and Russian fleets trapped the Turkish navy in the Bay of Navarino on October 20. In the surrounding confusion, fighting broke out, and as a result the Turkish fleet was destroyed. This unexpected and dramatic event changed the entire course of the Near Eastern crisis. The Russian government immediately expressed its enthusiastic approval of the event; the British government, in contrast, was deeply disquieted. The policy of co-operation with Russia had been designed to restrain the menacing northern neighbor and not to bring about the destruction of the Ottoman Empire. After the death of Canning, the Duke of Wellington in 1828 became responsible for British policy. Reversing the stand of his predecessor, the general now allowed Russia and the Porte to settle their quarrels alone. That conflict was inevitable was shown by the reaction of Constantinople to Navarino. The Convention of Akkerman was denounced and a Holy War proclaimed.

The Russo-Turkish War, which finally commenced in April, 1828, proved anything but an easy victory for the Russian troops. Nicholas I, who insisted upon heading the campaign personally, showed that despite his military training he was an inept commander. During the Russo-Turkish hostilities the three allied powers, France, Britain, and Russia, maintained the fiction that this conflict had little to do with the Greek revolution. They, therefore, continued to negotiate on the question. With the assent of Russia and Britain, French troops were landed in the Morea in 1828, and the Egyptian forces were compelled to leave. Despite their surface co-operation, relations between France, Britain, and Russia were characterized by mutual distrust and suspicion. In April, 1827 Capodistrias was chosen as the first president of Greece. His election marked the victory of the Russian party and gave Russia the hope that the new state would be strongly under her influence. Inside Greece, French and British agents co-operated to block such an occurrence.

Despite the difficulties they encountered, Russian troops were finally able to march down the Balkan peninsula to Adrianople, where they arrived in August. The seizure of the city and the fact that Russian armies were now within striking distance of Constantinople offered Russia the possibility of attempting the conquest of the city and the destruction of the empire. This grave question was discussed at this time by a special committee appointed by the tsar. It was decided here that the maintenance of the empire was more to the Russian advantage than any possible alternative. Although the work of the committee did not influence the terms of the Treaty of Adrianople, which was signed on September 14, 1829 before the decision had been reached, the agreement reflected as a whole the same general policy. The empire was to be preserved, but it was to be kept in subjection to Russia. This principle was clearly expressed in a secret circular of May, 1830 in which it was stated that the terms of the treaty should make it clear to the Turkish government that: "if it is still able to live, it will be only the life that the emperor is pleased to allow it . . . ." [1] Despite these strong words, Russia was in fact in no position to effect the outright partition of the empire. Such an action could only have been carried out at this time against the strong opposition of Britain, France, and Austria and would certainly have led to the formation of a coalition against Russia. The performance of the Russian forces in the Balkan campaign had shown that Russia was not prepared to fight Europe.

Despite the fact that the Treaty of Adrianople was regarded as a moderate peace, Russia had indeed gained much. The provisions of the Convention of Akkerman were reaffirmed, and Russia

1. Barbara Jelavich, *Russia and Greece during the Regency of King Othon: Russian Documents on the First Years of Greek Independence* (Thessaloniki: Institute of Balkan Studies, 1962), p. 138.

TREATY OF ADRIANOPLE

now acquired a protectorship in the Principalities and special commercial privileges in the empire. The control she gained over the Sulina channel of the Danube, the one navigable arm, gave her dominion over the mouth of the river. Serbia received the autonomy promised in the previous agreement, and Turkey was compelled to pay an indemnity. Article X provided that Greece should become an autonomous, tributary state in accordance with a protocol that had been signed between the powers in March, 1829. The Russian victory over the Turks thus resulted not only in the securing of further advantages to Russian commerce and certain territorial gains, but also in further freedom from Ottoman control for the Serbs, Greeks, and Rumanians.

Although the Treaty of Adrianople provided only for the establishment of an autonomous kingdom, Greece received in the London Protocol of February, 1830 full independence but with restricted frontiers. After the refusal of Leopold of Saxe-Coburg to accept the throne, the crown was finally given to Otto, the second son of the Philhellene King Ludwig of Bavaria. The prince ascended the Greek throne in 1832 as King Othon. The attitude of Russia toward Greece after this date was determined by the policy she had adopted at the time of the Treaty of Adrianople—that of preserving the empire intact, but in a state of dependence. Although the drawing of the Greek frontiers, which left most of the Greeks outside of the state, was bound to become again an international question, Russia acted to maintain the integrity of the lands of the Porte. Moreover, after the assassination of Capodistrias in 1831, Russia had little chance of securing the predominance of her partisans in the Greek government. Her interests in the new kingdom thus never became as important as her links with the Principalities, Serbia, or later, Bulgaria. Her aims within Greece remained, in general, limited to the securing of a diplomatic position of balance against the rival parties of the British and French. French influence in Athens was particularly disliked because of the revolutionary tendency of French politics and because of the links that country had with Egypt. The Russian government repeatedly pressed for the establishment of a strong monarchical regime in Athens, and the granting of a constitution was opposed on the grounds that

GREECE IN 1832

Black Sea

Adriatic Sea

MACEDONIA

●Adrianople

Constantinople

Sea of Marmora

Thessaloniki

EPIRUS

THESSALY

Aegean

LEMNOS

Sea

CORFU

Ionian Sea

MYTILENE

CHIOS

SAMOS

Athens

CYCLADES

DODECANESE

PELOPONNESUS
(MOREA)

Original Greek Kingdom 1832

RHODES

CRETE

it was first necessary to set up an orderly government and ac-
custom the people to the new political conditions.

On one issue, however, the Russian government in its relations
with Greece remained firm—that of religion. This question in
future years was to determine the Russian attitude toward King
Othon. Although Russia had been forced to accept a Catholic
king, because of the lack of a satisfactory alternative, she remained constantly concerned about the status of the Orthodox

church in the state. When in 1834 the Greek church was separated from the Patriarchate of Constantinople, the position of Othon, a Catholic, as head of the national institution was obviously not satisfactory. Thereafter Russia continued to press Othon to secure the promise that at least his heirs would adopt the Orthodox faith.

The Greek question, as a major disturbing element in international relations, now receded into the background until its revival in the 1890's. The other major powers also had no wish to see a strengthening of the Greek nation. The growth of Greek merchant sea power was as little favored by Britain as by Russia. The establishment of a strong Greece or of a revived Byzantine Empire was to the advantage of no major government. When in subsequent years King Othon was to attempt to win popularity among his people by a policy of expansion abroad, he was met with the united opposition of the Mediterranean powers.

Despite the Russian government's loss of influence in Greece after the death of Capodistrias, its position, in contrast, in the Principalities was assured through the Convention of Akkerman, which was reaffirmed in the Treaty of Adrianople. The Russian protectorate established at this time lasted until the Crimean War. In accordance with the agreements existing between Turkey and Russia, the hospodars in both Wallachia and Moldavia were to be elected for terms of seven years and they could be deposed only with the assent of Russia. In addition, the wishes of the Russian government were to be taken into consideration by the administrations. A new statute was to be drawn up for each principality, which would regulate the form of its government. In the Treaty of Adrianople, Russia also received the right to leave her troops in the Principalities until the Porte had paid a heavy indemnity.

Under the able and enlightened direction of P. D. Kiselev, the Russian governor-general, the Russian representatives in subsequent years did attempt to introduce a good system of administration into the Rumanian lands. With the co-operation of the boyars, the great landowners of Moldavia and Wallachia, the so-called Organic Statutes were drawn up for each principality. These documents established separate but parallel institutions in each section. Both states were to be governed by a hospodar, now chosen for life, and an assembly composed of the highest boyars. In the period of the protectorate, Russia supported the political position of the large landowner, who, in turn, was able to extend his control over the Rumanian peasant. Domination of the political life of Moldavia and Wallachia was exercised through the Russian consuls in Jassy and Bucharest, who interfered constantly in Rumanian internal affairs. Despite the good intentions of many in the Russian service, the years of the protectorate won for Russia the dislike and distrust of those who, in the future, were to direct the country. Strongly supporting conservative forms of government, Russia could not hope to win the sympathy of the group that was rising to power and was also liberal and strongly influenced by France. The Rumanian national liberation movement, as a consequence, became directed as much against Russian protection as against Ottoman domination.

PERSIA AND THE CAUCASUS

The attainment of the major Russian objectives in the Balkans in the 1820's was paralleled by similar successes in the Caucasus and against Persia. The tripartite struggle over Georgia between Russia, Persia, and the Ottoman Empire had its origins in the eighteenth century, but this area of diplomatic conflict had always remained distinctly secondary in Russian policy to the developments in Europe and the Balkan Christian territories. Here, as elsewhere in the east, the Russian activities were determined by general European considerations, particularly by the relations with France and Britain.

Russian penetration in the Caucasian region commenced in the reign of Catherine; under Paul, eastern Georgia was annexed to Russia. Although the ruler of the state had requested Russian protectorship against Persia and the Ottoman Empire with the condition that he remain as sovereign, Paul decided instead upon outright annexation. Despite the fact that this measure went against the wishes of the peoples concerned, Alexander I confirmed the decision, which made the later administration of the land more difficult. Russian expansion into and beyond the Caucasus principally affected Persia, but also the Ottoman Empire, particularly in view of the strategic value of the territory. During the Napoleonic wars the Russian government continued its efforts toward the gradual penetration and control of the Caucasian states. A policy of seeking to obtain the co-operation of the ruling families was adopted, and Russia sought to win them by offering them high ranks and positions in the Russian state.

The strengthening of the Russian hold here alarmed Britain because it brought up the question of the control of Persia, which was part of the system of buffer states that British policy favored as a protection for India. The entire diplomatic situation at the beginning of the century was somewhat complicated by the fact that the French government too attempted to exploit Persia as a weapon against its European enemies, Britain and Russia. Under foreign impulsion, Persia twice before 1830 attempted to block Russian expansion toward her borders. First, in 1804 under French influence a war was inaugurated, but the Persian armies soon met with defeat. In 1807, after the Treaty of Tilsit, France joined with Russia, and thereafter Britain became the dominating power at the Persian court. In 1812 Persia met further reverses, and in 1813 she was forced, in the Treaty of Gulistan, to recognize the Russian rule over the disputed Caucasian states. After this defeat, Britain still remained predominant in Teheran and maintained her position with promises of subsidies and military assistance.

A second attempt to halt Russia was made in 1826, but again the Persian armies failed to win victories. In the Treaty of Turkmanchai in 1828 Russian possession of Erivan and Nakhichevan was recognized. These annexations brought into the Russian Empire large Armenian populations whose acquisition was to have a great influence on the Russian attitude ·toward the Armenian question in the 1890's. The Treaty of Adrianople, as has been mentioned, also had given to Russia Caucasian lands. Despite these military and diplomatic victories, Russia still faced a difficult and protracted struggle to enforce her control, particularly over the Caucasian mountaineers, who strongly resisted Russian domination. In 1830 the rebels found a real leader in the person of Shamil, who was not finally defeated until 1859. The Caucasian campaigns, which extended into the 1860's, had a great influence on Russian culture, and they strongly appealed to the Russian imagination despite their relative insignificance in international diplomacy. The poets Lermontov and Pushkin participated in the fighting; the music of Rimsky-Korsakov, Balakirev, and Borodin reflected the exotic quality the Caucasus and other Asian lands held in Russian eyes.

The area was eventually subdued, but Russian relations with Persia remained unsettled; and throughout the century their course was determined by the wider Russo-British rivalry. In Teheran, as in Constantinople, Russian and British diplomats vied in their attempt to control the government of the eastern state. In the 1830's the center of conflict shifted from the Transcaucasian lands to Afghanistan, and here Persia acted in the interests of St. Petersburg. In 1837, under Russian influence, Persia commenced a war against Afghanistan in an attempt to seize Herat, a point Britain regarded as vital to her control of India. As a result of this struggle and its ensuing complications, Britain in 1839 brought about the First Afghan War, which led to the establishment of her domination over the country and eventually to a war with Persia in 1856. Although in the 1830's the principal attention of the European diplomats was centered on the Straits and the Egyptian question, the involvement of Britain and Russia in Persia and Afghanistan always played a determining role in the formulation of policy by the great powers. The fate of Afghanistan again came into question in the 1870's when

Russia moved against Khiva, Bokhara, and Kokand as well as Transcaspia. The larger problem of the control of Persia, waged on both the political and economic level, continued throughout the century and up to the outbreak of the First World War.

THE EGYPTIAN QUESTION

The granting of independence to Greece and the signing of the peace with Russia did not put an end to the difficulties of the Porte. Sultan Mahmud II was still faced with the challenge of his ambitious and resourceful ally, Mohammed Ali. Although the ultimate aims of the Pasha of Egypt are a matter of conjecture, he had by 1830 built up what could have become the center of a future great Arabian empire, and he had the power necessary to challenge the sultan himself. He first added the Sudan and part of Arabia to his lands; he received Crete in payment for his aid in the Greek revolt. Unlike other Ottoman governors, he had modernized and developed his territories, and his finances were in good condition. His military forces, the best in the east, had been built up with the aid of French advisors. With these advantages behind him, in 1831 Mohammed Ali revolted and started upon the invasion of Syria in an attempt to join this province to his own lands. His son Ibrahim, the commander of his armies, quickly reduced the Syrian cities and fortresses and in December 1832 at the battle of Koniah destroyed the main Turkish army. Constantinople now lay before the Egyptian forces, and the great powers were again faced with the danger that the Ottoman Empire might collapse or fall into the hands of a strong power.

Although Russia was directly affected by this challenge to her predominance in Constantinople, the Egyptian venture in its final outcome served to reinforce her position at the Porte. Faced with the new threat, Sultan Mahmud first appealed to Britain for aid, but that country, deep in the reform crisis of 1832 and the problems involved in the Belgian revolution, refused to accept further commitments. France, because of her relations with

Egypt and her position in Algeria, regarded Mohammed's victories with a sympathetic eye. The Ottoman Empire was thus left with the sole alternative of accepting Russian aid. With reluctance and with the explanation "a drowning man in his despair will clutch at a serpent," the sultan in 1833 agreed to the presence of Russian soldiers and sailors at the Straits. Russian protection, however, did not spare Mahmud the humiliation of yielding to Mohammed's demands. In the Convention of Kutahia, Egypt received Syria, including the disputed district of Adana.

In this moment of Turkish defeat and isolation, Nicholas I sent to Constantinople an able and tactful statesman, Prince Orlov. Under the influence of the diplomat's conciliatory and charming manner, the sultan himself proposed a Russo-Turkish agreement and consented to the terms of the Treaty of Unkiar Skelessi. This pact, signed in July, 1833, had the effect of making Russia the guarantor of the Turkish Empire and marked the height of her influence in Constantinople. The terms of this treaty of peace and alliance provided that each partner should protect the other's lands and render aid in case of aggression. An additional article, however, limited the assistance to be given by the Porte to Russia to the closing of the Straits to armed vessels of other nations in time of war. Although this clause was secret, the British government learned of it four days later. The great significance for Britain lay in the interpretation of the article. If the agreement sealed the Straits to all warships, it was not dangerous, but if the Russian fleet were allowed to pass freely in and out of the Black Sea, without a similar privilege being allowed to the ships of her opponent, then Russia had indeed gained a major victory. In the following years Nesselrode was to give repeated assurances that the Treaty of Unkiar Skelessi was no more than the reaffirmation of previous agreements and that Russia had gained no new rights. The British government, ever suspicious of Russian intentions, did not fully accept his words.

With the privileged position of St. Petersburg reaffirmed, the Russian policy, adopted in 1829, of the preservation and control of the Ottoman Empire was given new strength. The Russian ascendancy in the east was reinforced in September, 1833 by the Treaty of Münchengrätz with Austria. As we have seen, the Holy Alliance of the three conservative powers had broken on the Greek question. Throughout this crisis Austria and Prussia had remained to a large degree aside; Russia had followed a policy of co-operation with Britain and France in the achievement of Greek independence. However, the increasing division of interest with Britain after Navarino and with France after the July revolution made the continuation of close co-operation impossible. To meet this situation, Nicholas once again was able to join his policy in Europe with that in the east. Seeking to preserve the *status quo* in both areas, he turned back to his original partners. In the Treaty of Münchengrätz both Austria and Russia agreed to oppose Mohammed Ali should he attempt to obtain further gains at the expense of the Porte and to seek jointly the maintenance of the Ottoman Empire. Should the empire, despite their wishes, collapse, they were to co-operate to arrange a new system and to maintain the balance of power. Prussia later adhered to the general policies of this agreement.

After the conclusion of the Treaty of Unkiar Skelessi, affairs in the east entered upon a period of relative calm. A Russo-Turkish convention signed in January, 1834 provided for the evacuation of the Russian armies from the Principalities and a cancellation of a portion of the Turkish debt arising from the Treaty of Adrianople. Russia thus emerged from the period of the prolonged eastern crisis, which had begun in 1821, in a considerably strengthened position. Control had in effect been established over the empire through the Treaty of Unkiar Skelessi. Although the Russian government did not claim that it had received new rights in regard to the Straits, it did believe that the pact obligated the Ottoman Empire to consult first with Russia in all crises, and to accept Russian assistance before that of any other power, a situation that meant, in the words of Lord Palmerston, that "the Russian Ambassador becomes the chief Cabinet Minister of the Sultan." With Russian armies stationed on the Prut and the Russian fleet only a few days sailing distance from Constantinople,

Russia believed that it had the military strength necessary to maintain these terms. Moreover, Nicholas, with the re-establishment of the bonds with Austria and Prussia, had brought his central European allies behind the eastern settlement, which was much to the Russian advantage.

The relatively strong increase of Russian power and influence naturally aroused the concern and hostility of Britain, who was most directly affected by the events. Although it was largely due to British negligence that the Porte had been led to accept Russian assistance, Britain resented the diplomatic defeat she had suffered at Constantinople. Thereafter the tone of British policy became more aggressive and dynamic, particularly under the direction of the Liberal foreign secretary, Lord Palmerston. An ardent exponent of imperial power and glory, he became the chief influence in the shaping of British foreign relations. His opinion of Russia was expressed in a letter to his brother, written in 1835, whose words also give a clue to his way of thinking:

The fact is that Russia is a great humbug, and that if England were fairly to go to work on her, we should throw her back half a century in one campaign. But Nicholas the proud and insolent knows this, and will always check his pride and moderate his insolence when he finds England is firmly determined and fully prepared to resist him.[2]

The British distrust of Russian intentions combined with the threat to British interests implicit in the Treaty of Unkiar Skelessi gave rise to a great deal of anti-Russian feeling among the British statesmen and the public. These feelings also characterized the attitudes of both British ambassadors to Constantinople before the Crimean War, Lord Ponsonby, who held office from 1831 to 1841, and his successor, Stratford Canning, who remained there from 1842 to 1858. The most effective publicist of Russophobia, David Urquhart, was first secretary at the embassy from 1836. The importance of the conflict between the British and Rus-

2. Seton-Watson, *Britain in Europe* (Cambridge: Cambridge University Press), p. 184.

sian ambassadors in Constantinople in the following years cannot be overestimated. After 1833 the sultan always found in the British embassy firm support and encouragement for resistance to Russia.

In the 1830's the principal concern for Britain in her relations with the other powers in the eastern question was the protection of her rich possession, India. At this time events in Afghanistan and Persia, as well as at the Straits, led the British statesmen to fear that the Russian government intended a giant pincer movement to force Britain out of these areas and perhaps eventually to rob her of her costly prize. Relations with France and the rise of Egyptian power were also seen in this context. France, having increased in strength in the western Mediterranean after the conquest of Algeria, was thus seen as a potential enemy. Britain had won the duel with France for colonial supremacy in the eighteenth century, but the danger of a revival of the conflict was always present.

The increased power of Mohammed Ali was viewed with apprehension for the same reasons. With the introduction of the steamship and the growth in trade with the Orient, the British laid more weight on the possibilities of developing further the trade routes through the Red Sea and Suez as an alternative to the long stretch around South Africa. The erection of a modern powerful state, controlling this area, was viewed with great disfavor. A great Arabian empire was an equal danger to that presented by Russia. Moreover, the diplomatic possibilities in the situation were also menacing. France openly favored Egypt's power and growth. There was always the chance that Russia might join with France and Egypt, and Britain would be faced by a coalition that she could not defeat.

To meet these potential threats to their empire, the British statesmen launched an active policy in the Ottoman Empire. They now sought to bolster the power of that state so that it could remain as an effective buffer against the threats of its neighbors. Ottoman control of the routes to India was judged the most advantageous of the alternate possibilities for the protection of British interests. The British representatives, therefore, now pressed for the introduction of a program of reform within the empire that would strengthen the state as a military power and also conciliate the subject peoples so that they would not seek an independent existence. In 1835 British officers were sent to aid in the reform of the Turkish army. Due to quarrels that arose in this connection, the Turkish government finally dismissed these advisors and appointed instead Prussian officers, among them Helmut von Moltke. Britain also constantly advised a policy of resistance to Egyptian demands. In 1838 the very favorable commercial Treaty of Balta Liman was signed. Despite the fact that its provisions were not faithfully fulfilled by the Porte, it did signify a diplomatic victory and showed the increase in influence that Britain had won at Constantinople.

Although Mahmud gladly listened to advice on resistance to Egypt, he wished to proceed one step further and initiate a policy of revenge. He had never accepted the Peace of Kutahia as final, and he waited only for the proper moment to go to war with his rebellious vassal. Despite his strong pleas he was not able to win British support. The British government wished to reform and strengthen the empire but not bring about a war. It was justly feared that a severe crisis would lead Russia to implement the Treaty of Unkiar Skelessi by rushing to the aid of the Porte, by occupying the Straits, and by remaining there indefinitely.

The British aims were thus clear. They would uphold the Ottoman Empire as the best guarantor of British interests in the area. They also wished if possible to secure the abrogation of the Treaty of Unkiar Skelessi and its replacement by a general European agreement. The Russian plans, in contrast, were not so clearly formulated or vigorously pursued. Like Britain, the Russian government wished to support the Ottoman Empire and maintain the *status quo* in the Near East. The tsar desired also to exploit the opportunity presented by the French and British differences of opinion over Egypt to improve his own diplomatic position. Austrian and Prussian support was assured through the Treaty of Münchengrätz. If now Britain could be brought into this system, France would be isolated in Europe. The eastern question, which usually served to drive Russia's potential adversaries together, could now be used to divide them.

It is interesting to note that despite his dislike of liberal and constitutional governments, Nicholas I showed a great preference for working with Britain. It was France, with its revolutionary past and its sponsorship of subversion abroad that bore the chief weight of his disapproval. Throughout his reign, from the Greek crisis to the Crimean War, the tsar sought to solve the successive eastern crises, if possible, by agreement with Britain. The Russian policy in the Egyptian crisis of 1839 to 1841 was thus that of co-operation with Britain to the exclusion of France. The fact that both Russia and Britain favored the upholding of the sultan's power made such an agreement possible.

At the end of April, 1839 Mahmud precipitated the renewed crisis when his armies attacked Egypt. This rash act resulted in the resounding defeat of the Ottoman forces and the desertion of the entire fleet. At this grave juncture Mahmud died, to be succeeded in June by the sixteen-year-old Abdul Mejid. The great nightmare of the diplomats, the collapse of the Ottoman Empire, again appeared to be at hand. The powers were particularly apprehensive that Russia would now go to the aid of Turkey under the terms of the Treaty of Unkiar Skelessi. Austria, who, despite the Münchengrätz agreement, had no desire to see Russia act, proposed collective action. Nicholas I at first balked at the idea of a conference that would subordinate Russian interests to the desires of the majority of the powers. Nevertheless, in July, 1839 the Russian ambassador in Constantinople also signed a joint note addressed to the Porte that requested the Ottoman government not to take independent action, but to consult with the powers.

The decisive step toward co-operation with Britain was taken in September when P. I. Brunnov was sent to London to propose Russo-British co-operation. Russia at this time offered not to seek the renewal of the Treaty of Unkiar Skelessi, which was to lapse in 1841, and agreed that no attempt would be made to defend Constantinople by the occupation of the Straits without the agreement of the other governments. The closure of the Straits was also to be made part of the public law of Europe. Russia's intention was that France be excluded from any agreement that might be made.

Although Palmerston was not able to accept these terms at once, negotiations continued. France and Britain were now in disagreement on general policy in Europe. Finally, spurred partly by the fear that France might negotiate a Turkish-Egyptian peace, Palmerston joined with Russia, Prussia, and Austria in July, 1840 to negotiate the "Convention for the Pacification of the Levant" with the Porte. This agreement set the terms for a settlement of the Egyptian question. The exclusion of France from the negotiations marked a break between the French and British governments and a reversal of former British policy. When Mohammed Ali refused to accept the terms dictated by the powers, on September 14 the sultan deposed him. During the crisis the French government pressed Egypt to yield, particularly when it became obvious that the Egyptian forces could not withstand the allied attacks. British, Austrian, and Turkish naval squadrons defeated the Egyptian fleet, and a successful rebellion broke out in Syria against Egyptian rule. Although there were rumors of war and a French attack on the Rhine, there was little that France could do in its position of diplomatic isolation and in view of the Egyptian defeats. In November, 1840 Mohammed was forced to yield. In the peace the Porte received back what it had lost at Kutahia, but Mohammed Ali retained his independent position in Egypt with the recognition of his hereditary right to rule the country.

France rejoined the European concert in July, 1841 and signed the Convention of the Straits with Britain, Russia, Austria, and Prussia. Russia now allowed the Treaty of Unkiar Skelessi to lapse, and the Porte passed under the joint patronage of the powers. It was also agreed that the Straits would be closed in time of peace to the warships of all countries and that this settlement could only be changed by a European conference. This agreement, a victory of British diplomacy, placed the Straits for the first time under international control. The Russian gains of 1833 had been annulled, and the Ottoman Empire remained as a great buffer state protecting the routes to the Orient.

In the next years the Russian government attempted to continue and to extend its policy of co-operation with Britain with the aim of isolating France. The Russian statesmen did not see the abandonment of Unkiar Skelessi as a diplomatic retreat; they, too, were for the preservation of the *status quo* in the Near East, and the new treaty served this purpose well. Peace was thus preserved in the Egyptian, as in the Greek, crisis because the principal opponents, Russia and Britain, found a ground of common agreement in the upholding of Turkish power. The great issue, that Russia should not fall heir to the empire, remained in existence. Neither Austria, Britain, nor France could allow Russian control over the area; it was an issue on which all would fight. Russia, well aware of this condition, continued throughout the 1840's to base her policies on the principles adopted at the time of the Treaty of Adrianople.

THE REVOLUTIONS OF 1830

Despite the surrender of the privileged position won in the Treaty of Unkiar Skelessi, Russia had made considerable gains in the years after the accession of Nicholas I. Similar diplomatic successes were also characteristic of her policy in Europe proper in the same period. Here Russian interests called for the maintenance of the political and territorial conditions of 1815, which were so much to her advantage. The Vienna settlement was challenged twice between 1830 and 1850 by national and revolutionary forces. In the first crisis, in 1830, Russia was able to repress the movements directly dangerous to her, and in the second, in 1848-1849, she was able to reassert her position as final arbiter in the political balance in central Europe. Although the ideological emphasis in Nicholas' foreign policy becomes more pronounced in the affairs of continental Europe in comparison to those of the east, it must be remembered that Russian interests were bound more closely to the maintenance of the *status quo* in Europe proper than in the Ottoman Empire.

The revolutions of 1830 commenced in France with the overthrow of Charles X and the accession to the throne of Louis Philippe of the house of Orleans. Despite the fact that Nicholas I himself had warned against the repressive measures that Charles X took in the last days of his reign, the tsar was not willing to admit the right of the French people to change kings. With the Decembrist revolt still fresh in his mind, he was disturbed by any sign of the renewal of revolutionary activity. His anger was not directed so much against Louis Philippe as a person; he had met him in 1815 at Neuilly and had found both the man and his family highly sympathetic. It was the challenge to the principle of legitimacy and the danger of the influence of the movement on Russia that he feared. He was also concerned that the revolution would initiate a new wave of French imperial expansion and possibly a revision of the treaties of Vienna.

At the time that the July revolution occurred in Paris, Metternich and Nesselrode were by chance both in Bohemia. They were thus able to meet and come to an agreement on how the new events were to be met. In the so-called *chiffon* of Karlsbad, they declared that their two governments would not intervene in French internal affairs unless France inaugurated an active policy abroad. This agreement marked the recommencement of practical co-operation between the two conservative powers against the forces of revolution, a policy that had been interrupted by the eastern crisis. Both statesmen were chiefly concerned lest France again take up the Napoleonic tradition and initiate a new age of imperial expansion.

Nicholas I, in contrast to the more conciliatory attitude of his minister, immediately attempted to adopt positive measures against the revolutionary movement. He instructed the military governor of Kronstadt not to admit to Russian ports any French ships flying the tricolor, which now replaced the white flag of the Bourbons as the official French emblem. He also applied similar petty and vexatious measures to hinder the activities of French citizens in their relations with Russians. Determined on strong action, he then dispatched General Dibich to Berlin to try to persuade Frederick William III to mobilize his forces on the Rhine. With territories bordering on France and Belgium, the Prussian government had no desire to see its lands become a battlefield and, therefore, declined to follow a provocative policy. Nicholas met a similar check in his attempts to block the recognition by the powers of Louis Philippe's title. Four months after Austria, Britain, and Prussia entered into relations with the new regime, Russia finally followed. Despite the formal acceptance, Nicholas I always regarded Louis Philippe as a usurper and not as the legal king of France. Kingship could come only by inheritance; the position could never be changed or legalized by a revolution.

Despite the apprehensions of many statesmen, Louis Philippe soon proved himself an entirely safe ruler. A moderate in politics and chiefly interested in maintaining his own power, he embarked upon no adventures and he did what he could to conciliate the tsar. Although pressed strongly by popular opinion on the Polish and Belgian questions, he was able to maintain the peace and refrain from crusades in the interest of Belgian or Polish freedom. Nevertheless, he was not able to establish a satisfactory relationship with Russia. As we have seen, in the eastern question the Russian government had followed a policy that had as its aim co-operation with Britain and the isolation of France.

The revolutions of 1830 had thus brought a new king to the throne of France. The next major upset to the Vienna pattern occurred in the Netherlands, where the Belgian population rose against their king and demanded separation from Holland. The union of the two peoples, which had been supported by Britain in an attempt to raise a barrier against France, had not been a success. King William openly favored the Dutch section of his kingdom, despite the fact that it represented only a third of the nation. Dutch officials dominated the administration, and the tax system was organized to the detriment of the Belgians. On September 26, 1830 the revolutionary parties were able to set up a provisional government in Brussels. King William, faced with the revolt, at once appealed for assistance to the four powers that had constituted the Quadruple Alliance. Nicholas I, who received the request on October 15, was naturally ready to intervene immediately to protect the rights of a legitimate monarch faced with a rebellion of his people. Once again he turned for support to Berlin and Vienna. Prussia, however, declined to act without the co-operation of Britain; Austria, despite her conservative principles, also showed no eagerness to intervene. In this question Nicholas I based his call to strong action not on the immediate issue of the union of the two peoples but on the general principle of change through revolution. "I am not fighting Belgium here," he declared, "it is the general revolution . . . which threatens us if we are seen to tremble before it." [3] Russia alone, however, could do little. The final outcome of the revolt rested more in the hands of the statesmen of Paris and London.

The British capital thus became the center of the negotiations on the Belgian question. Britain, more directly concerned in the matter than Russia, was chiefly afraid that if the Belgian territories were separated from Holland, they would either be annexed by France or formed into a state that would become a French satellite. It was clear that a strong party in France favored annexation and that there were influential pro-French groups in Belgium. The Wellington government, which was in office at the time of the revolt, did not favor the establishment of an independent state. The Liberal administration of Grey, which took power in 1830, was in contrast willing to approve this settlement.

The London Conference of the powers, which opened on November 4, succeeded first in arranging an armistice between the Belgian and Dutch forces and then proceeded with a discus-

3. J. A. Betley, *Belgium and Poland in International Relations, 1830-1831* (The Hague: Mouton, 1960), p. 43.

sion of the terms. Nicholas I was willing to accept a new administrative relationship between the two states, but he insisted that
William must remain the king in both sections. He favored the
separation of the territories with perhaps the heir to the Dutch
throne, the prince of Orange, established as viceroy in Brussels.
He also believed that the decisions of the conference should be
backed by force, and he prepared his own troops in Poland for
this purpose.

In these circumstances, the attitude of the French government
was of first importance. France now had the choice of co-operating with the powers or of attempting to exploit the situation to
gain more territory. Louis Philippe, despite pressure at home,
chose to follow a moderate path and to co-operate with Britain.
He therefore supported the establishment of an independent Belgium under a separate ruler. This proposal was strongly in opposition to the Russian insistence that William's position be protected, but Russia was not able to act because of the outbreak of
the Polish revolution in November. Austria alone was not strong
enough to stand up for the rights of legitimacy and she too was
involved with the events closer to home. With the major opponent of an independent Belgium neutralized, the powers on December 20 finally agreed upon the establishment of an independent Belgium; in the following month it was decided that the new
state should be declared neutral and that this condition should be
guaranteed by all of the states. The choice of a ruler proved less
difficult when Louis Philippe did not press the candidacy of one
of his sons. Prince Leopold of Saxe-Coburg, the final choice of
the powers, entered Brussels in July, 1831. Determined to protect
his rights, William despatched an army into Belgium in August.
In reply to this display of force, France sent troops and a British
fleet enforced a blockade. Although William was thus compelled
to withdraw, he did not officially accede to the settlement until
1839. The Russian attitude toward the new state also remained
distinctly unfavorable. The Russian signature was affixed to the
treaties establishing Belgian independence and neutrality, but the

tsar did not thereby signify his approval of the act. A minister was not sent to Brussels until 1852.

The revolution in Poland in November, 1830 faced Nicholas I with an event far more serious than the change of monarchs in Paris or the separation of Belgium from Holland. Both of these questions had involved matters of principle and the maintenance of the Vienna settlement, but Poland reflected upon the tsar's prestige as a monarch and upon the integrity of his empire. After the Congress of Vienna, Grand Duke Constantine, as viceroy, became the effective ruler of the kingdom. Influenced by his Polish wife and his advisors, he was sympathetic to Poland and to its institutions. At the time of the Decembrist revolt he protected the rights of the Poles accused in the conspiracy to be tried according to Polish procedures. Nevertheless in the eyes of the Poles, he remained a Russian administrator and as such was not popular. Nicholas I, although it could not be expected that he would ever be well-suited to the role of a constitutional monarch, allowed himself to be crowned king in May, 1829 and he took the oath to support the constitution. This position of subservience to Russia and the Russian tsar, no matter how enlightened the domination might have been, could never have been acceptable to the politically active and nationalistic Polish gentry. Moreover, the majority regarded the true boundaries of their state as those of Poland before the partitions. They, therefore, saw with increasing dissatisfaction the Russian measures taken to assimilate the Western Provinces into Russia proper. The mobilization of troops on Polish territory and the possible use of Polish soldiers against the Belgian revolution also caused consternation. The revolutions in Paris and Brussels had already contributed to an increase in Polish restlessness. The rebellion, which broke out in November, thus expressed the desire of the Polish leadership to be freed from Russian rule and to re-establish the conditions of the early eighteenth century.

The rebels were at first considerably aided by the weak attitude of Constantine. Faced with the revolt, he chose to withdraw the loyal troops from Warsaw and to wait. The revolutionary forces thus gained time to organize, and they were able to place remarkably many men in the field. In the end the forces were numerically not too far apart. The Polish insurgents, 100,000 strong, faced Russian armies numbering about 120,000. The Polish troops, however, were considerably hampered by a lack of equipment. Moreover, the revolution, which began without adequate preparation, was further troubled by a division of leadership. Since the political right and left could not agree on the question of land reform, the revolution never gained the support of the mass of the peasantry.

At the beginning of the rebellion the Polish leaders immediately sought assistance from abroad. Since the Polish Kingdom had been created as part of the Vienna settlement, they hoped that the powers would be compelled to intervene. In reply to their requests, they received expressions of sympathy but no practical aid. The revolution had indeed been badly timed. The British government, chiefly concerned with the Belgian question, did not wish to endanger its relations with Russia although many liberals felt great sympathy for the cause of Polish freedom. Louis Philippe, despite the French tradition of the support of Poland against Russia, could also do nothing. The Polish revolt served instead greatly to assist the French government in the Belgian problem. Without foreign intervention the Polish revolution had little hope of success.

Once again in firm control of the country, the Russian government abolished the Polish Constitution of 1815 and replaced it with the Organic Statute of February, 1832. Had this new arrangement been faithfully executed, the Poles would still have enjoyed a favorable political position within the Russian state. Although the Kingdom was now declared an "indivisible" part of the Russian Empire, the guarantees of civil liberties, a free press, the inviolability of person and property, and freedom of religion were retained. Rights of local government and the use of the Polish language were similarly kept. These provisions were, however, ignored or violated by the succeeding Russian administrators. The country now fell under the rule of General I. F. Paskevich, who had commanded the troops that crushed the Polish revolt. Unsympathetic to Poland's particular position, he worked against the maintenance of autonomous Polish institutions and special privileges. The policy of repression, which he instituted, resulted in the growth of the underground political organizations that again in 1863 were to challenge the Russian rule.

After the defeat of their forces in Poland, large numbers of the Polish leaders fled abroad. Thereafter the Polish emigration was to exert influence on international diplomacy far out of proportion to its real strength. The center of Polish activities became Paris; the Hotel Lambert was the gathering point of the conservative elements of the Polish leadership. Here Czartoryski, the former comrade of Alexander I and the recognized Polish leader, organized what was in effect a state in exile and conducted a foreign policy worthy of an established government. The left groups, although in opposition to Czartoryski, also continued a policy of active opposition to Russia. Many co-operated with the radical movement Young Europe, organized by Mazzini. Henceforth in every great European revolutionary action, Polish participants could be found. The direction of all Polish activity, whether liberal or conservative, was in every circumstance highly anti-Russian. The Polish exiles were very successful, particularly among liberal circles, in building a picture of tsarist Russia as the embodiment of all that was reprehensible and reactionary in politics. The Polish emigration as a group added immensely to the numbers of those whose activities Nicholas I principally feared—the revolutionary who worked underground through secret societies to destroy the autocratic political system of Europe, that of Russia in particular.

The revolutions of 1830 thus succeeded in Paris and in Brussels, but failed in Warsaw. Similar movements in the Germanies and Italy were also suppressed, largely through the agency of Austria. Although France at first protested, Louis Philippe was not able to prevent the Austrian government from re-establishing the old order in Italy, which had also been threatened in this year of revolution. Austria acted with similar vigor in the German states. She used the occasion of the Hambach National Festival of May, 1832, an event organized by journalists and attended by around 25,000, to act against the growth of liberal and national movements. She was able to push through the federal diet the Six Acts, which limited the right of assembly and subjected the press and the universities to strong controls. The right of intervention in the affairs of states threatened by revolution was also reaffirmed. Austria thus brought central Europe and Italy back to the conditions of 1815.

Though the revolution in Paris and the division of the Netherlands had been opposed by Nicholas I, Russia as a power was not adversely affected by either event. The accession of Louis Philippe had not resulted in the revival of French imperialism across the Rhine or the sponsorship of liberal and national revolutions. The revolt in Poland had been quelled, but at a high cost to Russia. Austria had suppressed the resurgence of the spirit of revolution in her neighboring lands. Moreover, the revolutions had served to point out again to the conservative monarchies, particularly to Austria and Russia, that they should co-operate in European affairs. Divided in interest in the eastern question, they needed to follow a policy of mutual support in order to protect their political systems and their empires. The settlement of 1815 was to the maximum advantage of both powers; neither could benefit from the spread of national or liberal sentiment. With the adoption by Russia of a policy of preserving the *status quo* in the Ottoman Empire, the great issue separating Vienna and St. Petersburg was removed. Russian and Austrian interests both in the east and in Europe could thus be covered in one general agreement.

The Treaty of Münchengrätz, signed in September, 1833, has already been discussed in connection with the Egyptian crisis. It marked the formal renewal of the policies of the Holy Alliance, which had shattered on the Greek issue. In October, 1833 Prussia joined her neighbors in the Berlin Convention, whose articles were an open reaffirmation of the spirit of the old agreement. Here again the three monarchs supported the right of any ruler threatened by revolution to appeal for outside aid. They also agreed that should one of the three signatories, when engaged in the suppression of such a revolt, be threatened by an outside power, then the two other partners would come to her assistance. These agreements became the basis of Russian continental policy until the Crimean War.

With the conclusion of the agreements of Münchengrätz and Berlin, the Russian government had again established in Europe a political system that was not only in line with Nicholas' ideological convictions, but that also served to protect Russian state power. Prussia stood guard on the Rhine; Austria took over police duty in Italy and Germany. Russia guaranteed the preservation of the *status quo* in the east. Together the three powers were guarantors of the Vienna settlement and of each other's territorial possessions and conservative forms of government. Faced by this combination, which was united on lines of interest and ideology, Palmerston attempted to erect a counter-alliance of France, Britain, Portugal, and Spain. The agreement was, however, never the counterpart of the conservative alliance since Britain and France were not joined by the same ties of common interests and needs that united the conservative empires.

After 1833 the three courts continued a policy of mutual cooperation despite numerous petty disagreements between statesmen and rulers. As a result, central European affairs assumed an appearance of outward calm until the great revolutionary year of 1848. The single important disturbance was the Austrian annexation of Cracow in 1846, an act carried through with the approval of the other partition powers. At this time, but particularly during the reign of Frederick William III, Russo-Prussian relations were particularly close. Nicholas I, married to the Prussian king's daughter Charlotte, valued his family ties with the Prussian court and remained always a great admirer of the Prussian military tradition. In this relationship it was clearly Russia who predominated. Although Prussia could withstand Russian demands on minor issues, she stood always in the shadow of St. Petersburg, particularly as long as she remained in a position of rivalry with Vienna over German affairs. This situation was slightly altered in 1840 when Frederick William IV came to the throne. Unlike his father, the new ruler not only failed to develop close personal ties with the tsar, but he became increasingly drawn toward liberal ideas. Under the influence of his liberal advisors, he considered a change in Prussian institutions and a policy of closer co-operation with Britain. Such a change of political orientation naturally involved great dangers to Russia. If Britain should find a friend and ally in Berlin, Russian policy in the east would be paralyzed and her vital western front would be endangered. This close relationship of ideology and national interest in central Europe was clearly shown in the revolutions of 1848.

THE REVOLUTIONS OF 1848

Although the revolution of 1830 had resulted in the Polish rebellion, which had directly challenged Russian power, the movement in 1848 presented an issue of potentially greater danger to the Russian government—that of the unification of central Europe, possibly under liberal and national forms of government. As has been mentioned, the settlement of 1815 in central Europe had been to the Russian interest. The area, split in three political directions, allowed the Russian government a wide field in which to manoeuvre. The maintenance of the Austro-Prussian rivalry in German affairs and the protection of the independence of the states of the second rank was the best policy open to Russia. Moreover, the ideological unity of central Europe protected Russia from political influences from the left that might affect either her own population or that of Poland. The alliance of the three conservative courts, whose aim was the maintenance of the *status quo*, also assured the Russian government of the support of two of the four other major powers. This extremely favorable situation was threatened by the wave of revolution that began in

January, 1848 in Italy and that had spread by March across Europe to the borders of Russia itself.

The revolutionary tide caused little surprise to Nicholas, since during his entire reign he saw the spirit of revolt behind every unpleasant event. Like Metternich, he expected that some time a great political catastrophe would hit them all. Nevertheless, the fall of the July Monarchy in February, 1848 was a shock to the Russian court. Grand Duke Constantine reported in his diary: "It was as if we had all been struck by lightning." [4] Nicholas was delighted at the fall of the man he regarded as a usurper and saw in this act of retribution the hand of God and a justification of his own stand. As in 1830 he thought of direct and immediate military action, and he called upon his ally Prussia to co-operate with him. The feelings of the conservative courts remained similar to their apprehension in 1830—that revolutionary France might again initiate aggressive moves toward the Rhine or might patronize revolutionary movements in Italy or Germany. Nicholas I thus sought to organize a coalition to meet these threats. He wished Prussia and Russia to handle France; Austria was to deal with Italy.

Nicholas' desire for immediate action met with little response in Berlin. Instead, Frederick William IV suggested a meeting, the purpose of which would be the strengthening of the Germanic Confederation. Further action on the part of Prussia was made impossible when in March the revolution spread into the Germanies and into Berlin. On March 18 Frederick William IV was forced to concede to the revolutionary demands; already on March 13 Metternich had fallen from power in Vienna. Thus in March, 1848 all of central Europe stood under the control of the revolution. Nicholas I had to meet not the problem of a movement in distant Paris or Turin but on his very doorstep. His great conservative allies had also fallen victim to the dangers he had foreseen. The Holy Alliance had been defeated by the forces of rebellion; Russia stood alone in Europe.

4. A. S. Nifontov, *Russland im Jahre 1848* (Berlin: Rütten & Leoning, 1954), p. 228.

The events of March thus destroyed the Vienna settlement in central Europe and faced Russia with the general condition that would be of the greatest danger—the possibility that the center of the continent might unite under general theories that might ultimately lead to the destruction of the tsarist autocracy and the defeat of the Russian state. Although the map of 1815 was most favorable from Russia's point of view, the Russian government had not at all times looked with disfavor on a degree of consolidation in the area. Still, it had no desire to see one power dominate. From 1848 to 1851 three alternate solutions to the problem of German unification were offered; each was in turn defeated. Despite the Russian interest in their suppression, these movements failed primarily because of the inner rivalries within central Europe itself, that is, because of the split between conservative, liberal, and socialist political factions and the conflict for power between Prussia, Austria, and the smaller monarchies, rather than through foreign intervention.

The first solution, that of a liberal, national Germany, which was offered by the Frankfurt assembly in 1848, was that least desired and most feared by Russia. This Germany would be ideologically inimical to the Russian autocracy. Pro-Polish, it would tend in time naturally to ally with Britain or France. The strong bulwark of Russia against Europe, the Prussian army, would fall into the hands of the enemy. A second solution, offered by Austria in 1850, that of the incorporation of the entire Austrian Empire into the Germanic Confederation, to form an empire of 70 millions, was preferable to the Frankfurt proposal largely because the federal form and conservative basis of this union would make it more compatible with tsarist Russia. The third possibility, the unification of Germany, or at least of the states north of the Main river, under the leadership of Prussia, was for Russia the preferable solution, provided that the Prussian government remained conservative in form and oriented its foreign policy eastward. An autocratic Germany, united with Austria and Russia under the Holy Alliance, was thus the preferable alternative should it prove impossible to maintain the settlement of 1815.

In 1850 Russia opposed Prussian moves more because of Frederick William's liberal inclinations and his actions in the Schleswig-Holstein affair, rather than because of any direct opposition to the principles involved.

Before the threat offered by the March revolution in the Germanies, there was little that the Russian government could do. Although the tsar had been most bellicose in January and February, when the revolts occurred in Italy and France, the advice of his counsellors, who pointed out the financial and military conditions of the country, calmed his crusading zeal. An isolated Russia could indeed do nothing. In March Nicholas I gave vent to his feelings in a strongly worded manifesto, which ended with the declaration: "God is with us. Understand ye people and submit; for God is with us." Although this statement was understood abroad as a call for war against the revolution, such was not its intention. Nesselrode was forced to issue an explanatory circular in which he stated categorically that Russia would not intervene in the affairs of other nations as long as they did not interfere in Russia.

Although the policy of nonintervention in central European affairs was in contrast to his previous actions, Nicholas I was hampered by the unsatisfactory state of his own country and his military unpreparedness. The dangers of the general situation also became immediately apparent, particularly in regard to Poland. On March 17 the foreign minister of the new government in Prussia, Arnim, called for the restoration of an independent Poland. On March 28 Czartoryski appeared in Berlin. Prussian liberals at the same time called for a union of free Poland, liberal Prussia, France, and Britain. The possibility of a crusade of liberal Europe under Prussian leadership against autocratic Russia was also discussed. Russia thus faced the danger that she might find Europe united against her and that she might have to deal with revolutionary uprisings in Poland and in her own territory. At this time she could also call on no other power for assistance; Austria, with similar interests, was herself unable to handle her domestic rebellion.

The gradual withdrawal of this threat was due not to Russian actions but to the internal conflicting forces of the German revolution. Prussian enthusiasm for Polish freedom ended when the conflicts in Posen led the Prussian government to abolish the Polish administration that had been established on the basis of liberal, national principles. Even more significant was the split within the revolutionary forces on ideological grounds. Unlike the revolutions of 1830, the movement in 1848 contained a strong socialistic and radical element, which soon came into conflict with the moderate liberals. Moreover, the preserve of the old conservative tradition, the army, remained intact in most of the states. With the passage of time, therefore, the revolutionary groups became divided against each other, whereas the counter-revolution gained in strength and unity of purpose. The Russian government could thus afford to maintain its position of enforced waiting until it could intervene effectively on the side of its choice. The victory of Russia, for in the end she was called upon to act as judge and final arbiter of the central European settlement, thus came not so much from the wisdom and strength of the Russian statesmen, as from the division and lack of a common purpose within the revolutionary forces.

Active Russian intervention in the revolutionary situation was first exercised in the area of most immediate concern—the Danubian Principalities, which were under Russian protectorship. In June an insurrectionary movement, directed against Russian predominance, swept through the province of Wallachia. Despite the fact that the revolutionary government had reached some understanding with the Porte, Russian troops marched into the country and put down the revolt. This action in a land within the Russian political orbit called forth protests from both France and Britain, but caused no further diplomatic repercussions. The second action, the intervention in the affairs of Schleswig-Holstein, by contrast, involved negotiations with the other powers and affected greatly the course of the German revolution.

The Schleswig-Holstein question, a quite complicated issue, became the first international question arising from the revolutions of 1848 in the Germanies. The two duchies, of which Holstein was German and Schleswig predominantly so, belonged to the Danish crown. Holstein was a member of the Germanic Confederation; Schleswig was not. Both duchies wished to remain politically united. Unfortunately, the entire question of their status was opened at this most inopportune time by the problem of the succession in Denmark and the actions of Danish nationalists who wished to form a centralized state. A revolt broke out in the duchies, who then appealed for assistance to the Frankfurt assembly as the successor to the German diet. At the end of April, Prussian troops, acting in the name of the assembly and joined by soldiers from other German states, invaded the duchies. In this situation the King of Denmark, Frederick VII, appealed to the powers. Quite naturally, the tsar was sympathetic to the Danish king. Here was clearly a case of a rebellion against a legitimate monarch and a violation of the treaties of 1815. The entire international balance in the Baltic area was also affected when the victorious Prussian troops pressed into Jutland and thereby brought into question the continued independent existence of Denmark. The governments of both Sweden and Britain were vitally concerned with the status of the area, which dominated the entrance to the Baltic Sea. Prussia thus found herself faced with a coalition of powers who were determined to maintain the *status quo*. In the humiliating armistice of Malmö of August, 1848, the victorious Prussian troops were forced to turn back. This pact in no way settled the problem of the duchies. Instead the entire issue remained a point of conflict between Berlin and St. Petersburg and contributed to the eventual option of Russia for Austria in the German question by 1850.

The acceptance of the armistice by Prussia, which was done without consultation with the Frankfurt Assembly, did nothing to ease the internal German situation. This question had meanwhile become an issue in German politics, far out of proportion to its real importance. The revolt of the duchies had become deeply enmeshed with the German national question and had become a symbol to the German liberal. For the great powers the issue was the balance in the Baltic and the maintenance of treaties; for the German nationalist foreign hostility signified the determination of the others to prevent German unification.

By the fall of 1848 the anti-revolutionary forces were able to regain power everywhere. After the destruction of the socialist strength by the French army, France, too, received a political system more acceptable to Nicholas I. In the Habsburg lands the power of the Austrian army slowly began to assert itself. Nicholas rejoiced greatly at the news of the defeat of the Sardinian armies at Custozza and the subsequent securing of Italy under Austrian control. In June, General Windischgrätz had taken Prague; in October he recaptured Vienna from revolutionary control. In December the incompetent Emperor Ferdinand was replaced by his young nephew, Franz Joseph. Thereafter the Austrian policies were influenced predominantly by the counsels of an extremely able statesman, Prince Felix Schwarzenberg, who also proved most adroit in his dealings with the tsar. With the accession of the new monarch, in whom Nicholas I proclaimed a fatherly interest, Russo-Austrian relations gradually tightened at the expense of the ties between Russia and Prussia.

Throughout the revolutionary crisis, Nicholas I remained dissatisfied with the actions of Frederick William IV. The vacillating, unstable, and liberally inclined character of the Prussian king was hardly found sympathetic by the tsar, who erred on the side of impetuosity, strong action, and intensity of feeling. Certainly, Nicholas I could never obtain in Berlin the same unswerving support of conservative ideals that he received in Vienna. This difference, of course, reflected the divergent interests of the two German courts. Like autocratic Russia, the Habsburg Monarchy as such could only lose by the introduction of liberal, national ideas into central Europe. Because of its preponderant Hungarian and Slavic populations, Austria could never use the weapon of nationalism in the interest of state power. Prussia, nationally homogeneous, could, in contrast, find its power enhanced should it assume a position of leadership in a liberal, national movement. In 1849 and 1850 the Prussian government was not yet strong enough, nor was the international situation favorable, to exploit this advantage in order to defeat its Austrian rival. In these two years the victory went to the combined forces of Austria and Russia; in 1866-1870 this situation was to be reversed in the Prussian favor.

The Austrian armies were able to restore imperial control in Italy and Austria, however, Hungary remained in rebel hands. The Hungarian revolution had commenced in March, 1848, and by October Vienna and Budapest were at war. The danger of the Hungarian revolt was intensified in Russian eyes by the participation of large Polish forces and by the activities of General Joseph Bem, who had been one of the leaders of the Polish rebellion of 1830. The establishment of an independent Hungary was thus correctly regarded as the forerunner of renewed revolutionary activity in Poland. Therefore, in May, 1849 Nicholas I, in answer to an Austrian appeal, agreed to send troops into Hungary. His intention was to defeat the "enemies of order and tranquility in the whole world" as well as to aid the monarchy.

In June, 1849 the main Russian forces entered Transylvania. Together the Russian and Austrian armies numbered around 270,000 in comparison to the Hungarian forces of about 170,000. With their advantage in size, the allied armies were able to defeat the revolutionary forces by the end of August. Refugees from the Hungarian revolt thereafter fled in great numbers into Turkish territory, where the protection offered them by the Porte resulted in a diplomatic crisis in Constantinople. The joint campaign, instead of producing a feeling of comradeship, resulted in much bitter feeling between the two armies. Each held the military qualities of the other in low esteem; the Russians felt they had been cheated by the Austrian commissary. The vindictive punishments meted out to the captured Hungarian leaders, many of whom were delivered by the Russians to the Austrians, were bitterly resented. The estrangement between the military leaders, however, did not affect the political support that Russia continued to offer Austria in central European affairs.

The re-establishment of control over her empire now enabled

Austria to turn again to the German scene. Meanwhile Frederick William IV had again aroused Russian distrust by his actions in the Schleswig-Holstein affair, which had reopened in April, 1849. He was also further compromised in the tsar's opinion both by his failure to make a clean break with the revolution and by his failure to return his kingdom to the political conditions prevailing before the March revolt. In April, 1849 he had, however, refused the crown of the united Germany offered to him by the Frankfurt Assembly.

Although the liberal movement of 1848 collapsed with this refusal, ideas and plans for German unification did not. Frederick William IV proceeded to attempt to unite at least the northern German states under Prussian leadership; he first approached the kings of Hanover and Saxony. The Erfurt Union (as the Prussian plan was now called), which aimed at the ultimate unification of central and northern Germany, aroused at once the antagonism of Austria and the states of the second rank, such as Bavaria, Württemberg, and Baden. Under the able leadership of Schwarzenberg, the Austrian government now attempted to resurrect the old federal diet at Frankfurt and to gain the support of the south German states. With the German powers thus ranged against each other in 1850, Russia was able to intervene decisively and to arbitrate the German settlement.

The issue that brought the Austro-Prussian clash into the open involved the Electorate of Hesse-Cassel, where the elector and his assembly had quarreled. The elector appealed to the Austrian-dominated Frankfurt diet for assistance, and Prussia claimed an equal right to interfere since her military road to her Rhenish provinces ran through the state. In this crisis the position of Russia was determined by considerations already mentioned: the revival of the Baltic problem, the tsar's dislike of Frederick William's politics, and the Russian belief that Austria was militarily the weaker of the two German powers. Faced with Austrian and Russian opposition, Prussia was forced into a humiliating surrender. At Olmütz in November, 1850 Edwin von Manteuffel, the Prussian representative, and Schwarzenberg agreed upon the restoration of the pre-March conditions in Germany. The political organization of central Europe most advantageous to Russian interests was thus re-established. Later, at Dresden, the Russian government also secured the defeat of Schwarzenberg's proposal that the entire Habsburg empire be brought into the Germanic Confederation, thus bringing to an end the Austrian dream of the "empire of seventy millions." Russia had thus seen defeated the major schemes for the unification of central Europe. The settlement of the revolutions of 1848 was therefore a victory for conservatism, the Habsburg Empire, the small German monarchies, and Russia.

The restoration of 1850 was in the interest of Russian policy, yet it cannot be demonstrated that this was the goal of Russian diplomacy throughout the revolutionary years. Nicholas appears to have been influenced by immediate events and to have made his decisions on a day-to-day basis. The defense of conservatism and the Russian position in Poland remained, however, constant preoccupations. The division of forces within Germany saved Russia from the necessity of taking strong action or of resorting to outright military intervention. Moreover, at no time was Russia faced with the necessity of vetoing German unity outright, although political unification was a danger to her. It was instead enough to support the re-establishment of Habsburg power through assistance in Hungary; Vienna then undertook the task of thwarting the expansion of Prussia. In 1848 and 1849 Russian interests demanded the preservation of the Austrian Empire for the same reasons that the continued existence of the Danubian state was a political necessity for the German empire in 1914. Russia needed an ally of a similar ideological pattern. With the re-establishment of the division of central Europe and the securance of Austrian domination in Italy, the conditions of 1815 were again in effect. The Holy Alliance was apparently again an effective diplomatic combination. Outwardly Russia appeared to have achieved a position of new power and prestige.

Undoubtedly much of the influence which Russia was able to exert in international affairs, particularly in central Europe, was due to a gross overestimation of Russian military strength. In the period after the Napoleonic Wars Russian troops fought only the Turkic border tribes in Central Asia and the revolutionary forces in Poland and Hungary. Although here she enjoyed an advantage at all times in manpower and matériel, her victories had not been impressive. Her opponents, however, remained hypnotized by the mass of the Russian territory and the size of the Russian army. As long as these arms were not tested on a major battlefield against modern enemies, Russia could still win diplomatic victories on the basis of her presumed strength. The weakness of her internal system and its effect upon her military potential was not to be demonstrated until the Crimean War.

However, in 1850 Russia did indeed still appear to be the most powerful continental state. In the preceding years she had suppressed the rebellion in Poland, come to the aid of Austria, and, finally, had dictated the re-establishment of the old order in central Europe. The combination of the three northern courts remained the strongest diplomatic alignment; France and Britain, separated by constant petty quarrels, formed no adequate counterweight. When Schwarzenberg died in 1852 and was succeeded by Buol, Russia lost a sympathetic statesman, but the significance of the change was not at once apparent. Prussia, although similarly torn between an eastern and western orientation, continued to base her policy on co-operation with St. Petersburg. Moreover, Nicholas I never lost hope that he could reach an accommodation with Britain over the eastern question. We have seen how he had even sought to bring her into the Holy Alliance. France, Nicholas' chief opponent in his own opinion, after 1848 went through a series of political changes. The election of Louis Napoleon as president for life and his assumption of the position of emperor in 1852 were clear violations of the treaties of 1814 and 1815. Nevertheless, the European powers did nothing, and Russia and France engaged in a petty interchange concerning the way in which Napoleon should be addressed. The revolutionary influence of Napoleon's ideas on Europe were to appear only after the Crimean War. Thus in the early 1850's Russia appeared to have won a most favorable diplomatic position and to have the power to protect her own interests both in Europe and in the east.

THE CRIMEAN WAR

After the signature of the Straits Convention of 1841 a period of relative inactivity followed in the Near East. In 1843 King Othon of Greece, as the result of a military coup, was forced to accept a constitution, but this event caused no serious international complications. The first major diplomatic incident that arose was a result of the defeat of the Hungarian revolutionary forces by the Austrian and Russian armies. At this time approximately 3,600 Hungarian, and 800 Polish refugees crossed into Turkish territory. Austria and Russia immediately demanded their return, a move that was in accord with their treaties with the Porte on extradition. Unwilling to agree, the Ottoman government appealed to France and Britain, both of whom prepared their fleets for possible action in aid of the empire. In the course of the negotiations the British fleet on November 1, 1849, using the excuse of bad weather, moved into the Dardanelles in violation of the Convention of 1841. Palmerston, realizing the implications of the act for the future, at once apologized. Both Russia and Britain thereafter agreed that both the Dardanelles and the Bosphorus must remain closed to their fleets. The question of the refugees was settled with the withdrawal of the Russian demands and the granting of amnesty by Austria to some 3,000 of them. Others, such as Kossuth, emigrated or became Moslems and entered the Ottoman service. The crisis was thus amicably settled with no further repercussions.

A second incident, the "Don Pacifico affair," occurred in January, 1850, when in support of the claims of a Portuguese Jew whose house had been burned by a Greek mob, a British squadron applied a blockade to Greece. The act followed a long series of minor disagreements between the governments of Lord Palmerston and King Othon. At this time the French and Russian governments joined together to protest the highhanded British methods. The episode, which caused a break between London and Paris, thus was in the Russian interest in that it brought about a division between her potential rivals in the east.

Although no major crisis involving the fate of the empire took place in the 1840's, the problem of the future of the Turkish state always remained in question. Nicholas I, in view of his successful co-operation with Britain in the past, tried repeatedly to continue this policy and, if possible, to bring Britain into a closer and more definite arrangement with Russia. He did not seek the dismemberment of the Ottoman Empire, but he had no faith in its durability. He thus wished to make a firm agreement with Britain that would obligate that power to consult with him first should the eastern question again open. He also wanted to negotiate a partition treaty to be applied should the Turkish state collapse. His approaches met with little success, largely because of the British aversion to accepting prior commitments or treaties of a general nature. The tsar also seems never to have understood the constitutional limitation on the actions of a British cabinet, which could not without parliamentary consent make agreements that would bind its successor. As a result, Nicholas I appears to have believed that he received in his conversations with British statesmen in 1844 and 1853 more firm commitments than he actually had.

In 1844 the tsar visited Britain, where he discussed the eastern situation in detail with Lord Aberdeen. As a result of these conversations Nesselrode, in a later trip to London, drew up a memorandum, which he communicated to the British foreign secretary, that stated that both powers would co-operate to preserve the *status quo*. Should this prove impossible, they would come to an agreement on what should be done next. Although this was not the firm pact that Nicholas I had hoped for, the tsar now believed that he had obtained prior arrangements with

Britain as well as with Austria and Prussia to deal with an eastern crisis.

In 1853 Nicholas I again attempted to approach the British government in order to obtain a more detailed agreement. Once again Aberdeen, whom the Russians much preferred to the belligerent Lord Palmerston, was in office as prime minister with Lord Russell as foreign secretary. In January and February Nicholas I held a series of conversations with Sir Hamilton Seymour, the British ambassador in St. Petersburg. Again the tsar warned of the impending collapse of the Ottoman Empire and the necessity for a prior arrangement. He then offered a wide plan of partition based upon familiar lines: Wallachia, Moldavia, and Serbia would be under Russian protection; Crete and Egypt might go to England. It was assumed that Austria would support the Russian position. Seymour also reported that the tsar stated: "Constantinople must not belong to any Great Power, nor must there be a new Byzantine Empire: still less could he allow Turkey to be partitioned into small Republics, as asylums for the Kossuths, Mazzinis and other revolutionaries of Europe."[5]

To these open overtures the British government was entirely unresponsive. They had no interest in, nor did they expect the imminent collapse of the empire. They saw in Nicholas' attitude only the desire to hasten the demise of the Porte and to extend Russian power. London continued to believe that Turkey could be reformed.

The Russian attempt to strengthen the ties with Britain coincided with the rise of a dispute between France and Russia over Catholic and Orthodox rights in the Holy Places in Palestine. Despite the fact that Nicholas I looked upon France as the most dangerous of the powers, the interests of the two states clashed on few points. There had certainly as yet been no occasion for an open quarrel after the settlement of the Egyptian question. The clash between the Christian churches was, however,

5. Seton-Watson, *op. cit.*, p. 306.

an issue of deep significance for both governments. The protection of Orthodoxy had always been one of the bases of Nicholas' policy. Napoleon III needed the support of the Catholic church for his internal policies and to maintain himself in power. The prestige of both rulers was thus deeply involved.

The conflict commenced as a result of the gradual loss of rights suffered by the Orthodox before a militant Catholic offensive. In the first half of the nineteenth century, because of the anticlerical influence of the French revolution, the Catholic position had been weakened in favor of the Orthodox. After 1840, with the growth of the Ultramontaine party in France, the situation was reversed. Large numbers of French pilgrims appeared and the Catholics pressed their claims vigorously. Soon open fighting broke out between the two religious groups. Both the French and Russian governments then put pressure on the Porte, each in the interests of its own church. The French based their claims primarily on the capitulations of 1740; Russia on the Treaty of Kuchuk Kainardji. The Russians threatened with their army on the border of the Principalities; the French with their Mediterranean fleet.

Before these rival pressures the Porte, as was its custom, wavered. When the French threats appeared the more convincing, the sultan in December, 1852 made a judgment in favor of France. The Catholic monks received the key to a door of the church of Bethlehem and the right to replace at the birthplace of Christ a star that had been removed by the Orthodox in 1847. Nicholas I answered this blow to his prestige by mobilizing two army corps and sending Prince A. S. Menshikov as a special envoy to the Porte to discuss the entire question. In this dispute Nicholas I felt diplomatically secure because of his Prussian and Austrian allies and because of what he regarded as his understanding with Britain.

In February, 1853 Prince Menshikov arrived in Constantinople; the object of his mission was to block the French in the question of the Holy Places and to re-establish Russian prestige. His objectives were thus in many ways similar to those of Prince Orlov in

1833. However, unlike his tactful predecessor, Menshikov was an arrogant and overbearing diplomat. Instead of achieving his goal of reasserting Russian influence in the Turkish capital, he brought Britain and France together to face what they now regarded as an attempt of Russia to control the empire. Menshikov first forced the replacement of the Turkish foreign minister Fuad with Reshid, who was regarded as being more favorable to Russia. He then presented the Russian terms. Although ostensibly in Constantinople to settle the religious dispute, he now demanded what amounted to the recognition of a Russian protectorate over the 12 million Orthodox subjects of the sultan, and a treaty similar to that of Unkiar Skelessi. The basically religious question of the Holy Places had thus now been turned into a dispute over the survival and domination of the entire empire. The eastern question had thus been opened again, but in a manner unfavorable to Russian interests.

At Constantinople Menshikov faced the opposition of a very formidable adversary in the person of the British ambassador Stratford Canning, now Lord Stratford de Redcliffe, a recognized Russophobe. His instructions advised him to counsel moderation and reform to the Porte, but he was also given the right to call the fleet from Malta in an emergency. The presence of a strong man of anti-Russian inclinations considerably strengthened the hands of those in the Ottoman government who favored resistance to Russia. Stratford now wisely advised the Porte to separate the issues of the Holy Places and the protectorship of the Christians. In May a compromise solution on the religious question was reached, and the debate over the Holy Places played no further part in the relations of the powers. Firm resistance was, however, offered on the other Russian demands.

Since his proposals had not been accepted in their entirety, Menshikov left Constantinople on May 21. Ten days later Nesselrode issued a strong declaration, threatening the Porte with an occupation of the Principalities, an action that was carried through in July. Simultaneously, the British and French fleets were ordered to Besika Bay. From here they could easily enter the

Straits. The major opponents now stood face to face. British and French sea power lay off the Straits; Russian land power was concentrated in the Balkans. Russia was opposed by the diplomatic combination she had hoped to avoid; the policies of separating France and Britain in the eastern question and of co-operating with Britain had both been abandoned. Nor was the issue of the conflict clear. Nicholas I, in sending Menshikov to Constantinople, had not sought to destroy the empire but, at the most, to re-establish the conditions of the 1840's and what he regarded as the rights assured to Russia in previous treaties. The questions involved were in no sense great enough to warrant a war against the western powers.

In this moment of stress Russia turned to her allies. Basing her hopes on the agreements of Münchengrätz and Berlin and on the assistance rendered in 1849, the Russian government believed that it could count on Vienna. However, once again the division of interests between the two states in eastern affairs became apparent. Austria had no interest in increasing Russian power in the Balkans. Moreover, she feared that support of Russia would lead to French intervention in Italian affairs. Her control in that peninsula remained at all times precarious. In an impossible diplomatic situation the Austrian government, under the leadership of Buol, saw its interests tied with those of the west, but it was well aware of the dangers of antagonizing Russia. Throughout the Crimean War the Austrian policy of hesitation and half-measures won Austria the disdain of both sides.

Sentiment in Prussia was also divided; the humiliations of Olmütz and the Schleswig-Holstein affair were not forgotten. As usual, those with liberal inclinations favored co-operation with the west, whereas the conservatives stood behind the Russian alignment. As a result, Prussia adopted a policy of strict neutrality, which won her the lasting gratitude of St. Petersburg. During the Crimean War the Russian government did not have to fear that Prussia would join the allies and thus face Russia with the threat of a direct overland invasion. In contrast, Austrian neutrality always contained such a possibility. Prussia reaped the rewards of her restrained neutrality after 1856.

Not only was Russia without the active support of a strong ally, but she was also in no condition to enter upon a major war. The catastrophic state of Russian finances was reflected in the army, which, because of the cost involved, had not been equipped with modern weapons. The Russian network of railroads had not been developed to the south and Russian communications between the north and center of the country and the Black Sea were very bad. The bureaucracy, which was characterized by graft, corruption, and inefficiency, had not the ability to prepare the nation for a national crisis. The Crimean War was to demonstrate how thoroughly Nicholas I had failed to develop the internal organization of his country in order to enable it to keep pace with its international position and its external claims and commitments.

The summer of 1853 was filled with great diplomatic activity. Since Vienna held the key to the future, attention was concentrated on this city. For Russia, in particular, the Austrian attitude was bound to be decisive. Austria and Prussia together protected the Russian western frontier; the Austrian armies stationed in Transylvania could nullify Russian action in the Balkans. Russian armies could not march toward Constantinople if the danger existed that they might be cut off by Austrian action in the Principalities. Yet without a Balkan invasion the Russian government had no possibility of defeating the Turks or ending the war with a victory. Since Russian naval power could not hope to challenge France or Britain, Russia could menace Constantinople only by land.

In its approach to Vienna, however, the Russian government met only with rebuffs. Not only was the debt of gratitude for 1849 ignored, but Russia had also more recently supported Austria in a quarrel with the Porte over Montenegro. Before Russia had occupied the Principalities, she had invited Austria to act with her and to take Bosnia and Serbia. Vienna had refused to co-operate and had advised against the move. Austria certainly had every reason to prevent the crisis from developing further. In an attempt to save the situation, Buol and the ambassadors of the powers in the Austrian capital drafted the "Vienna Note" of July 28, 1853, which in effect reaffirmed the Russian rights under Kuchuk Kainardji and Adrianople. Russia accepted the proposal at once, but Turkey, by suggesting amendments that were unacceptable, in fact rejected it. The Porte, convinced that Britain and France would give their support, now was eager for a Holy War and a showdown with St. Petersburg. The effect of the apparent willingness of Russia to accept mediation was undermined when it became known that the Russian interpretation of the Vienna note was such that she would have more rights of interference in behalf of the Christians than was originally intended. Nicholas himself did not know exactly what had been gained at Kuchuk Kainarji. Although the tsar later withdrew this "violent interpretation" at a meeting with Franz Joseph at Olmütz, confidence in his sincerity of purpose was weakened.

Meanwhile, despite the continued diplomatic negotiations, the situation grew more critical. At the end of September, without consulting the cabinet, Aberdeen and Clarendon ordered the fleet to Constantinople. Confident of British backing, the Ottoman government on October 4 issued an ultimatum to Russia to evacuate the Principalities; on October 23 Turkish troops crossed into Russian territory. With the British fleet at the Straits and Russia and Turkey thus at war, public enthusiasm for participation in the conflict increased in both France and Britain. It took only a perfectly legitimate act of war on the part of the Russian fleet to make the final decision almost unavoidable. With the deliberate aim of provoking a Russian attack, the Ottoman government sent a squadron into the Black Sea. On November 30 at Sinope the Russian fleet met and annihilated the Turkish force. About 4,000 men were lost. Despite the full legitimacy of the Russian action, the western press dubbed it the "massacre of Sinope" and branded it a Russian outrage. Stratford de Redcliffe was delighted with the battle: "for that means war. The Emperor of Russia chose to make it a personal quarrel with me: and now I am avenged." [6]

The war still took long in starting. In January, 1854 the allied fleets entered the Black Sea; in the next month diplomatic relations were broken. At the end of February the allies sent Nicholas I an ultimatum giving him two months to evacuate the Principalities. The tsar did not bother to answer this communication, but on March 20 he despatched Russian troops across the Danube. Thus by slow stages the battle was finally engaged. The issue on the allied side was straightforward: the prevention of Russian preponderance over the Ottoman Empire. For Russia the reasons for the war were not so clear. At the time she had no immediate desire to partition the empire, although Nicholas I had repeatedly sought to provide for such an eventuality. The Russian government was also fully conscious of its own weaknesses and of the dangers of a coalition war. It had been, nevertheless, pushed into the conflict by a series of events that involved Russian prestige. The test of strength in the Near East between Britain and Russia, which had been years in preparation, was now to be fought under circumstances of maximum advantage to the British. Although it may well be argued that such a conflict was at some time inevitable, it was certainly a failure of Russian diplomacy, and of Nicholas I personally as the responsible head of the government, that the war came at a moment so unfavorable for Russian interests.

With the war now under way, the choice of a battlefield remained to be made. Since Russian sea power was inferior, it was obvious that it would be the allies who would determine where the armies would meet. Because of the attitude of Sweden, a Baltic campaign was not deemed advisable. Neutral Prussia closed that area. A Balkan venture remained a possibility, but here Austrian actions prevented that region from becoming a battlefield. In April, 1854 Prussia and Austria signed an alliance in which each guaranteed the other's territory and both agreed

6. *Ibid.*, p. 320.

to allow no further Russian expansion in the Balkans. Prussia later gained the adherence of the German diet to this agreement. Thereafter Prussian influence was directed toward the preservation of Austrian neutrality. With her position in central Europe secure, the Austrian government next turned to the Turks and made an agreement on the Principalities. To the intense indignation of the Russian government, whose armies were winning victories, the demand was then made that the Russians evacuate the Principalities. After the forced withdrawal of the Russian troops, Austria occupied Moldavia, and Austrian and Turkish troops together held Wallachia. As long as Austria remained neutral, it would be impossible for the allies and Russia to meet in combat in the Balkans.

With the Principalities in its hands, the Austrian government continued its efforts to find a basis for peace. On August 8 the allies and Austria issued the Vienna Four Points, which, because they eventually became the basic terms of the peace, are of immense significance. The declaration contained the following provisions: (1) the Russian protectorate over the Principalities and Serbia was to be replaced by a European guarantee; (2) the navigation of the Danube was to be made free; (3) the Straits Convention of 1841 was to be revised; (4) a five-power guarantee of the Christians of the Ottoman Empire was to substitute for the Russian rights in regard to the Orthodox. Since the Russian armies had not yet been defeated in battle, Nicholas rejected the proposals.

With all other possible areas eliminated, the allies were left with the Russian Black Sea coast as the only available area for combat. Thus the Crimea, with Sebastopol as the main objective, was selected as the point of invasion. Although this land was remote from their home base, Britain and France had absolute command of the Black Sea, and sea transport at that time was preferable to overland carriage. In September, 1854 a combined force of British, French, and Turkish troops landed, to be met by about 35,000 Russian defenders. Later in the campaign Sardinian troops also joined the allies. The first engagement on the Alma resulted in a defeat for the outnumbered Russians, but delay and divided council prevented the victorious troops from exploiting their gains. The Russian forces were thus given time to reassemble and to fortify Sebastopol more strongly. The siege of this city thereafter became the central point of the military operations of the war. Although the Russians were able to hold the position for eleven months, they were unable to dislodge their opponents; unsuccessful attempts were made at Balaklava in October and at Inkerman in November. Finally in September, 1855, after its long resistance, Sebastopol was finally captured by the allies. The only bright spot in the Russian military picture in the war was in the Caucasus where Russian troops took Kars in November, 1855. Nicholas I was spared the knowledge of the final defeat of his armies, in whom he had shown such intense interest and pride. On March 2, 1855 he died, leaving his country in a disastrous internal condition and faced with a war against dangerous opponents.

*　　*　　*　　*　　*

With the death of Nicholas Russia lost the unique position in Europe that she had won in 1814. Another century was to pass before Russian military power and prestige was to enjoy a similar advantage. Nicholas' entire reign has in retrospect been harshly judged, particularly because of his blind failure to institute some kind of internal reform. Although it is indeed difficult to justify his internal administration, the thirty years of his leadership in foreign policy do not present such a dark picture despite the final catastrophe. Until 1854 Russian policy in the east had been quite successful. The Russo-Turkish war had ended in a Russian victory; the Treaty of Unkiar Skelessi was an undoubted diplomatic triumph. The policy of co-operation with Britain in the Greek and Egyptian questions had led to solutions satisfactory to Russia and had prevented France and Britain from forming a united front against her. In central European affairs his success was even more marked. Certainly, his recognition that liberal and national movements could be potentially dangerous to

Russia was correct. He also kept Germany divided and Poland in political bondage. Although this condition was not to the benefit of the Poles or Germans, unreformed Russia could not be expected to welcome the formation of modern national states on her doorstep. The Crimean War, thus, did indeed mark a failure of policy, but the weakness of the system lay in the internal affairs of Russia. The new tsar, Alexander II, was to take this lesson to heart and, in concentrating on the domestic needs of his country, was to commit a blunder in foreign relations far greater than any in his father's reign in allowing the consolidation of central Europe.

IV

Alexander II

The reign of the new tsar, Alexander II, commenced under the most unauspicious of circumstances. Ascending the throne at the age of 37, he was, however, better prepared for this high position than his father had been. Keenly aware of the deficiencies of his own training for the demanding office, Nicholas I had associated his son with him and given him administrative duties. Alexander II had also functioned as regent in his father's absence. Unlike many royal heirs, Alexander II showed no signs that he did not fully share his father's basic political principles, although the weaknesses of the system had been shown in the Crimean War. Despite the fact that reforms were inaugurated under his administration and that he did initially follow a policy of alliance with France, he accepted these changes because of immediate necessity. At the end of his reign he returned to the old principles, particularly in foreign policy, and favored a rebuilding of the former conservative coalition.

Nevertheless, Alexander's reign as a whole is chiefly notable for the internal reforms in the state. The necessities of the domestic situation determined the shape of Russian foreign relations for the greater part of the period. The Crimean War had shown with great clarity how far Russia was behind the western states in military power; without a fundamental change in its basic structure it was apparent that the vast empire could not be maintained intact. The new reforms were therefore initiated much in the spirit of those of Peter the Great, although with less of the vigor and direction of purpose of that monarch. The reforms of the 1860's quite understandably concentrated on the question of serfdom since it was in this aspect that Russian society now differed markedly from that of the rest of Europe. Serf labor and a serf-based economy had also proved inefficient and uneconomical. Although there was little or no approval of the idea of serfdom itself, the problem remained of how this condition could be changed without at the same time severely damaging the position of the gentry, who in turn were the support of the autocratic system. The question was discussed and debated by various committees and the entire matter was energetically pushed by Alexander II with the argument that "it would be better to abolish serfdom from above than to wait till it will begin to liberate itself from below." The final measures of 1861 were a compromise between the interests of the gentry and the serfs. Although the conditions of emancipation differed in the various regions of Russia and among the categories of peasants, in general the former serf received land, somewhat less in extent to that which he had previously cultivated for his own use, in return for a sum of money to be paid to the government in forty-nine annual installments. The state then in turn indemnified the landlord. The village community and not the individual received actual jurisdiction over the land and held the responsibility for the redemption payments. The peasant was thus bound to his community as he had formerly been tied to his landlord. Instead of receiving real personal freedom, he remained in a special status where he was freed from the old bonds of serfdom, but he retained many of the former limitations on his free activity. His social and legal position still set him apart from the others.

The emancipation of serfs required other reforms closely linked with this fundamental social change. New regulations for local government and for legal proceedings were enacted; in the 1870's military reforms followed. Despite the fact that Alexander II supported these changes, it is to be noted that he did not surrender any of his political powers. Russia remained an autocracy and the support of conservative, legitimate governments was to become again, after a brief entente with France before 1863, a determining consideration of foreign policy. The peasant emancipation was in the end neither an economic nor a social success. The land the peasant received was too small in extent and his payments were calculated too high. Nevertheless, these acts did bring social conditions in Russia more in line with those of her western neighbors. The reforms also for the moment served to calm internal criticism. Reform from above without revolution was accomplished despite the weaknesses of the autocratic regime that were exposed in the Crimean War.

The Crimean disaster and the subsequent concentration of Russia on internal development removed her from an active, aggressive role in European affairs for almost twenty years. During this period the map of Europe was remade and the balance of forces on the continent was radically altered. The first part of the reign of Alexander II thus contrasts strongly with that of Nicholas I, who, as we have seen, intervened actively wherever Russian interests or those of the conservative order were affected. The change reflected not only the weakness of Russia as a power, but also the disinclination of the new tsar and his ministers to continue the role of the "gendarme of Europe," the defender of the conservative order and the treaties of Vienna.

THE PEACE OF PARIS

The first sad duty that Alexander II faced was the liquidation of a war he could not hope to win. In September 1855 the fortress of Sebastopol, despite a brave and able defense, fell to the western allies and the Russian troops were forced to withdraw in the Crimea. This victory, although welcomed as the first major success of the campaign, did not bring France and Britain much further. Obviously they were in no position to launch a major invasion of Russia, particularly as long as both Austria and Prussia remained neutral. Moreover, the French government had now become reluctant to press forward the expensive campaign in the Crimea. Britain, with more at stake in the defeat of Russia in the area, preferred to continue the war. The French proposal that the allies should call for a general uprising of the Russian subject nationalities in Finland, Poland, and the Caucasus was, however, strongly opposed. The separation in aims and objectives of the two major allies was here clearly apparent.

Because of the deadlock on the military level, the position of Austria remained decisive for all of the combatants. In November the allied powers with Austria agreed upon a new protocol based upon a strengthened interpretation of the Vienna Four Points. The full demilitarization and neutralization of the Black Sea was now demanded; Austria also obtained the provision that southern Bessarabia be returned to Moldavia, thus removing Russia from the Danube river shore. When the Austrian government agreed to enter the war should these terms be rejected, Russia was forced to accept. Austrian participation on the western side would have made a true invasion of Russia possible; the Russian statesmen also feared a rising of their minorities. The hostile attitude in Vienna throughout the war had aroused Russian anger, but it was this final action that was most bitterly remembered and most strongly influenced the subsequent decisions made in St. Petersburg.

Although the Russian diplomats subsequently went to the peace conference with the expectation of meeting British and Austrian hostility, they had some hopes of receiving support from France. As had been the case in Vienna in 1814, the war coalition had showed signs of cracking even before the fighting had ended. Throughout the war France had maintained indirect connections with St. Petersburg, and at the conference itself the basis for the subsequent friendship was laid. It was soon shown that Austria and Britain had more interest in checking Russia in the east than did France, who wished Russian co-operation for her own interests.

The peace conference that opened in Paris in February, 1856 was the first general European meeting of its kind since 1814. The powers who had fought in the war—France, Russia, Britain, Sardinia, the Ottoman Empire, and Austria, because of her actions at the end—sent representatives. Due to the opposition of Britain, Prussia was allowed to attend only the sessions concerning the revision of the Straits settlement, of which she was also a signatory power. Orlov and Brunnov represented Russia; Napoleon and Walewski were the French members. Clarendon and Cowley represented Britain; Cavour spoke for Piedmont, and Buol for Austria. Since the terms had been agreed upon beforehand, no great controversies threatened the success of the conference. In general, the Russian delegates sought to obtain a soft interpretation of the terms while the British attempted to impose as restricting a peace as possible upon their eastern antagonist. In the end the treaty was singularly mild when it is considered that the Russian government could not have continued with the war. The final terms reflected carefully the Vienna Four Points with their later modifications.

The section of the treaty that aroused the greatest resentment within Russia was undoubtedly that concerned with the demilitarization of the Black Sea since these stipulations reflected directly upon the Russian territorial integrity and upon her national honor. According to these, both Russia and Turkey were forbidden to maintain warships or arsenals on the shores of the Black Sea. The Straits were, of course, to continue to remain closed to warships of all nationalities, but open to the merchantmen of the powers. In the succeeding years the issue of the enforced neutralization of the Black Sea played a disproportionate role in the determination of Russian foreign policy. In fact, the breaking of these clauses became the chief single issue in Russian foreign relations until 1870.

The annexation of southern Bessarabia to Moldavia, who had lost it in 1812, removed Russian control from the mouth of the Danube in accordance with the Austrian desires. This action was certainly to the benefit of all of the powers since the Russian role of custodian of the navigable Sulina channel had been anything but praiseworthy. In the interest of her own Black Sea ports and her agriculture, she had allowed the channel to silt up and she had taken measures detrimental to the river trade. The administration of the Danube river was now placed in the hands of a commission of riverain states from whose number Russia was excluded. The question of Bessarabia, like that of the neutralization of the Black Sea, became henceforth for Russia a matter of national honor, despite the fact that the territory was not Russian in nationality and had been acquired only during the Napoleonic period.

The principal general issue leading to the Crimean War, the Russian claim to the protectorship of the Balkan Christians, was met by establishing the principle that the European powers jointly should assume responsibility in this question. The Ottoman Empire was also expressly admitted to the concert of the European powers and the governments promised to respect the independence and the territorial integrity of the Porte. It was agreed that should a conflict arise between one of the powers and Constantinople, the other governments would be consulted. These terms were an expression of the continued British hope and conviction that the Ottoman Empire could be reformed and reorganized into a political body acceptable to its citizens. On the vigorous prompting of Stratford de Redcliffe, the sultan on February 18 issued the reform decree of the Hatti-Humayun of 1856, which promised religious and legal equality for Christian and Moslem alike. In this respect this measure resembled the similar decree of the Hatti-Sheriff of November, 1839, whose promises had never been fulfilled.

The Russian government was also forced to give up its protectorate over Serbia and the Danubian Principalities. Serbian autonomy was reaffirmed, but Turkish garrisons were allowed to remain in the country. The question of the ultimate political organization of Moldavia and Wallachia brought up one of the major disputes of the conference and demonstrated the basic lack of unity between the Crimean allies. The issue was from the beginning of great interest and importance to Napoleon III, because he could by strengthening the Rumanian position serve French national interests and also forward his ideas on the national organization of Europe. Under the Russian protectorate, as we have seen, the liberal elements of the Rumanian leadership had been educated in Paris and had turned to France for inspiration and ideas. The ruling boyars in the country regarded themselves as linked to France in culture and civilization and wished to be regarded as an outpost of that nation in eastern Europe. At the congress Napoleon, therefore, supported the program of the liberal, national party and called for the union of the Principalities under a foreign prince. This plan met with the strongest opposition from Vienna, which did not wish to allow the formation of a strong state, linked with France, on the lower Danube. The effect that this action would have both on the balance of political power in the immediate area and on the Rumanian nationals under Austrian control was considered. This position was supported by the Porte, which naturally wished to avoid any further infringements or limitations on its sovereignty in the territory. Britain at first maintained a moderate position, but she also preferred not to allow a weakening of Turkish power. Faced by this division among its adversaries, the Russian government decided to support the French stand, chiefly in order to separate France from Britain. When it was found impossible to achieve an acceptable arrangement at the congress, the powers decided to refer the Rumanian question to a special commission to be appointed to study the problem. It was also agreed that assemblies would be elected in both Principalities in order to determine the opinion of the population concerned.

In other sections of the treaty Sweden obtained the demilitarization of the Aland Islands. Cavour was also allowed to speak at the conference on conditions in Italy, in particular in regard to the Kingdom of the Two Sicilies and the Papal States. In April, 1856 the British, French, and Austrian governments signed a treaty of guarantee in which they agreed to go to war should Russia break the treaty. Although this pact was in theory secret, Napoleon communicated it to the Russian government. Its conclusion had no further significance in international diplomacy.

Despite the fact that Russia lost the right to maintain armaments on the Black Sea, that she yielded southern Bessarabia, and that she was forced to abandon her general claims to act as the protecting power of the Balkan Christians, the treaty brought no great changes in the map or any clearly apparent shift in the basic balance of political power in the Near East. To many at the time the results seemed hardly to justify the losses in men and matériel; over a half million died in the war, the majority of disease and lack of care. The finances of all of the participants had been gravely affected by the burden of fighting at a great distance from the centers of the countries involved. Nevertheless, the Crimean War was perhaps the most decisive single conflict of the entire period since Peter the Great, because it created the general political conditions that ultimately brought about the national unification of central Europe and a radical change in the European balance. The results of the Crimean War were thus not to be seen in the terms of the Treaty of Paris but in the history of the next fifteen years.

The war and the conditions of the peace had also a profound effect upon the position of Russia as a great power and upon the opinion that was held of her military capacity. The ineptness of her fighting forces had shown both to the west and to the Russian statesmen the hollowness of her claims to military might. Not only had the Russian armies proved incapable of winning battles on their own soil, but the Holy Alliance, the diplomatic combination on which Russia had relied, had proved no guarantee of international security when it was tested. After 1856 St. Petersburg was no longer able to play the predominant role that it had enjoyed in European affairs since 1814. The center of European diplomacy now shifted back to Paris, and the chief protagonist on the European scene became Napoleon III.

THE FRANCO-RUSSIAN ENTENTE, 1856-1863

After the war the task of guiding Russian foreign policy fell into the hands of a new minister, A. M. Gorchakov. Nesselrode, who now left office, favored the return to the conservative alliance system despite the Austrian betrayal because he believed that Russian policy must remain "monarchical and anti-Polish." In many respects, Gorchakov was better fitted to the changed conditions than was his predecessor. Of an ancient and pure Russian lineage, he was more acceptable to the nationalists who had deeply resented the place occupied by those of German nationality in the Russian army and bureacracy. His prior career had centered on posts in Stuttgart and Vienna. Since his appointment in Württemberg also necessitated his attendance at the diet of the Germanic Confederation in Frankfurt, he had come to know Bismarck as a colleague. His chief position had undoubtedly been the post of ambassador in Vienna, which he held during the difficult days of the Crimean War. There he had come into strong conflict with Buol and he returned to St. Petersburg determined to obtain revenge for what he regarded as a flagrant betrayal of faith on the part of Austria. With this attitude he was well qualified to lead in the inauguration of an anti-Austrian orientation in foreign relations, a course of action that fitted with the convictions of most of the influential Russian statesmen of the time.

The policy that Gorchakov directed and implemented at the commencement of his period in office was referred to by his colleagues as that of *recueillement,* based on the minister's words, *"La Russie ne boude pas, mais se recueille."* It was recognized that for a period of years Russia would of necessity be forced to devote its principal strength to internal reform and reorganization. The Crimean War had demonstrated the weakness of the state and had shown again that an invasion by a hostile coalition of the powers of Europe was always a possibility that must be reckoned with. In these circumstances, the policy of Nicholas I would have to be abandoned until Russia was again strong enough to assume wide commitments. Thus Russian armies could no longer remain poised to intervene in European affairs; nor could Russia defend conservative causes all over the map of Europe. Foreign policy would henceforth be conducted on the clear assumption that foreign adventures should be avoided and that for a period Russia could not play a great role in European affairs.

Despite these considerations it was also recognized that because of her continental position Russia could not, like Britain, maintain a policy of diplomatic isolation. In addition, Russian aims did include certain limited goals, such as the breaking of the Black Sea clauses of the Treaty of Paris and the regaining of southern Bessarabia. Russia thus needed an alliance system of some kind, even though she intended to maintain a defensive policy. The previous tie with Austria had proved valueless. Prussia had acted in Russian eyes as a true friend, but in 1856 Prussian power was not highly rated. The Russian statesmen did not believe that alliance with Berlin alone was sufficient to offset the dangers of a hostile coalition. Britain remained the chief Russian opponent in the east; moreover her avoidance of general treaties, as had been shown in the negotiations with Nicholas I, rendered her unsuitable for Russian purposes. France alone of the powers therefore appeared to be a possible ally. In considering and in accepting the idea of co-operation with the French government, Gorchakov and the tsar reversed the entire course of Russian relations as they had been carried on under Nicholas I and inaugurated a new period in Russian diplomacy.

The policy of working with France, which Russia now

adopted, signified the abandonment of two fundamental bases of policy that had been maintained since 1815—first, the defense of the territorial settlement of Vienna, and, second, the protection of legitimate monarchs against revolution. Instead Russia now entered into a period of co-operation with Napoleon III, who actively sought to remake the map of Europe on national lines and to break the Vienna settlement. The French emperor thus stood in opposition to all that Nicholas I had held sacred in international relations—the sanctity of international treaties and the necessity for the rulers of Europe to make a common stand against revolutionary movements. In agreement with France, Russia was now to enter upon a period in which she would accede to, or actively aid in, the breaking of international agreements by revolutionary methods.

The Russian willingness to co-operate with France was a result not only of her need for an ally but also of her altered relations with her neighbors after the Crimean War. The Napoleonic policy of national unification affected at first primarily the Habsburg Empire. Russia was, after 1856, perfectly willing to accept a severe weakening of Habsburg power, and she welcomed the chance to secure revenge for the Austrian attitude during the war. However, even more important, Russia had changed her general attitude toward the Vienna settlement. Since the Russian government now openly sought to break the restrictions imposed upon her by the Treaty of Paris, it could no longer be expected to be the enthusiastic upholder of the sanctity of other international guarantees, particularly of those that benefited Austria. In order to destroy the clauses detrimental to Russian interests in this new treaty, modifications in the settlements of 1815 could be accepted. Moreover, alliance with revolutionary France no longer held the dangers to Russian internal policy of the previous era. Russia itself was undergoing a period of reform and change. Gorchakov prided himself on his liberal inclinations. Thus, once the Russian government abandoned its attempt to maintain the old conditions intact, France, as the center of change and new political ideas, no longer appeared in so dangerous a light.

Although no formal alliance was signed, Russia worked with France in international affairs with varying degrees of co-operation from 1856 to 1863. The entente was carried forward through a series of meetings between diplomats and rulers and through agreements on specific questions. The Russian government throughout these years attempted to use this policy of co-operation to divide France and Britain and to secure the humiliation of Austria. Within the period of the entente five revolutionary movements occurred in Europe—in the Danubian Principalities, Italy, Serbia, Greece, and Poland. In all but the final revolt in Poland, the Russian government either supported the changes or remained neutral. It thus concurred in the overthrow of established regimes and in the policy of the unilateral breaking of international engagements. In the following pages the three events in the Balkans, the unification of the Danubian Principalities, the change of dynasties in Serbia, and the overthrow of King Othon in Greece will be discussed together. The events in Italy and Poland will be described separately, although these occurrences overlap in time those in the east.

1. The Balkans, 1856-1863

The first major diplomatic event after the end of the Crimean War was the unification of the Danubian Principalities and the formation of the Rumanian state. The Russian protectorate over the territories, established after 1829, had, as we have seen, won Russia the enmity of the liberal, national groups. The Russian intervention in the revolutions of 1848 had caused particularly bitter resentment. Yet it was the program of those who had been foremost in their opposition to Russian domination that the French government now supported. At the peace conference Napoleon III championed the position of the Rumanian liberals, who wished a united state under a foreign prince. Russia, because of her new political orientation, in the next years followed the French lead and sponsored the attainment of the Rumanian national desires, although this action was in strong contrast to her previous position in the Principalities. In the negotiations, the French and Russian governments received support also from Sardinia and Prussia. The chief opposition to Rumanian unification lay, as before, in Vienna and Constantinople. Britain, however, because of her desire to support the Ottoman Empire also worked against the Rumanian national ambitions. The chief issue was the form of government to be given the two Principalities and the degree of unity to be permitted. In July, 1857 elections were held in the Principalities in accordance with the agreement reached at Paris. In the elections, which were characterized by extreme corruption, the vote went against the unionist party. The obvious fraudulent character of the whole transaction led to a major crisis between France and Britain, which was intensified by the rivalry of the ambassadors of the two powers in Constantinople. However, in August, 1857 a compromise solution was agreed upon between Napoleon III and Queen Victoria, accompanied by their ministers, in a meeting held at Osbourne. Britain accepted the annulment of the elections; in return Napoleon agreed not to press for the unification of the Principalities. Although this arrangement satisfied the powers, it was difficult to enforce because of sentiments of the Rumanian elector. After a more honest election held in September, 1857 the assemblies in both provinces again proceeded to vote for unification and a foreign prince. Thus the powers were forced to meet again and draft another convention affirming once more the separation of the Principalities. In the winter of 1858-1859 a third election resulted in the choice of assemblies who then elected the same man, Alexander Cuza, as hospodar (governor) in both provinces. This clear violation of the will of the great powers and of the treaties was only maintained because of the general international situation and the events in Italy. Austria, with her attention occupied elsewhere, could not actively intervene. France as usual remained the friend of the Rumanian nationalist. Under the circumstances, the powers agreed to accept the double election, but only as an exception, and they insisted upon the con-

RUMANIA IN 1861

tinued separation of the two provinces in administrative matters.

Cuza was thus able to retain his governorship over the two Principalities, but he had great difficulty in internal affairs. In order to secure support for his domestic policies, he gained the consent of the Porte in the spring of 1861 for the unification of the administrative apparatus and the assemblies of the two provinces. Thus he secured the real unity of the state. Rumania had, therefore, been created with French support and because the events in central Europe precluded intervention by the powers hostile to the development. In the question of Rumanian unification, Russian policy in this period underwent a gradual change.

Although at first favorable to the French position, the Russian government, after the double election of Cuza, gradually stiffened its outlook. It was certainly no more to the Russian than to the Austrian advantage to have the establishment of a united Rumanian state, particularly if it were liberal in politics and tied to France in international affairs. The national movement on the Danube also exerted the same attraction on the Poles that it did on the Austrian Slavic and Magyar subjects.

In 1866 the final stage of the program of the Rumanian nationalists of the 1850's was accomplished with the expulsion of Alexander Cuza and the election of a foreign prince, Charles of Hohenzollern-Sigmaringen. This revolt, carried through because of internal political conditions in Rumania, was strongly opposed by Russia, who withheld recognition of the new ruler for two years. However, again the powers did not act, although the event openly violated existing international treaties. In the next years Russian-Rumanian relations remained, in general, bad. The Russian government retained its desire to regain southern Bessarabia, which it continued to regard as part of the lands legitimately belonging to the Russian crown. It was clear that the territory would be retaken at the first opportunity.

Although the unification of the Rumanian Principalities was to prove disadvantageous to Russia in the next years, events in a neighboring state, Serbia, proved more favorable to Russian interests. Here Prince Alexander Karadjordjević, who had not supported Russia to the extent desired by his people, was replaced by the pro-Russian Miloš Obrenović. After his death two years later, his son Michael Obrenović continued his father's policies of seeking to remove the remaining rights in the state of the Porte, which was still the suzerain power, and, if possible, of extending the Serbian territories. Because of the Russian entente, the French government supported the Serbian national policy. France also co-operated with Russia in coming to the aid of the Montenegrins in their uprising against the Porte in 1858. An extension of the Montenegrin boundaries was obtained because of the intervention of the two great powers. Therefore until 1863, when the Franco–Russian alignment finally broke, France did assist Russia in the Balkans by favoring the national aspirations of the two Balkan Slavic states who were at the time in close relation with Russia.

The third important political upheaval that occurred in the Balkans involved the expulsion of King Othon of Greece in the winter of 1862-1863. The internal politics of the kingdom had been complicated since its founding by the rivalry of the powers for predominant influence in the country and by the fact that the state as established in 1830 contained within its boundaries only a minority of the Greek people. In 1844 Othon accepted a constitution and with it limitations of his political power. Thereafter he relied for political support on Kolettes, the head of the French party. Both the king and his minister pursued the one aim that was desired by all the Greeks and that would assure them the backing of their people—the national expansion of their country. In this policy they were principally opposed by Britain, who in Greek affairs as elsewhere upheld the rights of the Ottoman Empire. During the Crimean War the relations between Greece and Britain were particularly bad, largely as the result of the desire of the Greek government to use the opportunity to gain more territory. To prevent Greek action against the Porte, British and French fleets were sent to Pireus in 1854. King Othon had thus by 1860 antagonized the western powers. Russia was also not satisfied with his rule. As has been mentioned, from 1832 until the expulsion of Othon the Russian government in its relations with Greece placed great emphasis upon the question of religion. When Othon, who had no children of his own, failed to designate an heir of the Orthodox faith, or one who could be expected to be converted, he lost the support of St. Petersburg. Thus when a revolution forced his abdication in 1862, he found that none of the great powers regretted the event.

With the expulsion of the Greek king, France, Russia, and Britain as the protecting powers were faced with the problem of finding a successor. Here the British government with its fleet in the Mediterranean was in the most advantageous position to influence the choice. Moreover, it could and did use its possession of the Ionian Islands as a lever to insure the return of a suitable candidate. Although Britain had decided to relinquish the islands, it was made clear that this would be done only if the new king won British approval. Finally, the powers agreed upon the name of Prince William of Denmark, the second son of the future King Christian IX of Denmark. In 1863 he became King George I of Greece. The religious issue was settled by the postponement of the question for another generation. The new king was also to govern under a constitution of a very liberal character. The change of regime in Athens thus did not fulfill the Russian desire that an Orthodox king should rule Greece. In the negotiations the French government followed willingly the British suggestions and demonstrated that in questions involving Greece there was little chance of separating the two western powers.

The seven years after the Crimean War thus witnessed revolutionary changes in three Balkan states. In each case the Russian government had approved or supported armed revolts against legitimate rulers as well as actions in violation of international agreements. Autocratic Russia was clearly not the firm supporter of legality in international relations that she had been in the previous reign. The alterations in the conditions in the Balkans, however, brought no immediate repercussions in general European or Russian politics. In contrast, the revolutionary movements that took place concurrently in Europe proper had a deep significance for the future of the Russian state.

2. Italy and Poland

Napoleon III had gladly supported the unification of the Danubian Principalities, however, his chief interest lay in the national unification of two other peoples—the Poles and the Italians. Since friendship with Russia demanded the temporary abandonment of Poland, he, therefore, concentrated on Italian unification. He pursued this aim with particular vigor after an attempt was made upon his life by the Italian nationalist, Orsini, in January, 1858. In meeting with Cavour at Plombières in July, 1858 he agreed to support the unification of northern Italy under Piedmont in return for the Italian provinces of Nice and Savoy. Thereafter he turned to Russia to assure this nation's neutrality. In March, 1859 Russia signed a secret agreement promising to maintain an attitude of benevolent neutrality in a future war between France and Austria. In this tense situation the Austrian government made the mistake of delivering an ultimatum to Piedmont, thereby precipitating on her own initiative the conflict that both Napoleon III and Cavour wanted. In the resultant war between Piedmont (which was supported by France) and Austria, Russia played her role of benevolent neutrality to the full satisfaction of France and she concentrated troops on the Austrian border. She also acted to restrain the enthusiasm of the smaller German states who wished to go to the aid of Austria. Russia and Britain together put pressure on the Germanic Confederation not to act to assist their member state.

Despite the initial military victories that he won and the support he received from Russia, Napoleon III was not content with the course of events. Like Russia, he did not fully approve of the rapid progress of the revolutionary movement in the Italian peninsula. At the outbreak of the war, revolts had overthrown the governments in Tuscany, Parma, and Modena. Moreover, the attitude of Prussia was not clear, and the French government was well aware that Russia would not act against Berlin. Moreover, the Austrian strongholds in northern Italy remained unconquered, and the German states were clearly restless under their enforced neutrality. With these considerations in mind Napoleon III met with Franz Joseph at Villafranca in July and made an agreement that in effect halted the Italian national movement at the half-way point.

Although the great powers were now in agreement on the question, the forces of Italian nationalism, like those previously in Rumania, made a compromise solution impossible. Parma, Modena, Tuscany, and Romagna proceeded immediately to vote union with Piedmont, and the revolutionary movement took hold throughout Italy. The expedition of Garibaldi, who in May, 1860 landed in southern Italy and then marched up the peninsula, brought an end to the reactionary Kingdom of the Two Sicilies. The campaign of Garibaldi with its clear leftist and revolutionary implications caused great concern in Russia. The Kingdom of the Two Sicilies had always enjoyed particular Russian favor. When the armies of Piedmont occupied the Papal States, relations were broken between Turin and St. Petersburg, not to be re-established until August, 1862. The unification of Italy thus took place in face of the clear disapproval of Russia, despite the fact that her original agreement with France had made the event possible.

The entire episode of the Italian unification thus cast a deep shadow over Franco-Russian relations. The ousting of long-established dynasties in the Italian states was bound to disturb the Russian court. It was also quite obvious that the policy of friendship with France and enmity to Austria could have dangerous repercussions within the Russian controlled lands, particularly Poland. The old vision of France as the patron of revolution and the friend of free Poland again became apparent. In 1862 the firm supporter of the French alignment, Kiselev, was replaced as ambassador in Paris by Baron Budberg, a Baltic German, and a proponent of the Holy Alliance. Even before the outbreak of the Polish insurrection, the policy of alignment with France had thus been modified.

It was, however, undoubtedly the Polish insurrection that broke decisively the ties between Paris and St. Petersburg. With the accession of Alexander II, reforms had been introduced in the administration of Poland as well as in Russia. Changes in the government of their country, nevertheless, in no way met the demands of the Polish leaders who, as in 1815 and 1830, wished a complete end to Russian domination. As in the previous decades, the Polish national movement remained divided between the so-called Whites, under Czartoryski, who sought aid from France and Britain and were essentially conservative, and the

Reds, who wished to establish a democratic republic through a national uprising. The aim of both groups was the re-creation of a completely independent Poland with the pre-partition boundaries. Quite obviously these ideas could not be understood in St. Petersburg. By 1860 Poland had become in Russian eyes an inalienable part of the Russian crown possessions and the Western Provinces were regarded as clearly Russian in character. Although the liberal Russian leaders favored the granting of a wide measure of autonomy to Congress Poland, no responsible Russian statesman considered the re-establishment of prepartition Poland. Such an event could occur only after Russia had been defeated in a war against a coalition of European powers. The international aspects of the problem made the Russian government particularly sensitive to the interference of other governments in Polish affairs.

Under the viceroyship of General Michael Gorchakov, the brother of the foreign minister, a policy of further concessions was inaugurated. In 1861 and 1862 the Polish statesman Marquis Alexander Wielopolski sought to implement a program that would have established a regime in conformity with the statute of 1832, which had not been put into effect. The Polish politician, however, was extremely unpopular among his own countrymen because of his espousal of co-operation with Russia. A series of demonstrations against Russian rule were held, which showed the strong feelings of the Polish nationalists. In an attempt to suppress this agitation, Wielopolski introduced special measures, which led to the drafting into the army of the young men most prominent in the national movement. This action was the occasion of the outbreak of a revolt in January, 1863.

The Polish revolutionary movement of 1863, in contrast to that of 1830, had very little chance of success from the outset. The revolutionaries had no adequate arms or supplies, and their forces numbered only about 10,000 as against 80,000 Russian troops. Without foreign intervention, the movement was from the beginning doomed to failure. Hopes for a rising within Russia were soon dashed; the Polish peasants also failed to rally in strength to the national cause. Fighting against impossible odds, the revolutionary forces soon were defeated, and the country was subjected to a far more extreme measure of control. The Polish kingdom was incorporated into Russia and a policy of Russification was introduced. Instruction in the schools was thereafter given in Russian with the exception of the classes in religion and in the Polish language. In an effort to undercut the Polish gentry and middle class and win the support of the peasantry, the Russian government introduced a system of peasant emancipation in Poland far more beneficial than that in effect in Russia. The peasants paid no redemption dues and secured rights in excess of those allowed in Russia.

Although the Polish revolutionaries were unable to obtain concrete outside assistance, both France and Britain did offer encouragement and moral support to the movement. At the outbreak of the revolt Napoleon III had attempted to concert with Britain on common action. Throughout the rebellion the two powers had together sponsored a series of protests, which were delivered to St. Petersburg. These measures, unsupported by any actions of a practical nature, in no way aided the insurrection, but they did convince the Russian government of the impossibility of the policy of co-operation with France. The French support of national unification movements, which Russia had approved in Rumania and, initially, in Italy, had now inevitably also affected Poland. Moreover, the role of the Catholic clergy in the Polish revolt had been particularly active; the position of France as a Catholic power was an added danger.

In this crisis, in which the powers of the Crimean coalition were again united on a single issue, Russia found once more that Prussia was the only power that would stand by her. At the beginning of the revolt in February, Russia and Prussia signed the Alvensleben Convention, in which it was agreed that Russian forces could pursue Polish rebels into Prussian territory. Although this agreement was never implemented, it remained a sign of the solidarity of the two powers in the Polish question. Certainly, Prussia had even a greater interest in the maintenance of the partition of Poland than did her neighbor. Bismarck expressed an obvious fact when he stated that it would be impossible for Prussia to hold her Rhineland territories against France with a free Poland at her back. The rebellion demonstrated once again to both states the practical value of their continued friendship.

The Polish insurrection therefore served the double purpose of completely discrediting the policy of co-operation with France and of re-emphasizing the value of close political connections with Prussia. As long as that state remained under conservative political leadership, Prussia was indeed the ideal ally for autocratic Russia. She provided a barrier between the revolutionary west and the Russian lands. With no interests in the Balkans, she did not compete with Russian objectives in the area. Close family ties and old traditions bound the two courts closely together. Moreover, after 1814 Prussia had to an extent existed in the Russian shadow; at no time did she take a stand in opposition to St. Petersburg in vital matters. The single great qualifying factor in the assessment of the value of Prussia as an ally was her actual military strength. The Russian statesmen seriously doubted if Prussia alone was a strong enough ally to protect Russia from the danger of the formation of a hostile coalition and to save her from invasion. This consideration was to play the major role in the Russian attitude toward the unification of Germany in the next years.

The Franco-Russian entente, which had lasted from 1856 to 1863, thus ended. With Russian consent Napoleon III had gained the unification of Rumania and Italy. In return Russia had received little more than the satisfaction of securing the humiliation of Austria. Her interests in the east had not been pushed forward nor had she obtained a revision of the treaty of 1856. The rise of nationalism in Europe, aided and abetted by the Napoleonic policies, had ended with a rebellion in her own lands. The policy of co-operation and alliance with Paris was now abandoned, to be resumed again almost thirty years later under greatly altered circumstances.

The Russian dislike for and distrust of French policy had by this time also come to be shared by Britain. Napoleon's restless temperament and the combination of idealism and strongly practical considerations in his policy awakened British suspicion. Quite obviously the national reorganization of Europe, if carried out in the manner Napoleon intended, would have resulted in French hegemony in Europe. The British in particular feared that the emperor would attempt to annex Belgium, Luxembourg, and territory on the Rhine in the way in which he had taken Nice and Savoy during the period of Italian unification. The French-British entente, which had lasted since the Crimean War despite numerous differences of policy, received a severe blow when Britain in November, 1863 rejected a French proposal for the summoning of a European conference whose purpose would be to discuss general European questions and, if necessary, to revise the treaties of 1815. British fear of possible French aggression in areas of vital interest led the British statesmen, like the Russian, to look with favor on any diplomatic combination which might provide a counterweight in Europe to France. Thus Prussia, under the brilliant leadership of Bismarck, was able to exploit a general situation which had been prepared by the mistakes of French policy.

THE UNIFICATION OF GERMANY

With the suppression of the Polish revolt and the disintegration of the political ties of both St. Petersburg and London with Paris, the stage was set for the unification of Germany under Prussian leadership, the single most fateful event of the century for Russia. Although the genius of Bismarck as a statesman is without question, it must also be recognized that the international situation was most favorable for the realization of his objectives. For both Britain and Russia the chief danger to the peace and stability of Europe now appeared to be France under the leadership of Napoleon III. In such circumstances the building up of central Europe as a counterweight to this restless, unstable power would obviously be an advantage to both countries. For Russia a strengthening of Prussia or a furthering of German unity would provide a more effective shield for Poland; for Britain this condition would offer better protection for Belgium. Neither power foresaw the consequences of its actions. Russia, as we have seen, throughout the sixties remained preoccupied with the problems of internal reform; Britain after the death of Palmerston in 1865 entered a period of withdrawal from active intervention abroad and also concentrated on the domestic problems connected with the passage of the reform bill of 1867. Bismarck, therefore, inherited a diplomatic situation in which two of the great powers were deeply involved in questions of internal political reform, while a third was isolated and regarded with suspicion and distrust.

For Bismarck the relations between Berlin and St. Petersburg remained always of first importance. Throughout his career he sought continually to follow a policy of close collaboration and to maintain the traditional dynastic ties. As ambassador in St. Petersburg from 1859 to 1862, he had come to know the country and its principal statesmen. Because of his temperament and political convictions Bismarck as a person was also entirely acceptable in Russia. Throughout his own career Bismarck had always to meet the opposition of the Prussian liberals, who were pro-British and pro-Polish in inclination. Their victory in Prussian politics would have constituted a real danger for Russia. Therefore the protection of the position of Bismarck became a consideration of Russian policy during the years of German unification. In the 1870's Russo-Prussian relations were made difficult by the antagonism that developed between Bismarck and Gorchakov, but these feelings were not apparent at the beginning. After the great Prussian victories, Gorchakov, always vain and superficial, came to resent the successes of his colleague. The slow realization of the great significance of the unification of Germany also contributed to strengthen the dislike of the Russian minister and his assistants.

The unification of Germany was accomplished through a series of three wars in which Russia in every case maintained a position of benevolent neutrality in favor of Prussia. Without this attitude on the part of St. Petersburg toward Berlin, which was, after all, in contradiction to her policy since 1815, which had been to maintain a balance in Germany, it is difficult to imagine how the Prussian efforts could have met with success. Although the Prussian military establishment was in fact far more potent than was actually believed at the time, Prussia could not have withstood a two-front war or a conflict with a coalition. Only the abandonment by Russia of the traditional policy of enforcing the division of central Europe and of active intervention in the political affairs of the small monarchies made possible the subsequent Prussian actions. It is to be noted that in the two crucial conflicts, the Seven Weeks War and the Franco-Prussian War, Russia, in tying down Austrian forces on the Galician frontier, did in fact also render military assistance.

The first war, which arose over the vexed question of the duchies of Schleswig-Holstein, originated in a revival of the same issues that had played such a major role in the revolution of 1848 in Germany. Once again the German states saw in the question a problem of German nationalism; the other powers regarded it in the light of the necessity of maintaining the balance of power in the Baltic. In addition to the national and constitutional problems involved in the relation of the duchies to the Danish monarchy, the question of the succession to the Danish throne, since King Frederick VII had no direct heirs, was again brought up. The duchies, governed by the Salic law, would accordingly go to the Duke of Augustenburg, whereas Denmark proper would be ruled by Prince Christian of Glücksburg. In May, 1852 the powers had attempted to avoid future conflict by agreeing that both the duchies and the kingdom should together be inherited by Christian. Although Russia, France, Britain, Austria, Prussia, and Sweden signed the pact, the two German powers were not enthusiastic about the decision. The entire situation became more tense with the continuing rise of Danish and

German national feeling and its involvement in the dispute. In 1863 a new Danish constitution was drafted which provided for the incorporation of Schleswig into the Danish state in violation of the previous treaties. In answer the German diet sent an ultimatum to Denmark. At this critical moment, Frederick VII died and was succeeded by Christian IX. Pressed by his Danish subjects, the new king accepted the constitution. The diet then sent troops into the duchies in December, 1863.

War was now being waged between the diet, which favored the candidacy of Prince Frederick of Augustenburg, and the Danish monarchy. The small powers of Germany supported, in general, the actions of the diet. In contrast, Prussia and Austria, who continued to stand for the Treaty of 1852 and the candidacy of Christian IX, now separated their actions from that of the other German powers. On their own initiative, and ignoring the diet, they sent their troops into Danish territory. In the resultant fighting Denmark was defeated and forced to cede the disputed duchies. In the Convention of Gastein in August, 1865, the German powers divided the provinces, with Austria receiving the right to administer Holstein while Prussia took Schleswig. The successful acquisition of the duchies by the two powers at this time marked a strong contrast to the events of 1848-1850.

The Austro-Prussian victory and the loss of the territory by Denmark was certainly not welcomed by the other powers, but the swiftness of the event had precluded intervention. Moreover, Britain hesitated to act. She had no ally with a continental army on which she could depend and only about 20,000 troops that she could use. She was also extremely suspicious of French intentions and feared that Napoleon would use the struggle over the duchies as an opportunity to take territory on the Rhine or in the Low Countries. A strengthening of the German powers was preferable to this. Russia too had no ally, but again in contrast to 1849 and 1850 she felt no desire to check Prussia. In fact, the chief concern in St. Petersburg at this time appears to have been that war would break out and that the Prussian armies would be unable to withstand the French. Prussia as a barrier against the west would then fall. At the time that the troops entered Schleswig-Holstein, Gorchakov assured the German minister Redern that although war might occur, Russia would not join. "She will never march against Prussia," he declared.[1]

The disunity of the great powers also allowed Prussia, in the second episode, to settle the long struggle for the control of the German lands with Austria. Britain in 1866 and 1867 was chiefly concerned with her internal reform problems. In addition, a strong reaction to the meddling and provocative policies of the government of Lord Palmerston had set in. Britain, thus, for the moment played a less active role in continental politics. France remained a problem, but Bismarck assured her initial neutrality by vague hints of later compensation. Italian support was gained through an alliance and the promise of Venetia. The Seven Weeks War, which originated in a dispute over the duchies, resulted in a sudden and disastrous defeat of the Austrian armies. Only with great difficulty was Bismarck able to pursuade his king not to press the victory but to remain content with the removal of Austria from the German political scene. The Treaty of Prague of August, 1866, in accordance with Bismarck's desires, thus cost Austria no territory and only a small indemnity. The chief significance of the peace was that it ended the long duel for supremacy in Germany and it marked the dissolution of the Germanic Confederation. Prussia was now free to organize Germany north of the river Main; the four south German states, Bavaria, Baden, Württemberg, and Hesse, remained independent.

Thus, once again the Russian government had allowed Prussia to move forward and to increase substantially her power and political position. The Prussian activities this time, however, aroused great concern in the Russian court, where members of the tsar's family had close links with the German dynasties. Although Alexander II felt closely tied to Prussia because of his mother, his wife was from Hesse-Darmstadt. Others in the court were linked with the rulers of such states as Hanover and

1. W. E. Mosse, *The European Powers and the German Question* (Cambridge: Cambridge University Press, 1958), p. 172.

Württemberg. The outright Prussian annexation of Hanover, Cassel, Nassau, and Frankfurt was also unpopular. When Prussia formed the North German Confederation out of the lands north of the Main, the Russian government was also concerned about the liberal character of the constitution of the new organization.

Since the political framework of central Europe, which Prussia had now overturned, had been part of the Vienna settlement and was thus the concern of all of the powers, Alexander II proposed the holding of a conference to discuss the question. In reply to the tsar's request, William sent General Otto von Manteuffel to St. Petersburg to argue the Prussian claims. In his conversation with the Prussian general, the tsar first protested strongly over the dispossession of the small German monarchs, who, he argued, held their power from God just as surely as did the rulers of Prussia and Russia. In answer to these protests, Manteuffel emphasized the conservative aspects of Prussian leadership in Germany and he argued that a strong political organization in the area was the best guard against revolution. He thus returned to the basic emphasis of the former Holy Alliance—the conservative monarchies should remain united against liberal and revolutionary dangers. He also let it be understood that Prussia would support any Russian attempt to break the Black Sea clauses of the Treaty of Paris. Although Russia now accepted the Prussian victory and the new conditions in northern Germany, the hope remained that the southern states would retain their independence and that the tripartite division of Germany would be preserved despite the enormous strengthening of Prussia.

The severe defeat suffered by the armies of the Habsburg Monarchy forced that state to reorganize its internal structure, which it did in a manner that was to have an enormous effect on its subsequent relations with Russia. The expulsion of Austria from Germany and the national unifications of Rumania and Italy, events that were accomplished against the strong opposition of Vienna, made the further maintenance of her old political organization impossible. The monarchy was now encircled by national states; in internal affairs the Slavic and Magyar inhabitants of the empire were increasingly discontented with their status. Some compromise had to be made with the forces of nationalism. The empire met this problem by coming to terms with the strongest and most active of their minorities—the Magyars. In 1867 the state was in effect transformed into a partnership of the dominant nationalities: the Germans and the Magyars. Under the *Ausgleich* (Compromise), the lands belonging traditionally to the Hungarian crown were divided from those of Austria, and henceforth the two sections were joined only in the person of the emperor and by common ministries of war, foreign affairs, and finance as related to the first two offices. Although this political arrangement was made necessary by the pressure of events, it was to be highly detrimental to the future relations of Russia and Austria. Magyar policy in their lands became ever more nationalistic and was directed toward the further subjugation of their own Slavic and Rumanian inhabitants; in the empire as a whole the Magyar statesmen blocked reform measures. In foreign policy the memory of the Russian intervention in 1849 ensured that policies originating in Budapest would be anti-Russian. Magyar nationalism thus came increasingly into opposition to the rising Slavic national consciousness of the years after 1870, which, in turn, was to find a patron and supporter in tsarist Russia.

The clash of Magyar, Slavic, and German national feeling was further accentuated by the diplomatic consequences of the events of the sixties. The Habsburg Monarchy had lost her hegemony in Italy, and she had been forced out of Germany. Her Polish frontier was stable, and Rumania was united. She thus had left only one direction in which she could hope to make conquests—southeast toward the Balkans. The late nineteenth century witnessed a revival of imperialism and the desire for the acquisition of territory among all the powers; the Dual Monarchy, without effective naval power and hemmed in by her neighbors, could only direct her national energies toward the territory of the Ottoman Empire. Whereas before Austria had in general supported the maintenance of that state, she became henceforth more willing to participate in its partition. The territories first under consideration were the provinces of Bosnia-Hercegovina, which were inhabited by a South Slavic population. Like Russia, Vienna again became concerned with the fate of the Balkan Christian and his relations with his overlord. With the revival of a strong Balkan policy on the part of the monarchy, the question of the possibility of agreement with Russia again came into question. If the two powers could agree on a line of partition, which Bismarck always favored, conflict could be avoided. If, however, both governments sought influence and control over the same lands and peoples, a major clash would be inevitable. It was this issue that was to become and to remain the most dangerous single question for the peace of Europe in the coming years.

By 1866 Bismarck had thus succeeded in uniting Germany north of the Main; the four southern states, however, remained out of the union. After the Peace of Prague, Prussia proceeded to make defensive and offensive alliances with these monarchies, who were also brought into the Zollverein. The final stage in the unification of Germany would, of necessity, be their incorporation into the Prussian organization of north Germany. This policy could obviously be carried out only against the strong opposition of France. After the Austro-Prussian war, Napoleon III immediately sought to claim the compensation to which he believed himself entitled by the Prussian gains. In the next years he turned his attention to lands on the Rhine, to Luxembourg, and to Belgium. Although he was able to persuade the King of Holland to agree to the cession of Luxembourg, that ruler in the end backed down because of his fear of the reaction of the other powers. After this failure Napoleon remained unsatisfied and discontented with his role in European affairs.

Despite the tremendous shift in the balance of power occasioned by the Prussian victories, it is interesting to note that the state that continued to arouse the suspicions and fears of the others remained France. Moreover, despite frequent efforts, Napoleon III was unable to take his country out of its position of diplomatic isolation. Britain held firmly to its policy of non-involvement. Negotiations were initiated with Vienna, but the Dual Monarchy's interests were now primarily in the Balkans, an area where France could offer little assistance. The renewal of ties with St. Petersburg foundered as usual on the rocks of the Polish problem and the revolution. In 1867 the tsar visited the Paris exhibition of that year. Not only was he coolly received by the French crowds, but he was also shot at twice by a Pole. It appeared quite clear that a conservative Prussia-Germany was a needed safeguard for autocratic Russia. The general diplomatic situation thus remained highly favorable for further Prussian moves.

The Russian option for Prussia in central Europe received another confirmation when in March, 1868 the assurance was given that Russia would station troops on her border with Austria should war break out with France. Russia would in this manner perform for Berlin the service that she had rendered Paris in the Franco-Austrian War of 1859. Although no written engagement was made at this time, Bismarck could assume that Russia would not join with France. In addition, the Russian government used its influence with the southern German states to encourage them to co-operate with Prussia. Russian influence and military power were thus in effect put at the service of Bismarck in the last stage of German unification.

By 1870 both Prussia and France were ready for a decisive trial of strength. Although the Prussian diplomatic position was at this time undoubtedly superior, her military power was still in question. France, because of her great past and her military traditions, was usually judged the stronger, but neither power had tested its armies on a major battlefield since 1815. After that date Prussian military strength had not been rated highly; she was regarded as the weakest of the major powers, if not as a state of the second rank. Russian and British statesmen had in the past been principally worried lest a war between the two states result in such a severe defeat of Prussia that France would again be able to dominate central Europe. The final conflict was provoked by

French mishandling of the candidature of Prince Leopold of Hohenzollern-Sigmaringen to the Spanish throne. Although Napoleon III had been willing to accept the prince's brother as ruler of Rumania in 1866, he chose to make a major issue of the question at this time. Although neither William nor the prince's father would consider the acceptance of the Spanish invitation, Napoleon insisted that the Prussian king issue a statement renouncing the candidacy for all time. In the conversations that followed, both Napoleon and Bismarck showed themselves willing to allow the question of French and Prussian power to be settled on the battlefield. The final French declaration of war on July 19 reflected the desire of both governments to determine in this manner the question of continental supremacy.

Once the fighting commenced it soon became apparent that the three other powers, Russia, Britain and Austria, would remain passive. The British attitude was reinforced when Bismarck published a draft treaty that indicated clearly Napoleon's previous attempts to annex Belgium. The Russian position had been determined by the promises of 1868 and by an additional assurance given in the previous July that Russia would cover the Austrian border with 300,000 men. This move allowed Moltke to concentrate an extra 100,000 troops against France. Throughout the war Russia exercised strong pressure on Austria to prevent her from beginning military preparations. The tsar promised to guarantee Austrian territorial integrity as long as that country refrained from warlike moves. Although Russia considered proposing a conference and European mediation, the idea was dropped after the Prussian victory at Sedan. Thereafter the Russian government concentrated on securing some advantage from her efforts on behalf of Prussia.

At the beginning of the war the Russian statesmen had not expected that the independent existence of the southern German states would be at issue, but the magnitude of the Prussian victories soon led them to abandon any hope that the division of Germany could be maintained. The Prussian desire to annex Alsace-Lorraine and the encouragement given by Bismarck also influenced her decisions. In October, 1870 at a meeting of his council of ministers, Alexander II declared his intention of denouncing the Black Sea clauses of the Treaty of Paris. On October 31 Gorchakov issued a circular note to the powers announcing the unilateral Russian action. Although this move aroused widespread protests, particularly on the part of Britain, little could be done. France had been defeated; Prussia had promised her support in 1866 and 1870. Britain could not act alone. Finally, a conference of seven powers was held where in effect the Russian action was approved and a new Straits settlement was drawn up. In the new agreement of March, 1871 the principle of the closure of the Straits was again affirmed, but the Sultan was allowed the right "to open the said Straits in time of peace to the vessels of war of friendly and allied Powers, in case the Sublime Porte should judge it necessary in order to secure the execution of the stipulations of the Treaty of Paris of the 30th of March 1856." The chief advantage that Britain had received from her victory in the Crimean War was thereby annulled. Both Russia and Turkey were free to build arsenals and maintain fleets on the Black Sea.

THE THREE EMPERORS' LEAGUE

Germany was thus united under Prussian leadership with Russian support. The event was concluded on a high note of friendship between the two countries. At the end of the war William telegraphed the tsar: "Prussia will never forget that she owes it to you that the war has not taken on extreme dimensions." Alexander II replied: "Let the friendship which unites us assure the happiness and glory of our two countries." [2] Despite the optimistic tone of this exchange, Russia now faced an entirely new situation in central Europe; she could no longer play between three political elements. The Habsburg Monarchy had also been drastically altered in its fundamental composition. The question

2. *Ibid.*, p. 355.

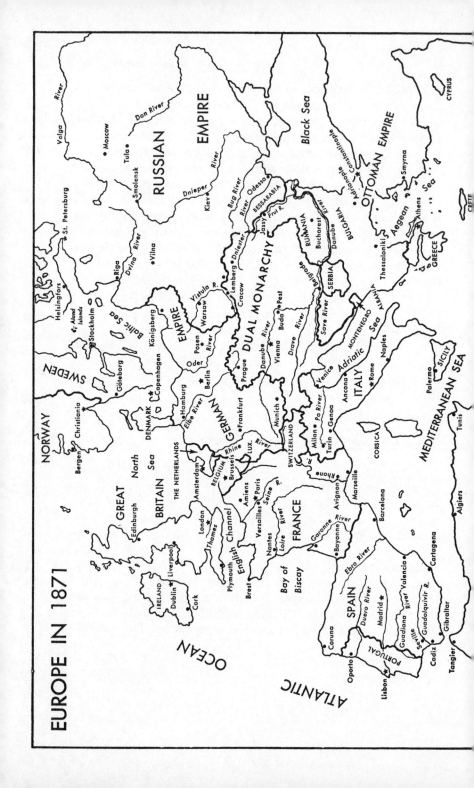

EUROPE IN 1871

remained whether Russian hopes would be fulfilled and the new Germany would remain the loyal friend that Prussia had been in the past—whether the empire would indeed save Russia from the dangers of a European coalition and offer support in the east.

After 1870 it did initially appear that the unification of Germany would make possible the reformation of the Holy Alliance on new and stronger foundations. Although no formal treaties were signed, the three emperors in a series of visits placed their relations on a co-operative basis and agreed upon the principles to be followed in foreign policy. In August, 1871 William I and Franz Joseph met at Ischl; in June, 1872 officers of the Habsburg armies visited St. Petersburg. In September, 1872 the tsar and Franz Joseph came to Berlin. Then, in May, 1873 the German emperor traveled to St. Petersburg, and in June Alexander II was in Vienna. In February, 1874 Franz Joseph completed the round by visiting the tsar in St. Petersburg. Although the monarchs were now clearly on close terms and the Austro-Russian breach had been at least temporarily healed, no true alliance treaty was negotiated between the eastern powers. In 1873, when the German emperor was in Russia, a military convention was drawn up between the staffs, but Bismarck later refused to countersign the document. During the visit of the tsar to Vienna, in the same year, a general consultation agreement, the Convention of Schönbrunn, was drawn up, which was little more than a restatement of the common conservative convictions of the rulers. William I adhered to this pact in October, 1873. The bonds of union between the members of the Three Emperors' League were thus extremely vague. However, a return had been made to the classical conservative alliance system.

Although Prussia had won a real military triumph over France in 1870, the antagonisms and fears of the previous period were not easily healed. Until the end of his career Bismarck's principal concern in diplomacy was the protection and preservation of the united Germany that he had created. The German Empire was a new political creation in Europe; what had been so recently built up could also be destroyed by a coalition of hostile powers.

Like Russia, Bismarck too became a victim of the "nightmare of coalitions." To meet this danger he concentrated upon the isolation of France and the creation of systems of alliance that would assure that Germany would always be one of three in the constellation of the five great powers of Europe. France, in particular, caused him increasing concern since it was apparent that after the loss of Alsace and Lorraine her participation in any enemy coalition would be a matter of certainty. Moreover, her unexpectedly quick recovery and the strong feelings of *revanche* everywhere apparent showed that she might take the opportunity to strike back sooner than expected. In 1875 a combination of circumstances led to a war scare, which showed the uneasiness of the entire situation.

In order to test the general diplomatic situation, the French foreign minister, Decazes, in April, 1875, circulated among the capitals a report of his ambassador in Berlin concerning the possibility of a German preventative war against France. In answer the British government made representations in Berlin and, more important, Alexander II in a visit to Berlin, accompanied by Gorchakov, made it quite clear that Russia would not remain passive in such an event. Bismarck, who had not been contemplating aggressive action, reacted violently to this outside intervention. The episode demonstrated that, first, the era of adventure was over and Germany could no longer move freely in foreign relations and, second, combined French, British, and Russian co-operation against Germany was possible. The incident did, moreover, provide Gorchakov with the welcome opportunity to play the arbiter of Europe and to balance between the two rival powers.

Therefore, in the first years after the unification of Germany it did seem as if the Russian hopes and expectations would be fulfilled. Russia had used the occasion of the Franco-Prussian War to secure the abrogation of the Black Sea clauses of the Treaty of Paris; thereafter she had been able to join again in the Three Emperors' League with her former partners of the Holy Alliance. In the war scare of 1875 Gorchakov had seen the confirmation of his expectation that Germany and France would remain permanently estranged and that Russia could play between them. In addition, in the years when affairs in Europe were dominated by the German question, Russia had been able to conquer great stretches of territory in Asia. The real test of Russian policy, however, had yet to come. It was only in the revival of the eastern question after 1875 that the Russian government was to learn the diplomatic consequences of its support of the consolidation of central Europe.

THE ASIATIC FRONTIERS

Although Russia in the first twenty years of the reign of Alexander II adopted a passive role in the affairs of the continent and the Near East, this same period was characterized by a recommencement of Russian expansion in the Middle and Far East. As a result, by 1885, in the reign of Alexander III, the Russian eastern boundaries had become stabilized, with a few small exceptions. The ease with which Russia accomplished the rounding of her Asiatic borders despite her military weakness was due to the poor quality of her opponents. China, from whom she won territory along the Amur, was also under pressure from the western powers; in the Middle East Russia faced only disunited, semi-barbarous states. Although she eventually came into conflict with Britain on the borders of Afghanistan, both governments were forced to seek a compromise because of the impracticability of contemplating a war in a remote area under the diplomatic circumstances of the time.

1. The Far East

The great Russian expansion over the Urals and across Siberia to the Pacific was accomplished before the reign of Peter the Great.

A fortress was constructed at Okhotsk in 1647 and Kamchatka was occupied in the 1690's. Expansion southward was limited when Russia signed the Treaty of Nerchinsk with China in 1689. In this agreement, the first concluded by a European power with Peking, the Russian government accepted a boundary that excluded it from the Amur valley. Chiefly interested in participating in the wealthy China trade, the Russians preferred to concentrate on the establishment of a profitable commercial relationship. Thereafter a mutually advantageous exchange of goods was indeed inaugurated, with the Russians specializing in the disposal of their Siberian furs, but they also offered leather, hides and cloth from Europe and Russia, as well as glassware. In return, they received silk, cotton cloth, tea, porcelain, sugar, and other luxury items. In this commerce China always had more valuable goods to offer than did Russia. In 1727 the Treaty of Kiakhta allowed the Russians to send a caravan of not more than 200 camels to Peking every three years and to establish an Orthodox mission of four priests and six students of the Chinese language in the capital city. These agreements, providing for the settlement of the boundaries and for commercial relations, lasted until 1858.

Excluded from the Amur valley, Russian activity in Siberia and the northern Pacific remained of necessity limited. The government supported and equipped voyages of discovery and exploration in the region, but little was done to develop or to settle the vast and inhospitable territory. As in the earlier period, the initiative for the extension of Russian activity came from private individuals, traders, soldiers, and adventurers. In 1799 Alaska was reached, and subsequently expeditions were sent down the Pacific coast of North America. In every case only a very limited number of men participated in these operations, which, because of the nature of the territory, involved little more than the occupation of lands that were either uninhabited or occupied by extremely primitive tribes. The Russian government, although willing to accept lands and sources of income that were offered without cost or danger to its European policies, was nevertheless extremely reluctant to take any steps that might lead to international complications, particularly in an area where it had no vital interests at stake.

The further development of the Siberian lands was, throughout the eighteenth and nineteenth centuries, limited by three factors: the lack of adequate communications, the bitter climate, and the difficulty of acquiring sufficient provisions. These problems led to a consideration of the advisability of acquiring the Amur river valley, despite the treaties with China. It was hoped that communications with the Pacific could be improved and that food for future settlements could be grown. The inauguration of an energetic, aggressive policy began with the appointment of Nicholas Muraviev in 1847 as governor-general of eastern Siberia. Without consulting his government, Muraviev proceeded to establish posts along the Amur on what was legally Chinese territory. He also sent an expedition to the island of Sakhalin. His activities met with little approval in St. Petersburg. Nesselrode did not want to involve his country in complications in the Far East. However, in moving against China at this time Russia was in fact paralleling the imperial policies of the western nations. In 1842, after the Opium War, the Chinese had been forced to open their trade to the European powers.

After the Crimean War the renewed conflict of the British and French with China from 1856 to 1858 allowed Russia the opportunity of legalizing and extending her conquests. In 1858 Muraviev signed the Treaty of Aigun with a local Chinese commander, who was in fact not authorized to conclude such an agreement. This treaty gave Russia territory on the north bank of the Amur and provided for a joint occupation of the Ussuri region. At the same time Admiral Putiatin negotiated the Treaty of Tientsin with the Chinese government, which extended to Russia the same commercial privileges that had previously been extorted by the British, French, and American governments. In 1860, N. P. Ignatiev, who was the Russian representative in

ASIA (RUSSIA AND CHINA) IN 1860

ALASKA
to 1867

Kolyma River

Anadyr R.

RUSSIA

Lena River

Yakutsk

KAMCHATKA
Annexed
1697-1732

Petropavlovsk

KURILE ISLANDS
To Russia 1711
To Japan 1875

1853

Nikolaevsk

SAKHALIN
ISLAND
Russian
1875-
1905

AMUR
1858
Aigun

DISTRICT

Amur River

USSURI

DISTRICT
1860

Ussuri River

Lena River

Lake Baikal

Irkutsk

Kiakhta

Harbin

Vladivostok

MANCHURIA

Mukden

Yalu River

KOREA

JAPAN

Tokyo

Pekin

CHINA

Peking, used the desperate situation of the Chinese government to gain the highly advantageous Treaty of Peking. Here the territorial provisions of the Treaty of Aigun were confirmed and, in addition, Russia received the enormous stretch of territory between the Amur, the Ussuri, and the Pacific Ocean. New trading privileges were also granted. With the acquisition of this land the Russian government proceeded with the construction of Vladivostok, which, since it was frozen only from December to March, allowed them more favorable port facilities on the Pacific. With the opening of the Suez canal in 1869, the voyage from Odessa to Vladivostok was reduced to forty-five days.

The acquisition of the Amur territory and the extended trading rights did not, however, result in an immediate development of the Siberian region. The great problems of food and transportation remained unsolved. The middle course of the great river remained covered with ice an average of 173 days of the year; the land did not prove suitable for the growing of adequate provisions. The government, moreover, showed little interest in promoting the colonization of the land or its real economic development. The long journey overland remained an immense obstacle. Because of the extreme hardship of travel by land, trade and passenger service between Russia and her Pacific lands remained primarily by sea.

Although the Amur question was settled peacefully and to the Russian advantage because of western pressure on China, a second dispute involving another sector of the long and turbulent Russo-Chinese border threatened to end in war between the two countries. In 1862 a revolt broke out among the Mohammedan tribes in Chinese Turkestan where the peoples were of the same racial stock as those in Russian Turkestan. Their able leader, Yakub Beg, was able to establish a regularly organized state. The British government sent a mission to his court and his troops received training from British and Polish officers. The inability of the Chinese government to control the situation alarmed the Russian government because of the possible effect of the movement on its own tribesmen. The strategic importance of the area, the Ili valley, was immense, since this was the great "Gateway of the Peoples" through which the early invasions of Russia had flowed. In 1871 Russian troops entered the territory and occupied Kuldja. At the same time they assured the Chinese government that the move was only a temporary measure. In 1877-1878 the Chinese troops were able to put down the rebellion, and they then requested that the Russian armies withdraw.

In the winter of 1878 the Chinese delegate, Chung-hou, arrived in Russia for nine months of negotiations. On September 15, 1879 the Treaty of Livadia was signed, which constituted a major Russian triumph. Russia received most of the territory in question, including control of the passes through the Tien Shan mountains, an indemnity of 5 million roubles for the expenses of the occupation, and increased commercial privileges. When the Chinese diplomat reached home with this unfavorable document, he was promptly imprisoned and condemned to death. Although the sentence was subsequently commuted after widespread protests abroad, China did not accept the treaty and prepared for war. At the same time a new delegate, Marquis Tseng, was sent to St. Petersburg to negotiate a revised settlement.

The crisis over the Kuldja territory placed the Russian government in a difficult position. The primary Russian interests were, as always, clearly in Europe and at the Straits. The Russo-Turkish War of 1878 had just been concluded, and again Russian military weaknesses had been exposed. Although the possession of the Kuldja territory would give Russia a welcome strategic advantage, she was not in a condition to go to war over the question. Therefore, in the negotiations that now commenced, considerations of prestige and commerce were placed first. In the final Treaty of St. Petersburg of February 24, 1881, Russia accepted a much reduced territory, but received instead an increased indemnity of 9 million roubles as well as added commercial privileges. The entire incident, despite the final Chinese victory, embittered the relations of the two nations for the next years. Moreover, the Chinese, having now apparently imposed their will upon a European power, became more confident. They had, it seemed, as the British ambassador in St. Petersburg concluded, in fact achieved much: "China has compelled Russia to do what she has never done before, disgorge territory that she had once absorbed." [3]

During the reign of Alexander II, the Russians also attempted to come into closer commercial and political relations with Japan. In 1855 in the Treaty of Shimoda, which was patterned after the pact made between the United States and Japan of the previous year, they did receive the right to trade at three ports. The agreement also provided for a division of the Kurile Islands and a joint occupation of Sakhalin. In 1875 this treaty was modified, and Japan surrendered her claims to Sakhalin in return for full control of the islands. In general at this time the relations of the two countries remained good, although limited in extent.

The gains in territory made in the Far East were to an extent balanced by the liquidation of the Russian possessions on the North American continent with the sale of Alaska in 1867. The American settlements had been set up and administered by the Russian-American company, which had been chartered in 1799 in order to exploit the fur trade of Alaska and the North Pacific. In the reign of Alexander I, the company had extended its activities down the California coast. The establishment of Fort Ross in 1812 marked the furthest point of extension. The Pacific undertakings of the company had first met with the opposition of the Spanish government, later with that of Britain and America. Not only did these activities threaten international complications, but the affairs of the company itself did not prosper. Fort Ross was finally sold in 1841.

The Russian government, which at no time showed much interest in the North American territories, after the Crimean War decided that the possessions could not be defended. During the war a Franco-British squadron attacked Petropavlovsk, and it was quite apparent that the weak Russian Pacific fleet could not protect Alaska. Moreover, Russian-American relations were quite good, due principally to the fact that at the time both the United States and Russia were in conflict with Britain. The

3. Demetrius C. Boulger, *The Life of Sir Halliday MacCartney* (London: J. Lane, 1908), p. 351.

Russian government thus entertained the hope that the sale of Alaska would both increase the friction between Britain and the United States and also win Russia a friend on the Pacific. Negotiations, which commenced in 1854, ended in 1867 with the purchase of Alaska by the United States for $7,200,000.

2. Central Asia

Parallel to the Russian expansion in the Far East, the 1860's also witnessed the inauguration of an active policy of conquest and annexation in Central Asia. In contrast to those in the Far East, these conquests involved military operations. Moreover, in this field the Russian foreign office and the military stood in direct conflict. The military commanders in the field, usually with the support of their superiors in St. Petersburg, favored an aggressive, forward policy, but they were usually opposed by the foreign ministry, which saw clearly the dangers of such activities for its policy in Europe and, in particular, for its relations with Britain. The chief military problem for Russia in the area remained what it had always been—the difficulty of controlling a border territory inhabited by nomadic, semi-barbarous tribes. In 1864 in an attempt to enclose the Kazakh steppe, two forces were sent out, one from Orenburg and another from Semipalatinsk. In September the two columns finally joined in an assault on Chimkent. The entire area was then joined to Russia under the governorship of General Cherniaev. With the conquest of the steppe, the Russian forces now found themselves confronted with the three relatively settled communities of Khiva, Bokhara, and Kokand. In an effort to calm foreign apprehensions of future Russian actions, Gorchakov on November 21, 1864 issued a statement intended to pacify the powers. He explained that the Russian actions had been made necessary by the need to acquire a settled frontier, and he gave assurance that further advances would not be undertaken because the assimilation of territory occupied by "more regularly constituted states, would exact considerable efforts and would draw us from annexation to annexation into infinite complications. . . ." [4]

This policy, however, proved impossible to maintain. Not only were the ambitious Russian generals on the scene difficult to control, but the political leadership of the three khanates also proved unstable. Further advances were embarked upon almost at once. In 1865 Cherniaev took Tashkent; three years later General Kaufmann captured Samarkand. By 1869 both Bokhara and Kokand had become Russian protectorates. In 1873 a large expedition under General Kaufmann was sent against Khiva, and that state too became a Russian protectorate. In 1876, after an uprising, the territory of Kokand was formally annexed to Russia.

With the subjugation of the khanates, the attention of the Russian commanders next turned to Transcaspia, a territory also inhabited by nomadic peoples, the Tekke Turkomans. Again the chief intention of the action was to achieve a settled, stable boundary. In 1877 serious operations were commenced in the region, and in 1881 the Turkoman capital, Geok Tepe, fell to General M. D. Skobelev, who was to become one of the great popular military heroes. The subsequent extension of Russian military conquests and the fall of Merv in 1884 brought the Russian armies closer to the Indian border and to the buffer territory of Afghanistan. From this time onward relations with Britain became increasingly tense, and in 1885 a major crisis developed between Britain and Russia over this area.

The period when the official Russian policy was, therefore, that of *recueillement* had thus in fact resulted in the acquisition of great stretches of territory in the east. It is to be noted, however, that during the reign of Alexander II these advances were made only when they involved no danger of a war with a major military power. Territory was taken from China when that state was pressed by the west; when Peking threatened to fight over Kuldja, Russia backed down. The middle eastern khanates, mili-

4. Richard A. Pierce, *Russian Central Asia, 1867-1917* (Berkeley: University of California Press, 1960), p. 20.

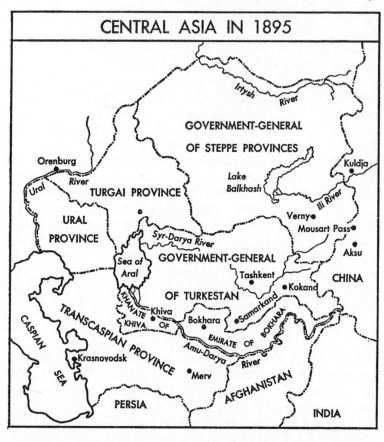

CENTRAL ASIA IN 1895

tarily extremely weak, were conquered, but Alaska was sold when it was judged indefensible. The Russian policy of maximum acquisition with minimum risk was also shown in the attitude taken toward the unauthorized actions of individual Russian commanders. Undoubtedly, Russian officers did often violate instructions in their activities on the frontiers. When their actions, although contrary to orders, were successful, the government was not hesitant about taking advantage of the gains. Since medals and promotions went to the successful, the general or officer in command in a territory was certainly encouraged to press forward. Russian conquest and the occupation of disputed territory thus proceeded without a definite plan or pattern and with little constructive direction from St. Petersburg.

With the conquest of the khanates and the Transcaspian lands Russia acquired what was in fact a colonial area adjacent to her own territory. Although great hopes were held for the possibilities of the economic exploitation of the area, particularly as a source of raw cotton to avoid the British monopoly, these expectations were not immediately fulfilled. The reluctance of the ministries of foreign affairs and finance to become enthusiastic over the eastern conquests is quite understandable under the circumstances of the time. The new lands in the Middle and the Far East, all of Siberia in fact, were difficult to defend and were economically unprofitable for the government unless further huge sums were invested in their development. Since finance was the major problem of the Russian government, the treasury had difficulty enough providing for internal needs and the defense of the vital western frontiers without acquiring new burdens in Asia. The outer fringes of the Russian Empire could thus never play the major role in Russian policy that, for instance, India played in the determination of British actions. The colonial areas thus had a relatively minor place in the formulation of general policy.

In addition, in the nineteenth century the eastern frontiers never succeeded in engaging the interest of the politically significant sections of the Russian public as did the west and the Near East. The defense of the Russian western frontier was vital to the very existence of the Russian state; official Russia felt itself, and, indeed, was, a part of European civilization. The Near East also attracted Russian attention and interest not only because of the power considerations of the area but also because of the pull of past Byzantine and Orthodox tradition. Constantinople, rather than Samarkand, Delhi, and Peking, held the imagination of the Russian and awakened his passionate enthusiasm. For this reason, the wars and the conquests of the east, although they did make military heroes of the generals involved, did not balance in the Russian mind the humiliation of the defeat of the Crimean War or the extension of Prussian power in northern Germany. Russian prestige, severely shaken by the events of 1856, thus demanded a victory in the Near East or continental Europe, not the acquisition of additional eastern territories.

THE RUSSO-TURKISH WAR OF 1877-1878

Although the Russian government did secure much new land in Asia and the abrogation of the Black Sea clauses of the Treaty of Paris, it was also quite clear by 1875 that Russia had for almost twenty years played the role of a bystander in the great events of Europe. Leadership in continental policy had been assumed first by Paris and after 1870 by Berlin. The great accomplishment of the past decade, the unification of Germany, had been carried out with Russian approval, but without the control of events shown in 1849 and 1850. Moreover, although Gorchakov was able to play the role of arbiter in 1875, it had become apparent that the united Germany under Bismarck was not the compliant Prussia of the earlier period. The faithful friend and true ally of the days of Alexander I and Nicholas I had become the greatest single military power of the continent.

Russia had originally adopted the policy of *recueillement*, as has been emphasized, in order to concentrate on domestic reform. Although great changes were accomplished in the internal organization of the state and in the status of the majority of the people, these events had brought in their train severe dislocation and discontent. Since criticism of internal affairs was judged dangerous to the government, more freedom of comment on foreign policy was allowed as a safety valve. Public attention was then drawn away from failures at home, and popular feeling could find expression in attacks on other governments and not direct its attention to the methods and policies of the autocratic regime.

Those who disliked the policy of abstention from European affairs, therefore, were able to express their views in print. The Russian foreign ministry thus found itself increasingly under open attack from those in the Russian public and government who wished the resumption of a glorious national policy.

The program of Gorchakov and the foreign ministry remained after the unification that which it had before—the policy of *recueillement*. Gorchakov's chief assistant during the major part of his career as foreign minister, A. G. Jomini, summarized this policy in 1876: "Russia has been unified for a long time in her greatness and her national unity. Her territorial security is perfectly in order due to her defensive resources and to the lessons she has given invaders. What is now necessary is the development of her internal life, her productive resources, her prosperity, her culture, her commerce, her industry—all things which require peace. Her foreign policy should thus be purely preventative and defensive." [5] Although this course of action was indeed the wisest for Russia, the problem remained whether it could be maintained. The danger lay in what Jomini described as *"l'affreux chaos oriental,"* where Russian prestige, historical tradition, and national power were alike involved.

During the reign of Alexander II the moderate policies advocated by the foreign ministry were often under attack by many nationally minded groups and individuals, but the place of prominence, certainly in foreign eyes, was occupied by the Panslavs. Although this term was used to designate men of widely varying beliefs, the Panslavs all reacted strongly against the negative role that had been previously played in foreign affairs and called for the resumption of an active program in which Russia would exploit her position as the greatest of the Slavic nations. In the reign of Nicholas I, the Slavophils, with their emphasis on the unique qualities of Russia in comparison to the west, had been precursors of the movement. Their ideas received little sympathy from

5. *Russia in the East, 1876-1880: the Letters of A. G. Jomini to N. K. Giers*, edited by Charles and Barbara Jelavich (Leiden: Brill, 1959), p. 44.

official quarters since both Nicholas I and Nesselrode could not well support a doctrine that would threaten the continued existence of the Holy Alliance. Russia also in their opinion was part of, and not apart from, Europe, and they could not favor an idea having revolutionary implications.

The defeat of the Crimean War, with its severe blow to the Russian national pride and the resultant reaction against the predominance of the German element in the administration, provided a good background for any program that would emphasize Russian power and leadership. The goal of all the Panslavs, although their individual programs differed, was the assumption by Russia of the leadership of the Slavic peoples; their liberation from foreign, that is Habsburg and Turkish, control; and their organization into political units closely allied to St. Petersburg. In 1858 the Moscow Slavic Benevolent Society was founded. Its aim was to assist the southern Slavs of the Ottoman Empire to achieve their freedom from Moslem control. This organization brought to Russia students from the Balkans, chiefly from Bulgaria, and carried on activities of a publicist and educational nature. Branches were later opened in St. Petersburg and Kiev. In 1867 the Moscow branch held a Slavic Ethnographical Exhibition which attracted attention in the west. The goals and general beliefs of these and related groups won the interest and support of influential individuals in the Russian court and society. Moreover, gifted and influential writers and journalists were drawn into the service of the cause.

In addition, the program of the Panslavs did correspond well with the Russian actual position in the Balkans. After the Peace of Paris Russia could no longer pose as the sole protector of Orthodox Christianity since the treaty specifically assigned that role to the powers together. Moreover, by 1870 the major non-Slavic Orthodox peoples, the Greeks and Rumanians, had been freed from Turkish rule. The next territories in question were those inhabited by Serbian, Bulgarian, and Montenegrin peoples —all of whom were Slavic. Although religious unity remained a consideration of policy, the emphasis could now be shifted to the racial tie with Russia. A program calling for a common policy among the Slavic peoples could also be used by Russia as a practical foreign policy weapon against both Austria-Hungary and Britain.

The ideas of the Panslavs naturally aroused the fears of the other powers. The British could not allow the establishment of a great Slavic state; the Austrians saw the program quite correctly as directed toward the destruction of the Danubian Monarchy. The two writers who obtained the widest public attention, R. A. Fadeev and N. Ia. Danilevsky, did indeed express opinions that were bound to arouse apprehension. In his book, *Opinion on the Eastern Question*, published in 1869, Fadeev argued that Russia should seek the destruction of both the Ottoman and the Austrian empires—that the road to Constantinople lay through Vienna. He emphasized the eternal enmity of Slav and Teuton and prescribed a solution by force. Danilevsky, in *Russia and Europe*, which appeared in the same year, pictured the great struggle of Roman-Germans against the Slavs. He too favored Russian leadership in the liberation of the Slavs and he called for a great Slav federation with Constantinople as the capital. Two of the foremost Russian journalists, I. S. Aksakov and M. N. Katkov, also joined the ranks of the Panslav publicists. Through the writings of these and other men the ideas of Panslavism received a wide audience in Russia and commanded the respect especially of those who believed that Russia should embark upon a glorious national policy.

The outbreak of a revolt among the peasants of Hercegovina in 1875 once again opened the eastern question and created conditions in which the nationalist and the Panslav could exert a strong influence on foreign relations. Although the new eastern crisis was in many ways similar to those in the past in that it was again caused by the revolt of the Balkan Christians against Moslem misrule, the general European diplomatic situation had profoundly changed. Austria-Hungary, now excluded from central Europe, showed a greater interest in Balkan affairs and a willingness to acquire new territory and influence. Moreover, well aware that the program of the extreme Panslavs would result in the breakup of their state, the Austrian and Magyar statesmen regarded St. Petersburg with renewed suspicion and distrust. In addition, contrary to the hopes of the Russian government, Prussia-Germany after 1870 proved a worse and not a better ally in the eastern question, due principally to the altered relationship of Vienna and Berlin after 1870. Since with the incorporation of Alsace-Lorraine into the empire, it could be assumed that, henceforth, France would remain a national enemy, Germany could not afford to estrange Austria because of that nation's strategic position. For the same reason Germany also could not allow a severe defeat or weakening of the Habsburg Monarchy that would eliminate that state from the ranks of the great powers since such an occurrence, given the French position, would put Berlin at the mercy of St. Petersburg. German policy in the Balkans, which was thus determined by considerations of general European interest, led her in the future to aid Austrian attempts to confine Russian power and to prevent the acquisition by Russia of significant gains in the area. This was not the role that Russia had envisioned for the unified Germany.

In the face of the new uprising of a Slavic Christian people, the Russian government, as in past crises, had two alternatives of action—it could follow a policy of co-operation with other governments, or at least with its allies in the Three Emperors' League; or it could seek to deal with Turkey alone. In this situation Alexander II, who made the final decisions, received conflicting advice. The foreign ministry, under the increasingly feeble and senile leadership of Gorchakov, the ministry of finance under Reutern, and also the ministry of war under Miliutin, throughout the crisis all advised caution. These men were chiefly concerned with the progress of the great reforms, and being in responsible offices they saw that Russia was in no condition to launch a war or adopt dangerous courses of action. They were opposed within their own departments and in the government in general by those with nationalist and Panslav convictions who wished Russia to resume an active policy. Of particular importance was Ignatiev because of his position as ambassador at Constantinople; his policies also received the strong endorsement of the tsar's brother, Grand Duke Michael. At the beginning of the crisis the moderate elements were able to maintain control, and Russia entered into negotiations with Germany and Austria-Hungary to attempt to solve the Balkan problem by peaceful mediation.

From 1875 to 1877 the powers therefore made repeated attempts to calm the revolt by compromise and by advocating programs of reform. The situation was further complicated by the attitude of the British minister Disraeli who wished to exploit the crisis in order to break the Three Emperors' League. As long as this coalition existed, he recognized: "There is no balance, and unless we go out of our way to act with the three Northern Powers, they can act without us, which is not agreeable for a state like England." [6] The British attitude tended to encourage Turkish resistance and therefore to make a negotiated settlement more difficult. The initiative for reform came always from the conservative powers.

The first of a series of reform proposals was drawn up by a consular commission in August, 1875. When these failed to secure acceptance, Andrassy, in December, 1875, issued with Bismarck's approval a program providing for land and tax reform and religious equality. Although the Porte accepted the note, the insurgents did not. In May, 1876 Gorchakov, Bismarck, and Andrassy together formulated the Berlin Memorandum. Here the conditions of the Andrassy note were restated, and an armistice of two months was suggested. France and Italy also accepted these terms, but Britain rejected them. Disraeli, wishing to make use of the crisis, then ordered the British fleet to Besika Bay. These British moves were interpreted in Constantinople as signifying support, and an intransigent attitude was maintained. Meanwhile, however, the internal situation in the Turkish capital deteriorated. In May, 1876 Sultan Abdul Aziz was replaced by Murad V under circumstances that appeared to foreshadow the breakdown of

6. William Flavelle Monypenny and George Earle Buckle, *The Life of Benjamin Disraeli* (New York: Macmillan, 1920), VI, p. 13.

the state at the center. The events in Constantinople naturally affected the decisions of the leaders of the subject nationalities.

Of the Balkan states Serbia had been most deeply concerned with the ultimate fate of the revolt in Bosnia-Hercegovina, since the declared aim of the insurrectionists was union with their neighbor. Although the Serbians received no official encouragement from the Russian government, they were given enthusiastic support and material assistance by the Russian Panslav circles. The Slavic Benevolent Committee collected funds throughout Russia, and volunteers streamed into Serbia to aid in the liberation of a brother Slavic people. In May, 1876 General Cherniaev, the hero of Tashkent, arrived to take command of the Serbian armies. The entrance of both Serbia and Montenegro into war with Turkey in June and July was thus initially welcomed with hope and approval by those in Russia with strong national or Panslav views. Unfortunately, the first feelings of exaltation were soon replaced by bitterness and recrimination when it became apparent that the Russian volunteer groups contained a high proportion of misfits and incompetents. Moreover, the Serbian armies soon proved themselves incapable of defeating the Turkish forces. In October, 1876 Russia was forced to intervene to save Serbia by imposing an armistice upon Turkey. Meanwhile, Russian attention and patronage was turning increasingly to another South Slav nation, the Bulgarians. Henceforth it was to be on these peoples, and not on the Serbs, that the Russians were to base their Balkan policy.

In the period after the Crimean War the Bulgarians, even more than the Serbians, had enjoyed the particular attention of the Panslavs. The Moscow Slavic Benevolent Committee had been most active in educational efforts on their behalf; with Russian support the Bulgarian church was able in 1870-72 to separate from the Greek-dominated Patriarchate of Constantinople and to form its own national ecclesiastical organization, the Bulgarian Exarchate. The Bulgarians, like the Serbs, were thus encouraged to look to Russia for aid against the Ottoman Empire. In 1876 the Bulgarians joined in the insurrection, but with little success. In their effort to repress the revolt, Turkish irregular troops committed a series of atrocities, which aroused all of the powers; over 10,000 Bulgarians were reported killed. The massacre greatly increased the pressure on the Russian government to assist the Balkan Slavic people. A similar reaction took place in London after the publication in 1876 of Gladstone's pamphlet, *Bulgarian Horrors,* which denounced Turkish misrule in eloquent terminology.

During this period, when the uprising against the Porte spread through the Turkish lands, the powers had continued to negotiate. Since the attitude of Austria-Hungary remained of crucial concern for Russian policy, Gorchakov again sought to come to terms with that power. In the Reichstadt Convention of July, 1876, it was agreed that should Serbia be defeated in the war with Turkey, the two powers would intervene to restore the *status quo* and to try to obtain administrative reform. Should, however, the Turkish armies be defeated, a real partition of the empire was to be effected, but no large Balkan state was to be erected. Bulgaria, Rumelia, and Albania were to be established as autonomous states; Constantinople was to be a free city. Russia was to acquire southern Bessarabia and territory in Asia Minor; Austria-Hungary, for its share, would receive Bosnia-Hercegovina. Greece would be given Thessaly and Crete.

Despite this agreement the Russian government remained unsure of its diplomatic position. Its two principal opponents in eastern affairs remained the Dual Monarchy and Britain. The Crimean War had shown that Vienna could not be relied upon. Moreover, Bismarck at this time made it quite clear that if a war should occur between Austria and Russia, he would not allow Habsburg power to be crushed. Germany thus would not return in kind the Russian favors of 1866 and 1870. The Russian option for Prussia in central Europe would not be repaid by support for Russian policy in the east at the expense of the Danubian Monarchy.

Meanwhile, the diplomatic negotiations continued, although few concrete results were obtained. In December, 1876 a conference of ambassadors in Constantinople produced yet another reform proposal, which the Porte again rejected. The attitude of the Porte and the failure of powers increased the pressure of those in Russia who favored a war with Turkey. The circumstances of 1828 were thus again in effect; since the great powers could not bring about a settlement by negotiation, the only alternative appeared to be a solution by force and a Russo-Turkish war. To provide for this event the Russian government concluded two more agreements with the Dual Monarchy. In January, 1877 the Budapest Convention was signed, which provided for the maintenance of an attitude of benevolent neutrality by Vienna in return for the provinces of Bosnia and Hercegovina. In March a further agreement was concluded, which, in general, reaffirmed the provisions of the Treaty of Reichstadt. Despite these documents, which cleared the way for a Russian conflict with the Ottoman Empire, relations between Vienna and St. Petersburg remained tense and suspicious. After a final attempt by the powers to find a peaceful solution met with failure, Russia on April 24 declared war on Turkey.

Throughout the war the chief danger for Russia came from Britain, the power with the greatest interest in the maintenance of the Ottoman Empire and the possible organizer of a coalition against Russia. Certainly Disraeli and many in Britain were eager and willing to accept another open trial of strength. The central question at issue between St. Petersburg and London remained, as it had been throughout the century, that of the control of Constantinople and the Turkish Straits. On June 30, 1877, when the Russian armies crossed the Danube, the British fleet was ordered to Besika Bay. A condition of acute tension existed between Russia and Britain from the beginning of the crisis until the Congress of Berlin, which met one year later.

Because of the general diplomatic conditions, the Russian government, when embarking upon the war, expected and hoped for a quick victory in their campaign in the Balkans. An agreement was signed with Rumania in April, 1877, which provided for the Russian transit across the country in return for a guarantee of

Rumanian territorial integrity. Although the Rumanian government offered supporting troops, Russia only accepted their use later in the war and after military failures of its own. With the outbreak of the fighting the direction of policy in Russia became divided and confused because of the conditions under which the war was fought and the split of the government into three sections. The tsar accompanied his army into the field, where he soon fell under the influence of the nationalist and Panslav military groups as well as of Ignatiev, who joined him there. Gorchakov, too old and feeble for camp life, remained in Bucharest, largely excluded from affairs of state despite his official capacity as foreign minister. Routine business was handled by N. K. Giers in the foreign ministry in St. Petersburg.

Despite initial optimistic hopes, the Turkish campaign brought no triumphant progress toward Constantinople. As in the Crimean War and the Russo-Turkish War of 1828, grave faults were soon apparent in the organization and conduct of the campaign. A real disaster was suffered at Plevna in July and September. Nevertheless, the Russian forces were finally able to defeat the even less efficient Turkish army. In December Plevna fell, and on January 20 Adrianople was taken. Once again, as in 1829, Russian armies stood at the gates of Constantinople, and a decision had to be taken concerning the fate of the Ottoman Empire. The issues remained what they had been in the previous eastern crises: how far Russia could extend her power and control in the Near East without provoking the formation of a hostile coalition and a major war.

On January 31, 1878 an armistice was signed between Russia and Turkey and negotiations for a settlement commenced. Britain, apprehensive over the fate of the Porte, in February despatched her fleet into the Dardanelles. On March 3, 1878 the belligerent states finally agreed on the terms of peace. The Treaty of San Stefano, whose content was largely influenced by the ideas of Ignatiev, created conditions in the Balkans that appeared to assure future Russian control of the Ottoman Empire. Although Russia did not take either the Straits or Constantinople, the agreement provided for the creation of a great Bulgarian state extending from the Black Sea to the Aegean and dominating the Straits. It was assumed by the powers that this Greater Bulgaria would be a Russian vassal state. The new Bulgaria was to be given an elected prince and an assembly and to be allowed to maintain a militia. A Russian army of occupation was to remain in the country for two years. Other stipulations in the treaty provided for territorial gains for the other Balkan states, but no mention was made of the Austrian acquisition of Bosnia-Hercegovina, despite the treaties that had been concluded before the war. The peace thus both violated previous international agreements, and it signified an upset of the power balance in the Balkans, which neither Britain nor Austria-Hungary could accept.

The reaction of the powers to San Stefano made it apparent to the Russian government that insistence on its maintenance could lead to a war against a hostile coalition. The attitude of Germany was made clear through previous statements on the necessity of maintaining the Danubian Monarchy. Although there was in March and April much enthusiasm for resistance, Alexander finally allowed himself to be convinced, by arguments emphasizing Russian military and financial weakness, that Russia must retreat. In the second half of May, Ignatiev left office, and his influence was replaced by that of the conciliatory and moderate Peter Shuvalov, who represented the views of the foreign ministry. It was he, therefore, who was sent to London to try to arrange terms with the British government. In the Protocol of May 30 the major problem was settled by the Russian abandonment of the scheme of the establishment of a great Bulgaria. The British government simultaneously scored a second diplomatic triumph. Using the extreme weakness of the Porte, Britain forced upon that government, on June 4, the Cyprus Convention, which compensated London for the Russian gains in the war. In return for a pledge that Britain would guarantee its Asiatic territories, the Ottoman Empire ceded the strategic Mediterranean island. In prep-

aration for the forthcoming congress, Britain also made an agreement with Austria to the effect that both would co-operate at the meeting. It was thus Britain, not Russia, that held the highest cards in the coming weeks.

On June 13 the third great European congress of the century opened in Berlin under the presidency of Prince Bismarck. The great powers were again represented by their chief ministers: Disraeli and Salisbury for Britain, Andrassy for Austria-Hungary, Waddington for France, and Corti for Italy. Although Gorchakov went as the chief Russian delegate, the burden of the negotiation was taken by Peter Shuvalov. The final agreement, signed one month later, restored the balance of power in the Near East. Since the main lines of settlement had been drawn by private arrangements prior to the congress, the delegates did little more than implement the previous agreements. The principal question of concern, the fate of Greater Bulgaria, was met by a division of the territory into three sections. The first,

Bulgaria proper, became an autonomous principality; the second, Eastern Rumelia, was placed under a Christian governor and was to be semi-autonomous. The third section, the Macedonian lands, was returned to Turkish rule. It was assumed by the powers that Russia would dominate the autonomous Bulgaria but that her influence would only be equal to that of the other powers in Rumelia. Russia received, in addition to her right of preponderant influence in Bulgaria, southern Bessarabia, Kars, Ardahan, and Batum, which was to be made into a free port. To compensate for the Russian acquisitions, Bosnia-Hercegovina was handed over to Austro-Hungarian occupation and administration. If Vienna had at the time pressed for the annexation of the provinces, her wishes would undoubtedly have been met. Andrassy, however, reflecting Magyar views, was not eager to secure the inclusion of more Slavic peoples in the Danubian empire.

The Berlin settlement also brought about other great changes in the map of the Balkans. Although each state received some increase in territory, these gains were satisfactory to none, and therefore led to further minor conflicts. Montenegro, Serbia, and Rumania received additional lands along with full independence from the Porte. Montenegro was almost doubled in size, and in 1881 received access to the sea with the acquisition of the port of Dulcigno. The assignment of two purely Albanian districts to Montenegro resulted in an uprising in the area and a return of the districts to Moslem rule. Rumania, deprived of southern Bessarabia in direct violation of the Russo-Rumanian agreement of 1877, received in consolation the poorer, non-Rumanian territory of Dobrudja. Greece, who was promised a border rectification in the treaty, eventually acquired Thessaly and a part of Epirus. Serbia, now abandoned by Russia, turned to Vienna for diplomatic support. Blocked from expansion westward by the Austrian occupation of Bosnia-Hercegovina, her aspirations were directed southward and she was given Pirot and Niš.

Although the engagements of 1856 and 1871 in regard to the Straits were reaffirmed in the Treaty of Berlin, the congress witnessed a major development in the question. On July 11 Salisbury made this statement: "The obligations of Her Britannic Majesty relating to the closing of the Straits do not go further than an engagement with the sultan to respect in this matter His Majesty's independent determinations in conformity with the spirit of existing treaties." The exact meaning of the declaration was vague, but it did signify that Britain would honor the closing of the Straits at her convenience. The determination of whether the sultan was acting independently or under Russian influence would be made in London. The Russian delegate immediately responded that the closure of the Straits was a European principle, binding on all, and that it was not subject to unilateral interpretation. The British action, which nullified the security that Russia had gained through the international agreements, caused great concern in Russia. Thereafter it was necessary to seek additional diplomatic support to maintain the Russian position on the problem.

Despite the fact that Russia had indeed gained much in the treaty with the establishment of a satellite Bulgaria, the reannexation of southern Bessarabia, and the acquisitions in Asia Minor, the final treaty was interpreted in Russia as a great defeat. When compared with the wilder aspirations of the Panslavs, it was certainly not a diplomatic victory, but it is doubtful if more could have been achieved under the circumstances. Gorchakov, sensing the popular reaction, pushed as much of the responsibility on Shuvalov, his fellow delegate, as possible. The chief scapegoat, however, for the anger of the Russian public became Bismarck, the "honest broker" of the Berlin Congress. Although he had usually voted with Russia at the meetings, Germany, under his leadership, had not played the role that Russia wished her to play. Berlin had not been the firm and faithful ally of Russia against the other powers in the eastern question; the unification of Germany had not freed Russia from the nightmare of a hostile coalition. Also, instead of Gorchakov playing arbiter between France and Germany, Bismarck had sat as judge in a contest between Russia and her opponents. Thus, after the Congress of Berlin, there occurred much the same shift in opinion that had taken place after the previous congress at Paris. Russian animosity became directed not at Britain, the chief competitor, but at a German power which had previously been regarded as a friend and ally. The Russian reaction against Berlin was expressed in a press war in the spring of 1879 and in a series of minor incidents. In August, 1879 the tsar wrote the kaiser an angry letter, but the two rulers subsequently met and patched up the quarrel. However, the basic theme of the Panslav, the inevitable conflict of Slav and German, appeared to receive justification. Although the Panslavs as a body of opinion were never to exert the same influence on the formulation of foreign policy, the Balkan crisis left bitter feelings behind and helped establish a frame of mind that later was to have unfortunate results.

The Congress of Berlin and the eastern crisis had thus accomplished Disraeli's objective of the breaking of the Three Emperors' League. Gorchakov and those with similar convictions in the foreign ministry now called for a return to the policy of *recueillement* and noninterference in European affairs. They wished to ally with no power, but to maintain a program of "free hands" and isolation. This proud policy appealed to the nationalist, but it was not practical under the circumstances. The Russo-Turkish War, like the Crimean War, although it ended in victory, again demonstrated Russian military weakness. Moreover, two immediate dangers faced the Russian government after the congress. In the treaty, the Porte had been given the right to send troops into Eastern Rumelia. The Russian government feared that if this action were carried out, it would precipitate another Balkan revolt and a reopening of the eastern question. In addition, the British declaration at the Congress of Berlin brought up again the problem of the closure of the Straits. However, although Russia could ill afford to stand alone, her choice of allies remained limited. Republican France was unacceptable both from a military and an ideological standpoint; Britain as before could not be considered. There remained only the two German courts, Berlin and Vienna, despite the fact that the conservative alliance had not functioned to the Russian satisfaction in the crisis of the 1870's.

Although Gorchakov continued to oppose any agreement with

Austria and Germany, Shuvalov, Giers, and P. A. Saburov, who was to become the Russian ambassador in Berlin, now advocated a renewal of the former diplomatic alignment. The tsar supported the negotiations with the central powers in order to avoid a condition of isolation and also to gain support for the Russian interpretation of the Straits agreements. It was decided at the same time that Russian policy would thereafter remain defensive and that the chief concentration would be on the solution of the Russian internal problems. Adventurous actions, such as the Russo-Turkish War had been, were, in the future, to be avoided. The Russian government, therefore, accepted in principle the renewal of the Three Emperors' League. The subsequent negotiations, nevertheless, proceeded slowly because of the hesitant attitude of Austria-Hungary, who saw few advantages for herself in the arrangement. The final agreement was not signed until 1881, after Alexander II had been assassinated by a terrorist organization.

*   *   *   *   *

The reign of Alexander II thus witnessed a major re-drawing of the map of Europe and a revolutionary readjustment of the power relationships of the large states of Europe. These years also saw the extension of the Russian boundaries to enclose huge stretches of land in the Middle and Far East. In the Treaty of Berlin, Russia, in addition, reacquired southern Bessarabia and won lands in Asia Minor as well as a protectorate over the new Bulgarian state. In internal affairs a period of major reform and domestic reorganization had been inaugurated. The age of Alexander II was therefore an active and a creative period. Despite the difficulties of readjustment, very substantial gains had been achieved in both foreign and domestic politics. It is interesting to note, however, that despite these obvious successes, the general feeling at the conclusion of the reign of Alexander was not optimistic, particularly in regard to foreign policy. Perhaps the principal cause of the relative disillusionment was the discrepancy between Russian hopes and what had actually been achieved. The great reforms provided no final answer to the domestic crisis; with the rise of radicalism it appeared that more problems had been created than solved. The Russo-Turkish War had again demonstrated that in comparison with the other powers Russia was not in a financial and military sense the equal of her competitors. Moreover, the single great national enthusiasm of Alexander's reign had been the crusade in the Balkans for the Christian Slavs. Instead of achieving a victorious and glorious peace, the Russian government had been called before the powers to account for her actions and had been forced to abandon her maximum program, an act humiliating for a major power.

The profound significance of the major event of these years, the unification of Germany, was slow in dawning upon the Russian awareness. This miscalculation, however, was shared by other governments. It was only in the crisis of 1876 to 1878 that it became evident that the new Germany was not the old Prussia. Russia now found on its doorstep a nationally minded, militarily powerful state with an economic, political, and social system far stronger than that of autocratic Russia. The industrialization of Germany, which commenced around 1865 and became fully apparent in the 1890's, increased the military differential between the two states. Central Europe, which in the days of Alexander I and Nicholas I had been a virtual power vacuum, could now no longer be controlled from St. Petersburg. As long as Bismarck directed German policy, the consequences of the change were not wholly detrimental to Russia. Educated in the Prussian tradition and fully aware of the need for Russo-German friendship, Bismarck endeavored throughout his career to maintain the old conservative alignment. It was thus only during the reign of Alexander III that the full significance of the new situation was finally realized.

V

Alexander III

Alexander III, who ascended the throne in 1881, ruled for the relatively short term of thirteen years. Nevertheless, his reign was to bring about a basic realignment in Russian foreign policy. Influenced by the horrible events of his father's assassination, Alexander III, in his internal policies, abandoned further reform and returned to the reactionary system of Nicholas I. The last of the Russian autocrats, the tsar, upon assuming power, rejected the draft of a constitution that had been approved by his father, thus blocking the further immediate political evolution of the country. In foreign affairs, he did, however, favor the continuation of the negotiations that led to a re-formation of the conservative alliance with Vienna and Berlin.

Born in 1845, Alexander III was the second son of Alexander II. When his brother Nicholas died of tuberculosis in 1865, he became the heir to the throne. He also later married his brother's fiancée, the Danish Princess Dagmar, the daughter of Christian IX. Of only moderate abilities and retiring in manner, Alexander preferred to live a life of calm and retirement with his family at Gachina away from the world of politics in St. Petersburg. Because he was not expected to inherit the throne, his training had not been as intensive as that of his brother, but he had in the persons of the historian Soloviev and his tutor Pobedonostsev two able teachers. Pobedonostsev, in particular, influenced the formation of the tsar's political ideas in a strongly conservative direction. He repeatedly urged Alexander to consider his role as tsar in the paternalistic tradition of that of the father of a family and not to be misled by demands for constitutional reform, which, he argued, was not the true desire of the mass of the people.

To his conservative convictions Alexander III also joined a strong Russian nationalism. In the 1870's he was believed to share the ideas of the Panslavs, but later as tsar he quite obviously did not adhere to their full teachings. Like the Russian nationalists in general he maintained a strong dislike of Austria-Hungary and Britain. In April, 1881 he commented: "I understand only one policy. . . . To exact from every situation all that is needed by and is useful to Russia, to disregard all other considerations, and to act in a straightforward and resolute manner. We can have no policy except one that is purely Russian and national; this is the only policy we can and must follow." [1] Although such remained his intention throughout his reign, it was not always easy to determine what was best for Russian interests. He obviously shared in the enthusiasms of the nationalists. He read with particular interest the articles of the gifted journalist, Katkov, who called for a strong and assertive national policy. His chief advisors, in contrast, were against any adventures abroad. His reign, unique in the annals of the tsars, to the end remained an unbroken period of peace despite the occurrence of severe crises in the Near and Middle East. This condition was made possible by the realization

1. Florinsky, *Russia*, II, p. 1088.

within Russia of her military impotence and by the general desire of all of the powers in the 1880's to avoid armed conflicts.

Throughout his reign Alexander III was associated in foreign policy with one principal minister, N. K. Giers. Although the tsar inherited Gorchakov from his father, that statesman, now in his eighty-third year, was clearly senile and incapable of administering his office. Despite the fact that many expected Alexander III, because of his nationalist leanings, to appoint Ignatiev, he finally in 1882 officially named Giers to the position he had actually held since the Congress of Berlin. The son of a frontier postmaster and of Lutheran, Swedish-German ancestry, Giers rose to high office chiefly through diligent work and moderation of character. His career was immensely aided by his marriage in 1849 to Olga Cantacuzino, a Rumanian and a niece of Gorchakov. He served first in the Danubian Principalities, Egypt, and Persia; later he was the Russian representative in Bern and Stockholm. In 1875 he returned to St. Petersburg as Gorchakov's deputy and Assistant Foreign Minister. In character and training he proved an excellent second for his impulsive and overbearing master. Faced throughout his career by constant opposition, particularly from the nationalists, he was able in general to maintain his position and to keep his country from involvement in conflicts for which it was ill prepared. In foreign policy he favored the program adopted at the end of the reign of Alexander II of the emphasis on internal development and the remaking of the alliance with the conservative powers.

THE REVIVAL OF THE THREE EMPERORS' LEAGUE

Alexander III faced, at the time of his assumption of power, an international situation that, although more favorable than that which his father had met in 1855, had, nevertheless, been profoundly altered by the creation of the united Germany. Berlin, not St. Petersburg or Paris, was now the center of continental diplomacy. Moreover, in Bismarck, the diplomatic genius of the age, the Russian statesmen found a formidable opponent. Fortunately for the tranquillity of central Europe, Bismarck, as one of the chief pillars of his policy, favored the continuation of the close ties between St. Petersburg and Berlin that had characterized Russian-Prussian relations throughout the century. Although the links between the courts were never as strong under Alexander III as they had been during the reign of his father, Bismarck, as long as he remained chancellor, tried to maintain the atmosphere of the Holy Alliance. He continued to insist upon the necessity of co-operation between the conservative powers against the revolution, although these arguments in an era of increasingly competitive nationalism tended to take on a hollow ring.

The treaty marking the renewal of the Three Emperors' League was finally signed on June 18, 1881. The pact obligated the partners to maintain an attitude of benevolent neutrality should one of them become engaged in a war with a third power. In the eastern question they agreed upon a policy of consultation and agreement should changes take place. The three states also declared their adherence to the principle of the European and mutually obligatory character of the Straits settlement. Austria gained the right to annex Bosnia-Hercegovina when an advantageous moment should arise; the three powers agreed not to oppose the eventual union of Bulgaria and Eastern Rumelia. The agreement thus offered advantages to each of the contracting parties. Germany gained the assurance that Russia would not join France should war break out on the Rhine. Russia could now depend on the support of her allies for her interpretation of the closure of the Straits and, in addition, for the eventual unification of the Bulgarias. Austria-Hungary received confirmation of her domination over Bosnia-Hercegovina.

Although the three courts of the Holy Alliance were once again joined by a specific agreement, the basic relationships between the powers had greatly altered. In the 1880's the difficulty experienced in the revival of the alliance was chiefly caused by the changes in the Danubian Monarchy that had been brought about by the unification of Germany and the transformation of the internal structure through the *Ausgleich*. Under the Holy Alliance the three powers had clearly enjoyed a community of interest in central Europe and in their sharing of the lands of partitioned Poland. Moreover, prior to the era of the national unifications each power had primary interests in geographic areas which did not directly conflict with the other partners and where they needed the assistance of their allies. Prussia wished to guard her position and lands on the Rhine against France; Austria was interested in maintaining her domination over the Italian peninsula; Russia had her eastern policy to protect against Britain. However, by 1870 Austria had been expelled from Italy and Germany was dominant on the Rhine. Although Russia still needed allies in the east, she had less to offer in return. Moreover, the Dual Monarchy, who now turned southeast and whose policy was greatly influenced by the Magyar views, had adopted courses of action in the Balkans that would inevitably conflict with those of Russia. The former community of interest of the three northern courts was, therefore, by the reign of Alexander III not what it had once been. The balance of strength between the partners had shifted and the number of issues on which they could render each other assistance had sharply diminished.

In addition, the old bonds of common conservative ideology had lost much of their significance and validity. It is interesting to note that as the tide of revolutionary activity in Russia rose, the role which the prevention of such movements played in Russian foreign policy became submerged. In the period between 1814 and 1854 the Russian support of the principle of intervention in the internal affairs of other states to prevent the overthrow of the legitimate ruler had been predicated on the assumption that it would be Russian armies that would march into other countries in support of their rulers. In that period the Russian government itself was never in the position of having to consider that foreign armies might be called upon to enter St. Petersburg to save the tsar. By the reign of Alexander III it was, however, the Russian ruler who was in danger, but it is certainly impossible to imagine that the tsar would have put his signature to a treaty that would have allowed the armies of Germany and Austria-Hungary to invade Russia in order to suppress a revolution. Yet this basis was the only practical foundation for a real conservative alliance designed for the protection of the monarchical system. By the end of the nineteenth century it was quite clear that the principle of nationalism had triumphed over that of political ideology even in that state which was the one most directly menaced by revolutionary agitation.

It was indeed the power of the national idea that first divided and then broke the alliance of the conservative courts. The belief of the Panslavs in the inevitability of final conflict between Slav and Teuton has already been discussed. Even the moderate Russian nationalists now recognized that Russia could not regain her former position in Europe without a reversal of 1870. Although the unification of Germany had been the right solution for the German people, it had obviously been wrong for the Russian state. The assumptions of the Panslavs of the basic rivalry of Russia with the central powers was shared by influential circles in both Germany and Austria-Hungary. In the Habsburg capital many, particularly among the military, foresaw and prepared for what they were certain would be a great war with Russia over the Balkan and Slavic questions. In Germany, too, similar groups wished a continuation of the active policies of the 1860's and the acquisition of additional territory and power by the new German Empire.

Despite the desire of Bismarck to preserve the lines to St. Petersburg, the position of Germany within the framework of the Three Emperors' League was quite different from that of Prussia in the Holy Alliance. As we have seen, before the Crimean War and the unification of Germany, Berlin had accepted the lead and direction of St. Petersburg in matters of vital importance because of the apparent vast military superiority of Russia. After 1870 united Germany was obviously the stronger power, certainly as long as Russia was not in alliance with France and had not come to terms with Britain. Russia could thus not dictate to

Germany after 1870 in the manner that she had dealt with Prussia in 1850. In addition, although Bismarck supported a Russian alliance, his primary interest was in the preservation of the Habsburg Monarchy. He feared two possibilities: first, that if Austria were defeated in a war that involved Germany, she would then join with France. Russia could thereafter dominate the situation by threatening to join the enemies of Germany in a new Kaunitz coalition. Second, he foresaw that if Russia went to war and defeated Austria, thus removing her from among the states of the first rank, then Germany would be in an equally dangerous position. Thereafter, she would be placed between France and Russia and without a real ally to the south. Isolated on the continent, she would be at the mercy of her neighbors. Bismarck saw quite clearly that the dangerous issue in European diplomacy was that of the eastern question. He would have preferred that Russia and Austria-Hungary simply partition the territory into spheres of influence. When this proved impractical, he attempted to keep his two neighbors in some sort of an alliance arrangement and to restrain both from adventurous policies.

The maintenance of peace in the first part of the reign of Alexander III was immeasurably aided by the determination of the two principal statesmen in Germany and Russia to try to avoid open conflicts and to mediate disagreements. Both Giers and Bismarck shared the belief that the main task for their respective governments was the concentration on internal consolidation and development; they were both opposed by those in their own countries who wished a greater emphasis on foreign policy. Giers in particular had a difficult time because of the strong reaction against Germany after the Congress of Berlin. Even men such as Peter Shuvalov, who had been sympathetic to the German cause, now regretted the French defeat. The Russian attitude was expressed also in the adulation and attention shown those who adopted an openly warlike attitude. The popularity of General Skobelev, the hero of Geok Tepe, who supported a war of Russia against Austria in aid of an uprising that had broken out in Bosnia in 1881, was an example of the popular feeling. The maintenance of a policy of co-operation between the two countries thus became increasingly difficult, despite the basic interest of both states in the maintenance of peace and the preservation of the conservative alliance.

Throughout the duration of the Three Emperors' League, which was renewed in 1884 but finally expired in 1887, Russia was part of a very complicated pattern of alliances devised by Bismarck to control the international situation. Primarily concerned with the protection of the gains of 1866 and 1870, he feared the formation of a coalition of those powers that had been directly injured by the unification of central Europe. Since after the annexation of Alsace-Lorraine France was to be reckoned as definitely in the enemy camp, he took steps to ensure that Paris would not become the center of diplomatic combinations directed against Berlin and would remain, if possible, isolated. The first alliance in what was to be an intricate network was concluded soon after the Congress of Berlin. The Dual Alliance of October 7, 1879 between Germany and Austria-Hungary was a defensive alliance directed against Russia. Should Russia attack either power, the other signatory must come to its partner's assistance. Should Germany become involved in war with France, Austria was obligated only to maintain a benevolent neutrality unless Russia entered. This treaty was renewed periodically and lasted until the outbreak of the war in 1914. It existed parallel with and was not replaced by the subsequent Triple Alliance. The partnership was of particular value to Austria-Hungary, who was now protected against an outright Russian aggression in the Balkans. Having secured its chief objective, the Dual Monarchy thereafter saw no need for extending its commitments. The negotiations for the Three Emperors' League were thus prolonged by the Austrian hesitations. As we have seen, this alliance was finally concluded in June, 1881. The agreement was strongly favored by Bismarck since it brought Russia into an alignment he could control. As long as Russia remained alone in Europe, the danger existed that she might join France. The alliance also served to moderate and contain the actions of the two Balkan rivals.

On May 20, 1882 a further combination, the Triple Alliance, was concluded, which brought Italy into the Austro-German camp. Since she too wished to be a colonial power, Italy was greatly disturbed by the French annexation of Tunis. The agreement that was signed at this time was thus directed primarily against France. Under its terms Germany and Austria were to assist Italy in the event of a French aggression; Italy would render similar aid to Germany. All the members of the alliance were obligated to join in a war should one of their number be at war with two great powers and to remain neutral if with only one. Thus Italy would be neutral in a conflict between Russia and Austria-Hungary, but would join should France and Russia fight Germany and Austria-Hungary.

In June, 1881 the network of alliances radiating from Berlin was lengthened by the conclusion of a treaty between Austria and Serbia. It will be remembered that although Panslav doctrines had called for assistance to all of the Slavs, practical military aid had been rendered only to the Bulgarians after the Serbian defeat of 1876. At the Congress of Berlin the Russian government had told the Serbs to turn to Vienna. As a result Prince Milan had been forced into a position of dependency on Vienna and the treaty of June, 1881 in effect made Serbia a vassal state. In return, Austria-Hungary agreed to support Milan in his desire to assume the title of king and made vague promises of support for Serbian aspirations in Macedonia.

The final agreements in this pattern were concluded in 1883 by both Germany and Austria-Hungary with Rumania. Angered over the Russian seizure of Bessarabia in violation of the treaty of 1877, the Rumanian government looked abroad for aid against further Russian encroachments. The agreements with the German powers, thus, promised support should Russia attack Rumania. In return, Rumania was obligated to assist Austria-Hungary in the same circumstances. The weakness in the partnership lay in the Rumanian national claims to Transylvania and the increasing policy of Magyarization practiced in the area by Budapest. However, as long as the Rumanian government saw its chief danger as coming from its northern neighbor, alliance with Vienna and Berlin was necessary.

This system of alliances joined four of the five powers of the continent of Europe but isolated France. Because of her imperial policies, Britain was also drawn into a policy of co-operation with the Triple Alliance. The wave of renewed imperial expansion after 1870 brought France and Britain into conflict over North Africa. With the French acquisition of Tunis in 1881, the fate of Egypt came next in question. The British involvement with France over this state and the rise of tension with Russia over Afghanistan made it impossible for the British government to pursue policies contradictory to those of the Triple Alliance.

Although the Bismarckian system of alliances was impressive, the question remained whether they could preserve the peace in a major crisis. The chief point of danger was still in the Balkans, but the situation in Central Asia as well was becoming increasingly tense. The ability of the alliance network to fulfill its intention was to be tested in the next years when Britain and Russia came close to conflict over the Afghan border question and when Russia's satellite Bulgaria challenged Russian overlordship.

THE AFGHAN BORDER DISPUTE

The value to Russia of her renewed alliance with Berlin and Vienna and the support that she thus gained for her interpretation of the Straits agreement was soon to be demonstrated by the events in Central Asia. The steady pattern of Russian conquest and expansion in the area had been watched with care and increasing apprehension in London. Once again, as in previous periods, the alarmists in Britain saw in the Russian actions a carefully conceived plan designed to take India. The fact that these advances were made despite repeated official Russian assurances that such action would not be taken naturally increased the doubts felt concerning Russia's reliability and honesty. Even if this condition was the result of bad communications and disobedient commanders, the fact remained that Russian troops were approaching the routes to India. The Russian capture of Merv in 1884 brought Russia dangerously close to the border of Afghanistan.

Because of its location between India and the Russian possessions in Central Asia, the preservation of Afghanistan as a buffer state was undoubtedly to the interest of both Russia and Britain. The political instability of the state and the nature of the country as a whole, however, made this aim difficult to accomplish. At the time of the Russian advance into Kokand, the Amir of Afghanistan, Shir Ali, had requested British assistance, which was denied. After the conquest of Khiva, he again appealed to Britain, but was unable to obtain any direct assurances of aid. Under these circumstances he turned to St. Petersburg, and in 1878 he received a Russian mission in his capital. But, at the same time he refused to receive one from Britain. The British government, fearing that Russia would establish a protectorate, opened the Second Afghan War of 1878-1879, which ended in the deposition of Shir Ali. Although thereafter Afghanistan was in theory a neutral buffer state, it was in fact a British protectorate.

Because of the political shift in Afghanistan, Russia and Britain now stood face to face over a common border for the first time in the entire period under discussion. The issue in dispute between them was the line to be drawn between their empires, which met at this point. The exact border of Afghanistan was exceedingly difficult to establish because it ran through a wild region inhabited by tribes who were under the general jurisdiction of the Amir of Afghanistan. In 1884 the Russian government agreed to the formation of a boundary commission that was to investigate the question on the spot. In September a British representative was sent, but when he arrived in Afghanistan he found that his Russian counterpart was delayed, nor did he appear in the next months. In the meantime the Russian forces slowly pushed forward in the territory under dispute with the objective of occupying as much land as possible. By February, 1885 the situation had become critical. In January the British had suffered a major setback in the Sudan when General Gordon and his garrison were massacred at Khartoum. Faced by the double pressure in Egypt and in Afghanistan, the British government gave priority to the Russian threat and made preparations in India for war. A Russian move towards Herat was particularly feared. On March 30 an open battle occurred between Russian and Afghan troops at Penjdeh, which increased the danger of the entire situation.

In this moment of crisis the value of the Three Emperors' League for Russia became apparent. Britain, who was without allies in the imperial conflict, could not hope to conduct a victorious war against Russia over Central Asian issues unless she could repeat the plan of the Crimean War, sail through the Straits, and initiate a campaign in the Caucasus. To prevent the opening of the Straits to British warships, Bismarck used pressure at Constantinople. He was supported not only by his allies, Austria and Italy, but also by France. Under the circumstances, both the British and Russian governments were virtually forced to arbitrate the conflict; neither was in a position to fight over the issue, and a real military engagement under the existing military and diplomatic conditions was virtually impossible. Although both powers agreed to arbitration, the question was finally settled by direct negotiation in the treaty of September, 1885, which set the Russian-Afghan boundary. Russia received the greater portion of the territory under dispute, but British predominance in Afghanistan was recognized in return. In March, 1895 a final settlement of the Pamir boundary was reached and a strip of Afghan territory was maintained between the territories of Russia and India to serve as a buffer zone.

Despite British fears to the contrary, there is no indication that Russia had any real designs for the conquest of India or that plans were ever made for the incorporation of that territory into the Russian Empire. The value of the land as a weapon against Britain was, nonetheless, thoroughly appreciated. Without adequate naval power to challenge British domination of the seas, Russia could only directly threaten British interests by pressure in Central Asia and in the eastern Mediterranean. Certainly,

Russian troops could never be landed on British soil the way British armies had been despatched to the Crimea. Therefore, in every major Russian-British crisis plans were made for an invasion of India, principally to exert pressure on Britain to aid in the accomplishment of Russian policy in other areas. The British sensitivity over the fate of the "jewel" of their empire made such threats effective. The Russian government during the period under consideration never had the military capacity or the desire to carry out such a great undertaking.

THE BULGARIAN CRISIS

Although the Central Asian problem was thereby solved in a manner acceptable to both sides, a major crisis followed in the Balkans in connection with internal events in Bulgaria which did not end in an equally satisfactory solution for the Russian government. After the Congress of Berlin the great powers had assumed that the autonomous Bulgaria under a foreign prince would be a Russian satellite and stand in a colonial relationship to St. Petersburg. The establishment of this state as a dependency had been the single great gain for Russia at the Congress of Berlin and the justification of the Russo-Turkish War. Control of the area was also most important from strategic considerations since the land formed a bridge to Constantinople. It was thus vital for the success of Russian policy in the Near East that a stable, friendly government be maintained in Sofia, which would look to Russia for instructions and would be a loyal ally in time of war.

The Russian government was also convinced that in its task of directing the administration of the new state it had to deal with a population that would welcome its benevolent, tutoring hand. Panslav enthusiasm for the Balkan Slavs had in the war concentrated itself on the Bulgarians; it was optimistically assumed that similar sentiments were felt in Bulgaria. And indeed after the liberation of the country from Turkish control there was a great fund of gratitude toward Russia, although it was not as much as Russia thought. The Bulgarians after the war expected to gain their freedom; they did not wish merely to change masters. They were therefore willing to accept direction and advice but not dictation. The Russian government thus met again in a liberated Balkan people a response it neither expected nor understood. Russia had, undoubtedly, in the case of Bulgaria, as previously in Greece and Rumania, expended large sums and had lost many men in wars against Turkey; and she expected to be repaid with eternal gratitude. The Balkan states, in contrast, recognized their debt to Russia, but they felt themselves independent political entities tied to no particular camp. They wished to remain free to align with whatever group best suited their interests and to regulate their internal affairs on the basis of purely domestic considerations.

The first years of the Russian protectorate over Bulgaria passed relatively smoothly. A new government was established under Russian direction with the Russian army in occupation. A draft constitution was drawn up in Bulgaria and then sent to Russia. This first document called for the establishment of a strong executive branch and was therefore conservative in form. The draft was examined by the ministries concerned and by a special commission and then it was returned to Sofia. In Bulgaria a constitutional assembly was summoned, which proceeded to examine this proposal. The constitution, which the Russian government offered only as a suggestion, was then subjected to thorough examination and debate. In this assembly the two political parties, the Liberals and the Conservatives, which together were to dominate the political life of Bulgaria, took shape. The issue that divided them was the balance between the executive and the legislative branches of government. The final form adopted for the constitution was extremely liberal in character, with the Liberals winning their demand for a strong legislature. The country was also to enjoy full civil liberties and the preponderant assembly was to be elected by universal manhood suffrage. It is interesting to note that the form of government adopted by Bulgaria was in great contrast to that in Russia. The Russian government stood sponsor for a regime whose people enjoyed rights far in advance of those of the Russians themselves.

Though the assembly altered the draft constitution presented by the Russian government, it did elect the prince designated by the controlling power. There were, in fact, few candidates available for the position. The final choice of Alexander of Battenberg was determined largely by the fact that he was acceptable to all of the powers. He was related to the British royal family, but he was also a nephew of the tsar. In selecting him the Russian government expected that he would follow its suggestions and directions. Alexander himself had little training for his future position as head of a Balkan state; in politics he was conservative, and he disliked the liberal constitution under which he was obliged to govern.

As had previously been true in the Danubian Principalities, Russian influence and control in Bulgaria were exercised through the Russian representatives in the state. In addition to the usual diplomatic agents, Russia had also a large number of military officials in the country. In the Bulgarian army all officers above the grade of captain were Russian; the Bulgarian minister of war was a Russian officer. These men were thus under the jurisdiction of the Russian war ministry, and they were expected to consult St. Petersburg on questions of policy. The diplomatic representatives, in contrast, were under the authority of the foreign ministry, and they sought their instructions in his office. Unfortunately for the success of Russian policy in Bulgaria, although the war and foreign ministries did often consult on common problems, adequate measures were not taken to ensure that the military and diplomatic agents in Sofia co-operated and co-ordinated their policies. Thus in time a difficult situation developed. Representatives of the two branches of the Russian service entered into competition with each other and joined opposite camps on domestic issues in Bulgaria.

The first major political issue involved the determination of Alexander of Battenberg to amend the new constitution. In this conflict the prince naturally allied with the Conservatives against the Liberal opposition. He was able to gain support for his views from the Russian consul, A. P. Davydov, a friend of Giers. However, General Parensov, the Russian minister of war in Bulgaria, in contrast, supported the Liberals and the constitution, with the approval of Miliutin and the Russian war ministry. In the end Prince Alexander resorted to a *coup d'état* to set aside the constitution, an action that he carried out without first notifying the Russian government. Thereafter, the Russian officials shifted roles. K. G. Ernrot, who was sent to replace Parensov, supported the prince and the Conservatives. Khitrovo, who became diplomatic agent, joined the Liberals.

Meanwhile, Alexander III had become tsar of Russia. Although he approved of the prince's action because of its conservative motivation, he was even more firmly determined than his father had been that Bulgaria should accept Russian direction. Moreover, although there had been a degree of sympathy and affection between the Bulgarian prince and Alexander II, no such feelings characterized the relationship of the new tsar and his cousin. Alexander III expected to be treated with the respect due the ruler of a great country, not as a relative. He also thought of Bulgaria purely in the terms of a satellite state. His stronger policies were to be introduced at a most inauspicious moment in Russo-Bulgarian relations. With time the Bulgarian political leaders had become increasingly resistant to Russian pressure and more eager to escape from Russian tutelage. Although the Bulgarians were grateful for past Russian military assistance and diplomatic support, they as a group had little admiration for Russian political thought or government. It is interesting to note that when the Panslav organizations brought Bulgarian students to be educated at Russian schools, these young men came primarily into contact with the elements of the Russian youth who were particularly dissatisfied with Russian autocracy. In Russia they also read and became acquainted with the western social and political philosophies that were the basis of the Russian revolutionary movement. Panslav educational efforts thus produced the opposite effect to that originally intended. Study in Russia had shown the degree to which that state lagged behind the west and not its capability of assuming the leadership of the Slavs. The Bulgarian political leaders, whether educated in the east or the west, thus turned toward western Europe for inspiration.

Before continued Russian pressure and interference in the political life of Bulgaria, Alexander adopted the only possible course of action by which he could maintain his independence. He joined with the two political parties to form a common front against Russian domination. He also restored the original constitution in order to win Liberal support. In reprisal, Russia withdrew two of her chief representatives, but she took no further action. Bulgarian defiance, however, lost for the new state Russian diplomatic support abroad. In its negotiations with other governments, Russia ceased in its efforts to further Bulgarian national interests. Whereas previously Russia had included the eventual unification of Bulgaria and Eastern Rumelia among its own foreign policy aims, this event was now firmly opposed. Alexander of Battenberg, because of his refusal to be a puppet ruler, had completely lost the Russian confidence.

The prince was able to resist Russian pressure on his state and to unite his people on this issue, but his position was not easy. It was extremely difficult for any Bulgarian government to withstand Russian pressure since it was impossible to obtain the support of any foreign government. Austria and Britain were sympathetic to the show of independence, but because of the general diplomatic situation they could not offer concrete assistance. Moreover, at the Congress of Berlin they had recognized that Bulgaria was within the Russian sphere. Bismarck, in particular, stood strongly behind the maintenance of the Berlin policy because he feared lest further Balkan complications should upset his delicate balance of alliances. In June, 1884 he commented bluntly that if Prince Alexander "would be something other than a Russian viceroy, then he has misunderstood his position." [2]

In September, 1885 a revolt broke out in Plovdiv, which

2. Stählin, *Geschichte Russlands*, IV/1, p. 528.

brought the entire issue of Russian control in Bulgaria again on the international scene. Despite the separation of the two Bulgarian provinces at the Congress of Berlin, the movement for national unification had proceeded in Eastern Rumelia after 1879, at first with the enthusiastic aid and assistance of the Russians. When the Russian officials subsequently reversed their stand, the Bulgarian nationalists continued their activities despite Russian opposition. On September 18, 1885 a group of revolutionaries deposed the governor-general of Eastern Rumelia and announced the union of their province with Bulgaria. Alexander of Battenberg was thus faced with a difficult decision. His position in Bulgaria demanded that he accept the leadership of the national movement. Like Cuza in Rumania and King Othon in Greece, he had found that it was only in the furtherance of national issues that he could unite his nation and gain support for his rule. If he refused to recognize the union, he could probably not remain as prince of Bulgaria. However, the international situation was clearly unfavorable for the event. Russia had made her negative attitude quite clear. Moreover, in August, 1885 Alexander had met with Giers at Franzenbad and apparently at that time gave assurances that he would not take steps to further the national cause. Russian disapproval of the revolt was expressed at once. On September 21, when it became apparent that Alexander would accept the headship of a united Bulgaria, the tsar ordered all of the Russian officers out of the country. He announced also that he would not recognize the unification as long as Prince Alexander and his government remained in office. Since the Bulgarian army was now deprived of all of its higher officers, it appeared that the Bulgarian state was militarily virtually defenseless.

The Bulgarian union was in fact saved by the thoughtless and ill-managed acts of King Milan of Serbia. Increasingly unpopular in his own country, he feared the effect upon his own position of the increase in power and prestige that the union gave his neighbor state. With the Bulgarian army apparently in a state of total disorganization, an ideal situation appeared to have presented itself. Milan therefore declared war on Bulgaria on November 13, despite an Austrian warning to the contrary. Because of the internal conditions in Bulgaria, the powers expected to witness a quick Serbian victory. To the surprise of all, the Bulgarian army not only defeated its opponents on its own soil, but it prepared to invade Serbia itself. In this crisis the Austrian government intervened to save its protégé and forced the conclusion of a peace between the states on a *status quo ante* basis. The Bulgarian victory, nevertheless, had saved the union.

Despite the intense opposition the Russian government felt towards the prince and the unification of Bulgaria, it was recognized that Russia could not afford to precipitate a major Balkan crisis over the event. Although Bismarck maintained his position of support of Russian control in the country, Britain and Austria-Hungary were openly delighted at this blow to Russian prestige and power. A compromise solution was finally agreed upon. Alexander of Battenberg was recognized as the governor-general of Eastern Rumelia, in theory only for five years, and the provinces were to remain administratively separate. The prince, however, almost immediately violated this agreement and joined the two assemblies. The united Bulgaria was thus created.

Although Bulgarian unification was achieved, the Russian government did not cease in its efforts to regain political control and if possible to oust the prince. Alexander III, who placed the entire question on a personal and emotional basis, was particularly bitter. The Russian leaders also appear to have held the illusion that the "Bulgarian people" were for them and that only the prince and his regime prevented a reconciliation. Conspiracies directed against the person of Alexander and against his government, therefore, received assistance from St. Petersburg. On the night of August 20, 1886, with the foreknowledge of Giers and the tsar, a band of conspirators entered the prince's room and forced him to sign a document of abdication. They then transported him out of the country and left him in Bessarabia. The provisional government established thereafter by the revolutionaries proved only of short duration. After three days the government was again taken over by loyal forces under the leadership of Stefan Stambolov, who then invited Alexander to return to his country. Thus only eleven days after the kidnapping, the prince again crossed the border. Here confused and exhausted, he made a disastrous mistake. Under the apparent impression that Russian support for his return might be forthcoming, he telegraphed the tsar: "As Russia gave me my crown, I am prepared to give it back into the hands of its Sovereign." [3] This message not only enraged the Bulgarian leaders, but it also gave the tsar the welcome opportunity of accepting this offer of abdication. When the Russian government in reply indicated its disapproval of his continuation in office, the prince appointed a regency and then left the country.

Russia now had the opportunity of once again establishing its influence; however, the mistakes of the past were repeated. General Nicholas Kaulbars, who was sent from Russia to deal with the situation, resorted to the same measures of pressure and violence that had alienated the Bulgars in the past. When the newly elected Bulgarian assembly proceeded with the choice of a new prince against Russian opposition, Kaulbars and the Russian officials all were recalled from the country; a complete break in diplomatic relations followed. In the next years the Russian government tried repeatedly to isolate and hinder the activities of the Bulgarian government in foreign affairs. This attitude accounted for much of the difficulty that the Bulgars met in attempting to find a new prince. Finally, in December, 1886 the name of Prince Ferdinand of Coburg was suggested, and in July, 1887 he was formally elected to replace Alexander of Battenberg. In the first years of his reign he was unable to obtain the recognition of any of the powers, and his tenure in office seemed indeed precarious. Nevertheless, the new Bulgarian state under the political guidance of Stambolov had shown the internal strength necessary to throw off the domination of Russia and to bring about the unification of the nation, despite the fact that it enjoyed the outright military support of no great power.

3. Charles Jelavich, *Tsarist Russia and Balkan Nationalism* (Berkeley: University of California Press, 1958), p. 258.

The tremendous blow to Russian prestige in eastern Europe resulting from the successful national revolution and again from the election of Ferdinand had strong repercussions within Russia. As a result Giers, personally, was forced to face the great crisis of his career as foreign minister because of the attacks launched on his policy by the nationalist press. The most effective opposition was offered by the publicist Katkov, whose articles in the *Moskovskii Vedomosti* (Moscow News) were read by the tsar. Katkov's position was also supported by Pobedonostsev and Saburov, of whom the latter now entered the camp of the nationalists despite his previous advocacy of alliance with Austria-Hungary and Germany. In March, 1886 Katkov made the error of publishing the terms of the agreement of 1884 of the Three Emperors' League. This document was secret, but its contents had been communicated by Saburov to the journalist. Alexander was greatly enraged over this breach of trust, and Katkov never again enjoyed similar influence. He died the next year.

Though Giers was able to withstand this storm, it was also apparent that a modification would have to be made in the policy of alignment with the northern courts. The Austrian attitude in the Bulgarian crisis made a continuation of the Three Emperors' League impossible, despite Giers' advocacy of its maintenance. Alexander III was now quite unwilling to co-operate with Vienna. He was, however, ready to continue close relations with Germany. The firm attitude taken by Bismarck against Alexander of Battenberg won general Russian approval; it was Vienna not Berlin that stood in the enemy camp. Alexander III himself commented:

Germany and Russia, closely associated, would put everything in order, would maintain tranquility and peace everywhere, would avert the revolution and be the masters of the world. Unfortunately Austria stands between us.[4]

In May, 1887 negotiations were therefore commenced with Germany alone by Paul Shuvalov, the Russian ambassador in

4. Stählin, *Geschichte Russlands*, IV/1, p. 548.

Berlin. During these discussions Bismarck, after communication with Vienna, read to the Russian representative the contents of the Dual Alliance with Austria. He argued that since the German position had consistently been that Austria must be upheld, this defensive alliance with Vienna did not preclude an agreement with Russia. Bismarck again emphasized in these conversations the old formula of the necessity of mutual support among the conservative powers. The Reinsurance Treaty, concluded on June 18, 1887, brought the German chancellor the assurance of Russian neutrality should France attempt to reverse the decision of 1870. In return, Germany agreed to support Russian interests in Bulgaria and at the Straits. The "preponderant and decisive" interests of Russia in Sofia were recognized, and Germany agreed not to allow the restoration of Alexander of Battenberg. Aid was also promised should Russia endeavor to re-establish "a regular and legal government" in Bulgaria. In regard to the Straits, Germany promised Russia assistance should the tsar "find himself under the necessity of assuming himself the task of defending the entrance of the Black Sea." Although Bismarck in this agreement apparently assured Russia of wide support in the east, he thereafter proceeded to create through a system of counter-alliances a general diplomatic situation that would make it impossible for Russia to carry out an active policy either in Bulgaria or at the Straits and thus benefit from the treaty with Germany.

The Reinsurance Treaty was only one in a wider framework of alliances encouraged by Bismarck in order to meet the double threat of the collapse of the Three Emperors' League in the east and the revival of French revanchism in the Boulanger movement in France. Before the conclusion of the agreement with Russia, Bismarck had already tightened his western alliances. With strong German approval Britain and Italy on February 12, 1887 signed the first Mediterranean agreement, which was devised to protect the *status quo* in the Mediterranean and Black Seas. Later Austria-Hungary and Spain adhered to this agreement, which was directed primarily against the extension of French control in North Africa. Although Germany did not formally become a member of this combination, she was connected with it through her allies of the Triple Alliance. This later pact was renewed on February 20, and Italy was allowed further advantages. The Reinsurance Treaty, the third in the series, was, as we have seen, concluded in June. The further deterioration of the Balkan situation after the election of Ferdinand of Coburg in July led directly to German sponsorship of a fourth agreement. Since Bismarck had in the Reinsurance Treaty promised Russia German support in Bulgaria, he now needed a combination that would assure that these promises need never be kept. Using again the instrumentality of the Mediterranean agreements, in which Germany did not participate, he supported the conclusion of the second pact of December, 1887. Here Italy, Britain, and Austria-Hungary joined to preserve the *status quo* in the Near East and thus to block Russian moves against Sofia. With this agreement in existence, Bismarck could with safety publicly support Russia. Since the Russian government was faced with a front of the other powers in the eastern Mediterranean, she could not act, and henceforth the Bulgarian problem as an international issue slowly lapsed. It should be noted that although these agreements, as the later diplomatic arrangements, remained secret in detail, the existence of the alignments and their participants were usually known.

The Bismarckian system of alliances and counter-alliances thus brought Europe through the year 1887. It was a complicated pattern and perhaps unnecessarily complex. Peace was, after all, maintained not so much through the existence of the agreements as because of the fact that none of the major powers wished to, or was prepared to, enter a major war. The preservation of the system also depended on the continuation in office of Bismarck. His ability to control German diplomacy, let alone European, came seriously into question in 1888, the year of the three emperors. First, William I, under whom Bismarck had served for so long, died. He was succeeded by his son, Frederick III, who was expected to favor the liberal, pro-British trend in Prussian policy. When he died from cancer of the throat after only three months in power, his son William II succeeded to the throne. Although more conservative in politics than his father, the new emperor was also more intolerant, aggressive, and headstrong. It was perhaps inevitable that the young ruler, who wished to be more than a figurehead, should clash with the man who had been for so long accustomed to directing German policy unhindered.

Agreement and alliance with Russia had, as we have seen, always been a central theme in Bismarck's policies, although after 1870 St. Petersburg had been subordinated to Vienna. The maintenance of this friendship had also been the constant preoccupation of Russia, even when the lines to Vienna were down. It has been shown how in so many respects Russia and Prussia, and later Prussia-Germany, had complemented and paralleled each other. They had common interests in the partitioned Poland, in the upholding of the conservative order, and they were strategically necessary to each other as long as Russia remained in conflict with Britain and Germany with France. These conditions remained valid in 1888. Under the new regime Bismarck continued therefore to emphasize the stern necessity of Germany's friendly relations with her eastern neighbor, particularly in view of the attitude of France. He also saw that, even if Germany should win a future war against Russia, little would be gained since:

This indestructible empire . . . would after its defeat remain our natural and revengeful opponent just as France is today in the west.[5]

These convictions were initially shared by the new emperor, but Bismarck met increasing opposition within the German foreign ministry from those who felt that the Russian agreement conflicted with Germany's obligations under the Triple Alliance.

The entire question of German-Russian relations was reviewed at the time of the scheduled renewal of the Reinsurance Treaty in 1890. The negotiations were commenced in Germany in February by Shuvalov, who then went back to St. Petersburg. When he returned to Berlin in March, he found the situation entirely altered. Bismarck was no longer chancellor, and the emperor had

5. *Ibid.*, p. 569.

accepted the advice of those who opposed the renewal of the agreement. Alexander III received the news with indifference; he had never felt any great enthusiasm for the pact although he had understood its advantages for Russian policy. However, for Giers the German rejection was a bitter blow. Throughout his career as foreign minister he had always supported the alignment with Berlin even though this position had won him the dangerous opposition of those with Panslav and strongly nationalist beliefs. Although the German government would not now renew the Reinsurance Treaty, Giers sought to obtain some kind of substitute. He was willing to drop the sections concerning Bulgaria and the Straits; he also declared that he would be satisfied with a simple exchange of letters. He was primarily concerned with securing something on paper that would justify the continuation of his policy. The Russian proposals met with no response in Berlin, where Bismarck's successors were bent upon strengthening the ties with Britain. With great reluctance Giers and his associates were now forced to consider a complete change of policy and the formation of the alignment previously pressed by the nationalist opposition—that of alliance and co-operation with Republican France. The diplomatic situation that Bismarck had labored so long to prevent had thus been created. Russia and France both stood alone. Neither had any outstanding quarrel with the other, but both faced dangerous opposition from their neighbors. A policy of collaboration under such circumstances could not long be avoided.

THE FRANCO-RUSSIAN ALLIANCE

The formation of a Franco-Russian alliance had long been supported by the nationalists in both France and Russia; however, many considerations still hindered its accomplishment. The chief link between the states remained the fact that both were now diplomatically isolated and faced the danger of seeing their policies, whether offensive or defensive in intention, blocked by the combination of the Triple Alliance and Britain. France and Russia thus had the same potential enemies, but they did not have similar immediate aims and interests in foreign policy. Russian interests were still primarily concentrated in the Balkans, where the chief opponents were Austria-Hungary and Britain. Russia had no quarrels with Germany nor did she wish to antagonize that military giant. France, in contrast, had no important Balkan goals; she was thus unlikely to lend active or enthusiastic assistance to Russian projects in the east, certainly not as long as her principal enemy lay across the Rhine. She had certainly no interest in fostering Russian antagonism to the Danubian Monarchy over the fate of the small states of the Balkans where she had nothing at stake. French policy remained in this period divided in that the government sought to carry on an active continental policy against Germany and also a colonial program against Britain. Her chief opponent, however, always remained the German Empire. The strong nationalists wished to prepare for a war of revenge and to regain Alsace-Lorraine; the moderates feared that Germany would launch a preventive war for the purpose of eliminating French power once and for all. The chief aim of the negotiations with Russia in French eyes was thus to obtain the support of the Russian armies against Germany's eastern frontiers in time of war, although the French had few illusions about the actual military strength of Russia at the time. The Russian government naturally had no great enthusiasm about fighting Germany for French aims on the Rhine when no outstanding issues stood between St. Petersburg and Berlin.

The ideological issues of the past century also continued to hinder closer political relations. Certainly, the Third Republic and tsarist Russia stood poles apart. Despite her value as an ally, France remained for the conservative Russian the center of revolutionary movements of all colors and the patron of Polish nationalism. Little respect was felt for the reliability and stability of the French regime itself. The repeated scandals and internal crises in Paris did nothing to alter this view. The incompatibility of the two systems of government was chiefly a matter of concern to the Russian officials; the French, with nothing to fear from tsarist autocracy, were interested chiefly in securing the assistance of the Russian armies, less in the ideological implications of the question.

In both France and Russia, as has been mentioned, the strongest support for an alignment came from the extreme nationalists. Neither group had much sympathy or interest for the aims of its counterpart, but they recognized that they needed each other. If the immediate issues were put aside and only general long-range questions were considered, then Germany was the principal enemy of Russia as well as of France. It was clear that Russia too had lost by the decision of 1870 and that the new Germany threatened the claims of both Paris and St. Petersburg to continental supremacy. The Russian Panslav, foreseeing an inevitable clash of Slav and Teuton, realized that a French alliance was necessary to secure the realization of his dream of a great Slavic empire; the French nationalist, bent on a policy of *revanche*, saw that France could only regain its former role as the great nation of the continent with the destruction of Germany, a project feasible only with Russian co-operation. Both nations thus had the common aim of the reversal of the achievements of Bismarck. Alexander III in 1891 uttered these convictions:

In case of war between France and Germany we must immediately throw ourselves upon the Germans in order not to give them time to defeat France at once and then turn against us. We must correct the mistakes of the past and crush Germany at the first opportunity.[6]

Despite these considerations, the negotiations between France and Russia were initiated because of the actions of Germany, which left the Russian government no other alternative. At the time of the dropping of the Reinsurance Treaty, the advisors of William II had not believed that a Franco-Russian alliance was possible because so many issues separated the two countries. They were chiefly concerned with tightening the connections between Germany and Britain through the Triple Alliance. When on July

6. V. N. Lamzdorf, *Dnevnik, 1891-1892* (Moscow, 1934), p. 299.

1, 1890 an agreement was signed in which Germany received
Heligoland in return for the abandonment of claims to lands in
Africa, it appeared as if the policy of co-operation with Britain
was well under way. At the same time the German government
undertook measures to ameliorate the position of the Poles who
were under German domination. It thus appeared that German
policy had taken the course that had caused so much concern
in other periods, that of co-operation with liberal England and
the adoption of measures in support of Polish nationalism. A
liberal and pro-Polish Prussia in alliance with Britain had always
been recognized as a danger to Russian policy; Germany following the same course made the maintenance by Russia of a diplomatically isolated position impossible. The existence of ties between Germany and Britain were underscored at the time of the
renewal of the Triple Alliance. The Italian premier, Rudini, in a
speech in June, 1891 implied that Britain had joined the combination of the central powers. If this were indeed true, then both
France and Russia were faced in Europe and overseas with a solid
block of preponderant military and diplomatic power. Thus, although Russia and Germany had no outstanding immediate differences between them, it appeared that Berlin was firmly attached
to the camp of the Russian opponents.

Even before 1890 the groundwork had been laid for Russo-
French co-operation in the financial field by an ill-advised act of
Bismarck made before he was forced out of office. In 1887, in
reprisal for action taken against German interests in the Russian
Baltic provinces, he made it impossible for the Russian government to secure loans in Berlin. Russia, thereafter, turned to Paris,
a far better money market, and the necessary funds were readily
obtained. This economic relationship, which the French government manipulated for political ends, remained until the fall of the
tsarist regime when the French were left with much worthless
paper on their hands. Nevertheless, the loans strengthened the
relations between the two governments and gave France a large
stake in the Russian economy. It also took the financial weapon

out of the hands of the German government and gave it to the French.

The actual negotiations for an agreement were, nevertheless, slow in initiation and in completion. In July, 1891 the improved relations between the two countries were demonstrated during the visit of a French squadron to the Russian naval base of Kronstadt. On this occasion the tsar stood at attention during the playing of the Marseillaise, the hymn of the revolution, the ban on its performance in Russia having been lifted for the occasion. The first written agreement between the two powers was contained in an exchange of letters in August, 1891. The stipulations reflected the hesitancy of the Russian government to accept really effective obligations in regard to France. It was merely agreed that the two signatories would "confer on every question of a nature to threaten the general peace." Should either power be threatened by aggression "the two parties agree to come to an understanding on measures which the realization of that eventuality would make it necessary for both governments to adopt immediately and simultaneously." These statements, the first stage in the Franco-Russian alliance, were thus quite limited in extent. The agreement could also be directed against Britain as well as against Germany.

The significant and central agreement for the alliance was not negotiated until a year later. Since the chief bond between France and Russia was the military assistance that they could render each other against Germany, it was proper that the chiefs of staff should be primarily concerned with the drawing up of the arrangement. In August, 1892 General Boisdeffre and his Russian counterpart, General Obruchev, agreed upon a far-reaching military pact, which, after its ratification, was to form the basis of the Russo-French alignment that brought both nations into the First World War. In the conversations concerning an agreement the French showed they were primarily interested in ensuring that at the commencement of hostilities the Russian army would immediately launch an attack upon Germany's eastern frontier and not simply remain on the defensive. The French government feared a military situation in which the German armies would enter Paris while the Russians concentrated on the Balkans and Austria-Hungary. The final agreement, which was directed clearly against Germany, met the French demands. It was stipulated that if France were attacked by Germany, or by Italy backed by Germany, Russia would come to the aid of France. France assumed similar obligations towards Russia in case of a German attack or an Austrian aggression backed by Germany. Mobilization by any member of the Triple Alliance obligated both Russia and France immediately to call up their troops. It was further agreed that at the outbreak of hostilities France would immediately employ 1,300,000 men in action against Germany while Russia should enter with 700,000 to 800,000 in order "that Germany will have to fight at the same time in the east and in the west." The duration of the agreement was to be the same as that of the Triple Alliance.

This pact, initialled by the two chiefs of staff, still required the approval of the tsar and the French government. The ratification was long delayed because of continued hesitation in Russia, particularly on the part of Giers, to enter into an openly anti-German agreement. Throughout the negotiations the alliance received the strong support of the Russian ambassador in Paris, Mohrenheim, who did all he could to promote good relations between the countries. The tsar's distrust of the French regime was strengthened again by the Panama Canal scandals of 1892, when it was shown that members of the government were involved in financial irregularities in connection with the construction of the waterway. In this period Giers again tried unsuccessfully to initiate some kind of discussions with Berlin. In October, 1893 a Russian squadron visited Toulon amid scenes of enthusiasm and rejoicing. The renewed friendship with Russia had won the strong acclamation of the French public, which felt that their country had won a strong ally against Germany. Finally, in December Giers was able to notify France that his government accepted the agreement. On January 4, 1894, with the French approval, the Franco-Russian alliance was established.

This agreement has received much study and much adverse criticism because it contributed to the creation of the alliance system that eventually brought the European states into a major war over a relatively minor Balkan incident. However, it is difficult to see how such an alignment could have been avoided in the early 1890's. Russia could not afford to stand alone, particularly in the face of the Triple Alliance working in co-operation with Britain. It should also be emphasized that the agreement was a strictly defensive alliance, and it was certainly not followed by any immediate attempts by Russia to turn it into an offensive weapon. In fact in its first years the agreement caused France to join Russia in a policy of peace and the maintenance of the *status quo* in the Near East. Nor were there any indications that the alliance would remain firm and lasting; other similar engagements had been terminated, and the international situation was to take many turns before 1914.

The alliance did, however, divide the continent into two camps, Triple Alliance against the Franco-Russian alliance. As before, the two danger areas remained the Rhine, where French and German interests clashed, and the Balkans, where Russia and Austria stood in opposition. Although the next years were to be dominated by imperial rivalry, these two areas never lost their significance. It is also interesting to note that in the long view in the formation of both alliance systems it was the stronger power that saw its freedom of action ultimately hampered. Under the relatively firm rule of Alexander III, Russian policy in the east remained under control. When this situation changed during the reign of Nicholas II, the French government found itself allied to an unstable government, whose balance and wisdom in a time of crisis could not be relied upon. France in 1914 went to war to defend Russian Balkan policy over an issue in which she had no direct interest and one that was certainly not worth the risking of her national existence. In the same manner Germany after the conclusion of the Dual Alliance became increasingly dependent upon her Austrian ally, but that power underwent a process of disintegration and division similar in degree to that in Russia.

Because of this relationship it was to be the Balkans and not the Rhine that was to be the area of chief significance. The danger in the situation increased after the turn of the century when, because of their failures in internal policies, neither Russia nor Austria-Hungary could afford to suffer humiliations abroad. The alliance relationship thus forced both France and Germany to support their allies, even when the latter pursued dangerous and provocative policies.

* * * * *

Despite the fact that the reign of Alexander III lasted but a short time, it perhaps constituted the most significant period of the century in regard to tsarist diplomacy. Although the unification of Germany had occurred previously, the policy of alliance with Berlin had been continued through the Three Emperors' League and later through the Reinsurance Treaty. The dropping of that agreement by William II in 1890 marked the end of the policy of co-operation and friendship that had been maintained by Berlin and St. Petersburg almost without interruption since the reign of Catherine the Great. The importance of this realignment was as great for Germany as for Russia and for the same military and strategic reasons. The area of greatest significance for Russia was that occupied by Prussia and partitioned Poland. It was from here that Europe could effectively launch an invasion of Russia that could endanger the existence of the state. Thus in comparison to central Europe, the Near, Middle, and Far East always remained sideshows. The great achievement of 1814 had been the securing of the conditions of maximum security through the control of Congress Poland, the tripartite division of the German lands, and the maintenance of military superiority in eastern Europe. The Holy Alliance had aided Russia in that it joined together the three conservative monarchies for the preservation of the system established by the Congress of Vienna. This highly favorable situation was changed in 1870 with the emergence of the united Germany, but as long as the diplomatic ties were kept between Berlin and St. Petersburg, the Russian western frontiers were safeguarded. This entire structure fell in 1890 when Germany not only abandoned the line to St. Petersburg but also sought a policy of exclusive alignment with the Russian adversaries: Britain and Austria-Hungary. The Russian government then faced the possibility that conflicts in Asia and in the Balkans could result in a direct invasion of Russia. It was not the Crimea that was now in danger but St. Petersburg and Moscow.

The decision to abandon the Reinsurance Treaty was made in Berlin, not in St. Petersburg; the Russian foreign ministry had wished to keep it. The Russian government thereafter followed the obvious course when it with reluctance concluded the agreement with France. Even with the alliance with France Russia was still at a disadvantage in relation to her neighbor, since behind Germany stood the Triple Alliance in co-operation with Britain. In the next years this superiority of Germany over Russia was to increase at a steady pace. The enormous advantages that the accelerating tempo of industrialization offered the German military establishment were not paralleled in Russia. Although Russia too entered a period of industrialization in the 1890's, her internal structure, in contrast, rapidly deteriorated. Economic change led to social and political unrest and not to an increase of national power. It was this combination of military weakness and political maladjustment that was to lead in 1917 to the collapse of the regime.

The reign of Alexander III marks, thus, the end of the great period of Russian diplomacy in the nineteenth century. Four rulers, Alexander I, Nicholas I, Alexander II and Alexander III, together with their three chief statesmen, Nesselrode, Gorchakov, and Giers, had, despite inevitable mistakes, nevertheless kept Russian prestige high and her policy on an even keel. In the next reign, under Nicholas II, this continuity and direction were lost. Instead, the negative elements of the preceding years joined with the growing internal chaos to lead Russia into adventures for which she was not prepared.

VI

꒰꒦꒰꒦꒰꒦

Nicholas II

In October, 1894, at the young age of twenty-six, Nicholas II succeeded his father, who died of a kidney disease. Like Alexander III he had been educated under the guidance of Pobedonostsev, and, in the tradition of his predecessors, he accepted the basic policies and principles of Russian autocracy. With only a limited education, his preparation for his office also suffered from the fact that he had not been adequately initiated into the conduct of state affairs and had himself not held important positions in the government. In 1890-1891 he made a long journey, accompanied by his brother George and his cousin Prince George of Greece, to Greece, Egypt, India, China, and Japan, then home through Siberia. His subsequent interest in the east was thus influenced by his travels. A firm believer in autocracy and in the divine origins of his own power, he was to prove a bad constitutional monarch. He was, however, in temperament in no way suited to the role of an absolute ruler. Well-meaning, but weak, unstable, almost childish in his reactions, he fell too easily under the influence of the last person who talked with him. This lack of determination was to prove especially unfortunate in the field of foreign policy, where the tsar had to make the final decisions.

Throughout his reign Nicholas II was always open to the influence of those around him but particularly to that of his wife, Princess Alice of Hesse-Darmstadt. A granddaughter of Queen Victoria, the empress was brought up in England, and her manner was that of an Englishwoman. She and her husband always corresponded in the English language. Stronger in character than the tsar, she interfered increasingly in state affairs, where her influence was always in the direction of the strengthening of the conservative forces.

The greatest tragedy in the lives of the couple centered on the health of the heir to the throne. After a succession of four daughters, a son was finally born in 1904, but it soon became apparent that he had hemophilia, inherited from his mother's family. Both Nicholas II and his wife often associated with adventurers and even outright charlatans, but it was through their child's sickness that the most disastrous of these advisors, the monk Rasputin, gained a dominating position in the Russian government. The fundamental weakness of character of the tsar and his inability to keep order in his own house reflected itself in the foreign and internal policies of the empire until the destruction of the regime in 1917.

In foreign affairs Nicholas II inherited from his father the French alliance, of whose existence he learned only after his accession. During the first years of his reign he not only maintained, but even tightened the bonds of this agreement. In 1896 he travelled to France; in 1897 the French president Faure returned the visit. In 1899 the alliance was strengthened through the provisions that the military agreement should be of indefinite duration and that the pact in general should be extended to cover the "maintenance of equilibrium" rather than only "the maintenance of peace." The existence of this alliance, however, in no way hindered Nicholas II from considering and discussing agreements with Germany or Austria-Hungary. Like the previous tsars, Nicholas II felt a strong sense of dynastic kinship with the court of Berlin, despite his dislike for William II. In his meetings with the German emperor and in their correspondence, Nicholas II showed himself personally willing to accept a policy of co-operation, even when such an agreement would have meant a violation of the French alliance.

This reign also witnessed the Russian initiative in an event that must be recorded here since it falls outside of the subjects discussed in the following pages. In August, 1898 the Russian government called upon the other states to meet in a conference to limit armaments. Like the proposals of Alexander I, this summons was greeted with much suspicion and derision. Russian actions in the Far East at the time seemed to indicate that Russia herself was following anything but a peaceful policy; the weak economic structure of the country obviously made it advantageous for her to seek to limit the weapons of her neighbors, since she could not hope to rival their capacity for arming. Nevertheless, a meeting was held at The Hague in 1899. Although no disarmament agreement was reached, the governments attending did attempt to regulate the conditions of warfare and, more significant, an international court of arbitration was established. A second meeting in 1907 also failed to result in a limitation of arms, but problems of international law were more successfully handled.

It is extremely unfortunate that the tsar with the least capabilities of real leadership should also have been backed by the weakest of foreign ministries in the century. If Nicholas II had been associated with a statesman of the caliber of Bismarck, or even Giers or Nesselrode, Russian foreign policy might have taken an entirely different course. Instead, the conditions of the past century were in fact reversed. We have seen how, since the Congress of Vienna, four tsars were served by three chief ministers. Each of these had been trained thoroughly in his duties by his predecessor and had enjoyed considerable experience in diplomacy before assuming the office of foreign minister. This system had provided continuity and unity of policy. In contrast, Nicholas II was served by eight different ministers before his fall in 1917. None of these were men of unusual capability. Giers, who remained in office after the death of Alexander III, died in 1895. A. B. Lobanov-Rostovsky, who followed him, was an experienced and able statesman, but he died after little more than a year in office, to be succeeded by M. N. Muraviev, a man of much less ability, who served until 1900. His successor, V. N. Lamzdorf, in office from 1900 to 1906, was a sober, hard-working administrator, but he lacked experience in service abroad. The next minister, the ambitious Izvolsky, in power from 1906 to 1910, adopted a more active policy but, as we shall see, suffered a humiliating defeat. He was followed by S. D. Sazonov, in office from 1910 to 1916, who owed his position to his relationship to Stolypin and who proved to be unable to maintain control of the affairs under his jurisdiction. B. V. Sturmer (July-November, 1916) and N. N. Pokrovsky (1916-1917) held office during the difficult final years of the reign.

The Near East in the 1890's

In the 1890's Russia, like the other great powers, entered upon a period of imperial expansion in the Far East. The shift of emphasis from the Near East and Europe to Manchuria and the Pacific was made possible because of the interest of all of the powers in similar enterprises and also their common desire to maintain the *status quo* in the area that had formerly been the center of dispute: the Ottoman Empire. Although a series of crises arose here, all of the governments showed a determination to settle matters peacefully and not allow an upset of the balance. In this endeavor, the lines between the Triple Alliance and the Franco-Russian alliance tended to disappear since no power now felt it could benefit by independent action. This policy of agreement was best represented by the Russo-Austrian understanding of 1897 in which the former opponents agreed to co-operate to maintain the *status quo*. The Russian desire to remove the Balkans from the field of diplomatic conflict had been shown already in the reconciliation that took place with Bulgaria in 1896. In this question, as in the concurrent Armenian and Cretan crises, the Russian government thus followed a course of action that was to contrast with its later policies in the Far East.

As we have already seen, a period of highly strained relations followed the accession of Ferdinand of Coburg to the Bulgarian throne. Despite the fact that diplomatic relations between the two countries had been broken, the Russian government continued to try to exert pressure on the country; and it also encouraged activities of a violent and illegal character against the new regime. Thus Ferdinand and his influential minister, Stefan Stambulov, were in constant danger of overthrow or assassination because of the actions of groups that enjoyed at least unofficial Russian support. Since none of the great powers had yet recognized the new ruler, the position of the Bulgarian government was most precarious. Under these circumstances, it became of utmost importance that Ferdinand marry. If he had an heir, there would be less temptation for his rivals to assassinate him. However, because of the stipulations of the Bulgarian constitution, which required that the heir be of the Orthodox faith, the prince had great difficulty in finding a bride. Finally he secured the acceptance of Marie-Louise of Parma, but only on the condition that their children be brought up as Catholics. Against strong Russian opposition, Ferdinand and Stambulov were able to amend the constitution. Subsequently, the prince married, and soon a son was born. Relations with Russia during this period remained tense and dangerous. A change, however, came in 1895 when Nicholas II became tsar and after Stambulov had been forced out of office and later assassinated. Ferdinand recognized clearly that Bulgaria could not continue indefinitely in a condition of diplomatic isolation. Moreover, she needed the support of a great power for her national aspirations for the acquisition of lands still in the control of the Porte. Because Bulgaria lay by common agreement in the Russian sphere, it was unlikely at the time that any other major government would lend assistance. For these reasons, Ferdinand finally decided to seek a reconciliation with St. Petersburg. As a first step, and against the strong opposition of his wife, the prince saw the necessity of meeting the Russian wishes on the conversion of the heir. As had previously been the case in its relations with Greece under King Othon, the Russian government now placed the first emphasis on the religious issue. Ferdinand, therefore, had his son, who had been christened a Catholic, re-christened in the Orthodox church. With this major obstacle removed, Russia then recognized the government of Prince Ferdinand, and relations returned to normal after the long break. Russia, however, was never again able to exert the predominating and dictatorial influence in Bulgarian internal affairs that had characterized the first years of her protectorate over the new state.

The change of attitude of Bulgaria toward Russia and the recognition that a reconciliation would have to be sought was at least partially occasioned by the development of the Macedonian problem in the 1890's. Bulgaria clearly could not afford to lose Russian support in an issue where previously she had enjoyed the patronage of St. Petersburg. For it was only with Russian assistance and pressure on the Porte that the Bulgarians in 1870 had obtained the right not only to establish a Bulgarian exarchate but also permission to extend the jurisdiction of that organization over any Macedonian territories in which two-thirds of the population voted for their inclusion. With these rights the Bulgarians had launched a highly successful educational and cultural offensive. Russian support of the Bulgarian claims had also been shown in the provisions of the Treaty of San Stefano where Macedonia had been a part of the Greater Bulgaria provided for in that agreement. Thereafter the boundaries of the Bulgaria of San Stefano became the national aim of the subsequent Bulgarian governments.

Naturally the maximum program of San Stefano and the Bulgarian cultural offensive in Macedonia met the opposition of both Greece and Serbia. The Bulgarian gains had been chiefly won at the expense of the Greeks, whose influence was exerted through the Patriarchate at Constantinople. Greek interest in the area was also increased when with the acquisition of Thessaly and part of Epirus in 1881 their national territories approached those of the disputed area. Serbian claims were also reinforced after the disappointments of the Congress of Berlin. Forced by Russia to acquiesce to the Austrian occupation of Bosnia-Herce-govina and to accept a position of subservience to Vienna, the Serbs could only direct their ambitions and salve their national pride in Macedonia.

In order to fortify their own position and to win converts to their cause, the opposing parties in the Macedonian dispute proceeded to organize. In the early 1880's the Bulgarians formed the Cyril and Methodius Society; the Serbian Society of St. Sava was organized in 1886 in answer. Those who sought an independent Macedonia established in 1893 the Internal Macedonian Revolutionary Organization (IMRO). Thereafter in 1895 the Bulgars set up the External Organization, whose intention was the annexation of the area by Sofia. In 1894 the Greeks entered the scene with the formation of their Ethnike Hetairia. The first and perhaps the chief result of the rise of national feeling in Macedonia was thus to destroy any hope of Balkan unity. Instead of concentrating on a policy of common opposition to the Ottoman government, the three states now engaged in bitter rivalry over this territory.

In addition to Macedonia, another section of the Ottoman Empire, Armenia, was also in the 1890's subject to violent national agitation. Here, as among other subject nationalities of the Porte, revolutionary committees were organized with the aim of securing independence or at least autonomy for their people. Unfortunately, in this case, the Armenian revolutionary leaders made a grave miscalculation. They believed that if they committed acts of violence against individual Turks, the Porte would reply with such extreme measures that the powers would be forced to intervene to rescue the Armenians as they had in similar cases come to the aid of the Balkan peoples. The plan worked only so far. Atrocities committed by Armenian terrorists did provoke a violent Turkish reaction; from 1894 to 1896 massacres were repeatedly reported. The powers, however, failed to react as expected. Although the British public proved sympathetic, the government did not act. Moreover, Russia, the upholder of the rights of Balkan nations, proved less receptive to the idea of Armenian freedom. With a large Armenian population of its own, which was also subject to national influences, the Russian government could not support a movement in the Ottoman Empire that might eventually react to its own disadvantage, particularly at a time when a strong Russification program was being pursued in regard to the Russian minorities. At this time also Russian influence had increased in Constantinople and Russia could gain no advantage from a further weakening of the empire. Although no serious crisis occurred over the question, the Armenian incident did lead to the formulation of plans to seize the Bosphorus should Britain take action. These were strongly supported by the Russian ambassador in Constantinople, Nelidov. In the end the powers did nothing for the Armenians beyond the usual recommendations to the Porte for reform. The entire question ultimately merged into the more serious problem of the Cretan uprising of 1896.

Although Greek in nationality, the island of Crete had not been joined with free Greece in 1830 because of British opposition. From 1824 to 1840 the island was under the control of Egypt; it then returned to direct Ottoman rule. The same condition of Turkish maladministration and national unrest developed here as in the rest of the Ottoman lands. Uprisings of the restive Christian population occurred in 1841, 1858, and from 1866 to 1868. These revolts were met, as ever, with the usual sequence of the formulation of reform programs by the powers, the acceptance of these plans by the Porte, and the subsequent failure of the Ottoman authorities to implement the measures agreed upon. However, even with the best will the Ottoman government would have had great difficulty in pacifying or conciliating the Cretans. They, like other national minorities, wished not reform, or even autonomy, but union with Greece. They naturally received a great deal of moral and material support from the mainland, although by the 1890's the Greek nationalist was more interested in Macedonia, where his claims were disputed by other states. Crete was clearly Greek and would inevitably one day join free Greece.

In February, 1896 the question was reopened when another rebellion broke out, which was supported strongly from the Greek mainland and by the Ethnike Hetairia. In February, 1897 the Cretan rebels declared their union with Greece. Although the Greek government was well aware of the international aspects of the situation, it was forced to send aid because of the great enthusiasm within Greece for the revolt. Prince George, the second son of King George I of Greece and, incidentally, the former companion of Nicholas II on his travels to the east, was sent to the island with an expedition of 1,500 men. This reopening of the eastern question and the new threat to Ottoman domains were received very unfavorably in St. Petersburg, despite the support the Russian government had previously offered the Cretans in the crisis of the 1860's. The continental powers also favored the Russian position on the maintenance of the *status quo*. The enforcement of this policy was rendered impossible by the lack of co-operation from Britain. The Cretan rebellion could only be checked if the flow of supplies from Greece were halted, an action that could only be carried out with the assistance of the British navy. When this could not be obtained, no positive action was possible. Meanwhile, political pressures in Greece mounted. Although entirely unready for war, the Greek government in April, 1897 launched an invasion of Turkish territory. The Turkish troops, better prepared than in previous years, soon inflicted a decisive defeat upon the Greeks. At the same time Russia took steps in both Serbia and Bulgaria to prevent them from joining with Greece. The powers then put pressure on both Greece and Turkey and compelled the belligerents to conclude an armistice. In September a final peace treaty was signed, which allowed the Ottoman Empire only a few token gains despite its military victory. Although the Greek armies were defeated, the Cretans lost little from this disaster. Instead they won the fulfillment of much of their program. They were not allowed to join Greece, but they received an autonomous status and, more significant, through the support of both Britain and Russia, they obtained the appointment of Prince George as their governor. The separation was thus largely a fiction, and it could be expected that the island would soon be integrated into the kingdom. The Cretans, in contrast to the Armenians, had thus been able to win great power intervention and had achieved most of their national aims.

With the settlement of the Cretan question a condition of comparative calm characterized the diplomacy of the Balkans for the next ten years. The desire of Russia for the maintenance of the *status quo* in the area had been shown in her attitude toward Bulgaria and in her co-operation with the continental powers in the Armenian and Cretan questions. A similar policy of inactivity was also now to the interest of Austria-Hungary, whose government faced grave internal political problems. Since both powers had primary interests in other directions, Russia and the monarchy were able to come to an understanding. In April 1897, during the Greek crisis, Franz Joseph, with his foreign minister, Goluchowski, visited St. Petersburg where an agreement was concluded that put the Balkans "on ice" for the next decade. Both powers agreed to co-operate to preserve as far as possible the *status quo* in the area and to maintain the closure of the Straits. The problems raised by the possibility of the further disintegration of Ottoman rule in the peninsula were also discussed, but no definite plans were made beyond the mutual recognition of the fact that the balance should be preserved. In October, 1903, the two rulers met again at Mürzsteg. Here they discussed the new outbreaks that had occurred in Macedonia, and they drew up a reform program. Although their co-operation did little to settle the Macedonian problem, it did signify a continuation of a policy which removed the Balkan area from the international diplomatic arena until 1908. With her southwestern front secured through an understanding with her opponent, Russia was then free to turn her attention to the Far East. Without the agreement of 1897, the Russian government would not have been able to embark upon the adventurous and dangerous course that was now to be followed. The pact that brought peace to the Balkans thus led to war in the Far East.

THE FAR EAST TO 1905

Although Russian activities in the Near East thus showed a desire to retain conditions as they were and to co-operate with other powers, the policy adopted in Far Eastern affairs was to lead in an entirely different direction. For the first time in the century under consideration, the problem of China and the Far East in general was to occupy the central position in Russian diplomacy. Here Russian activities paralleled those of the western European states, who, after 1870, entered upon a new era of overseas conquest directed towards Asiatic and African lands. At the end of the eighteenth century European imperialism as a movement had slackened. Of the two major powers concerned, France had become absorbed by continental affairs, and Britain was at least partially disillusioned with colonial conquest after the American Revolution. Despite this weakening of interest, the powers had, nevertheless, continued to protect and enlarge their colonial possessions. Concern over the approaches to India was, as we have seen, a determining aspect of British policy as directed toward Russia. French expansion in North Africa, involving chiefly assistance to Egypt and the annexation of Algeria in 1830, signified the continued imperial interests of France, which were also reflected in other parts of the world. The attitude of all the powers toward the Ottoman Empire and Russia's conquests in Central Asia were also examples of imperial policies. The shift after 1870 was thus one of intensity and commitment; the states involved embarked upon more active programs of expansion aimed at the control or annexation of great stretches of territory in Asia and Africa. The character of the movement was also strongly stamped by the influence of the industrial revolution. The advanced technology of the industrialized states not only gave them the facility to subdue more easily backward nations, but it also widened the difference between the civilizations of the conqueror and the conquered. In addition, the new economic development made colonial areas more attractive as places of investment, of trade, or as sources of raw materials. Much of the former disillusionment with colonies had been that they did not pay. Now it appeared that indeed a highly profitable relationship could be developed between the industrial nation and its dependencies. The intense competitive national pride that characterized the nations at the end of the century could also find expression in this field. National glory often provided sufficient incentive when economic gain was not immediately apparent. The actions of Europe in Asia and Africa, thus, reflected, and indeed became, an extension of European politics—its industrial civilization and its competitive state system.

The chief power who participated in this new movement was again the greatest of the imperial states, Britain. But others followed close behind. France, Belgium, Holland, Germany, Italy, and Spain all joined in the competition. The United States and Japan, despite the fact that they at one time had been the objects of colonial domination, now also sought to expand overseas. In this complex Russia occupied an interesting position. In Asia, as we have seen, she was herself an imperial power, but in her relationship to western Europe she was in a sense a semi-colonial dependency because of the character of her trade, German investments and French loans. By 1914 approximately $2,000,000,000 in French money was in Russian hands. It has already been mentioned how France used the money market to ensure Russian support for her policies. Nevertheless, the Russian government now joined the other powers and also tried to extend its control over peoples and regions whose economic and political organizations were inferior to her own.

Excluded because of her geographic position from a real share of the African cake, Russia naturally concentrated on expansion in Asia, where she enjoyed certain advantages over the other great powers because of her long history of dealings with the Oriental peoples. Moreover, at this time Russia could follow an expansionist or imperialist policy only in the Far East. Her borders in Central Asia had been settled by agreement with Britain; the pact of 1897 with Austria closed that area for further gains. In addition, even if she had not wished to adopt a forward policy in China, it would have been difficult to maintain her former attitude once the other imperial states commenced their attempts to control China. Russia could afford to neglect her eastern frontiers and territories only as long as the area as a whole remained a power vacuum. When Britain, France, Germany, the United States, and Japan entered the scene, the situation was entirely altered. The Russian opponents in Europe and the Near East now appeared on the Pacific. Therefore, although in fact the Russian actions were to be offensive, not defensive, in intention, it was virtually impossible for her to remain passive once other states threatened Chinese independence.

The general diplomatic situation was also very favorable to the commencement of an active policy. The French alignment gave Russia security in Europe and a ready money market. The Austrian pact of 1897 closed the dangerous eastern question for a period. Germany was most anxious to encourage the Russian government to turn east and away from the Balkans, where renewed rivalry between Russia and the Austrian Empire could again place Berlin in a difficult situation. William II, in his letters to the tsar, repeatedly pressed his cousin to take up the sword of Europe against the "Yellow Peril." It was certainly to the interest of Germany to encourage the Russians to involve themselves deeply in Chinese affairs, because they would there inevitably run up against British opposition. The Germans believed that they would then be in a position to play between the two and to make gains to their own advantage.

The growing problems arising from the necessity of defending Siberia and the Pacific possessions also played a large part in the Russian decision to press forward in the east. The old difficulties concerning the provision of adequate food supplies and communications still hampered the development and settlement of Siberia. The advantages to be gained from the securing of a port that would be ice-free all year were obvious, although it could be gained only at the expense of Korea or China. The great weakness of the Russian Siberian communications, from a military and strategic viewpoint, became, of course, far more significant once the European great powers and Japan commenced a policy of expansion in Asia.

In addition, certain economic considerations influenced the Russian attitude. It has already been shown that in its relations with China the Russian government had in the previous two hundred years been more interested in the development of trade relations with Peking than in territorial conquest. The 1890's witnessed the spread of the Industrial Revolution to Russia. Russian merchants, realizing that their industrial goods were not of sufficiently high quality to compete on the markets of the west, wished to find customers in the Middle and Far East. It was hoped that these eastern markets could be captured and secured before the British arrived. With only goods of a relatively inferior quality to offer, the Russians had little interest in promoting free-trade policies in their colonial areas. They were more concerned with establishing spheres of control where they would enjoy a monopoly and not face the competition of industrially more advanced nations. The amount of influence, however, that these economic interests could exert upon the decisions of the government is debatable. Although, as has been emphasized, commercial questions had always played a part in Russian policy in China, economic considerations at this time probably played a secondary role to those of political and military advantage.

Certainly, expansion in the east as an idea alone had a great appeal; Nicholas II himself was open to such influences. Many who were close to the tsar, such as Prince E. E. Ukhtomsky, believed in the Asiatic Mission of Russia. The colonial gains of all of the powers were justified by high-sounding claims about civilizing missions and the white man's burden; Russia was no exception. It is interesting to note, nevertheless, that the concept of Russian expansion in the Far East never won the real support of large sections of the Russian public. Only the Balkans, with the ultimate goals of the acquisition of the Straits and Constantinople, the Byzantine imperial city, greatly stirred Russian enthusiasm. The Far East remained more the concern of individuals and cliques, not a matter on which the Russian government could hope to win the same great popular approval with which such imperial activities were greeted in Britain or Germany.

The inauguration of an active policy in the east was largely due to the actions of the influential and able minister of finance, Witte, who thought of the question largely in terms of economic gain. Throughout his career in office, he advocated Russian expansion in Asia, but he favored a policy of gradual economic penetration. He thus came into conflict with those who wished to pursue the same goals quickly and with military means. Witte's first concern involved the construction of a trans-Siberian railroad. The need for such a line had been recognized in the 1870's, but it was only in 1891 that its construction was finally decided upon. Both Giers and Alexander III strongly supported the project, and it was the chief financial preoccupation of the government during the administration of Witte. Although the finance minister favored the line principally because of its economic advantages, he was not averse to drawing wider pictures for the impressionable tsar: "From the shores of the Pacific and the heights of the Himalayas Russia would dominate not only the affairs of Asia but those of Europe as well." [1] In 1891, as has been mentioned, the heir Nicholas, who was also accompanied by Prince Ukhtomsky, travelled through the east. At Vladivostok he was able to participate in the ceremonies inaugurating the commencement of the building of the railroad.

In the Far East, the chief areas of concern for Russia were Manchuria and Korea. Manchuria, whose territory extended as

1. B. A. Romanov, *Russia in Manchuria, 1892-1906,* translated by Susan Wilbur Jones (Ann Arbor, Mich.: J. W. Edwards, 1952), p. 47.

a salient into the Russian lands, was of particular interest after the decision was made to build the railroad to the Pacific. Quite obviously an immense advantage would be gained if it were possible to run the line directly across Manchuria to Vladivostok rather than to follow the curve of the border. Korea attracted Russian attention because of its warm-water ports. In both of these areas the chief Russian competitor for control was not to be either Britain or the nominal owner, China, but the rising new great power, Japan. Korea, strategically of vital concern for the island nation, brought about the first open duel of Japan and Russia. In the 1870's the powers had been able to extract commercial treaties here as well as elsewhere in the Far East. Although Korea was in theory an autonomous kingdom under Chinese sovereignty, the predominant influence was in fact divided between China and Japan. In 1884, a reform movement, which was pro-Japanese in direction, caused disturbances that led to the sending of troops by both controlling powers. In 1885 the two governments agreed to withdraw their troops and henceforth to act together should further intervention be needed. After a decade of continued rivalry between China and Japan, another rebellion occurred in 1894, this time pro-Chinese, and both Peking and Tokyo again dispatched troops. When the revolt was put down, Japan refused to recall her soldiers and war broke out. The Japanese victory in this conflict resulted in the conclusion of the Treaty of Shimonoseki in April, 1895. In this agreement Japan gained control over areas where Russia had a strong interest and which were coveted by the groups that favored an aggressive eastern policy. At this time Korea was declared independent; Japan annexed the Pescadores Islands, Formosa, and the Liaotung peninsula with Port Arthur. Commercial concessions were also gained. The Japanese victory, which completely upset the balance of power in the east, affected adversely the other European powers.

In this new situation the Russian government had a choice of action: the integrity of China could be protected, which would require the revision of the Treaty of Shimonoseki, or compensation could be demanded to balance the Japanese gains. The general situation in regard to China was thus reminiscent of that in regard to the Porte. Russia could either follow a policy calling for the protection of Chinese territorial integrity but at the same time attempt to dominate the government and expel the influence of other powers, or she could favor outright dismemberment in co-operation with other nations. Witte at this time still favored peaceful penetration and thus the adoption of the first alternative. Russia, he argued, should oppose partition until she was militarily stronger and could therefore gain more. Instead she should seek to obtain the dependence of China upon her and win concessions in this manner. In contrast, other ministers, including Lobanov-Rostovsky, preferred to secure immediate compensation in the form of a port in Korea and rights in northern Manchuria. In this first instance, the advice of Witte won out. Russia thus joined with Germany and France to force Japan to accept a revision of the treaty. Consequently the Liaotung peninsula with Port Arthur remained under Chinese jurisdiction. Britain, who did not join in this pressure upon Japan, now began to see the island as a possible ally against the combination of Russia, Germany, and France in the Far East.

With this diplomatic victory against Japan secured, Russia turned towards implementing the policy of establishing domination over the Chinese government under the guise of protection. The Russian government enabled China to pay her war indemnity to Japan by supplying her with funds obtained through French loans. In 1895 the Russo-Chinese bank was chartered, with Prince Ukhtomsky as chairman, and again French money formed the basis of Russian policy. The greatest gains, however, were made when in May, 1896 the Chinese statesman Li Hung-chang visited St. Petersburg for the coronation of Nicholas II. In the secret Li-Lobanov Treaty of June, 1896, Russia and China joined together in a defensive pact against Japan. In return for this protection, China was to allow a railroad to be constructed across Manchuria, which would shorten the route to Vladivostok by about 450 miles. This line, called the Chinese Eastern Railway, was to be controlled by the Russo-Chinese Bank because the Chinese refused to grant the concession directly to the Russian government. However, since Russia in fact owned the bank, it therefore really had the railway. The concession, which included some very unusual privileges, was to be for eighty years, when the line would revert to Chinese ownership without further compensation. The Chinese government also had the option of purchasing it after thirty-six years.

Despite the fact that this agreement on the surface dealt with railway matters, it established virtual Russian domination in Manchuria because of the conditions attached. The railroad company was allowed to maintain a police force, ostensibly to protect the line. It had administrative authority over the strip of land through which the line ran. Under the cover of this agreement, Russian soldiers were introduced into Manchuria, and the Russian government held practical jurisdiction over Chinese territory. Russia thus had established the basis for a possible future annexation of the entire province. With her interests in Manchuria now secured, the Russian government turned to Japan, and in 1896 the two powers established a condominium over Korea and agreed to co-operate to exclude other powers.

The Russian policy of seeking to maintain the territorial integrity of China proved difficult to uphold because of the activities of the other European great powers in the Pacific. In 1897 two German missionaries were murdered in Shantung. Using recompense for this incident as a pretext, the German government demanded Kiaochow and concessions in Shantung. The German action precipitated a round of outright landgrabbing by all of the powers. Despite the strong opposition of Witte, who continued to believe in the wisdom of the old policy and who did not wish to antagonize Japan, it was decided that Russia too would demand territory. Muraviev, now foreign minister, wished to take Port Arthur, and he secured the approval of Nicholas II for the move. In the spring of 1898 Russia was thus able to extract from the powerless China a twenty-five-year lease to the Liaotung peninsula and the right to build a naval base at Port Arthur and a commercial port at Dalny. Permission was given for the construction of another railroad, the South Manchurian Railway, to run from Dalny to Harbin, where it would link with the Chinese Eastern Railway. France and Britain at this time also used the opportunity to make gains at the expense of China. The policy of partition was accepted by all the great powers.

The absorption of the Liaotung peninsula by Russia, which had previously been denied to them, naturally was strongly resented by the Japanese. They were, nevertheless, willing to make an agreement that would signify their recognition of Russian domination in Manchuria in return for Russian acceptance of Japanese control over Korea. The reluctance of the Russian government to abandon all claims in Korea made such a pact impossible. However, in 1898 an agreement was made in which the particular position of Japanese commercial interests in Korea was recognized. The question of the political domination of the peninsula still remained unsolved.

The imperialist policies of the European powers finally provoked a strong Chinese nationalist reaction. The Boxer Rebellion of 1900 was suppressed by the European powers, who co-operated to meet this threat to their special privileges. The outbreak gave the Russian government the opportunity to send in troops to occupy Southern Manchuria and to increase its forces assigned to the Manchurian railroad. This strengthening of Russian military power in Manchuria and the subsequent threat that it offered to the interests of the other powers aroused chiefly the apprehension of Britain and Japan. France, the Russian ally, and Germany, who always encouraged Russian expansion, were less concerned. Britain, therefore, had to look outside the European political complex for an ally to aid in the halting of Russian penetration into China.

Britain, however, did first attempt to secure the co-operation of Germany, since obviously that power would provide the most effective counterweight to Russian expansion. Russia could not well devote her national energies or expend military strength in

China if she were threatened on her vital western front. More-over, negotiations were in process between London and Berlin on the possibility of reaching a more general agreement. The German government proved unwilling to fight Britain's battles in the east and believed that it could only gain advantages for itself from the Russo-British antagonism. With the negative German attitude, Britain was left with another alternative, that of seeking the support of Japan. Here she was successful in finding a government with similar interests in regard to Russia. Britain needed in particular an ally with a land army. The potency of the Russian threat lay in the fact that Russia did have territory adjacent to China and she could occupy Chinese territories with large forces. The British fleet could obviously not meet the Russian armies. The problem facing the British government was thus similar to the one it had met in Central Asia and at the Straits. She needed the support of a power like Japan with an army in Asia, or one like Germany who could threaten Russia on another front.

Like the Russian government, the Japanese statesmen were divided among themselves on the policy to be adopted. Repeated attempts had been made and were to be made to obtain an agreement with Russia on the basis of the Korea-for-Manchuria bargain. In 1901 the Japanese former premier, Prince Ito, travelled to St. Petersburg to attempt to make a Russo-Japanese agreement, but he was unable to gain a clear recognition of Japanese predominance in Korea. The Japanese government, therefore, finally decided upon the conclusion of an alliance with Britain. During the initial discussions over the terms the inclusion of Germany was considered; but when the wider conversations between Berlin and London failed, this combination was abandoned.

The British-Japanese alliance of January, 1902 was a major diplomatic event for both powers, and it signified the abandonment by Britain of the policy of "splendid isolation" that it had so long followed. She now signed a pact of a general nature, whereas before she had consented only to join in agreements designed to solve specific problems. The pact, a defensive alliance, obligated both partners to preserve a position of neutrality should one of them be engaged in a war with a third power, but to join in the conflict should another state enter. Through this agreement Britain gained an ally against further Russian expansion in China; Japan received support for her claim to domination in Korea. The joining of the two principal Russian opponents in the east should have warned the Russian government of the necessity of adopting a moderate policy. Instead, Russian actions became increasingly irresponsible.

The lines of division on policy within Russia remained, meanwhile, much as they were before, except that Witte was supported by the foreign ministry, now under Lamzdorf, in his desire for the adoption of a gradual extension of control in China. In opposition, the war minister, Kuropatkin, although recognizing the dangers to Russian policy in Europe caused by the eastern adventures, supported measures leading toward the eventual annexation of northern Manchuria. The position of the regular officials of the government was, unfortunately, at the time being challenged by the influence exerted upon the tsar by a small clique that stood for an outright aggressive policy in the Far East. Of particular significance was Alexander Bezobrazov, whose most interesting exploit concerned the organization of a company for the exploitation and development of a timber concession on the Yalu river. This undertaking, far from being a purely economic move, was to be an instrument for the penetration and eventual control of Korea. Although the obvious significance of such a venture for Russo-Japanese relations was clear, the tsar nevertheless provided the money for the undertaking. Nicholas' involvement in the Orient always also received the strong encouragement of William II, who took every occasion to emphasize the support that Germany would lend to the Russian "great task" in Asia. Russia's destiny, wrote William II in 1895, was "to cultivate the Asian continent and to defend Europe from the inroads of the Great Yellow Race. In this you will always find me on your side ready to help you as best I can . . . the great future for Russia [is] in the cultivation of Asia and in the Defense of the Cross and the Old Christian European culture against the inroads of the Mongols and Buddhism. . . ." [2] Later he commented: "Therefore it is evident to every unbiased mind that Korea must and will be Russian."

Meanwhile, the diplomatic negotiations among the powers in the Far East centered around the question of the Russian forces that had entered Manchuria during the Boxer Rebellion. Under pressure from the other governments, Russia finally agreed to withdraw her troops in three stages. With the completion of stage one, the operation was brought to a halt. By 1903 the adventurers and those who wished an aggressive policy had in fact taken over the direction of Russian policy. The defeat of Witte and the moderates was greatly aided by the support given the opposition by the minister of interior, V. K. Plehve, a bitter opponent of the finance minister. In May, 1903 Plehve stated his convictions: "Russia has been made by bayonets not diplomacy . . . and we must decide the questions at issue with China and Japan with bayonets and not with diplomatic pens." [3] The minister also thought that "a little victorious war" with Japan would do much to calm the revolutionary agitation within Russia. In May Bezobrazov was made a state secretary and thus assumed much control in eastern affairs. At the same time Admiral Alekseev was appointed regent over the districts of the Amur and Kwantung. He received with this post powers that previously had belonged to the responsible officials in St. Petersburg. With the clear victory of his opponents, Witte was forced to resign.

Although negotiations continued between Japan and Russia in 1903 and 1904, it was apparent that no agreement could be reached. Both states prepared for war. Faced with a constantly increasing buildup of Russian military power, the Japanese in

2. William II, *Letters from the Kaiser to the Czar*, edited by Isaac Don Levine (New York, Frederick A. Stokes, 1920), pp. 10-13.
3. B. H. Sumner, *Tsardom and Imperialism in the Far East and Middle East, 1880-1914* (London: Humphrey Milford, n.d.), p. 14.

ASIA (RUSSIA AND CHINA) IN 1904

February, 1904 opened the conflict with a surprise attack on Port Arthur. The imperial policies of both governments had now reached their logical conclusions.

The Russians at the outbreak of the war felt few misgivings, mainly because of their contempt for the Japanese, whom they referred to as "baboons." They, like the Japanese, were not averse to a trial of strength over the fate of Manchuria and Korea.

Despite the hopes of both belligerents, the events of the war did not unfold as expected. From the beginning the Russian military effort was hampered by bad leadership and by strong conflicts between those in charge of the operations. Although the trans-Siberian railroad was completed for most of its length in 1903, a section across Lake Baikal remained unfinished. The entire line was also only single track. Moreover, the Russian government was never able to make this war a popular one with the Russian people. It remained a war of the officials, and it never captured the imagination of the public. The Japanese met with similar disappointments. In order to achieve victory they recognized that they must engage and annihilate the Russian forces in Asia in a short time. A long war would allow the Russians to organize and mobilize their potentially superior resources and to bring men and equipment from Europe via the railroad. With more men and matériel on the spot in fighting condition, the Japanese forces did achieve initial great successes, but they did not attain their real objective.

The major battles on land and sea were, nevertheless, won by the Japanese. At the beginning of the war they had the advantage of a superiority in numbers of about 180,000 men to the Russian 130,000. They also were fighting much closer to their home base and their centers of supplies. Both Britain and the United States were sympathetic with Japan; the Russian ally, France, could do little to aid her. The war in the Far East centered on the Japanese attack on Port Arthur and on the campaigns in Manchuria. In January, 1905 after an unimpressive resistance the port city surrendered. The battles in Manchuria were of particular significance because of the relatively large number of troops involved. After a series of engagements in which the Russian armies were gradually forced back, the war in Manchuria came to a climax in the great battle of Mukden in February and March, 1905. Here the forces were about even, with about 300,000 soldiers engaged on either side. Once again the Russian troops met with a decisive land defeat.

The course of the conflict at sea was equally unfortunate for Russia. Much of her Far Eastern squadron was either sunk, damaged, or immobilized at Port Arthur at the beginning of the war. Later, Admiral Togo inflicted a defeat on the remaining ships. With the virtual destruction of its Pacific fleet, the Russian government was forced to bring its Baltic squadron to Asiatic waters; the closure of the Straits to warships prevented the use of the ships in the Black Sea. On the night of October 21, 1904, at Dogger Bank in the North Sea, the Russian officers mistook some British fishing boats for Japanese battleships and fired on them. This episode resulted in a major crisis between Britain and Russia. The British government in the war was naturally sympathetic to its ally. In contrast, the German government did all that it could to assist the Russian fleet, and it aided in the fueling and supplying of the vessels. After a nightmare voyage the Russian ships did manage to arrive in May in eastern waters only to meet with a naval disaster, the battle of Tsushima.

Russian naval power was thus erased and the armies beaten, but Russia had certainly not been rendered incapable of continuing the war. The military situation was, in fact, unsatisfactory to both sides. The financial burdens of the conflict weighed heavily in each country. The rise of revolutionary activity in Russia showed that troops might soon be needed to quell civil disturbances. Under these circumstances the proposal of President Theodore Roosevelt to mediate the war was accepted by the two powers. A final treaty was therefore signed at Portsmouth, New Hampshire, on September 5, 1905.

Agreement upon satisfactory terms was made difficult by the instructions given the Russian delegates, Witte and Baron Rosen, requiring that they surrender no Russian territory and agree to pay no indemnity. The Japanese government expected both. Finally a compromise was accepted, by which Russia, although not paying a money indemnity, did surrender rights in China equivalent to a high monetary compensation. She also was forced to agree to the surrender of half the island of Sakhalin. Japan received, in addition, the Russian lease of the Liaotung peninsula, along with Port Arthur, Dalny, and the Southern Manchurian Railroad, which had formerly been under Russian control. Manchuria was restored to Chinese jurisdiction; Korea, the point of contention, was declared independent, but was generally recognized to be within the Japanese sphere. In 1910 Japan formally annexed the peninsula. Thus, with the exception of Sakhalin, Russia did indeed surrender none of her national territory, but she did lose almost all that she had gained in the past decade of intense diplomatic and military activity in the Far East. Her armies had suffered humiliating defeats, and the peace, like that in connection with the Kuldja crisis, was a blow to Russian prestige. Asiatic armies and an Asiatic power had been able to overcome a European state.

After the defeat by Japan and with the concentration on internal reform after 1905, Russian policy again became limited and realistic in the Far East. In addition, since after the war Russian diplomacy was again to shift to the Near East, Russia was led by general considerations to seek a policy of agreement with her former enemies, Britain and Japan. A peaceful settlement of the remaining issues in the east would allow a full concentration on the other problems. Having failed to defeat each other, both Japan and Russia saw the wisdom of co-operating, this time to the detriment of the interests of China. In 1907 and 1910 agreements were concluded, which, if they had been signed in 1904, would have prevented the war. The Russian government now, with far more respect for Japan, agreed to a partition treaty. Japan retained full control in Korean affairs and in southern Manchuria and Inner Mongolia; Russia for her share was given domination over northern Manchuria and Outer Mongolia. In 1911, Outer Mongolia, with Russian support, declared itself independent of China and thereafter became a clear Russian dependency. A further treaty confirming and delimiting these spheres of influence was concluded in 1912. By collaborating with Japan in the partition of China, Russia thus made great gains of territory at no cost. The policy of co-operation with Japan at this time fitted well into the general Russian pattern of alliances that had meanwhile developed in Europe. On the eve of the First World War, Russia, Japan, France, and Britain formed a common front in an alliance that operated to the Russian advantage in Europe and Asia.

Although Russia therefore lost in the end comparatively little in the peace, the public reaction to the loss of the war helped precipitate events that led to a major change in the political structure of the empire. Once again, as in 1854-56, defeat in battle had brought to light the grievous faults and failures in the civilian and military apparatus. In 1905, however, in contrast to 1856, reform was forced upon the government by the active agitation of the people. Throughout the reign of Nicholas II discontent with the autocratic regime had spread widely among the population. Opposition stemmed not only from among the rural classes but also from among the social groups whose numbers had been greatly increased by the industrialization of the country—the workers and the middle class. In Russia, as in other European countries, both radical and liberal first joined together in a common effort to change the conservative regime of the tsar. Here, as elsewhere, liberal leadership and the classical program of that political philosophy, with its emphasis on constitutional government and civil rights for all classes, were first predominant. Internal agitation and the demand for reform were given impetus by the reports of the humiliating defeats and failures in the war against Japan. The revolutionary year 1905 commenced with the events of the "Bloody Sunday" of January when soldiers shot down workers who had come to petition the tsar. This disaster was followed by a wave of strikes and of peasant uprisings in the country. Although in March the tsar agreed to the summoning of an elective legislature, the disorders and violence increased during the summer. The revolutionary activity culminated in the great strike of October. Faced by this rebellion Nicholas II in the same month issued a manifesto, drawn up by Witte, which answered in essence the liberal demands. Russia was to receive a popularly elected legislature (the Duma), whose approval would be necessary for the passage of laws. Full civil rights were also guaranteed. With these changes, Russia now became a constitutional monarchy. In the next years, as in the period after the Crimean War when the great reforms were introduced, the prime attention in Russia was again concentrated upon the internal scene. The new regulations were not successful in meeting the domestic problems. In this situation of political instability and unrest at home, it was thus advisable that Russia be part of a strong external alliance system, which would provide protection at a time of internal crisis.

THE FORMATION OF THE TRIPLE ENTENTE

During the years when Russian attention was concentrated in the Far East, the other European powers went through a period of changing relationships. In the west, colonial questions centering upon Africa and the Mediterranean held the center of the stage. In this field, similar to the situation in the Near and Far East, the continental alliance lines of Triple Alliance and Franco-Russian alliance did not hold firmly. The tendency shown by the continental imperial powers to co-operate overseas was, of course, a great disadvantage to the one nation that had remained outside of either grouping, Britain. This power now conflicted with France in Africa and with Russia in the Middle and Far East. The Near East, it will be remembered, remained out of the international limelight for about a decade. Like Russia and Germany, Britain also always had to face the danger that the other states might unite to partition her possessions. The idea of a continental coalition against the British Empire, which Napoleon had in fact tried to form, was always a possibility. The existence of this state of tension between Britain and the alliance of France and Russia in the imperial field was of particular value to Germany, who hoped to be able to play between the rivals. Because of the apparently irreconcilable divisions between them, the German government never gave sufficient weight to the danger that Russia, France, and Britain might reverse this situation and combine against Berlin.

The most interesting of the diplomatic negotiations of the end of the century were those carried on at the time between Germany and Britain in an attempt to settle the terms for an alliance. The desire of the German government at the beginning of the reign of William II for such a combination has already been discussed. Certainly at this time the two powers did have many interests in common, and no great disputes divided them before the launching of the German naval program. They had much to offer each other; their combination in an alliance would join the greatest sea power with the strongest land power. They were also the two most highly industrialized states and each other's best customers. However, in many issues they did not have common interests. In the 1890's Britain, as has been mentioned, was anxious to acquire an ally who could exert pressure on Russia and limit her expansion in Asia. The British, with their military strength concentrated on the seas, could not render equal service to Germany. Germany might find her army fighting Britain's battles for her empire. Moreover, Germany expected to gain by Russian conquests in China, and she had done her utmost to encourage Russian efforts in the East. At the end of the century Germany's embarcation on a policy of overseas expansion and, in particular, her decision to build a "risk" navy provided a specific source of great friction between the governments. The rise of German competition in the overseas markets to the detriment of British trade also contributed to the increase of the conflict. Nevertheless, negotiations were directed towards an alliance. The British colonial secretary, Joseph Chamberlain, was a particular supporter of what he regarded as a "natural alliance." The first discussions in 1898 reached no definite conclusion. When the outbreak of the Boer War in 1899 clearly demonstrated to the British the danger of their isolated position, they made another attempt in 1901 to reach an agreement with Berlin. The negotiations this time centered entirely on the Asiatic question. Germany, averse to entanglements with Russia and feeling that under the circumstances Britain was bound to act with her in any given diplomatic situation, refused to accept terms that might eventually engage her in a war with the allied France and Russia for the sake of Britain's eastern possessions. With this refusal Britain turned, as has been explained, to the east to find an ally against Russia. In 1902 Britain concluded the alliance with Japan.

The French government, meanwhile, also reassessed its position. France too had no desire to face Germany in a war started by the Russian-British disputes over the control of China. Moreover, unlike Germany, France had a clear view of its own primary interests and major aims. Whereas Berlin now attempted to pursue an active policy both overseas and on the continent and finally gained the enmity of three of the five great powers, France gave a clear first priority to its continental position and to the German frontier. The French government was thus willing to compromise on its maximum colonial program in order to strengthen its continental position. From 1898 to 1905 Théophile Delcassé directed French policy; under his leadership a slow and gradual rapprochement was undertaken with Britain and Italy. In 1899 an agreement over the Sudan was reached with London. In 1900 a deal was made with Italy by which French rights in Morocco were recognized in return for French acceptance of the Italian claims in Libya. This pact with France lessened the dependence of Italy on the Triple Alliance for support for its colonial endeavors. In an even more significant agreement, signed in November, 1902, Italy further gave the assurance that she would remain neutral should France "as the result of direct provocation . . . find herself compelled, in defense of her honor or of her security, to take the initiative of a declaration of war." The Italians had thus for all practical purposes left the Triple Alliance.

The most significant of the French negotiations were, however, those begun with Britain, who now had no hope that a German alliance could be completed. The successful conclusion of these discussions produced the Entente Cordiale of 1904. In the agreement made at this time, Britain and France settled between them all of their outstanding colonial disputes. The heart of the pact was the recognition that Morocco should fall to France and Egypt to Britain. Other points of conflict in Newfoundland, Africa, and Siam were simultaneously settled. In 1904 Spain and France made a similar agreement delimiting their respective spheres of influence in Morocco. These colonial settlements profoundly altered the diplomatic scene. Through the instrument of these pacts, France was now linked with Britain, Spain, and Italy, the latter having in reality withdrawn from the alignment with the central powers. The French government also had the alliance with Russia, which had been strengthened in 1899; its new partner, Britain, was linked by a firm agreement with the great power of the Far East, Japan. Therefore, by 1904 France had succeeded in reversing the conditions that had existed in Bismarck's time; it was Paris and not Berlin that was the center of European diplomacy. It was naturally to the interest of France to round out her diplomatic system by drawing her two partners, Russia and Britain, into some kind of a combination. The danger of their continued antagonism had been clearly shown in the Russo-Japanese War. If France could end this contradiction in her alliances by bringing both powers into agreement, she would have regained the continental position that she lost in 1870.

By 1905 Russia, weakened by a lost war and an internal revolution, was also ready to negotiate. The Russian leaders recognized that they would need a period of peace and that a policy of retrenchment in foreign affairs would be advisable. The extreme financial distress in which the Russian government found itself naturally made it increasingly dependent on French loans, which Paris always used as political weapons. By this time Russia, as Britain had done previously, had conducted unsuccessful negotiations with Germany. With the exception of the issues involved in the Russian-Austrian quarrel in the Balkans, Russia and Germany had even less cause to disagree than did Britain and Germany. Certainly, as long as the Russian government had Britain as its chief opponent, it could not afford to antagonize Berlin.

Moreover, in the Near East and in China in the 1890's the three powers, Russia, France, and Germany, had co-operated with success. There was always the temptation for the continental powers to continue this policy and to combine in a coalition directed at the destruction of British world power. With the failure of the British conversations, William II, in reversal of his policy in 1890, sought actively to obtain an agreement with Russia. Since the German government was averse to the inclusion of France in preliminary discussions, the German emperor attempted to use his influence over the weak tsar to gain the type of agreement favored in Berlin. Two attempts were made in 1904 and 1905 by William II to negotiate a defensive alliance of the two countries; both failed because of the opposition of the Russian and the German ministries to the conditions formulated by their rulers.

After the Dogger Bank incident William II in October, 1904 sent to Nicholas II the draft of a defensive alliance. Article 2 of this agreement provided for the eventual adherence of France. Although the tsar approved the pact, both Witte and Lamzdorf insisted that it was in contradiction to the French agreement; Paris should first be consulted and not merely be asked to adhere later. When Germany refused, the two countries signed a limited agreement promising mutual assistance if war with Britain should break out as a result of the German fueling of the Russian Baltic fleet during its journey to Asia.

The second attempt at an alliance brought similar negative results. During a meeting on a yacht at Björkö in July, 1905 the two emperors placed their signatures on a treaty much like that suggested in 1904. Its clauses provided that: "If one of the two Empires is attacked by a European power, its ally will aid it in Europe with all forces on land and sea." When Nicholas II finally disclosed its contents to his ministers, they again rejected it as incompatible with the French alliance. They were not averse to a tripartite agreement, but they did not want a tie with Berlin alone. As a result the Björkö pact simply faded out of the diplomatic picture. The German government, calculating that a Russo-British agreement was not probable, was not greatly concerned over this failure. It did, however, mark the last chance before the outbreak of the war for the re-creation of something like the old alliance of the three northern courts. It must be remembered that Russia at the time was linked to Vienna through the Balkan agreements of 1897 and 1903. The conclusion of a pact between Russia and Germany would have signified that ties of a kind again bound the former allies. The possibility of the formation of a continental coalition died, of course, with the establishment of the British-French entente of 1904.

Although the Russo-Japanese war had increased the tension between London and St. Petersburg, relations improved rapidly after the peace. In fact, it is interesting to note that the major Russian animosity appears to have again been directed against Germany, who had encouraged Russian activities and who many, such as Witte, believed had "pushed" Russia into the battle. In 1907 and 1910 the major differences with Britain's ally, Japan, were settled. There were therefore no more points of conflict in Asia. At the same time, with enthusiastic French approval, relations were improved with Britain. Although in the past century Britain and Russia had often joined in pacts of a limited and definite nature, conflict and rivalry, as we have seen, had more often characterized their attitude toward each other. Both nations now had a common interest in bringing an end to their traditional antagonism. In Britain King Edward VII and his foreign minister, Sir Edward Grey, were anxious to make an agreement, largely because of the increasing competition of Germany in the naval field. The conversations were also enthusiastically supported by the British ambassador in St. Petersburg, Sir Arthur Nicolson. Alexander Izvolsky, now Russian foreign minister, strongly favored the policy, but he did not wish the understanding to have an anti-German direction. He notified the German government of his intentions, and he received its approval.

Finally, on August 31, 1907 an agreement was concluded, which settled the outstanding colonial disputes of the two signatories in Asia. The most significant section of the treaty involved the tripartite division of Persia, the area where British and Russian interests most directly conflicted. It was agreed that Russia would dominate in the north, Britain in the south, and that a neutral zone would be established as a buffer in the center. In addition, Tibet was recognized as under Chinese sovereignty, and both powers were to withdraw. Afghanistan was to remain under British control, but it was not to be annexed. Although the Russian government sought to obtain a statement on the Straits, the British refusal to consider this question postponed it for the future.

Despite the fact that this agreement dealt only with imperial questions, it, like the Franco-British agreement of 1904, had far wider political significance. Russia was now part of a block of states, including France, Britain, Japan, Spain, and even Italy, which were linked by treaties of varying kinds. She also had the agreement with Austria-Hungary. With this defensive alliance pattern were created the basic conditions that would allow her a period of peace in which to concentrate on internal reform. If adventures in foreign policy were avoided, Russia had nothing to fear from foreign pressure. The danger area remained, as throughout the entire century, the eastern question. The situation here was also affected by the new grouping of powers and the heightened importance that the maintenance of the Habsburg Monarchy was now to have for the German Empire.

Russia had not intended that the British pact have an anti-German significance, but the event profoundly disturbed the German government. The visit of King Edward to Reval in June, 1908 increased its fears of the degree of co-operation that actually existed between Britain and Russia. The new friendship of these two former enemies appeared to close the last link in the chain that the Germans believed was encircling their country. Instead of following the examples of the wise French and Russian governments who, when pressed, simply cut their foreign commitments and retreated where necessary, the German government instead tended to react with increasing vigor and to extend rather than to limit its fields of activity. Germany challenged France in the two Moroccan crises of 1906 and 1911 and lost. The naval program, which contested British rule of the seas, was also pushed. An active policy was maintained in the Near East and relations between Germany and the Ottoman Empire became more cordial. Under these circumstances the fate of Germany's sole major ally, Austria-Hungary, took on a new significance; less than ever could Germany afford to see the monarchy collapse from inner strife or from foreign war. The progressive weakening of the real power of that state because of its increasing national disintegration was, therefore, to have a major effect on international relations. Unfortunately for the peace of Europe, after 1908 both the Dual Monarchy and Russia again turned their attention to the Near East. Neither power, because of its weak internal condition, could afford a setback in diplomacy; both attempted to seek major advances. A new crisis was now to test the Russian diplomatic alignment and also the relations of Vienna and Berlin. The Balkans thus again became the center of European diplomacy and were to remain so until the outbreak of the First World War.

THE REVIVAL OF THE EASTERN QUESTION

Neither Russia nor Austria-Hungary could well afford a strong foreign policy; however, both states acquired foreign ministers who favored such a course of action. In 1906 Alexander Izvolsky replaced Lamzdorf; in the same year Aehrenthal took the same office in the Dual Monarchy. The relations of the powers had hitherto been determined by the agreements of 1897 and 1903, which called for the maintenance of the *status quo* in the Balkans. During the decade in which this policy was in effect, a major change had occurred in the diplomatic balance in the Near East. Germany had in the meantime become deeply involved in Ottoman affairs and had acquired a direct interest in the fate of the empire.

It has already been explained how throughout his career Bismarck had remained well aware of the perils involved in the eastern question for the united Germany. The Balkan area, which

he declared was not worth "the bones of a Pomeranian grena-
dier," he would have preferred to see partitioned between Austria
and Russia. Under no circumstances did he wish Germany to
become involved in a war over Balkan questions. In his alliances
with Austria-Hungary and Russia he attempted to restrain the competitive powers and to keep the balance between them. This careful and moderate policy was reversed by William II, and the
German government embarked upon a course of action that
brought it directly into the problems of the Porte and made it
a rival in Constantinople of Britain and Russia for dominant influence in the Ottoman Empire. The significance of German involvement in the question of the control of the empire was, thus, not
only that it was a new departure in policy but that it also was
bound to involve increased hostility with the states having traditional interests in Constantinople. German penetration before the
war was both economic and political in direction. In the 1890's
the chief German interests centered around the construction of a
railroad that was to run from the Persian Gulf to Konia; the
line would then join with the Turkish railways in Anatolia, which
were already under German control. The "Berlin to Bagdad"
railroad remained a point of diplomatic dispute until the eve of
the First World War. It affected German relations with both
Russia and Britain, whose interests in Persia were thus challenged.
In addition to furthering these concrete plans in order to achieve
an economic advantage, William II contributed to the suspicion
with which the German moves were met through a series of
singularly unwise statements concerning Germany's relations with
the Moslem world. Most inept from the point of view of international relations was his declaration in 1898 at Damascus in
which he proclaimed his friendship for the 300,000,000 Moslems
of the world, a needless annoyance to Britain and Russia,
both of whom had large populations of Moslem subjects, whereas
Germany had none. The activities of Germany in the Near East,
although she certainly had as much right to exploitation and
political control as did her rivals, naturally resulted in the increase
of the political importance of the Anglo-Russian entente of 1907.

Pressed by Germany in yet another field, the British government became more ready to strengthen the diplomatic ties with Russia and to overlook obvious Russian violations of the agreement concerning Persia.

Of far greater significance for the future course of events in the Near East was the process of weakening that the state structure of the Habsburg Empire was undergoing through the rise of national feeling among the Slavic populations. Although the Czech-German struggle was of major importance for the internal history of the monarchy, it was the South Slav question that was to have the strongest repercussions upon foreign policy. This problem was influenced by the successful conclusion of the national liberation movements of the Balkan peoples against the Porte. By 1900, as we have seen, the Rumanians, the Bulgarians, the Serbians, and the Greeks had all obtained independent or autonomous status, even though some of their people still remained under foreign rule. Only Albania, the most primitive and disorganized of the Ottoman regions, was yet without a separate political organization. These great victories of Balkan nationalism were bound to have an effect upon the nationalities of the Habsburg Empire, with, of course, the exception of the Germans and Magyars who enjoyed a privileged status. Although all of the peoples went through a period of similar national agitation, the South Slav movement alone will be discussed here since it involved Russian policy in the Balkans and led eventually to the great war of 1914.

The South Slavs in the empire were divided into three groups and lived in territories in both halves of the Dual Monarchy. The Slovenes, who inhabited chiefly the provinces of Carniola, Gorizia, Carinthia, and Styria, were governed from Vienna, and of the three South Slav peoples remained most loyal to the Habsburg dynasty. The Croatians lived both in Dalmatia, which was under Austrian control, and in Croatia and Slavonia, which were part of the Hungarian lands. The Serbs, the least numerous, were chiefly to be found in the Voivodina, under Magyar administra-

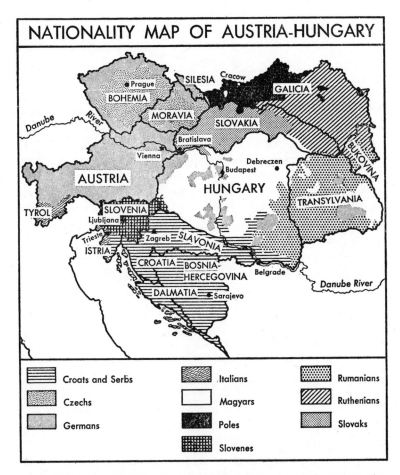

NATIONALITY MAP OF AUSTRIA-HUNGARY

Croats and Serbs

Czechs

Germans

Italians

Magyars

Poles

Slovenes

Rumanians

Ruthenians

Slovaks

tion. The occupied provinces of Bosnia-Hercegovina were inhabited by both Croats and Serbs. Although many political programs were formulated to deal with the question of the position of these national minorities within the empire, two in particular threatened the existence of the entire structure. The first involved the separation of the Croats and Serbs from the Habsburg Empire with the subsequent formation of an independent Croatia and the annexation by Serbia of her nationals and their lands. The second, far more significant because of its grander aspects, was the Yugoslav movement, which called for the union of the Serbs, Croats, and Slovenes of the monarchy to form a great Balkan state with free Serbia and Montenegro. Despite the fact that the Serbs were separated from the Croats and Slovenes by religion, past history, and general culture, this idea of Yugoslav unity held the greater appeal and was therefore of the greatest danger to Vienna.

To meet the problem of South Slav agitation, two practical courses of action were open to the monarchy, both of which involved the Kingdom of Serbia. As the stronger of the two free South Slav states, Serbia naturally exerted a great attraction on the subjects of the Dual Monarchy, particularly those under Magyar control. Like the other Balkan governments, the Serbian state had as its chief foreign policy aim the acquisition of all of its national lands still under foreign domination. Both the Serbian and the Yugoslav programs of the South Slav minorities of the empire, thus, received constant encouragement from Belgrade, although the accomplishment of these plans would result in the dissolution of the Dual Monarchy. To counter this danger the first possibility open to Vienna was the path of attraction and conciliation. Under the program of trialism, associated primarily with the name of the heir to the throne, Franz Ferdinand, the Slavic minorities were to be brought into the administration of the monarchy on an equal basis with the dominant nationalities. The logical extension of this plan would be to then bring Serbia, willingly or unwillingly, into the union, which would now include almost all of the peoples of the three South Slavic groups. The empire would then be firmly based on the geographic unity of the Danube basin and also upon a political balance of its three component peoples. Ultimately, of course, because of the population ratio, the empire would have become a Slavic rather than a primarily German and Magyar political entity. The chief weakness of this solution was that which had previously plagued all of the reform proposals for the Ottoman Empire. The privileged peoples, in particular the Magyars, were no more willing than the Turks had been to surrender their position; the other nations wanted not a share in the government but autonomy or even a separate political status.

The second possibility, the solution by violence, thus appeared to many the only possible way to preserve the empire. This alternative, which involved the forceful maintenance of the *status quo*, brought up inevitably the question of the disposition of the neighboring nation. An independent Serbia, following an irredentist program, would always form a center of leadership for dissident South Slav groups. Unless that land were either conquered and annexed or made a vassal, the Dual Monarchy would have on its borders a state whose national efforts were devoted to its destruction. From the point of view of Habsburg internal interests, the conquest of Serbia was a clear advantage; from the diplomatic standpoint it was a question of the gravest concern because of the links between Belgrade and St. Petersburg and the historic role of Russia as the protector of Balkan Orthodox Christendom.

Parallel to the increase in South Slav agitation in the monarchy, a new movement, Neoslavism, earned growing popularity in Russia, in particular among the liberals. This doctrine was especially relevant to the Slavs of Austria-Hungary, who were primarily Catholic. In contrast to the Panslavs, those who supported this program called not for a Slavic federation under Russian control but a true league of independent, constitutional Slavic states. Since this plan would lead ultimately to the political liberation of the Russian-controlled Ukrainians and Poles, Neoslavism as such received little sympathy among conservative political circles. The dissolution of the Habsburg Empire was one matter, that of the Russian another. After 1910 the emphasis returned to the basic Panslav idea that Russian military power should be used where possible to free the Slavic, particularly the Orthodox Slavic, peoples. The Neoslav idea, however, was significant in that it showed that the Slavic question as such and the liberation of Slavic peoples engaged the interest of Russian political circles from the left to the far right. This issue was thus one in which the government could ill afford to suffer defeats abroad.

Under these circumstances the relations of Vienna and Belgrade were of first importance to Russia as well as to Germany. This was the witches' cauldron that was to brew the First World War because it faced the four governments concerned with problems that were virtually insoluble by peaceful means. It could not be expected that the South Slav peoples, any more than the Poles, Irish, Bulgarians, Greeks, or other people under alien political authority, would give up their endeavors for independence; in the given situation it was inevitable that the Serbian government should help them whenever possible. On the other hand, the Habsburg government could not remain inactive, nor could one expect the German and Magyar peoples to surrender their position without a good fight. It has already been explained how Germany, by the beginning of the new century, found herself with only Austria-Hungary as a loyal ally. Her own security thus demanded that this state remain intact and with little diminution of its military power. At the same time, events in Russia brought that government into closer relations with Serbia than she had enjoyed at any time in their previous history.

After the establishment of Serbian autonomy at the beginning of the nineteenth century, Serbo-Russian relations had varied in their degree of closeness and cordiality. The low point was reached when at the Congress of Berlin the Russian government abandoned Serbia to the Dual Monarchy in return for the control of Bulgaria. During the next period Serbia became in fact a vassal state of the monarchy. After the defection of Bulgaria from the Russian camp, relations between Belgrade and St. Petersburg became closer. In 1903 a particularly bloody revolution brought about the overthrow of the Obrenović dynasty and the accession of Peter Karadjordjević. Although a change of policy was not at once evident, the new king did bring his country closer to Russia; and, more significant, he subscribed to the Greater Serbian program, calling for the assimilation of all of the Serbs into the state.

Under the brilliant leadership of the king's chief minister, Nikola Pašić, who wished to make Serbia the Piedmont of the Balkans, Belgrade naturally became a point of attraction for the dissident South Slavs in the Dual Monarchy. The national program also won the enthusiastic support of the Serbian people, who looked as in 1876 to Russia for practical assistance. The accession of the new dynasty and its adoption of a program of national advancement added to the already dangerous situation. Now in both Austria-Hungary and Serbia strong parties existed which believed that their own desires could only be fulfilled by the destruction of their neighbors. In both cases the support of an additional outside great power was needed. Without the firm backing of St. Petersburg, Belgrade could not stand up to or advance against the Dual Monarchy. Without Germany, Austria-Hungary could neither defend its own position nor move forward in the Balkans. This perilous game of four powers was played twice. In 1908 Austria-Hungary made a move to the detriment of the South Slav idea, obtained the support of Berlin, and inflicted a real humiliation on St. Petersburg. In 1914 a similar action brought about war, the destruction of the empire, and the eventual victory of the Yugoslav idea. The Bosnian crises of 1908-1909 thus offered a preview for the chain of events that were to lead to the catastrophe in 1914.

Relations between Vienna and Belgrade after 1903 became, as could be expected, increasingly difficult. As the first step in his foreign policy, King Peter of Serbia attempted to establish closer ties with Bulgaria. In 1904 a treaty was concluded between the two states, which aimed at the accomplishment of a customs union by 1917. Viewing this pact as inimical to her own Balkan interests, Austria-Hungary placed an embargo on Serbian exports and commenced the "Pig War" of 1906. (Pork was the chief item of Serbian foreign trade.) The Serbian government was able to withstand this pressure since it found other markets for its goods, notably in Germany. The chief point of friction between Serbia and the Monarchy was not, however, economic, but national. It concerned the provinces of Bosnia and Hercegovina. The Austrian occupation of these lands, which the Serbs regarded as their primary foreign aspiration, rankled. The extent of the Austrian investment in the area also showed that the monarchy did not intend to relinquish it again to the Porte. With every year Serbian hopes for its acquisition thus grew dimmer. Not only was it quite apparent that Austria-Hungary intended to retain the provinces permanently, but by 1908 that government had determined to change the status of the occupied provinces. The opportunity for such a move occurred after Izvolsky became the Russian foreign minister.

Immediately after his entrance into office, Izvolsky sought to embark upon a more active policy despite the obvious fact that Russia militarily was unprepared for such a course of action. He first made an entirely unsuccessful attempt to obtain the right to fortify the Aland Islands, and then he turned to the question of the Straits. The regulations that had been in force were in all probability the most favorable that Russia could hope to attain under the general circumstances of the time. The closure of the Straits did protect the Russian shores from invasion. However, the Russo-Japanese war had shown the difficulties that could be caused by the bottling up of the Russian fleet in the Black Sea. The long journey of the Baltic fleet to Asian waters had been made necessary because the Black Sea units could not be utilized. The ideal arrangement for Russia would be one that would allow Russian ships to sail freely in and out of the Black Sea but would deny equal access to other powers. It was precisely this unequal bargain that Izvolsky now sought to obtain. He was also under the impression, gained from the Reval meeting, that Britain would not oppose a change in the status of the Straits. France as an ally would not block his wishes. It therefore remained for him only to make an arrangement with Vienna.

Like Izvolsky, the Austrian foreign minister, Count Alois von Aehrenthal sought to commence his period in office with real accomplishments. His first action broke, in spirit at least, the agreements of 1897 and 1903. Without consulting Russia he announced in 1908 the building of a railroad that was to run from

Sarajevo through the Sanjak of Novi Pazar to Mitrovica, where it would join with the Turkish lines of Macedonia and thus eventually lead to the Aegean. The plan was regarded in St. Petersburg as a violation of the previous arrangements concerning the maintenance of the *status quo*. In answer the Russian government announced a plan of a railway to run from the Danube to the Adriatic.

The Sanjak railroad thus caused friction between the governments; but the two ministers were chiefly concerned about the questions of Bosnia-Hercegovina and the Straits, and here they could co-operate to their mutual benefit. Although they had previously discussed the possibility of acting in these matters, their final agreement was considerably hastened by the Young Turk Revolution of July, 1908. At this time Sultan Abdul Hamid was forced to put into effect the Constitution of 1876, and the status of the territories still under the suzerainty of the empire came into question. Bulgaria as well as Austria-Hungary was affected by the events. Thus when Izvolsky met with Aehrenthal in Buchlau, Moravia, in September, he found that he could quickly come to terms on the question of the Straits. Although the exact decisions reached at this time became later a matter of controversy, the two ministers did agree in general that Russia would support the Austrian annexation of Bosnia-Hercegovina in return for the aid of the monarchy in securing the opening of the Straits for Russia. With the support of Vienna ensured, the Russian minister continued his trip to the other capitals of Europe where he hoped to secure a similar favorable reception.

Once Izvolsky had left, Aehrenthal quickly proceeded to collect his side of the bargain. He first consulted with Ferdinand of Bulgaria, and they agreed on common action. On October 5 the independence of Bulgaria was proclaimed; on October 6 Austria-Hungary announced the annexation of the provinces. Izvolsky learned about the event in Paris. The Austrian action precipitated an immediate international crisis. The status of the provinces had been set by the Congress of Berlin; in theory it could be altered only by another conference. In 1870 Russia had unilaterally denounced the Black Sea clauses of the Treaty of Paris, but this move had been confirmed by an international gathering. Izvolsky in particular was affected by the Austrian action. His visit to London, which had taken place in the middle of October had proved a complete failure. The British government had demanded reciprocal rights of entry into the Black Sea and had conditioned its acceptance on that of the Turks. Russia could therefore not hope to obtain its part of the Buchlau bargain. Russia then proposed that a conference be called to discuss the annexations. The monarchy agreed only on condition that all the arrangements be made prior to the opening of the meeting, which would then just register the *fait accompli*. Since no power wanted to go to war over the matter, the annexation was in the end confirmed by direct negotiations between Austria and Turkey. In February, 1909 Austria-Hungary agreed to return the Sanjak of Novi Pazar and to pay compensation for the provinces. In April, in another agreement, Ferdinand was recognized as the king of an independent Bulgaria in return for a similar payment.

Meanwhile, however, tension continued to mount in the Balkans, where both Serbia and Montenegro made military preparations. The Serbian government, deeply resenting this tightening of the Habsburg hold on a South Slav territory, hoped to obtain Russian assistance and appealed to St. Petersburg. Austria-Hungary, who had not consulted her ally about the annexation before the event, turned to Berlin and was able to receive full support for her policy. On March 21 the German government delivered what was regarded in Russia as a virtual ultimatum that the Austrian annexation be recognized. After consultation, the Russian government decided that it was not in a position to risk war, and the desired acceptance was given. Without Russian aid Serbia was powerless to resist. Not only was she forced to accept the annexation but also to subscribe to a statement that she "undertakes further to change the course of her present policy towards Austria-Hungary and to live henceforth with the latter on a footing of good neighborliness."

The entire Bosnian episode was on the face a triumph for the diplomacy of the central powers and a defeat for Russia. Izvolsky was in particular deeply embittered, since this event put the stamp of failure on his career as minister. In 1910 he was replaced in office by Serge Sazonov and sent to Paris as ambassador. In this position he retained his resentment against the central powers and he worked for the strengthening of the Triple Entente. At the end of this crisis Russian anger was directed primarily not at Britain, who had prevented the Russian acquisition of commensurate gains at the Straits, or even at Austria-Hungary, who had undoubtedly played a clever trick, but at Germany, who had backed up the stand of Vienna with a stern warning to St. Petersburg. The strong support that Germany gave at this time also had an effect on Vienna. It was now clear that in contrast to the policy of Bismarck, the German government would risk a major war to support the Balkan interests of its ally and on an issue on which it had not been consulted beforehand. In contrast, Russia had received no aid from her allies.

The Austrian victory over Serbia naturally intensified rather than calmed South Slav agitation. At the time of the crisis and in the years thereafter the Austrian chief of staff, Conrad von Hötzendorff, strongly pressed for the destruction of Serbia. The failure of the Habsburg government to have recourse to the solution of violence at this time probably removed the possibility that it could be carried through at all without unleashing a general conflict. In 1908 Russia was unprepared for war; she also did not have the backing of her allies should she have wished to come to the aid of Serbia. Although only a surmise is possible, given the general diplomatic situation we may assume that Austria-Hungary could have reduced Serbia at this time. Later in 1914, when with far more justification she launched an attack on Serbia, the position of the powers had so altered that a localized war was no longer possible.

Although the Bosnian episode embittered relations between Berlin and St. Petersburg, there was certainly no break between the governments. In November, 1910 Nicholas II with his new foreign minister, Serge Sazonov, travelled to Potsdam. There the two rulers discussed the question of the Near East, and the Russians withdrew their opposition to the Bagdad railroad in return for German recognition of Russian predominance in northern Persia. The agreement was a blow to Britain, who had previously refused to negotiate on the railroad without French and Russian participation. The German government was, however, unable to obtain the written declaration that they wanted, which would have contained a Russian promise not to join Britain in policies hostile to Germany in return for a German guarantee not to support expansionist Austrian actions in the Balkans. At the meeting the tsar did assure William II that he would not follow an anti-German policy.

The annexation crisis thus brought to an end the policy of co-operation and the maintenance of the *status quo* in the Near East, which both Russia and Austria-Hungary had supported in the previous decade. Although the Habsburg government did indeed revert to its former passive attitude, it could no longer act in close concert with St. Petersburg. In fact, now deeply distrustful of Vienna, Russia attempted to form a front against further expected aggressive moves on the part of Austria. Negotiations were first entered into with Italy, who was deeply dissatisfied with the failure of the central powers to give adequate attention to her claims for a share in the division of the Ottoman lands in the Balkans. The Italian government was interested primarily in the Albanian territories, but it had received no support from Austria for these claims. In October, 1909 Nicholas II and Victor Emmanuel, accompanied by their foreign ministers, met at Racconigi, where it was agreed that a policy of co-operation would be pursued in Balkan affairs. The Russian government also agreed to support Italian claims in North Africa in return for aid in the Straits question. In 1911 Italy went to war with Turkey and as a result annexed Tripoli.

The Russian desire to erect a counterweight against Habsburg penetration southeast affected principally her relations with the Balkan governments. Sazonov, personally a weak leader, had no desire to precipitate another eastern crisis; he knew well how ill-prepared his country was to meet further Balkan disturbances. Nevertheless, he did not have a clear policy of his own nor was he able to exercise control over the activities of his subordinates in the eastern capitals, who proceeded to implement programs of their own. The Russian representatives in Sofia, A. Nekliudov, and in Belgrade, N. Hartwig, were able to work actively to form a Balkan alliance, which they hoped would operate against Austria-Hungary but which in fact led to war against the Ottoman Empire.

Like the great powers, the Balkan governments were influenced by the Young Turk Revolution and the resultant Bosnian crisis. They looked upon the events as an opportunity for them to acquire the remaining territories of Turkey-in-Europe, in particular in Macedonia. The states thus welcomed the interest and encouragement given them by the agents of the Russian government, but they wished to exploit this support to expel Turkey from the peninsula and not merely to block further Austrian moves. Under Russian sponsorship the governments entered into negotiations among themselves and a series of agreements was reached. The first of these, concluded in March, 1912, joined Serbia and Bulgaria in a mutual assistance pact, which on the surface appeared indeed directed against the monarchy. In a secret annex, however, provisions were made for a war with the Ottoman Empire. All the territories to be annexed by each power were described, with the exception of a disputed area that was to be left to the arbitration of the tsar. In May a similar pact was completed between Bulgaria and Greece which provided for mutual assistance in a conflict with Turkey. Because of the clash of the claims of the powers over Thessaloniki, no territorial division was agreed upon. By October Montenegro had joined in agreements with Serbia and Bulgaria, and the Balkan League was completed. Since the Ottoman Empire was at the time involved in war with Italy, it seemed a propitious moment to begin operations.

Although Sazonov was kept informed on the course of the negotiations, he appears to have been singularly blind as to their real implications. When the French president Poincaré visited St. Petersburg, he recognized at once that these were war alliances. In face of this threat to the general peace the powers were consulted, and with general consent Austria and Russia, acting in the name of the other powers, warned the Balkan states not to start a war with Turkey. The declaration, sent on October 8, arrived too late. On that same day Montenegro declared war on the Porte, soon to be followed by the other allies. Russia, who had been instrumental in forming the Balkan association, thus saw it fall completely from her hands. She was unable to control the actions of the Balkan states once they had come into agreement with each other.

Despite the initial assumption of the powers that the Turkish armies would hold, it soon became apparent that the Balkan allies would win a quick victory. By May, 1913 Turkey had indeed been virtually forced out of Europe and had been compelled to agree to the cession of all of her territory north of the Enos-Media line. The Porte was left with only the Straits, Constantinople, and a thin edge of surrounding territory. The co-operation that the Balkan governments had shown in fighting the war was not reflected in the making of the peace. The Bulgarian army, because of obvious strategic necessity, had been forced to concentrate its main forces against the Turkish armies marching northward from Constantinople. The Serbian and Greek armies had used the opportunity to occupy the portions of Macedonia that they wanted, and they showed no inclination to leave. Moreover, when in the peace negotiations Austria insisted upon the creation of an independent Albania, Serbia was deprived of territory she had been assigned in the pact with Bulgaria. She naturally then wished a rectification of her claims in Macedonia. In a gross overestimation of their own strength, the Bulgarians attempted to settle the dispute by launching an attack upon their former allies. As a result, Greece and Serbia, joined by Rumania and Turkey, now fought against Bulgaria. In the subsequent peace, Bulgaria, who could not withstand such a combination,

THE BALKANS IN 1914

was forced not only to surrender much of what she had gained in the first war but also to yield southern Dobrudja to Rumania.

As a result of the defeat of Bulgaria, Greece and Serbia received the major share of Macedonia. An independent Albania was also established in concurrence with the wishes of both Austria-Hungary and Italy. The monarchy wished to block Serbian access to the sea; Italy saw the land as a future colony. In October, 1913 the Habsburg government delivered yet another ultimatum to Serbia, whose troops continued to occupy lands assigned to Albania. Serbia and Montenegro were able, by the partitioning of the Sanjak, to obtain a common frontier. The peace also allowed Greece finally to obtain Crete and other Aegean islands. As could be expected, the Second Balkan War broke the Balkan League. In the subsequent years Bulgaria drifted towards the central powers; the states who had benefited by the treaties, Serbia, Greece, and even Rumania, despite her agreements with Austria-Hungary and Germany, tended to join with the entente powers. The expulsion of Turkey from Europe thus in no way ended with the reconciliation of the states who had once formed her old domains.

With the division of Macedonia, and the expulsion of Turkey from Europe, three chief issues remained unresolved: first, the relations of Serbia and Austria-Hungary; second, the Russian demands for a change in the status of the Straits; and, third, the rivalry over the control of the Ottoman government. In 1911 the Russian ambassador at the Porte, N. V. Charykov, again brought up the question of the Straits, but his proposals were not backed by Sazonov once it became apparent that the powers would oppose any changes. In 1913-1914 an incident occurred that involved the question of the control both of the Straits and of the government when the German general, Liman von Sanders, was placed in command of an army corps stationed at Constantinople. The German general's position in the Turkish army was balanced by the appointment of similar British and French advisors in other sections of the Turkish service. However, his presence in the city in command of the forces would give him and, therefore, the German government a strong position in a time of crisis. Although the Russian government had no immediate plans to take the city, its traditional stand had always been to oppose the control of any other power, be it Britain, France, or Germany. The problem was solved by the promotion of the general to a higher grade so that he could no longer be in command of a mere corps. On the eve of the war Russian interests in the Ottoman Empire were thus what they had been throughout the previous century. Russia was quite willing to pick up the Straits if this could be done cheaply, but she would not launch a war for their acquisition. In the empire as a whole, she opposed German control or primary influence in the same way that she had always previously sought to block British domination. The power that held the Straits must either be entirely independent or under Russian domination.

1914

The year 1914 commenced much as any other in peacetime in the past century of Russian diplomatic activity. Certainly, there were few if any indications that not only Russian autocracy but also the kindred dynasties of the alliance of the three northern courts were on the eve of destruction. In general the Russian international position appeared excellent; her military buildup was proceeding with rapidity. As a partner in the Triple Entente, Russia was associated with the stronger of the diplomatic alignments. The basis of the Russian alliance system remained the military pact with France. Although the two powers had few common interests outside of their opposition to Germany, this bond proved sufficient. They also had no serious points in dispute. As long as the conflict with the German powers was maintained, it was certainly the natural strategic alliance for Russia. Since Berlin stood strongly behind Vienna, Russia needed an ally who could put pressure on the German western frontier, or her position in the Near East would soon become untenable. In July, 1912 the alliance was broadened through a naval convention; in 1912 and 1914 Poincaré visited St. Petersburg. Relations with Britain were never so cordial, due principally to the repeated Russian violations of the agreement on Persia, which were caused largely by the familiar failure of the government to control its local agents. However, as long as the German naval program continued, Britain needed Russia. In 1914 a British squadron visited Kronstadt; discussions for a naval convention were underway when war broke out. By 1914 Russia had also, as we have seen, developed friendly relations with Japan and, in the Balkans, with Serbia, Montenegro, Greece, and Rumania.

Although Europe was indeed divided into two camps, there

was little to indicate that these alliance systems would last any longer than their predecessors. What the Germans chose to regard as an iron ring of encirclement was not so firm and tight as they believed. The traditional alliance for Russia had been the one with Prussia; the ties between the dynasties remained fast. There was, moreover, within Russia, despite Panslavist and Neoslavist enthusiasm, a strong current of sympathy for Germany based on the economic bonds that had developed between the countries and, more important, on the fact that so many of the Russian statesmen had been educated in Germany or had personal ties with that country. Despite the reaction against the system of Nicholas I, it was still true that a large proportion of Russian officialdom was of German background. In addition, both Germany and Russia, as well as Austria-Hungary, were still joined together by their adherence to the conservative order, although in varying degrees. All three monarchs were subject to liberal and socialist pressure within their countries, and none could afford a lost war because of their own deteriorating positions. Moreover, aside from the Franco-Russian military pact, the lines of the entente were loose. Britain was tied to France and Russia by colonial and naval agreements, not by political pacts. The points at issue between Germany and the Entente were primarily Alsace-Lorraine, naval competition, and, with Russia, the problem of Austria-Hungary. The first two questions, although extremely important, could with difficulty trigger a war which would simultaneously draw in all the other states. The relations of the three powers, France, Germany, and Britain, were thus much what they had always been in the entire century; there was no indication that a rearrangement of the alliance systems could not be made as they had so often been in the past century.

The danger spot for European peace in 1914 lay in the Balkans because the issues in this area could draw all the powers into a major war. The nineteenth century had been a century of peace in the sense that there had been no conflicts on the scale of the wars of Napoleon. The engagements had been localized and of short duration, or they had occurred on colonial battlefields. In every case diplomacy had remained in control. For instance, before Russia went to war with Turkey in 1877, she took care to make arrangements with Vienna; and she stopped when faced by the danger of a larger conflict. Bismarck, before proceeding against Denmark, Austria, and France, made efforts to ensure that he would only have to deal with one state at a time. In contrast, the political situation in the Balkans and on the Danube, given the European alliance systems, had by 1914 evolved in such a manner that it would have been very difficult to avoid a world war should the question of Austria-Hungary and Serbia turn into a duel for survival.

The recurrent Balkan crises since the time of Peter the Great have been discussed in the preceding pages. Here we have seen that the powers primarily concerned with the fate of the Balkan peoples were Austria and Russia, both Christian powers, allied by a common political ideology, with a basic interest in the defeat of Moslem power. Their quarrels originated over the preservation of the balance of political power between them, but neither had any interest in the fate of the Ottoman Empire aside from its role in the European equilibrium. It was Britain who became in the nineteenth century the chief upholder of Ottoman integrity. It has also been emphasized that this question was the one issue in foreign policy that captured and held the Russian imagination. The hold of the idea of the Byzantine heritage and the ultimate capture of Constantinople was apparent in Russian thinking during the entire period. Emotional and irrational considerations were thus here at work to an extent not true elsewhere. By 1914, however, the Ottoman Empire had been driven from Europe; the Orthodox and Slavic Balkan peoples had been liberated from Moslem domination, and this deed had been accomplished without a major war between the great powers concerned: Russia, Britain, and Austria-Hungary. Moreover, although the Russian government was still interested in the control of the Straits, this question had lost much of its former significance. Russian domination of the area or the closure of the Straits to foreign warships was of major importance when Russia was at odds with the western naval powers. The only way that these states could harm Russia was to sail into the Black Sea and land on her southern coast. However, in 1914 Russia was in agreement with these governments; instead the opposition came from Germany, whose army stood concentrated at the Russian front door.

With the removal of Turkey from Europe, the next state up for partition, should the national idea continue to win victories, was obviously Austria-Hungary. The relation of the South Slav movement to Serbia, the necessity of the maintenance of the Dual Monarchy to Germany, and the Russian attitude toward Belgrade have all been discussed. The situation was made even more critical by the fact that at this time not only was the Habsburg Monarchy politically weak, but the Russian government itself was in a position where it could not afford another humiliation in foreign policy. In 1905 Russia had been defeated by a despised Asiatic power; in 1909 she had been forced to give way before the strong stand of the central powers. By 1914 the Russian government felt itself militarily better prepared and it was also more certain of the support of its allies. It was nevertheless in no position to enter a major war, nor did it have any foreign policy aims worth such a risk. The destruction of Austria-Hungary or the complete domination of the Balkans was certainly not at this time a goal of immediate Russian policy. Russian real interests lay in the maintenance of peace and the development of her internal resources; her statesmen were well aware of this condition. A chain of events nevertheless occurred that, in fact, led Russian tsardom to gamble its existence for the sake of Serbia.

It is in the context of the mutual interconnection of the problems of Russia's relations to the Balkan Slavs, the South Slav question in the Monarchy, and Germany's dangerous strategic position that the assassination of Franz Ferdinand on June 28 should be viewed. The wisdom in scheduling a visit of the archduke to the Bosnian capital, Sarajevo, on the date of the Serbian national holiday is certainly debatable. The failure of the local authorities to take even elementary security precautions perhaps made them culpable. Nevertheless, the fact remained that the heir to the throne of the Habsburg Empire had been murdered by a member of a secret organization, whose membership included responsible officials in the Serbian government. The goal of the revolutionary organization was the establishment of a Yugoslavia and thus the dissolution of the monarchy. Serbia was the center of its activities. Under these circumstances both the Austrian foreign minister Berchtold and Conrad von Hötzendorff now determined upon the destruction of Serbia as an independent power. They were at first opposed by the Hungarian premier, Count Stephen Tisza, who was only won over with the promise that no more Slavs would be incorporated into the empire. At the same time the German government was consulted. Although it was not clearly indicated that hostilities would be initiated, the memorandum sent to Berlin did state "the necessity for the Monarchy to destroy with a determined hand the net which its enemies are attempting to throw over its head." Both William II and his chancellor, Theobald von Bethmann-Hollweg gave their approval along with the assurance that the German government would back the Austrian decisions. This "blank check" considerably strengthened the position of the monarchy.

The final step of the issuance of an ultimatum was delayed about three weeks. During this period the Habsburg government investigated the assassination, but it did not enter into correspondence with other courts concerning its possible courses of action. Austria-Hungary thus adopted in this crisis the same methods that she had successfully used in dealing with Serbia over the annexation of Bosnia-Hercegovina. She attempted to limit the affair to a matter between herself and Serbia, and she resorted again to the use of an ultimatum. In following this course of action, the Monarchy chose to play a very dangerous game and one that violated the traditions of the past century. It will be remembered that before annexing Bosnia, Austria-Hungary did consult Russia; in addition, her action at that time involved no more than a change of status in a territory that was already assigned by great power agreement to her sphere in the Balkans. The elimination of Serbia as an independent power and its reduction to a state of vassalage to the monarchy would, in contrast, result in a profound readjustment of the balance in the area, particularly when it is remembered that as a result of the Second Balkan War, Bulgaria had in fact joined the central powers. Control of the Balkans would thus fall to Austria-Hungary; Russia would be separated from her allies by the very combination that contributed to her downfall in the war: the front of Germany, the Dual Monarchy, Bulgaria, and Turkey. In previous Balkan crises, the German, Austrian, and Russian governments had recognized the necessity of maintaining a balance; Russia had always tried to conciliate Austria before moving forward. Now, however, no attempt was made by Vienna to make a deal with St. Petersburg. It is understandable that the central powers would have opposed a conference where they would have been outvoted.

Undoubtedly, the Habsburg government relied much on the effect that they hoped the assassination would have on other governments. On July 24 Berchtold told the Russian councillor of embassy in Vienna, "The pan-Serbian propaganda directly undermines our house, our dynasty. . . . The wiping out of this propaganda root and branch is a question of being or not being for Austria-Hungary as a great power." Berchtold added that Russia could "not desire the collapse of Austria-Hungary also in the interest of the preservation of the monarchical principle." [4] It should also be noted that Russia would never have tolerated the continued existence of a Polish state on her borders that would have maintained relations with her Polish subjects similar to those between Serbia and the Habsburg South Slavs. It was not however to be considerations of this order that were to determine policy. The Austrian ultimatum was the result largely of what that government regarded as the necessities of her internal order; Russia, in contrast, based her decisions on the general international situation and her past influence in the Balkans.

On July 23 the government of Austria-Hungary finally completed and delivered a forty-eight-hour ultimatum to Serbia.

4. Stählin, *Geschichte Russlands,* IV/2, pp. 1036, 1037.

The document, designed to be rejected, called upon Belgrade to suppress all anti-Austrian activities and to allow Habsburg officials to participate in enquiries concerning the assassination. The Serbs accepted most of the conditions but rejected the presence of Austrian officials. On July 28 the Dual Monarchy declared war on Serbia. The Serbian government had, quite naturally, appealed at the beginning of the crisis to the Russian government, which had advised moderation. When the ultimatum was delivered, Russia promised assistance. Once Serbia and Austria-Hungary were at war, the question was whether this conflict could remain localized or whether the alliance systems would draw all of the powers into the battle. Nicholas II, who was in constant correspondence with William II during the last days, attempted at first to order only partial mobilization against Austria-Hungary. Since the Russian army had no plans to deal with this situation, he finally ordered full mobilization on July 30. Because of the Schlieffen plan, which called for a knock-out blow against France before the Russian armies were fully prepared to fight, the German government then mobilized and declared war first on Russia on July 31 and then on France on August 3. On August 4 Britain entered; on August 6 Austria and Russia were also at war.

Thus, after almost two centuries of controversy over the fate of the Balkan peoples, the powers of Europe were drawn into war by this question. Certainly, when entering the conflict none of the three conservative courts wished to or expected to secure the destruction of the others. No precedent for such an occurrence existed; wars in the nineteenth century had been limited in their results. Even the Napoleonic wars had not brought about a real alteration in the European state system, and the governments of the old regime had in general been returned to power. The war of 1914 was to show that the three eastern empires were indeed linked both in regard to their foreign interests and their basic political structure. Within five years the three dynasties were to be replaced, after defeat in war and with the triumph in each nation of revolutionary principles.

THE FIRST WORLD WAR, 1914–1918

At the beginning of the war in August, 1914, all the major participants expected a short conflict; their military plans were based on this presupposition, which put a strong emphasis on the time factor. By the winter of 1914/15 each state saw its hopes for a quick victory defeated; all were faced with a war for which they were not prepared. Under these circumstances it became more important that the nations that were still neutral be won and also that the Allies compensate themselves for present losses with hopes of future gains. The governments thus sought to formulate their war aims and to make their claims for the future peace. This definition of goals was not easy for any power. The war had begun basically over the South Slav question in the Habsburg Monarchy and the balance of power; only France—in Alsace-Lorraine—had a concrete territorial aim. Nevertheless the powers did conclude a series of bargains to protect their positions for the future. The agreements of major concern to Russia involved primarily those concerning the partition of the Ottoman and Habsburg empires.

On September 5, 1914 Russia signed her first war agreement with the Allies. The three powers agreed not to conclude a separate peace or to set the terms for the peace without consultation. The powers then turned to the task of trying to gain other states to their side. The first whose allegiance was still in question was the Ottoman Empire. In the beginning of August an alliance had been concluded with Germany, but the Turkish government remained divided over the question of entering the war. After negotiations with both sides, the empire finally decided that it could gain more from the Central Powers. In September the Straits were closed, and in November Turkey was at war with the entente. The entrance of this state had the immediate effect of cutting the best line of communications between Russia and the west. Supplies in sufficient quantities could thus no longer be sent by the Allies, but it is indeed a question if, in view of military conditions on the western front, Russia would ever have received adequate war matériel even if this route had been open.

With Turkey now in the enemy camp, it was possible for the Allies to bargain with her territory. The first and most obvious claim to Ottoman land was Russia's. Finally the dream of the annexation of Constantinople and the Turkish Straits could be realized. In sharp contrast to her previous stand, Britain was willing to recognize this demand in return for Russian acceptance of British claims elsewhere. The French were at first hesitant, but finally in spring, 1915 the assent of both western powers was given. A year later, in the Sykes-Picot agreement of May, 1916, France and Britain divided Asiatic Turkey. Russia accepted this arrangement in return for recognition of her rights in Armenia and a part of Kurdistan. In other agreements the Allies made further bargains, and Italy was also assigned a share.

The disposal of the lands under Turkish rule was not difficult since the empire was an enemy and the powers had in the previous years already established spheres of influence over certain areas. The settlements that concerned lands in the Balkans, particularly those under Habsburg rule, proved more complicated since they involved the conflicting claims of friendly powers. The future of Serbia, in particular, was at stake when the French and British governments wished to use South Slav territory to entice Italy into the war. The former German ally proved a tough bargainer; she desired the Tirol, Istria, the Dalmatian coast, a protectorate over Albania, and a share in any division of Turkey or the colonies made by the Allies. The claims to Dalmatia, of course, ran directly counter to those of Serbia and conflicted with the Russian desire to gain Bulgarian support with the promise of a part of Serbian Macedonia, with Serbia compensated from Habsburg lands. In the end the Serbian interests were sacrificed for what the Allies thought was the necessity of Italian intervention. In the Treaty of London of April, 1915 Italy was given most of her demands, including Dalmatia.

The entrance into the war of the remaining uncommitted nations, Bulgaria, Rumania, and Greece, resulted from similar sets of agreements. In the negotiations with Bulgaria the Central Powers had the advantage of being able to promise Sofia Macedonia without selling out an ally. They also added the promise of Rumanian and Greek lands should those states join with the enemy. Bulgaria thus entered the war on the German side in October, 1915. Opposite conditions prevailed in regard to Rumania, whose national claims centered on the Habsburg lands of Transylvania, Bukovina, and the Banat. With the promise of these territories, Rumania joined the Allies in August, 1916. The entrance of Greece, which followed a state of civil war and Allied intervention in behalf of the party favoring their interests, came after the abdication of the king in June, 1917.

The last major political agreement into which Russia entered was that of February, 1917 with France. Here Russia agreed to allow France to settle her eastern border with Germany in return for the right to determine her own interests on the Russian western frontier. France thus in effect abandoned the Polish cause to Russian solution although in the previous century the support of Polish nationalism had been a main element of French policy. In August, 1914 the Russian government had issued a declaration to the effect that after the war an autonomous Poland, united with Russia through the tsar, would be created from the Polish lands of all the partitioning powers. This re-creation in an enlarged form of Congress Poland was unlikely to arouse much Polish sympathy because of previous experiences with similar assurances.

From the secret negotiations and agreements of the war period it can thus be concluded that the war aims of tsarist Russia encompassed the annexation and control of large areas along her borders in directions in which she had previously shown an interest. If victory had come and if indeed her allies had allowed her a free hand in the east, it could have been expected that the tsarist government would have annexed Galicia, Bukovina, Ruthenia, and the Polish lands belonging to Germany. Russia would also have taken control of large sections of the Ottoman Anatolian lands, including Constantinople, the Straits, Armenia, and

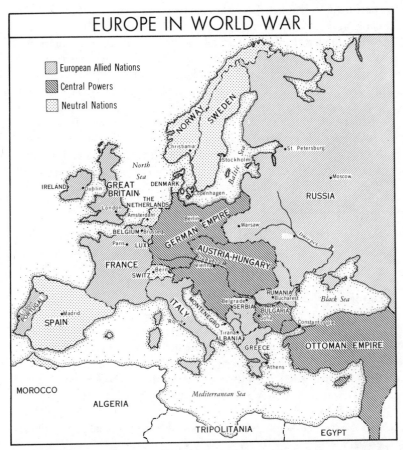

EUROPE IN WORLD WAR I

European Allied Nations
Central Powers
Neutral Nations

NORWAY
SWEDEN
Christiania
North Sea
Stockholm
Baltic Sea
St. Petersburg
IRELAND
Dublin
GREAT BRITAIN
DENMARK
Copenhagen
Moscow
London
THE NETHERLANDS
Amsterdam
Berlin
RUSSIA
BELGIUM
Brussels
GERMAN EMPIRE
Warsaw
Dnieper
Paris
LUX
AUSTRIA-HUNGARY
FRANCE
Bern
Vienna
SWITZ
RUMANIA
Bucharest
Black Sea
ITALY
MONTENEGRO
Belgrade
SERBIA
BULGARIA
PORTUGAL
Madrid
Rome
Sofia
Constantinople
SPAIN
Tirana
ALBANIA
GREECE
OTTOMAN EMPIRE
Athens
MOROCCO
Mediterranean Sea
ALGERIA
TRIPOLITANIA
EGYPT

Kurdish lands. Russian ambitions for territorial increases were, of course, no more extensive than those of her British, French, and Italian allies.

The carrying out of these agreements was, of course, entirely dependent on an Allied victory. Bearing the main weight of the fluid war in the east, the Russian military situation steadily deteriorated. Although great efforts were made in the field of war production, after the winter of 1914 the Russian armies suffered increasingly from disastrous shortages. As with previous Russian campaigns, the problems of supply and communications were not well managed. Initially, as in all the belligerent powers, there had been much enthusiasm for the war; the critics were a relatively small minority. The Russian public, like that in other lands, had no premonition of what lay ahead; few preparations had been made for a long conflict. After a century of relative peace, the memory of what a great war meant had largely been effaced.

Although Russia had in Britain and France allies with real military and naval power, she gained little direct assistance. Throughout the war Russian actions were carried out without real coordination or joint planning with the western powers. Despite her desperate need, military supplies could not be delivered because of the demands of the western front. At the beginning of the war, however, Russia did make a major contribution to the eventual Allied victory. The original Russian military plans had called for a major attack against the Habsburg forces in Galicia. A victory here would have protected the Russian Polish lands and have gained a desired territory. In answer to Allied pressure, in August, 1914 the Russian army instead launched a great offensive against East Prussia. Although this campaign ended with the disaster at Tannenberg in the same month, the Russian threat forced the German army to move two corps to the east, thus aiding in the French victory in the battle of the Marne. A Russian action in Galicia in this same period proved successful, and it also helped Serbia to resist Habsburg attacks. In 1914 also, it will be remembered, the Ottoman Empire joined the Central Powers.

In 1915 the Russian campaign in Galicia was reopened. At first it was successful, but a German-Austrian counter-offensive in May turned the tide. The Russian forces were compelled to evacuate their Polish and Lithuanian lands with enormous casualties. Millions of refugees joined the defeated forces in their retreat eastward. The situation in the Balkans was similarly dismal. In February, 1915 the Allies launched the ill-fated campaign in Gallipoli, first with a naval attack and then in April with an attempted land action. The failure of this effort against the Ottoman Empire influenced Bulgaria, who entered the war in October, 1915, an action that sealed the fate of Serbia. The year ended with the Central Powers clearly ahead in the east.

The tragedy of the war front was meanwhile being repeated at home. Nicholas II clearly lacked the force of character necessary for a wartime leader. In September, 1915 he made the great mistake of personally assuming the leadership of the army, thereby absenting himself from the capital for long periods. Control of the government fell into the hands of Empress Alexandra, who in turn was influenced by the incredible adventurer, Gregory Rasputin. The inability of the tsarist government to direct the country in a time of emergency was becoming increasingly apparent.

The year 1916 was to produce even greater disasters. In June the Russian armies under General Alexis Brusilov launched attacks that at first made great advances. These apparent victories, together with generous promises of future territorial gains, led Rumania to enter the war in August. However, the military fortunes shifted again; by December, 1916 the Central Powers were in occupation of Bucharest. Although the German and Habsburg armies had been able to gain impressive victories and inflict enormous casualties, in the winter 1916/17 the Russian army was able to maintain its front intact from the Baltic to the Carpathians. The strain of the constant defeats and the immense losses in men and equipment, however, had a great effect within the country. Throughout 1916 the increasing stress was apparent. The appointment of Boris V. Sturmer, whom many regarded as a German adherent, to the post of prime minister in February and foreign minister in July added to the disgust and distrust felt toward the tsar's government. The political opposition, well provided with examples of flagrant misgovernment, grew steadily during the war years. By the end of 1916 conspiracies against the regime began to be organized. One of these, in which members of the court were involved, resulted in the assassination of Rasputin in December.

By March, 1917 the opposition forces had gained enough strength to move against the tsar. Having lost control of the army and without sufficient personal support, on March 15 Nicholas II abdicated for himself and his son in favor of his brother Grand Duke Michael, who declined the position. The Provisional Government, which now controlled the state, was led by Prince Lvov, as prime minister, and Paul A. Miliukov, as foreign minister. Faced with the two-fold task of organizing a new, stable government and handling the problems of the war, this regime was to fail in both endeavors. Despite the disasters on the battlefields and the obvious need of the country for peace, the Provisional Government was determined to fulfill its commitments to its Allies and to stand by the war agreements. The spring of 1917 was a bleak time for the Allies; the war was not going well in the west. Although the United States entered the conflict in April, the decisive effect of this action was not realized at the time. Composed of representatives of the moderate and left parties of the Duma, the new regime, rent by factional disputes among its members, faced repeated crises. In July Alexander F. Kerensky replaced Prince Lvov; in September the government had to meet the dangers presented by the revolt of General Lavr Kornilov. Moreover, during the entire period of its existence, the Provisional Government had to compete with the rival political authority of the Petrograd Soviet of Worker's and Soldier's Deputies, a body which in September became dominated by the Bolshevik Party. In November a revolutionary movement, organized from this center, brought down the Kerensky government. The victorious Bolshevik leadership now embarked on a new path that led not only to a complete transformation of the political structure of the country but also to the initiation of a foreign policy which at least at first was quite different from that of the previous regimes.

The year 1917 thus witnessed the downfall of both the monarchical and the republican systems. The next year was to bring an end to the Romanov dynasty. In August, 1917 Nicholas II was sent to Siberia; the following July on Bolshevik orders he and his family were shot in the cellar of the house in which they had been imprisoned. The last members of the family suffered the very fate that the tsars from Alexander I through Nicholas II himself foresaw and feared if the revolutionary forces in Russia were not confined.

*   *   *   *   *

The entire reign of Nicholas II tends to fall under the shadow of the final catastrophe. Indeed there is a temptation to view the period in the terms of an inevitable last act of the drama of Russian tsarism. It is not difficult to emphasize the weakness of Nicholas II as a leader of government, the confusion of the administration, and the inability of responsible officials to see with sufficient clarity the probable consequences of the policies adopted. However, these characteristics had been present in previous regimes without severely endangering the state. Although it is true that the ministers of the tsar were not geniuses of statesmanship, they were no worse on the average than those who held similar offices in other countries. The question thus remains why Russia under Nicholas II failed to avoid a war for which she was not prepared and why, once in the fighting, the regime collapsed from the weight of the responsibilities placed upon it. The answer lies perhaps most completely in the fact that the last tsar was forced to pay the costs of a long series of mistakes and that the bill was presented suddenly in 1914-1918 for the entire account. In foreign policy, Sazonov, not Gorchakov, faced the consequences of the unification of Germany and the subsequent transformation of the Dual Monarchy. Nicholas II, not his four predecessors, had to accept the hard reality that the patronage of Balkan nationalism could involve the Russian government in deadly risks. Moreover, the new Russian alliance system, the Triple Entente, whose chief component was the Franco-Russian alliance inherited from Alexander III, had neither the military nor the ideological advantages for the tsarist regime of the old Holy Alliance in its various forms.

More significant was the internal failure. Throughout the entire century Russian military strength was not really equal to her foreign power commitments. Through wise diplomacy she had usually avoided military conflicts with the great powers, but when her armies did fight, they demonstrated that they were not up to the necessary standard. The military power of any state rests upon its internal order, its wealth, and its organizing abilities. Nicholas II thus also paid for a century of Russian maladministration that had failed to develop an internal system, whether liberal or despotic, that could produce the armies necessary to defend wide boundaries.

Part II

The Soviet Union

LENIN

STALIN

KHRUSHCHEV

BREZHNEV

VII

Lenin

The events of November, 1917 brought to power a revolutionary party with conceptions of human life and politics radically
different from those held by the tsarist regime. These views were
closely linked with and of great significance for the foreign policy
of the new government in the next years. To a large degree, but
never completely, they shaped and directed Soviet relations with
other states and determined Moscow's reaction to succeeding international crises. Even when Soviet policy was obviously decided by considerations of national interest in the traditional sense,
the actions taken were usually justified and explained in terms of
ideology. For these reasons a short review of the aspects of
Marxism-Leninism that involve foreign relations is essential before examining the events of the more than half a century since
the revolution.

The tsars in the nineteenth century also held a distinct view of the world in which they lived and of the role they believed they were destined to play in history. Adhering to the concepts of eighteenth-century enlightened despotism, they felt deeply that they held their power direct from God and that in turn they were responsible to him for their actions and the welfare of their subjects. Accepting as natural the division of society into estates, they tended to regard as virtually eternal the existing class structure of the state. No tsar, including Nicholas II, was truly sympathetic to a radical reconstruction of Russian society and the state to produce pluralistic institutions close to those of the west. As far as their duties as rulers were concerned, the tsars placed great emphasis on foreign affairs and national defense. Their goals remained the development and extension of Russian national power, but in a moderate and limited sense. Although by 1914 the empire was barely half Great Russian in nationality, the rulers saw their lands as a national unit and not as a state of nationalities. The entire world of ideas associated today with the concept of the welfare state and national self-determination was simply not present in their thoughts.

Despite the fact that they held firm views, Russian tsars and ministers were seldom doctrinaire. Cosmopolitan in background and attitude, they felt linked with the traditions of the European aristocracy. They did not pursue great ideological missions or airy national fantasies. The defense of the conservative order did indeed play a role in the foundation of the Holy Alliance and the Three Emperors' Alliance and in the support given the Habsburg Empire in 1849 and Prussia in 1870. However, in each case the action taken also conformed to what was considered at the time Russian national interests.

In opposition to these relatively simple and flexible attitudes, the triumphant Bolshevik Party held a far more intricate and detailed view of the world, one based essentially on the works of Karl Marx and Friedrich Engels as interpreted or altered by Lenin. Rejecting the entire framework fundamental to tsarist thinking, Marx developed a theory of history which, simply stated, declared that economic phenomena, that is, the economic conditions, the means of production and exploitation of economic resources, in a given period of history determine all other aspects of human life at that time. Thus at a particular historical moment the economic base will call for a certain structure of society and certain political institutions. In each case these will be a reflection of the interests of the dominant class.

In contrast to the essentially static nature of the tsarist view, Marx saw history as continually evolving and the economic substructure as being in a process of constant change. Thus in time as the economic base advanced, as new means of production or methods to exploit labor and resources were developed, the superstructure, which did not change as rapidly, would soon find itself out of harmony with its base. The means by which this discrepancy would be rectified, according to Marx, was through the class struggle. According to these theories, at each stage of development one class enjoyed a special position and was able to shape the state and its institutions in its own image and interests. However, once created, this class inevitably brought into existence its counterpart, an antagonistic class. Under capitalism the bourgeoisie needed a labor force to exploit the new means of production. Once in existence this proletariat was by its very nature a strong opponent of the predominant group. Marx saw capitalist society as developing toward a condition of polarization, with a few wealthy men at the top and a seething mass of discontented workers at the bottom. When this situation obtained, the capture of the state apparatus by the vast majority was easy to contemplate. After the proletariat came to power, it was assumed, the state would wither away. By definition an instrument of class domination, this institution would be superfluous once only one class remained.

Karl Marx developed his ideas by observing conditions in the industrial west in the third quarter of the nineteenth century. However, in the succeeding years social and economic development did not proceed in the direction that he had predicted. Instead wealth tended to diffuse through wider elements of society. Moreover, the "bourgeois" state, through programs of social legislation, proved that it could offer much to the proletariat. Inevitably these developments led to a split in Marxist and socialist thought. The numerically stronger elements, the basis of the European socialist parties and the Mensheviks in Russia, favored the formation of political parties that would then seek to gain control over and transform the state through regular legal processes. They believed in seeking better conditions through social legislation. In contrast, other groups emphasized the primacy of a revolutionary policy and the capture of the state by force. This split of the political left was to be of tremendous significance not only for internal developments but also for foreign policy in the European countries.

Of those who favored revolutionary methods, the most articulate and able proponent was undoubtedly Vladimir Ilich Ulianov, known as Lenin, the major author of the October revolution, both in a theoretical and a practical sense. Lenin was born in Simbirsk in 1870. His father, a bureaucrat of lower middle-class origin, received noble rank with his post as school inspector. In his youth Lenin was deeply involved in revolutionary activities. The execution of his older brother for similar actions had a deep effect upon him. Despite his engagement in illegal operations, he was able to complete his education and travel abroad. In 1895 he was arrested, sent to prison for fourteen months, and then exiled to Siberia for three years. After his return he moved to western Europe, where he became involved in the European socialist movement and in the development of his own ideas. In his writings Lenin emphasized or changed certain elements of Marxist doctrines to conform to the realities of the twentieth century and to Russian conditions. His chief contributions to socialist theory lay in his treatment of the "imperialist wars," the role of the Communist Party in leading revolutionary action, and the nature of the "dictatorship of the proletariat," the political order to follow the revolution.

Of Lenin's numerous works the most important for foreign policy is certainly his essay on *Imperialism*, published in 1916. Here and in other of his writings he argued that the contemporary capitalist states were in their highest stage of development, that of imperialism. In order to maintain their position and satisfy the demands of their working populations, these governments had conquered and exploited colonial areas. With the profits they had been able to maintain high wages and keep the workers contented. However, colonial lands were limited. Inevitably the capitalist states would be brought into a conflict over the division of the spoils. The resultant wars would create conditions favorable for revolution. In this situation Lenin foresaw that the role of the communist parties would be of determining significance. These organizations, the "vanguard of the proletariat," should use the chaotic conditions attendant upon modern wars to seize power. The aim was to replace the capitalist state structure with the "dictatorship of the proletariat." Once the remnants of the capitalist order had been swept away, then, and then only, could the state "wither away."

In the competitive political world of the twentieth century, the Marxist-Leninist program, from the beginning, had the great advantages that its doctrines could be simply and precisely stated and that it also provided a plan for action. Certainly at first, when it had not become so closely associated with Soviet state power, it also had an immense appeal to certain reforming elements of European society. By the end of the nineteenth century Marxian socialism had replaced the liberal national ideology that had represented "revolution" in previous decades. "Red" now meant communist or socialist—not the ideas generally associated with the French revolution. For Russia the victory of a party with such a program marked a complete turn of the wheel. Until 1917 that state had been generally regarded as the most politically reactionary and backward great power; thereafter to the rest of the world the Soviet Union represented the foremost revolutionary danger. After a century in which conservative, autocratic tsars lived in dread of bourgeois, liberal, national movements, we come to a period in which liberal, national, bourgeois western states similarly distrusted and disliked the revolutionary, socialist Soviet Union.

The figure of Lenin dominated the internal and external

policy of the Soviet Union in the early 1920's. Closely associated with him in the first years after the revolution was Lev Davidovich Bronstein, called Trotsky. He was born in 1879, the son of a Jewish farmer in the district of Nikolaev. Trotsky shared in many of the early revolutionary experiences of Lenin. He too was arrested and sent to Siberia, and subsequently made his headquarters in various European capitals. A theoretician, an eloquent speaker, and a gifted organizer, he appeared at first the natural heir of Lenin. In the spring of 1922 Lenin became ill; by March of 1923 he was paralyzed. The incapacity of the chief figure in the Bolshevik revolution brought up the dangerous question of succession. In opposition to Trotsky there now arose a triumvirate of leading Bolsheviks: Gregory E. Zinoviev, Leo B. Kamenev, and Joseph Stalin. Of the three Stalin at first appeared the least likely to emerge as a clear leader. His previous field of activity had been organization and administration. He had been a member of the Central Committee of the Communist Party since 1912; after the revolution he was closely involved with the nationality problem. In the spring of 1922 he became general secretary of the Party. After Lenin died in January, 1924 the struggle for power became more acute. First, the triumvirate was able to eliminate Trotsky; then Stalin with new allies moved against his former friends. In 1926 Zinoviev was removed from office. Trotsky meanwhile was sent to Central Asia and subsequently exiled. By 1928 Stalin held the strongest position in the Soviet government.

This shift in leadership, of course, directly affected the conduct of foreign affairs. After the revolution the predominant influence of Lenin and Trotsky was apparent. However, foreign policy decisions were made, as under the tsars, after consultation and discussion among the top members of the government. Issues were freely and openly debated with little limitation on the freedom of expression of the chief Bolshevik leaders. After 1922 disagreements over policy, particularly between Stalin and Trotsky, became more apparent. By the late 1920's Stalin was clearly the major figure in the Bolshevik hierarchy, but he did not have the absolute authority he was to wield later. The most dangerous situation to be faced by the new leadership existed in the first two years after the seizure of power when Lenin was in control.

THE NEW DIRECTION: BREST-LITOVSK

The first question facing the victorious Bolshevik government was the very practical problem of organizing a national administration and implementing the revolutionary declarations. At first the new regime was not very concerned about the offices and institutions connected with foreign affairs. Convinced that the Russian revolution was but the first of a great wave of similar upheavals, they confidently expected that the new international order of socialist states would produce a different system of foreign relations. Nevertheless, a Commissariat of Foreign Affairs was created with Trotsky in charge. The government then turned to its most pressing need—the restoration of peace.

An end to the war was now an absolute necessity both from an ideological and a practical standpoint. Slogans of peace and land had been intimately connected with the Bolshevik victory. Under the combined pressure of the German attacks and the Bolshevik peace propaganda the Russian armies were literally falling apart. In its first weeks in power the Soviet government itself embarked upon measures of demobilization. The growing political and economic chaos throughout the country demanded an end to the fighting. Moreover, Lenin himself, while still in exile in Europe, had been one of the leading advocates among socialist circles of an end to the capitalist war, an event which he believed could only come about through the victory of revolutionary uprisings throughout Europe.

Immediately after assuming power the Bolshevik regime had issued a call for a general peace. Its aim was to end the fighting in Europe, not to make a separate peace with the Central Powers. As a new diplomatic method, the Soviet appeals over the heads of the governments to the workers and the enemy camp had little attraction for the Allies. Not only was the source suspect, but with the entrance of the United States into the war the western states now hoped for a victor's peace. President Wilson's declaration on the Fourteen Points in January, 1918 was designed in part to counter the Soviet call for an immediate peace to be based on principles of self-determination and "without annexations or indemnities." Point V of Wilson's proposals called for the evacuation of Russian territory by foreign forces and acceptance of Russia by the other powers "under institutions of her own choosing."

In contrast to the Allies, Germany and Austria-Hungary were eager for an end to the hostilities. Hard pressed on the western front and desirous of opening an offensive in the spring, the German government welcomed an agreement that would allow it to transfer troops and to gain an assured source of raw materials. A cease-fire went into effect in November; in December a preliminary armistice was signed. At the end of that month negotiations for the terms of a peace treaty were initiated in the city of Brest-Litovsk. The delegations sent by the two sides typified the different natures of their governments. Germany was represented by Richard von Kühlmann, the foreign secretary, and General Max von Hoffmann; the Habsburg Monarchy, Bulgaria, and the Ottoman Empire also sent representatives. On the Soviet side the principal delegate was Adolf A. Joffe, who was subsequently replaced by Trotsky. He was accompanied, among others, by Anastasia Bitsenko, who had assassinated a tsarist officer, and by a worker, a peasant, a soldier, and a sailor, who presumably represented "the people." In the first weeks the Soviet government used the negotiations as a platform from which to make political speeches directed to the outside world and to the German army. The aim remained peace, but a peace followed by widespread insurrection after the Bolshevik pattern.

Once serious discussions began, the negotiations did not proceed well for the Soviet government from the practical standpoint. The Central Powers did indeed accept "self-determination," but as a principle to be applied to Russian territory. The

German government made it clear that it would decide the final fate of the Russian Baltic and Polish lands. A separatist Ukrainian government, the Rada, was recognized and peace was made with it in February. The extent of the German demands caused a division within the Soviet government. Trotsky left the conference on January 20 to discuss the question with the Soviet leadership. Faced with the extreme nature of the enemy conditions, some members of the government wished to abandon the negotiations and launch a true revolutionary war. In opposition to this solution, Lenin advised that the German terms be accepted. He recognized that the Soviet regime needed time to consolidate its hold on the country.

Accepting neither position, Trotsky returned to the meetings on February 10 with a novel solution of his own. He announced to the assembled delegates the formula of "no war, no peace." The Soviet government would simply stop fighting and no peace terms would be signed. With this declaration he left the conference. After recovering from their surprise, the Central Powers made the obvious move; the German offensive was resumed. Encountering little opposition from the demoralized Russian army, the German troops advanced swiftly. Faced with imminent disaster, the Bolshevik government was now forced to accept even stiffer terms for a peace. The military implications of this episode were obvious. Trotsky left his position as foreign commissar for the far more important War Commissariat, where he directed the organization of the Red Army, which was eventually to save the Bolshevik regime.

The Treaty of Brest-Litovsk, signed on March 3, 1918, left the Soviet government in effective control of only northeastern Russia and Siberia; the Polish and Baltic lands, as well as much of White Russia, were lost. The Ukraine was already under a separate authority. Finland's declaration of independence was recognized by the Soviet government in December, 1917; in Central Asia and in the Caucasus separatist movements held the real authority. In the peace the Ottoman Empire was able to regain the losses of 1878—Batum, Kars, and Ardahan. Rumanian troops were also in occupation of Bessarabia, the area Russia had annexed in 1812.

Despite the drastic nature of these territorial changes, the Bolshevik leadership, still confident that the expanding tide of revolution would soon make the peace terms obsolete, took the necessary measures, along traditional lines, to make the Soviet power base stronger. Of prime importance was the organization of a Red Army. First the ideological stand on the military was reversed. Discipline was reasserted; the whole population was made subject to service. In a move to assure the political reliability of the army, political commissars were attached to the troops. The extent of the national disaster together with the presence of foreign troops on Russian soil worked to the benefit of the recruiting efforts. Tsarist officers and former soldiers, no matter what their political persuasion, now returned to defend their homeland. Although the importance of drawing all elements of the population to its side was clear, the Bolshevik regime did not retreat on the political front. During this period of War Communism, the attempt was made to introduce into national life some of the theoretical aspects of Bolshevik economic doctrine.

The difficulties facing the Bolshevik government at this time were certainly enormous. It did nevertheless enjoy certain advantages over its adversaries, both domestic and foreign. Bolshevik propaganda certainly had a wide appeal to a war-weary population. Obviously no attempt was made to expound the intricacies of Marxism-Leninism. Instead simple phrases, such as *land, peace, bread, self-determination,* were repeated constantly. Moreover, during this period of crisis the regime itself held together. In the spring of 1918 the government was moved to Moscow, an area less open to western, specifically German, invasion. Despite the heavy territorial losses, the Bolshevik regime, like its tsarist predecessor in 1812, was able to maintain military control over the vital central area and to stifle any effective challenge to its political domination in this region. It was also to the Bolsheviks' advantage that they had inner lines of communication and that they held control of the major industrial areas.

Perhaps the greatest benefit enjoyed by the Soviet government, however, was the division of its adversaries. Opposition to Soviet control was to take two forms—a civil war directed against the regime by dissident Russian elements and an intervention by the Allies, Britain, France, the United States, and Japan. The leadership in the civil war, as could be expected, lay in the hands of the generals and statesmen of the former governments. The majority of them desired to return to the political framework of the period of the Provisional Government. Their followers ranged through the entire political spectrum—from monarchists to Social Revolutionaries to anarchists. They showed no more ability to cooperate in adversity than previously. They were backed by a halfhearted and hesitant Allied intervention. Although the war in Europe concluded in November, 1918, fighting continued on Russian soil well into 1920.

Civil War and Intervention

The main foreign policy objective after the acquisition of power for the Bolshevik regime was the regaining of control over the territories of the former tsarist empire and the expulsion of all foreign military forces. In internal affairs the chief emphasis had to be placed on the defeat of the armies of the political opposition. In 1918 Allied troops entered Russia through the ports of Archangel, Murmansk, Vladivostok, and Odessa. Centers of internal resistance, backed by foreign armies, existed in the Ukraine, southern Russia, the Caucasus, and Siberia. The first Allied intervention came through the Arctic ports. Quite naturally, during the winter of 1917/18 the French and British leaders had watched with apprehension the progress of the negotiations at Brest-Litovsk. Hitherto the eastern front had absorbed a large proportion of the German forces; the closing of that area of combat would have a highly negative effect on Allied strategy. The question of military intervention, either to back Soviet resistance to German demands or to overthrow the new regime and replace it with a government that would continue the war, arose at once. The western governments were also concerned over the fate of large stocks of munitions and equipment at the major Russian ports. As long as conditions were unsettled, the Soviet government too was willing to discuss the question with Allied representatives. Western assistance was a possible alternative should the peace negotiations fail or should German actions force a resumption of hostilities. The first British landing at Murmansk in June, 1918 was with the acquiescence of the Bolshevik government. By the summer of 1918, however, the Allied action had acquired a decidedly anti-Bolshevik coloration. The seizure of the port of Archangel in August by an American, British, and French force was in opposition to the Soviet authorities, as was the simultaneous occupation of Siberian territories by Japanese and American troops.

Of the three centers of major opposition that now arose to Bolshevik rule—the Ukraine, southern Russia, and Siberia—the politically most dangerous for the future of the state was the separatist organization of the Ukraine. Although throughout the previous century the Polish question and the Russian control of Polish lands had been a major theme in international relations, the tsarist government's domination over White Russian and Ukrainian territories had never been in question. The Ukraine, with a population of 35,000,000, had its own history and language, but no national movement of great European significance had occurred there in the modern period. A Ukrainian cultural center existed in Galicia in Austria-Hungary. However, Ukrainian nationalism was simply not an issue in diplomacy. After the revolution the area became a center of conflict and turmoil. The first separatist government, which had signed a peace with Germany, fell soon after the armistice. Thereafter Allied, Bolshevik, and Polish forces disputed control of the area. In December, 1918 French troops intervened through Odessa; in 1920 a Polish army captured Kiev. In the same year a Ukrainian Bolshevik regime was established with an administrative structure separate from that of Moscow and with its own foreign office. When the Soviet Union was organized on a federal basis in 1923, foreign policy again became the responsibility of the central government.

Southern Russia and the Caucasus region, in contrast to the Ukraine, became a center of military resistance by the White armies, first under General Lavr G. Kornilov and then under General Anton I. Denikin, and by the cossacks of the Black Sea and the Don River region. The entire Black Sea area was also of great concern to the Allies. In December, 1917 France and Britain, in an agreement reminiscent of the other secret treaties of the war period, divided the region into two spheres of action. France was assigned the Crimea, the Ukraine, and Bessarabia. Britain, following her traditional interests in Central Asia, was allotted the Don and Caucasus region, thus giving her control over the oil resources of the area. Assistance was then offered to General Denikin, and the separatist regimes that had been established in Georgia and Azerbaijan were recognized as independent. Despite the aid from the west the White armies of General Denikin, who was succeeded by General Peter N. Wrangel, could not stand against the Bolshevik forces. This front collapsed at the end of 1920: in November of that year Allied ships evacuated the remnants of the White forces from the Crimea to Constantinople. Also in 1920 the situation in the Caucasus was consolidated in favor of the Bolsheviks. Bolshevik regimes were established in Azerbaijan, Armenia, and Georgia; like the government of the Ukraine, they remained autonomous until 1923. A similar situation existed in Central Asia, where in 1924 the local regimes became five Soviet republics.

The intervention and civil war in Siberia met with a similar fate about the same time. Here the White Armies were led by Admiral Alexander V. Kolchak, whom both the White leaders and the Allied governments recognized as the head of the Russian state. The chief forces of intervention came from the United States and Japan. The initial impulse for the Allied action was provided by the problem of the Czech legion. During the war the Czech prisoners in Russian hands, some 40,000, had been organized into a fighting force. In the winter of 1917/18 the Allied governments wished to take them from Russia and bring them to the western front. The Soviet authorities agreed that they could be evacuated through Vladivostok and that they could remain armed. When fighting broke out between Czechs and Russians, Trotsky ordered the Czechs disarmed. Resisting this move, the Czech troops took command of towns along the Trans-Siberian railway and joined with local White forces. A situation thus developed in which the Allies could assist in rescuing some of the Czech soldiers and also aid the Whites. By early 1918 Japanese troops were already in Vladivostok. In the fall about 7,000 American troops and many more Japanese arrived. They occupied the line of the Trans-Siberian Railroad to Lake Baikal. Japanese forces were also in Manchuria.

Although the Siberian situation was considerably more complicated, the Red Army was able to assert its military superiority here also. In 1919 Admiral Kolchak was defeated, captured, and, in the next year, executed. In the spring of 1920 the American forces evacuated Siberia. The Japanese remained there until 1922 and in northern Sakhalin until 1925. Because of the complexities of the eastern situation the Bolshevik government preferred to set up a satellite Far Eastern Republic at first to control Siberia. In November, 1922, after the evacuation of the Japanese troops, this area joined the rest of the country. Not only were the Siberian lands regained, but the Bolshevik government was able to re-establish the pre-war Russian political domination over Outer Mongolia. Here in 1921 a pro-Soviet regime, the Mongolian People's Republic, was established with close ties to Moscow.

Despite the fact that in 1919 the Red Army was victorious over its White opponents, the Soviet government still had to face a major military threat from the west. The Allied forces were withdrawn from Murmansk and Archangel in the fall of 1919, but the French government continued to give military aid to the revived Polish state. Re-established under the headship of General Joseph Pilsudski, the independent Polish national state fully justified the Russian fears of the previous century. The leadership of the new nation soon showed that it desired not ethnic Poland or even pre-partition Poland but, if circumstances allowed, the re-creation in some form of the Polish-Lithuanian state of the sixteenth century with its vast Ukrainian and White

Russian territories. The Polish army, backed by France, could have presented a real danger to the Soviet regime had the Polish leaders chosen to co-operate with the White opposition. Under the impression that a White Russia would be stronger than a Red Russia, the Poles preferred to wait until the White forces were eliminated. In the spring of 1920 the Polish forces advanced, and in a great offensive were able to take Kiev in May. However, at that point the situation altered radically. The Ukrainians, even those desiring independence, disliked Polish occupation more than Great Russian. As traditional Russian enemies, the Polish forces, by their invasion, produced a patriotic reaction throughout the other areas. A Soviet counter-offensive launched in May quickly rolled the Polish army back. Only at Warsaw in August did the Polish line hold. Here the Poles were able not only to stop the Soviet drive but to regain the offensive. The Soviet forces were driven back beyond the Polish ethnic frontier. Having failed to achieve a military victory, the Soviet government now accepted a disadvantageous peace. The Treaty of Riga of 1921 provided for a line of demarcation which left approximately two and a half million White Russians and Ukrainians under Polish control.

INTERNATIONAL COMMUNISM: THE COMINTERN

Although the Bolshevik leadership succeeded in consolidating its control and in suppressing foreign invasion and civil war, its expectations of a widening of the revolutionary movement to encompass at least those states most disrupted by the war and the subsequent conditions of peace were not realized. At this time, it should be emphasized, the Bolsheviks believed that the expansion of the revolution was essential to the survival of their own regime. Germany was the focal point of Soviet attention. For the Marxists this state had always been the area of central interest. As a capitalist nation with a great concentration of industry and capital and with the Social Democrats as the strongest workers' party in Europe, Germany not Russia should logically have been the site of the first communist revolution. Moreover, the Social Democrats had been the strongest single party before the war, and Germany had been the center of European socialism. In the chaotic conditions of the immediate post-war period, some revolutionary action on the Soviet model could certainly be expected there.

After the signature of the Treaty of Brest-Litovsk, German-Soviet relations resumed a fairly normal course. Joffe was sent as ambassador to Berlin. In this period the Soviet government where possible continued to conduct a propaganda campaign directed at Germany, but, with its own internal problems, it was in no position to offer active aid to communist movements abroad. Joffe used his headquarters in Berlin as a center of revolutionary propaganda. His actions became so flagrant that he was expelled by the imperial government on November 6, 1918. When that regime was overthrown a few days later, Joffe waited at the border hoping to be called back by a new revolutionary authority. Both his and his government's hopes were disappointed. The new provisional government under Friedrich Ebert, moderate and socialist in composition, from the beginning showed itself primarily concerned with the reaction of the western victor powers. Apprehension was also felt over the nature of the Russian revolution. An offer of food from the Bolshevik government was rejected; regular diplomatic relations were not resumed.

Despite the negative attitude of the German government, Soviet hopes for Germany remained alive. It was expected that the German "March" revolution would soon be followed by a communist "October" revolt. Karl Radek, recognized as the German expert of the Bolshevik party, was sent to make contact with the left-wing socialists. Signs soon appeared that indeed the revolutionary movement might proceed. During the November upheaval workers' and soldiers' councils, similar to those formed in Russia in 1917, had appeared. Attempts were made to deal with them as if a dual governmental authority existed in Germany as it had in Russia in the period of the Provisional Government. Soviet expectations lay not in the activities of the majority of the members of the Social Democratic Party, who now seemed securely settled within the capitalist framework, but in fringe groups of the workers' movement. In 1917 the Independent Social Democrats had emerged as a faction opposed to the continuation of the war. To the left within this group was the so-called Spartacus League, under the direction of Rosa Luxemburg and Karl Liebknecht. In December, 1917 the left wing of the Independent Social Democrats became the German Communist Party.

In the future this new Communist Party, in close association with Moscow, was to make a series of disastrous attempts to seize power. The first occurred almost immediately, in January, 1919. At that time there were outbreaks in Berlin and other German cities, but there was no major uprising. With the co-operation of the army, the Social Democratic government easily suppressed this feeble rebellion. Rosa Luxemburg and Karl Liebknecht were arrested and then murdered by reactionary Free Corps soldiers. The Soviet anger at the German Social Democrats, who had shown that they would co-operate with the army and the Right to put down radical movements, was to be significant for the future. Karl Radek was also imprisoned, at first under severe conditions and later under what was little more than house arrest. Until his release at the end of the year he acted as a kind of unofficial Soviet representative and received visitors representing all sectors of German political life. Official relations between Berlin and Moscow were resumed in early 1920.

The single example in this period of a successful communist movement was the establishment of the regime of Bela Kun in Hungary in March, 1919. At the end of the war Hungary was in a desperate situation. Pressed by impossible demands from the victors, the moderate republican government in Budapest resigned in favor of a Social Democrat-Communist coalition. The resultant Bela Kun regime was of exceedingly short duration. Faced with the opposition of the Allies and the neighboring powers, the communist state soon came into armed conflict with Rumania and Czechoslovakia. As their troops entered Budapest in August, Bela Kun was forced to flee to Vienna.

Soviet hopes of a communist victory were blighted in two

other areas. As the victorious Soviet army advanced into Polish territory in 1920, there was discussion of the possible establishment of a communist government there. The Polish military triumph and the obvious lack of enthusiasm among the Polish workers killed any possibility of a revolutionary success here. In April, 1919 a Bavarian communist regime came into existence for a short period. Its suppression by the German army left this area a center of rightist political movements.

Coincident with the Soviet hopes for the spread of communist revolutionary activities was the move to establish a central organization to co-ordinate these actions, especially since the possibility existed at this time that the European Socialist parties would attempt to revive the Second International, the pre-war central socialist organization, and thus form a competing body. The congress that met in Moscow in March, 1919 to establish the Third International, commonly called the Comintern, was almost entirely a Russian affair. Because of world conditions delegations could not easily come from abroad. The majority of the thirty-five delegates were Soviet citizens, picked by the leadership of the Russian Communist Party, or foreigners present in the country. Delegates did come, however, from Germany, Austria, Norway, Sweden, and Holland. The German representative abstained from voting on the question of the establishment of the Comintern. Once this organization was set up Zinoviev became the president of the Central Committee, with Karl Radek as secretary. In this first congress the main targets of attack were the European socialist parties; Great Britain was denounced as the greatest imperial power and the main supporter of the capitalist order.

The second congress of the Comintern, held in July and August, 1920, was more truly international in character; foreign delegations did attend. As in the previous meeting the language was German. Most important for the future of the world communist movement, this congress adopted the Twenty-One Conditions as the basis for membership in the organization. Chiefly the work of Lenin, these rules laid the foundation for Soviet control. Foreign communist parties were henceforth expected to follow the Soviet lead in ideology, organization, and revolutionary strategy and tactics. The Soviet system was thus established as the model for world communism; all communists were to look to Moscow for direction. Again at this congress the Social Democrats were singled out as the chief political opponents.

As the major rivals for the leadership of labor and leftist movements, the Social Democrats were bound to be a target of attack. However, with the failure of the revolutionary action in Germany, the pursuance of a thoroughly hostile policy was not practical. Therefore in December, 1921 the executive committee of the Comintern in a change of policy called for the formation of united workers' fronts. Local communists were now encouraged to join socialist and labor organizations. The aim of this "united front from below" was to exploit the wider facilities of the larger organizations and to try to win support among their members and draw them into the communist camp. This policy operated not only in Germany but also in Britain, where British communists sought to join the Labour Party.

Although in theory the Comintern was an international organization, it became in fact a department of the Soviet state. The basis for domination was laid in 1920. Although in succeeding years the Soviet government repeatedly declared that the Comintern was a completely separate and independent body, it was perfectly clear that the same people who were running the Comintern were also in control in the Soviet state and party structure. Perhaps because of this close association the Comintern never became a really important element in world revolutionary activities. Although yearly congresses should have been held, only seven were ever convened. As the years passed the nature of the organization became clearer. The fourth congress, in 1922, strongly emphasized the duty of foreign communist parties to support the Soviet state. As the hope of revolution faded, the importance of upholding the one communist country in existence was increasingly emphasized.

During these first years of the Comintern's existence, two further attempts were made to bring about a revolution in Germany. In 1920 Zinoviev attended a meeting of the Independent Socialist Party at Halle. Here the Twenty-One Conditions were discussed. The majority of those present accepted the proposals and most of them joined the Communist Party. This organization now numbered 350,000 members and formed the only mass party the Communists were able to organize in western Europe at this time.

Having established this strong base, the party then proceeded to make a series of real mistakes. In March, 1921 riots broke out in many German districts, in particular in the Mansfeld coal area in central Germany. The army was sent in to restore order and to suppress political agitation. The Communist Party first called for revolt and then for a general strike. Although some clashes between workers and the police occurred, the entire movement was a decided failure. It was obvious that the Communists could not command the mass of the German workers.

A third and final attempt at revolt occurred in 1923. At this time the French were in occupation of the Ruhr, an action taken in reprisal for a German default on reparations payments. Economic conditions in Germany were rapidly declining. In this tense situation another uprising was planned. Again some street fighting took place, but the police and the army had no difficulty in maintaining control. The event had a bad effect both on German relations with the Soviet government and on the German Communist Party, which was banned in October, 1923. When it became legal again in 1924, its membership had dropped to about 120,000. After 1923 the attempt to introduce a communist regime into Germany by revolutionary action was abandoned. The Soviet government thereafter placed its main emphasis on establishing and maintaining friendly formal relations with Berlin.

Despite the obvious lack of success in spreading communism, the activities of the Soviet state and the Comintern in this direction caused real problems for Soviet diplomacy. In these early years Moscow was obviously both officially and unofficially a revolutionary center. Although the Soviet government in the 1920's was in no condition to render effective material aid to outside revolutions, the flow of propaganda to this end continued. Other governments naturally felt apprehensive about Soviet intentions; these fears were bound to play an important role in international relations. For its part the Soviet leadership also retained its revolutionary convictions. Although by the middle 1920's a general condition of calm reigned throughout Europe, many still awaited another wave of revolution that would sweep through Europe, occasioned either by an inner breakdown of the capitalist system or by another imperialist war. The Soviet constitution of 1924 was drawn so that other states could adhere to the central framework. However, until the day dawned when new revolts would bring more adherents to communism, the Soviet state was faced with the practical necessity of getting along with the capitalist and imperialist world.

RELATIONS WITH EUROPE

The establishment of even formal relations with the victorious western allies was to prove a difficult achievement. Formidable economic, political, and ideological barriers separated the Soviet Union in particular from France, Britain, and the United States. Not only had the Soviet regime as its first task signed a peace with the Central Powers, but the government had also refused to recognize the tsarist debts and it had nationalized foreign industries and banks. In the period of the civil war and intervention, an undeclared war in fact existed between the Bolsheviks and the three western powers and Japan. In the 1920's the question of the debt and the nationalized property dominated any negotiations that the Soviet government held with the western powers. In 1914 the tsarist government owed approximately four billion gold rubles to foreign governments and investors; the debt rose to twelve billion rubles by 1917. In 1914 80 per cent of these loans were carried by France, who was also the heaviest hit by the nationalization of foreign property. The total figure of the repudiated debt and the value of the confiscated property came to about seven billion gold rubles. This question became closely interconnected with the problem of German reparations and the loans given to the Allied countries during the war.

The ideological gulf went even deeper. Here the western leaders showed a great deal of confusion. As we have seen in the previous century, the western liberal capitalist states had sincerely felt that they held the key to future human progress in their unique political and economic institutions. Basic to their thinking was their faith in the effectiveness of representative institutions, private property, and civil liberties, backed by a general Christian and humanitarian ethic. In the nineteenth century new national states, whether in central Europe or the Balkans, did indeed adopt these institutions. After the First World War the western nations, in particular the United States and Britain, continued to be convinced that their ways of life were universally applicable and morally right. These states now found themselves challenged by another power with a rival program for future progress and human betterment, a program definitely not based on forms of western parliamentarianism and positively antagonistic to accepted European ideas on private ownership. Instead of representing shining lights of progress and civilization, the western states now found themselves castigated as politically and economically backward and as oppressors of their own workers and their colonial subjects. Great Britain in particular found herself designated the chief oppressor of suffering mankind. Even when the Soviet government made an effort to suppress this kind of revolutionary propaganda in the interests of better relations abroad, it was always met with an attitude of suspicion and distrust in western capitals. The fact that communist accusations were often based on fact, in particular on conditions in the colonial world, did not help matters either.

The Soviet government, of course, was not a participant in any of the conferences that drew up the post-war treaties. Thus the greatest European gathering since 1814, that at Versailles in

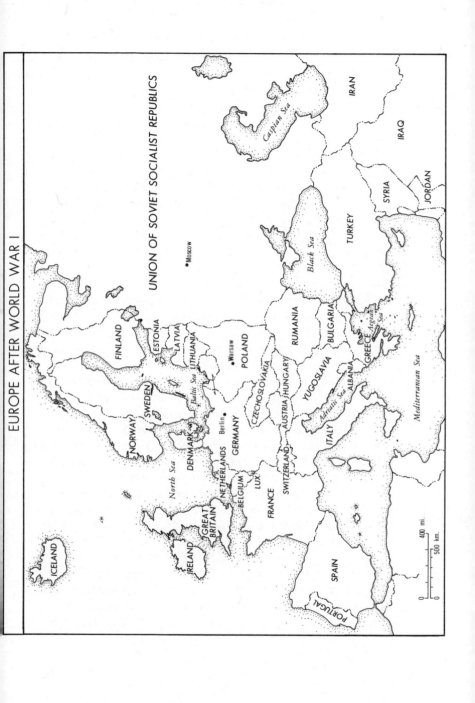

EUROPE AFTER WORLD WAR I

1919, was not attended by the power who had dominated the proceedings of the Congress of Vienna. In the future this fact was to be an advantage in that it allowed the Soviet statesmen to denounce freely what was indeed a very bad settlement. A just peace, one of fairness and conciliation, might have resulted in a unity of the capitalist, liberal states against the revolutionary menace. Instead the post-war map of Europe, which was largely the product of French hysteria for security, resulted in the creation of a general situation favorable to the Soviet Union in its time of weakness. Particularly important was the condition of Germany. With impossible reparation demands levied upon it, with the imposition of unilateral disarmament, and with a boundary settlement in violation of proclaimed Allied principles of self-determination, this power, potentially the strongest in Europe, could easily become a Russian ally. The two states rejected by the predominant west could come together; a solid capitalist front did not stand opposed to Soviet power.

The eastern European settlement, fraught with similar gross injustices, offered similar opportunities. Here, after the war the Soviet government met a situation radically different from the one that had existed in tsarist times, when Russia and the Habsburg Empire had shared in controlling the area and in maintaining a rough balance of power. Now Austria-Hungary, which at times had indeed been an enemy, but more often an ally, had been broken into its national components. Most impressive, however, was the fact that Russian influence was now completely excluded from the entire area. Tsarist Russia had gone to war for Serbia and to preserve her position in the Balkans. By 1919 not only was the Russian hold there broken but the Polish lands were lost also. Moreover, the Soviet government was faced in the area with a predominant France, who was not usually friendly to the Soviet regime in the immediate post-war period.

However, the situation did offer certain possibilities for Soviet action. In the peace settlement, again under French sponsorship, certain nations—Poland, Czechoslovakia, Rumania, and Yugoslavia—received disproportionate rewards. Poland then became

the center of a French security system that included the Little
Entente alliance of Rumania, Czechoslovakia, and Yugoslavia.
This French-dominated alignment, a revival in modern form of
the old Eastern Barrier, could operate against either Germany or
the Soviet Union. There were, nevertheless, great weaknesses
within the structure. Not only were there cleavages within the
alliances, such as that between Poland and Czechoslovakia, but
also the division caused by these pacts between victors and van-
quished left the entire area disturbed and unsettled. The dissatisfaction of Austria, Hungary, Turkey, Bulgaria, and also Italy,
kept the diplomatic situation fluid. Thus the settlement in eastern Europe, like that with Germany, assured the Soviet government that it would not be alone in desiring an alteration in the
political and territorial *status quo*. Although there was no basic
agreement among the defeated powers on the direction the
changes should take, they were united in not accepting the peace
terms. Although the comparison is in many ways faulty, Europe
had in a sense gone back to the 1860's. With the great powers
disunited, the way was free for the adventurers.

By 1921, when the Soviet government made a determined effort to establish regular relations with other governments, the
state already had a functioning Commissariat of Foreign Affairs
(*Narodnyi komissariat po inostrannym delam*, or *Narkomindel*).
Trotsky, as we have seen, became the first foreign commissar in
1917. The administrative apparatus of the former Provisional
Government was placed under his direction. The new leadership
had no wish to change the organization or personnel of these
offices immediately. As their first task under the Bolshevik regime, the officials were assigned the translating of Lenin's Decree
on Peace, which had been issued directly after the communist
victory. This document had denounced the war, called for a peace
without annexations or indemnities, and appealed to the peoples
of the world as well as to the governments. The foreign ministry
staff, who almost to a man had supported the war program of
the previous government, balked. On November 12 they called a
strike through their new union; on the same day most of them

were dismissed. Thus only a few minor officials from the old regime remained. A similar situation existed in the posts abroad. Most of the Russian ambassadors refused to surrender their positions; many of them continued to be recognized for many years afterwards by the governments to which they were accredited, and their embassies often became anticommunist centers. Other officials defected. Despite this loss of personnel, adequate replacements were soon found chiefly among the Bolshevik bureaucracy, but also from among the radical emigration which had left the country during Nicholas' reign and which now returned.

In March, 1918 George Vasilievich Chicherin replaced Trotsky as commissar for foreign affairs. A man of noble birth and a former archivist in the tsarist foreign ministry, Chicherin had first been a Menshevik and had not joined the Bolsheviks until 1918. Like the foreign ministers under the tsars, and indeed like many in similar positions in other countries, he was primarily responsible for the implementation but not the formulation of foreign policy. In this period, as later, policy was decided primarily by the Central Committee of the Communist Party and in particular by its Political Bureau (*Politburo*). As long as Lenin lived he remained its principal figure, but important roles were also played in foreign affairs by Trotsky, Zinoviev, Stalin, and others. Despite his subordination to those higher in the Bolshevik hierarchy, Chicherin did become identified with a definite line of policy. Representing a continuation of the element in tsarist thought that saw Britain as Russia's chief adversary, he desired a close connection with Germany. He also came to represent that policy which called for attacks on the Treaty of Versailles and the denunciation of the League of Nations as a "League of Capitalists."

In the first years of its existence the task of the Foreign Commissariat was indeed difficult. In early 1919 the Soviet government had no direct links with other capitals. The only true foreign representative in Moscow was the Danish Red Cross, which handled the interests of other nations. Contacts through revolutionary organizations were maintained with some Asiatic states, such as Afghanistan and Turkey. The first formal pact made with another state after the war was the Treaty of Tartu with Estonia in February, 1920. Agreements were subsequently made with Lithuania and Latvia. In this period the Ukrainian, Belorussian, Georgian, Armenian, Azerbaijanian, and Far Eastern Republics had their own foreign commissariats, as did two Central Asian republics, but only the Ukrainians sent representatives abroad. In 1924 these separate institutions were abolished and their offices absorbed into those in Moscow.

The prime Soviet desire after 1921 was to have normal relations with the great capitalist states. In that year the government adopted the New Economic Policy, NEP, which in some respects meant a return to private capitalism. With a new emphasis on improving the economic conditions of the country, the Soviet government was now most desirous of obtaining trade agreements and loans. For a country that had just repudiated its debts and nationalized foreign-owned property, the attainment of such an end would be no small accomplishment. The task was made more difficult by the fact that trade was a government monopoly. Two countries proved most difficult to approach from both an economic and a political standpoint—France and the United States. France, of course, had been the most injured by the Soviet actions. The United States, with its emphasis on the sanctity of international obligations, private property, and certain other legal and moral principles dear to the liberal heart, remained suspicious and hostile. The best opportunities for the Soviet government thus lay in Berlin and London. Both Germany and Britain wanted and needed trade relations and both were willing to consider political arrangements. In this early period the Soviet government often used commercial negotiations to precede or parallel political conversations.

A move toward a renewal of formal relations with Great Britain occurred even before the end of the civil war. The Allied blockade was lifted in January, 1920; in the next month an agreement was made on the exchange of prisoners. Negotiations for a trade agreement were commenced in May. The treaty resulting from these discussions, which was signed in March, 1921, did not signify the resumption of normal diplomatic relations, but it did allow the exchange of unofficial representatives and the continuation of trade negotiations. This agreement did nothing to settle the difficult question of debts and claims in connection with nationalized property. It also contained a clause in which both sides agreed not to allow hostile propaganda against each other. India and Afghanistan were expressly included in this prohibition.

Despite this advance, relations did not basically improve between the two countries. Britain remained a prime target of attack as the best example of the evil capitalist system. British extreme irritation at this type of propaganda in the colonial areas and the problem of the nationalized property prevented a further improvement of relations under the Conservative government in power at the time. At the beginning of 1924 the first Labour government was formed under Ramsay MacDonald. More sympathetic to the Soviet regime, the Labour Party had made better relations with Moscow part of its election campaign. In February, 1924 the British government thus formally recognized the Soviet Union, but ambassadors were not exchanged. Soon afterwards France, now under a leftist government of Edward Herriot, extended similar recognition, as did Japan and Italy. Unfortunately for British-Soviet relations, the Labour government lasted only nine months. In October, 1924 new elections were scheduled to be held. Toward the end of the campaign the British foreign office released to the press a letter allegedly written by Zinoviev to one of the leaders of the British Communist Party. The letter, inflammatory in character, called for the organization of cells in the British army and preparations for revolts in the colonies and Ireland. A protest was sent to the Soviet government. Although the letter was a forgery—an original was never produced—its publication contributed decisively to the Conservative Party's winning the election. The new Conservative government under Stanley Baldwin was not eager to pursue closer relations with the Soviet Union; a general treaty under negotiation was dropped.

Relations declined again precipitously in 1926. In May a general strike was called in support of British coal miners. Although the strike failed, the coal miners continued their efforts until November, when they too gave in. Throughout these events, which deeply shook the British public, the Communist Party was most vocal in its support of the labor movement. Soviet labor organizations sent money to the strikers, an action which the Conservative government regarded as interference in British internal affairs. The Soviet reply was to deny responsibility, as in the case of the Comintern, for the activities of their unions. The culmination of Soviet-British friction came in May, 1927 when the London police raided the offices of the Soviet Trade Delegation and the trading company ARCOS (All-Russian Cooperative Society Limited). Its papers were examined despite the delegation's supposed extraterritorial rights. Although no documents of real significance were discovered, the British government used this opportunity to break relations with the Soviet Union.

In contrast to Soviet efforts in Britain, attempts to improve relations with Germany were more successful. The Soviet government had been able to maintain some sort of connection with Berlin almost without interruption after November, 1917. In the period after Brest-Litovsk regular diplomatic relations had been established; later connections on some levels were never broken. Moreover, in the immediate post-war world, it was clear to both states that not only did they have much in common but also they could aid each other. Both were in an extremely weak and dangerous position politically and economically. Moreover, certain aspects of the territorial settlement in the peace treaties created a link between them. Most obvious was the formation of the independent Polish state with its large German, Ukrainian, and White Russian minorities and its diplomatic dependence on France. Again, as in the nineteenth century, a common German and Russian interest on the Polish question existed.

On the economic level also the two states had similar interests. In the period of the NEP the Soviet government wanted industrial equipment, especially machinery. German heavy industry, cut off from western and colonial markets by Allied policy, desired eastern outlets for its products. Soviet industry could benefit from German technological assistance, and Germany also obviously needed the food supplies and other raw materials that the Soviet lands could supply. Because of these mutual concerns, in 1920 the two countries exchanged representatives, who were subsequently given diplomatic privileges.

Most significant for Soviet-German relations was the attitude of the German right. The renewal of close connections with Moscow was appealing not only to the German industrialist in search of markets but also to the nationalist and to the military. After the defeats suffered at the hands of the Poles, Soviet army leaders became increasingly interested in German ties; in the fall of 1920 an initiative thus came from the Soviet side. In January, 1921 General Hans von Seeckt, the head of the German army, sent an emissary to the Soviet Union. In the next years other officers followed. For about ten years in an entirely unofficial manner, and outside of regular diplomatic channels, co-operation was maintained on certain matters between the Soviet and German high commands. The Soviet Union primarily sought technical assistance in the training of its troops and the organization of its war industries. The Germans wished to train men in tanks and airplanes on Russian territory and thus circumvent the disarmament clauses of the Versailles treaty. The assistance provided by both sides was moderate, but it reflected a real community of interest in this sphere.

Meanwhile, on the political level, relations improved, but only gradually. The Soviet interest was clearly to draw Germany away from any close connections with the western powers. What the Soviet Union had most to fear in Europe was the formation of a solid alignment of the capitalist states. Tsarist Russia, as indeed all the great powers, had previously had constant fears concerning European coalitions. Any moves by Germany toward reconciliation with the victor states were thus disliked. Although many in Germany, the so-called Easterners, favored a revival of the former close links to the Russian lands, opinion in Berlin was definitely divided. The persistence of Soviet attempts to revolutionize the country, which continued through 1923, did not provide a harmonious background for diplomatic relations. Moreover, a great many German politicians were convinced that it would be better for their country to follow a policy of fulfillment of the peace treaties and reconciliation with the west. The possibility of playing between the two camps was also seen. In practice, the German attitude toward the Soviet Union was largely determined by the actions of the two western powers, Britain and France, on the question of reparations and the territorial settlement. Particularly important was the final formulation of the reparations bill at 132 billion gold marks, an entirely unrealistic figure, in October, 1921 and the assignment of a part of the Upper Silesian industrial area to Poland, in flagrant violation of the principles of self-determination and of a plebiscite held under Allied supervision.

In May, 1921 Germany and the Soviet Union signed a trade agreement similar to that concluded the previous March between Moscow and London. In this pact Germany recognized the Soviet regime as the sole government of Russia. The Soviet government then wished to proceed with a political treaty establishing regular relations. The German leaders were not enthusiastic. The government, with Ebert as president and Walter Rathenau as foreign minister, preferred a policy of understanding with the west despite obvious difficulties. The Soviet diplomats were nevertheless able to attain their aim by a clever exploitation of the conditions surrounding the Genoa Conference.

Largely under the sponsorship of British Prime Minister David Lloyd George, the conference was called to meet in the spring of 1922. Its aim was to attempt to stabilize the European economic scene and to obtain a settlement with the Soviet Union. It was the first post-war conference to which Germany and the Soviet Union had been invited. Since France refused to include the question of German reparations on the agenda, the tsarist debts and the nationalized property became the main items of discussion. The Soviet representatives now countered the Allied claims by presenting their own bill for losses supposedly caused by the intervention. Countering the Allied sum of approximately 14 billion dollars, the Soviets produced one of 60 billion. Although the Genoa Conference failed, the Soviet representatives were able to use one aspect of the discussions to their own advantage. Article 116 of the Treaty of Versailles, drafted by the Allies in favor of a hoped-for future non-Bolshevik government, left the way open for such a regime to present a reparations bill to Germany. The German government now feared that the Allies would use the provision to gain support from the Soviet representatives. Although there was no Soviet intention to invoke it, the clause did provide a lever to persuade the reluctant German leaders to negotiate a political treaty.

On its way to Genoa the Soviet delegation, headed by Chicherin, had stopped in Berlin. Here discussions were carried on with German officials on the terms of a possible treaty. The German government, however, did not wish to sign such a document on the eve of the conference. Once at Genoa German fears concerning a pro-Bolshevik interpretation of Article 116 and of the possible formation of a front of the Soviet Union, France, and Britain against Germany caused a re-assessment of the situation. The Soviet representatives, ably playing upon German apprehensions, were thus able to persuade Rathenau to sign the Treaty of Rapallo, which was concluded on April 16. This pact re-established full diplomatic relations between the two countries and it provided for a mutual cancellation of all debts and claims. The question of reparations, tsarist debts, and nationalized property was thus settled. The signature of the agreement marked the failure of the Genoa Conference and of Allied policy. For the Soviet Union it assured that an economic front of capitalist states would not be formed. Germany had avoided what had apparently been a danger of diplomatic and economic isolation. Nicholas M. Krestinsky now became the Soviet ambassador to Berlin; Ulrich Brockdorff-Rantzau represented Germany in Moscow.

Despite these developments many in Germany remained dubious about the wisdom of Soviet ties. Moreover, events again tended to divide the governments. Communist attempts to promote a revolt during the French occupation of the Ruhr have already been described. Not only did the Soviet government not aid Germany in time of crisis, but the opportunity was exploited by the Communist Party to try to overturn the regime. The events of 1923 weakened the hand of those who wished an eastern policy. In May, 1924 the German police entered the premises of the Soviet trade delegation in Berlin ostensibly in search of a prisoner. They used the occasion to examine the files in the offices. In protest Krestinsky left and trade negotiations were interrupted. The matter was smoothed over by the diplomats, but it was apparent to the Soviet government that Germany did not intend to rely solely on the Rapallo connection.

In fact, the Ruhr invasion and the subsequent massive inflation led the German government, now under Gustav Stresemann, to adopt a contrary course. Convinced that the primary need for Germany was the improvement of its relations with the western states, he stood strongly for a policy of the fulfillment of the treaties. The success of this course of action was shown in the settlement of the reparations problem in the Dawes Plan and in the subsequent large American loans that were obtained. The apparent reconciliation of Germany and the victor states was not welcomed in Moscow.

The height of the Stresemann policy of reconciliation was reached with the signing of the Locarno pacts in October, 1925. The heart of these agreements was a treaty signed by France, Germany, and Belgium accepting their frontiers as permanent and providing for the demilitarization of the Rhineland. Although the agreement did not cover the German eastern frontier, France signed parallel pacts with both Poland and Czechoslovakia. As part of the general arrangement Germany joined the League of Nations in 1926.

Throughout the period of these negotiations the Soviet government urged closer political and economic ties on Germany. Although more concerned with the west, whence loans could be gained, than with the impoverished Soviet state, the German government had an obvious interest in maintaining the eastern relationship. On October 12, 1925 an important commercial treaty was signed. On April 24, 1926 the Berlin Treaty was concluded. Its terms guaranteed that neither signator would join in an attack on or an alliance against the other power. A reaffirmation of the Rapallo policy, it also resembled the Reinsurance Treaty of Bismarck's day.

EAST AND NEAR EAST

Although in the years after the Bolshevik revolution Soviet policy remained most concerned with events in Europe, it was also involved in Asian affairs, in particular in relation to the new Turkish state and to the civil turmoil in China. With Turkey the Soviet government tended to follow in the path of its tsarist predecessors. In contrast, in China communist ideological as well as great power considerations played an important role in Soviet decisions.

In the post-war period the Near East witnessed the final resolution of the issue that had been of prime importance in nineteenth-century diplomacy—the eastern question. The Soviet government was to have a major influence over the final settlement, although that had not been the intention of the Allies. At the end of the hostilities the Ottoman Empire, like the Central Powers, was the victim of a highly punitive peace treaty. In the Treaty of Sèvres of June, 1920 Asiatic territories of the empire were divided among the victors along the lines of the secret treaties. In eastern Anatolia an independent Armenia and an autonomous Kurdistan were established. In the west the Greek government was given the right to occupy the city of Smyrna and its hinterland for five years. A plebiscite, whose results could be foretold if the territory remained under Greek control, was to determine the final distribution of the territory. Under the cover of the mandate system France and Britain partitioned the Arab lands between themselves, with French influence preponderant in Syria and British dominant in Palestine and the Meso-potamian valley. The great nineteenth-century issue of the Straits was, as could be expected, settled along lines of British pre-war thinking. The Straits were now to be open almost without control to ships of war, obviously giving Britain free access to the Soviet southern shores. Ottoman sovereignty was limited in that the Straits area was internationalized and put under the control of a commission.

This peace, based on nineteenth-century imperial principles previously reflected in the Cyprus Convention of 1878, by its very drastic provisions produced a strong reaction in the Otto-man lands. Already a Turkish nationalist movement under the able leadership of Mustafa Kemal had arisen, with its base in Ankara. Two centers of political authority now came to exist in the country. Kemal refused to accept the treaty, but Sultan Mo-hammed VI did sign, an action that contributed to his final down-fall in 1922. These violent events gave the Soviet government a wedge for the establishment of relations with the nationalist regime.

Although Mustafa Kemal accepted the loss of the Arab prov-inces, he was determined to defend Anatolia. In April, 1920 he negotiated a military agreement with the Soviet government, which was, of course, deeply concerned with conditions in east-ern Anatolia. In October the Turkish army moved against the independent Armenian state, an action approved of in Moscow in view of similar Soviet problems with separatist Armenian move-ments. In March the nationalist regime made a peace treaty with the Soviet Union in which Batum was returned to Soviet control, but Turkey was allowed to keep Kars and Ardahan. The subse-quent co-operation of the two military forces made the Soviet reconquest of Caucasian lands easier.

Soviet military aid and advisors also contributed to Kemal's victory over the Greek army. The atheistic Soviet regime was not burdened by any sentimental considerations for Balkan Or-thodox Christians. In June, 1920 the Greek government made the unwise decision to try to widen its territorial control around

Smyrna and commenced an advance into the interior of Anatolia. In the fall of 1921 the Greek forces were decisively defeated and compelled to retreat to the sea. The Turkish capture of Smyrna and the precipitous flight of the Greek population followed. Subsequent agreements on an exchange of populations between Greece and Turkey and the final deposition of the Ottoman sultan brought the eastern question to a conclusion.

The Turkish military victories made a revision of the Treaty of Sèvres inevitable. A conference was therefore opened in Lausanne in November, 1922. The Soviet government was invited to participate, but only in those sessions concerning the Straits. The Soviet delegation, headed by Chicherin, supported what had been the tsarist position for most of the nineteenth century. Acutely aware of its weakness in the Black Sea and remembering that the Allied intervention had come through there, the Soviet government wished the Straits closed to all warships except those of the riparian powers. Turkey also was to have the right to fortify the area. The British position remained the maintenance of the provisions of Sèvres. When the Turkish representatives swung more to the British side, the Soviet stand was weakened. The compromise solution reached in the agreement of July, 1923 was actually more in the British interest. The Straits were demilitarized; outside powers were to be allowed to send ships into the Black Sea but with the limitation that no one power could despatch ships whose total tonnage was more than the Soviet Black Sea fleet. France and Britain, in alliance, could thus send in twice the tonnage. This agreement lasted until 1936, when it was replaced by the Treaty of Montreux, which allowed the Turkish government to fortify and control the Straits.

In addition to establishing good relations with the Turkish Republic, the Soviet government also carried on an active policy in regard to Persia and Afghanistan. In both countries the chief adversary remained the British Empire. Although in the agreement of 1907 Britain and Russia had partitioned Persia into spheres of interest separated by a neutral zone, the competition for control of the entire country continued. In 1915 in a secret treaty Russia had agreed that Britain could take the middle zone in return for Russian domination of the Turkish Straits. During the period of civil war and intervention the Soviet government had been separated from Persia by the White armies. With their defeat and the renewal of control in the Caucasus, Soviet influence could again be exerted in Persian politics. At first a revolutionary policy was pursued; a Persian Communist Party was organized and for a short time the independent Ghilan Republic in the north was supported. In 1921, however, in line with general policy, it was decided that an agreement with the Persian government would be a better alternative. In February a treaty was signed in which the Soviet government renounced the tsarist agreements, with the exception of some regarding Caspian fishing rights. At this time regular relations were also established with Afghanistan, with whom a treaty of friendship was signed in 1921. This state remained as a buffer between the Soviet Central Asian lands and India, but the Afghan king accepted a Soviet subsidy.

Despite the Soviet emphasis on Europe, in the 1920's events transpired in China that were of immense importance for Soviet policy. In 1912 the old Manchu dynasty collapsed. The new government of the Republic of China could not maintain control and after several years the county deteriorated into a condition of anarchy with rival centers and competing warlords holding the real political power. In this situation Soviet policy aimed in two directions. Diplomatic relations were desired with Peking, where a government existed that was still formally recognized by the powers. Political assistance was also offered to Sun Yat-sen's nationalist Kuomintang government at Canton in southern China, which was also under local warlord protection. In 1921 and 1922 the Soviet government sought first to negotiate with the Peking regime. However, as long as the situation in the Far East remained unstable, the Chinese government hesitated to conclude an agreement. It disliked the continuance of Russian domination in Outer Mongolia, and it sought complete control of the Chinese Eastern Railway. In 1923 Leo M. Karakhan came to Peking as the Soviet representative. In May, 1924 he succeeded in concluding a treaty that re-established diplomatic relations and provided for regulating the operation of the railroad in a manner that preserved Soviet authority. This settlement was not satisfactory to the Chinese, and in the summer of 1929 they attempted to seize the railroad by force. Soviet troops entered Manchuria and occupied two points. The railroad was subsequently restored to Soviet control, but diplomatic relations were broken.

Relations with Peking and after 1927 with the Chiang Kai-shek regime in Nanking were thus determined predominantly by Soviet interests in Manchuria and north China that paralleled those of the tsarist regime. In contrast, in dealing with the Kuomintang ideology, Marxist theory concerning backward and colonial areas in particular was to be of great importance. Obviously China in the 1920's had none of the economic or social prerequisites for a Marxist revolution; the contrast with Germany was strong. With virtually no industry, a Chinese proletariat could not be the base of the revolution. Nor did the country have the mass of disillusioned, impoverished but armed, soldiers and sailors who played such a role in the Soviet revolt. However, Lenin had dealt with exactly this problem in his works on imperialism where he had linked the colonial areas with the fate of the great capitalist states. He could thus call for an alliance of the proletariat of the advanced industrial lands with the oppressed classes of the colonial areas.

Marxist theory also provided a basis on which the Soviet government could support national movements in Asia led by the bourgeoisie. Since China, like other colonial areas, had yet to go through a capitalist stage of development on the road to socialism, parties aiming at this goal could in this sense be regarded as progressive and worthy of assistance. The achievement of national goals, which in Asia usually meant the removing of foreign, chiefly British, domination, would serve the further aim of cutting off a source of profits from a capitalist country. Once the idea of co-operation with national liberation movements was accepted, the problem remained of how this policy should be carried out. The communist parties in Asia were weak; should they join the stronger bourgeois national groups, they might be absorbed by them. To meet this danger the Comintern leadership adopted a policy which was first applied in China—that of the "united front from above." Communist parties could join bourgeois movements, but they were to remain apart and retain their separate organization.

On the strength of these decisions Soviet representatives were able to act with the Kuomintang. Although possessing great personal authority and prestige, Sun Yat-sen at this time headed a party that was little more than an association of politicians. With no real military power of his own, he was at the mercy of the warlords around Canton. Although he was not himself a Marxian socialist, Sun saw the advantages of working with the Soviet Union. In the summer of 1922 Joffe visited both Peking and Canton. In 1923 he reached an agreement with the Kuomintang, according to which Chinese Communists, whose party had been founded only in July, 1921, could join the Kuomintang as individuals but they were also to keep their separate political identity. For China the most important Soviet representative was Michael M. Borodin, an emissary of the Comintern, who arrived in 1923. Under his guidance the Kuomintang was thoroughly reorganized along the lines of the communist organizations. It now became a mass party, but its ideology was that of Sun Yat-sen and not of Lenin. At the same time the Chinese nationalists acquired an effective military force of their own. Both Sun and the Soviet representatives were interested in this aspect of the Chinese situation. In the colonial world the Soviet Union was primarily concerned with combatting Britain; southern China was a British sphere. The Soviet general Vasily K. Blucher, a hero of the civil war in Siberia, was thus sent to China. In 1923 a protégé of Sun Yat-sen's, the young officer Chiang Kai-shek, went to Moscow for training. When he returned to China he was placed in charge of the Whampoa Military Academy, which had just been founded. The new nationalist army was chiefly led by officers trained there.

The death of Sun in 1925 inaugurated a struggle for the control of his party between the left and right wings. At issue was also the position of the Communist Party in the organization. The conflict in views between the bourgeois national basis of the party and the radical left was now becoming increasingly apparent. By 1926, with military power behind him, Chiang was emerging as the leader of the movement. Some measures were taken against the Communists at this time. In the same year the Kuomintang leadership decided to launch a Northern Expedition against the warlords to widen its territorial base; Chiang was in command of this operation. Despite the moves that had been taken against them, the Communist Party strongly supported the Kuomintang and contributed to the victory through a propaganda campaign in the areas to be occupied. The Soviet military advisors assisted with the war plans. The campaign progressed with great successes and few casualities. By the spring of 1927 the Kuomintang forces were in control of most of China along the Yangtze River.

Parallel with the military advances, the tension within the Kuomintang mounted. In April, 1927 Chiang made a clear stand against the Communists and the left wing of the Kuomintang. His occupation of Shanghai was followed by a massacre of Communists in that city and elsewhere. In July the Communist Party was expelled from the Kuomintang and Borodin returned to the Soviet Union. Even the left wing of the Kuomintang purged its ranks of Communists.

This disaster to Soviet plans for China was thoroughly debated in Moscow. Chiefly under Stalin's influence, a new policy was adopted. The Chinese Communist Party, despite its small size and lack of preparation, was now directed to act against the Kuomintang. Although a series of small urban uprisings took place, the situation proved hopeless. Particularly significant for the future, however, was the occurrence of small peasant revolts in central China, notably the Autumn Harvest Uprising in September, 1927 under the leadership of Mao Tse-tung. With the failure of these revolts, Mao and his followers withdrew to the old bandit stronghold of Chingkanshan in Kiangsi Province. A final revolt was also organized in Canton in December, 1927. Several thousand participants were able to seize the city for three days and institute the Canton Commune. The nationalist army was able to suppress this rebellion with little difficulty. Having used Soviet and Comintern assistance to achieve victory, the Kuomintang now broke relations with the Soviet Union. The revolts had almost eliminated the Communists as an effective political force in China.

The Soviet program for China in the 1920's thus ended in a total breakdown. Relations had been severed with both the Peking regime and the revolutionary Kuomintang. Communist tactics in China had failed. In the summer of 1928, at the sixth congress of the Comintern, the Chinese question, among other issues, was debated. The original policy was reversed. Henceforth communist parties were directed not to co-operate in bourgeois-national movements like the Kuomintang; instead they should participate only in those actions which they themselves directed.

*   *   *   *   *

During the first decade after the Bolshevik seizure of power, the figure of Lenin predominated over all other Soviet leaders, even in the years immediately after his death. The spirit and methods of this period were to disappear with the gradual tightening of Stalin's hold on the system. At the time of the revolution most of the principal Bolshevik leaders had traveled outside of Russia. They regarded themselves as part of the world, not just the Russsian, socialist revolutionary movement. Even after their victory they were at first primarily concerned with the spread of the revolution rather than its immediate fate in Russia. They accepted the harsh terms in the Treaty of Brest-Litovsk on the assumption that the agreement would soon be overturned. Until his exile Trotsky argued for the idea of permanent or world revolution—that is, the belief that unless the movement spread, it would die. With the conviction that success was inevitable some time in the future and with his personal strength and popularity, Lenin was able to allow a great deal of freedom of discussion within the party without endangering his pre-eminent position.

Tolerance of disagreement did not extend to the recognition of a real opposition group, but it did allow a wider discussion of issues and possible alternatives among party members.

In assessing the gains and losses at this time in foreign relations a separation should perhaps be made between the interests of the Russian state and that of the victorious Bolshevik Party. Considered from the viewpoint of the nation, the war and the postwar period were a complete disaster. The change of regime and the subsequent controversies with the western powers meant that not only would the Soviet government not share in the spoils of the Allied victory, but also that it would be treated almost as an enemy power. The peace treaties resulted in the detachment of large areas of what had been tsarist territory. Moreover, in Europe and Asia, the Soviet Union was to be excluded from influence in areas such as the Balkans, where at least a partial sphere of influence had previously been held. In addition, in part because of the nature of the regime, the Soviet state was now without reliable allies and friends in what was a really dangerous period of national weakness. Germany, as we have seen, wished to keep a foot in both camps. The dangers of isolation for the Russian lands have been repeatedly emphasized in this account.

Taken from a party and ideological standpoint, the judgment is not so grim. The great achievement of the Bolshevik regime was the fact that it maintained its power in a period of civil turmoil and foreign intervention. If Marxist assumptions concerning the inevitable political future of mankind were true, the Bolshevik capture of the Russian state alone would be no mean accomplishment. In addition, despite the nature of its political system, the Soviet government was able to achieve some sort of working relationship with the capitalist states. On the ideological front the chief failure was the inability to organize successful revolts abroad, in particular in Germany and China. The next years, however, were to mark a reversal of this situation and to justify many of the predictions of the early Bolshevik leaders on the spread of world revolution, although not always in the form expected.

VIII

𐌋𐌋𐌋𐌋𐌋𐌋

Stalin

If Lenin had provided the ideological direction and early leadership to the Bolshevik movement, Stalin was to lead the Soviet Union before his death to the position of being one of the two great powers remaining after the disaster of the Second World War. The change in the character of the leadership with Stalin's rise to power was comparatively abrupt. Stalin, unlike Lenin, Trotsky, and other Bolshevik leaders, had no experience outside of his country. Born in 1879 in Gori, Georgia, Joseph Vissarionovich Dzhugashvili was the son of a shoemaker. He attended school first in local church establishments and then went to a seminary for Orthodox priests in Tiflis. After being expelled, he became active in revolutionary movements in the Caucasus. In 1912 he became a member of the Central Committee of the Party in St. Petersburg. He was arrested and in 1913 was sent into exile to Siberia, where he remained until 1917. His first duties after the revolution were organizational in nature; his reputation was based on his skill in these areas. Unlike his two great predecessors he was not a theoretician, although he was to prove to have definite ideas on foreign policy. As a man he preferred to live in seclusion; he did not mingle with the crowds or become a familiar public figure. Under his direction the relative openness and the internationalism of the Lenin period were bound to end.

With Stalin's assumption of power two changes important for foreign policy occurred. First, in a move against internationalism, Stalin now emphasized the importance of protecting and developing socialism in the Soviet Union. The resources of the Soviet state were not to be devoted to spreading or supporting revolution abroad; the internal development of the country along communist lines was to receive the chief attention. Second, together with this determination radical changes were introduced within the country. The New Economic Policy was replaced by the program of the Five Year Plans, whose aim was rapid industrialization and, as a base, the collectivization of the peasantry. This move was achieved against violent opposition and at the cost of another period of internal chaos. Stalin personally had little sympathy for the peasantry. In his eyes they were a remnant of feudal society doomed to disappear. Collectivization was completed by 1934, but only after a period of famine and with great loss of life. The violence of these changes at home necessarily had to be accompanied by a tightening of control within the state. The role of the secret police became more important and the last vestiges of opposition to Stalin were removed at this time and during the purges. In the 1930's the Soviet Union became a totalitarian state.

RUSSIA AND EUROPE, 1927-1933

Foreign policy in the period of the first Five Year Plan, 1928-1933, reflected the internal conditions. As in previous periods of stress at home, the state needed quiet abroad and peace in Europe; internal affairs took great precedence over foreign policy. Since alliances could not be contracted with other powers, efforts were made to assure at least the support of the communist parties. In a declaration of December, 1927 Stalin stated that the era of capitalist stabilization was over; a new and dangerous period could be expected. The sixth congress of the Comintern, meeting from July to September, 1928, echoed this judgment. The necessity of all communists as their first duty to defend the Soviet state, the world's only communist government, was strongly emphasized. In addition, a less flexible front was presented in regard to other political questions. The sixth congress not only denounced the policy of co-operation with bourgeois national liberation movements like the Kuomintang but also renewed and intensified the attack on the European socialist parties. Although under previous decisions it had been an accepted practice for communists to join in united fronts with socialists, these parties were now termed "social fascists" and denounced as the chief danger to communism.

Despite these tough words from the Comintern, the Soviet government itself followed a different course and in fact sought a détente in its relations with all the powers. With a difficult situation at home, it now chose to join in the pacts and conferences that were characteristic of the period and to present a peaceful face to the world. The cessation of an active role in colonial revolutionary movements aided in this endeavor. At this time also a new foreign commissar was chosen. Chicherin had been ill for several years, and was replaced in 1930 by Maxim Litvinov, a leading Soviet diplomat in the preceding decade who had often appeared as his rival. Although policy was still made by Stalin and in the Politburo, Litvinov, like his predecessor, did have certain ideas on foreign relations. In the ten years before the revolution he had lived in England and his wife was English. On the basis of his personal experiences he was less enthusiastic about the Rapallo policy and more inclined to co-operate with the western victor powers. He was also less antagonistic toward the Versailles settlement and associations attached to it, such as the League of Nations. During his period in office Soviet policy looked better to the western powers. At a time when Soviet interest demanded security, this representative spoke in the manner approved by the liberal westerner.

Most apparent was the new Russian attitude toward international organizations. In the late 1920's a great reaction against World War I occurred throughout Europe. The uselessness of the conflict was emphasized and a new view of its origins tended to undermine the bases on which the Treaty of Versailles stood. In a great effort to assure that another such catastrophe would not occur, there followed a period of attempting to prevent war by the signature of treaties and declarations and through disarmament conferences. Although in retrospect these activities seem amazingly futile, they reflected an extreme aversion to the recurrence of the events of 1914. While not a member of the League, the Soviet Union did join the Preparatory Disarmament Commission in Geneva in 1927. Here Litvinov, the Soviet representative, like Trotsky at Brest-Litovsk, used the opportunity for a massive propaganda effort. He urged radical measures— the immediate abolition of all military forces and the destruction of weapons of war. As could be expected, only militarily weak countries, like Germany and the Soviet Union itself, were open to such suggestions. The French, whose position in Europe depended on the maintenance of artificial barriers, were, of course, opposed. Although most powers were extremely sceptical of the Soviet position, Litvinov did achieve a degree of popularity in liberal and leftist circles.

The Soviet Union also accepted the United States-sponsored Kellogg-Briand Pact although she was not invited to be one of the original signatories. This agreement, which called for the renunciation of war as an instrument of policy, was ratified in July, 1929. Almost at once the Soviet government violated the principles of the agreement by sending its forces into Manchuria in the dispute over the Chinese Eastern Railway. However, in conformance with the spirit of the time, the Soviet Union became the sponsor of a regional treaty, the so-called Litvinov Protocol. In it the Soviet Union and her neighbors, Poland, Latvia and Estonia, all solemnly promised not to attack each other. Lithuania, the city of Danzig, Turkey, and Persia, but not Finland, endorsed the document. The illusory nature of these compacts was soon demonstrated.

From a more practical standpoint great improvements were gained in Soviet relations with the two greatest capitalist powers —Britain and the United States. Another Labour victory in 1929 made possible the restoration of relations with Britain in October, 1929. In 1930 a temporary trade treaty was signed. In 1933 the sixteen-year break in relations with Washington was ended. Both the United States and the Soviet Union now wanted an end to this abnormal situation. With the election of a Democrat, Franklin D. Roosevelt, a change was possible. Moreover, the United States was at this time suffering from the effects of the depression, and the possibilities of trade held attractions. For Moscow the principal consideration was possible American assistance in the Far East, where Japan was becoming increasingly more dangerous. In the period of the civil war and the intervention the American role as a check on Japan had been useful. Co-operation in this field in the future was desired.

For these discussions the Soviet Union sent its chief negotiator, Litvinov. As with other states, the problem of the tsarist debts and the nationalized industry proved a major barrier. Like Britain, the United States was also concerned about propaganda and subversion. The final agreement left the debt question open; the Soviet Union dropped claims for compensation for the intervention. The American demand for assurances on non-intervention in internal affairs was also accepted. Although ambassadors were now exchanged, no real improvement in relations occurred. The United States, on an isolationist course, was unable to be an aid in the Far East; impoverished Russia could not absorb significant amounts of American goods.

Relations with France until 1933 followed their previous course. Marked coolness continued to be their characteristic. In the same manner, the German link remained much as before. Although Berlin did not rely exclusively on the Rapallo association, the two governments were on friendly terms. The military cooperation continued; economic relations were good. The Soviet Union was able to secure credits from Germany, who in turn had borrowed from the west, and obtained needed machinery and other items for the completion of the Five Year Plan. At this time Germany provided half of the Soviet imports. Meanwhile, however, the Soviet trade partner was collapsing politically and economically.

The declarations given at the Comintern meeting in 1928 that the capitalist world was on the edge of a new crisis were indeed correct. The Great Depression of 1929 to 1934 created the mass poverty and unemployment so lovingly depicted in socialist literature as the inevitable accompaniment of the western system. Being itself in a period of economic readjustment and operating under a program that did not stress world revolutionary activity, the Soviet Union was not in a position to exploit the situation. Moreover, the increasingly authoritarian nature of the Soviet system alienated world liberal leaders. The police-state methods and the course of events in the country did not attract working-class and, in particular, organized labor's sympathies.

While the Soviet Union was thus prevented from using the world catastrophe effectively, another aspect of its ideological program, as enunciated in the same Comintern conference was to have a tragic effect on the political evolution of her best associate in Europe and on the fate of the only foreign mass communist party. The outcome took place at a time when the Soviet government could not afford foreign adventures or see the creation of a dangerous situation in central Europe. As could be expected, the depression in Germany, following years of foreign disasters and economic turmoil, had the most devastating political effects. The situation was ripe for the rise of political extremists. Conditions should also have been favorable for the strengthening of the communist cause. In conformance with Comintern directives the German Communist Party in the 1920's and early 1930's designated the Social Democrats as the chief enemy. In practice, this policy meant that the Communists would co-operate with the nationalists and the National Socialist Party of Adolf Hitler against the parties who supported the Weimar Republic, that is, the Social Democrats, the Catholic Center, and the Liberals. In voting with the extreme right the Communist Party thus not only hurt the socialists but also undermined the constitutional system itself.

One of the difficulties faced by the Communist leadership at this time was its apparent misjudgment of fascist movements. The Soviet Union had already entered into good relations with Mussolini's Italy. Fascism appeared not a competing ideology of great potential, but rather an extreme offshoot of capitalist doctrine. The Nazi Party was thus regarded as another bourgeois organization, not a competing revolutionary body. The very extremeness of its doctrines appeared a point of weakness. Should it come to power, it appeared that capitalism in Germany would collapse just that much faster. The Communist association with the German right was, of course, directed to the defeat of the rival Social Democrats, not to the victory of the nationalist parties.

The fate of the German Communist Party and the rise of Hitler is well reflected in the elections of the early 1930's. In 1930 the Communist Party, the third strongest in the country, had 77 deputies. In 1931 it joined with the Nazis in an unsuccessful attempt to bring down the Social Democratic government of Prussia. In the very significant elections of July, 1932 the Communists increased their representatives to 89, but the Nazis received 230 and the Social Democrats 133. Most important, in the polls 37.5% voted Nazi and 14.5% Communist. The majority of the German electorate thus chose candidates whose parties stood for the destruction of the Weimar Republic. Despite the growth of Nazi strength, the Communist Party still did not see the real danger. In January, 1933 by a regular, legal process Hitler became chancellor; new elections were then ordered. Thereafter in swift succession came a series of events that ended in the downfall of the Communist Party. In February the Reichstag (parliament) building in Berlin was burned; the Nazis blamed the Communists and launched a great campaign based on the Red Menace. Nevertheless, in the March elections the Communist Party was able to win 5 million votes. With the support of the Catholic Center, which joined the other parties of the right, Hitler was now able to gain from the Reichstag the right to rule by decree for four years. He immediately moved against all of the organizations on the left; Communist and Social Democrat alike went to prison.

With the collapse of the Weimar Republic, an event aided by Communist miscalculations, the Soviet Union saw arising in central Europe a government not only based on an anticommunist program, but with a leader who had not hidden his ideas on foreign policy. Three paragraphs from Hitler's book, *Mein Kampf*, published in 1923, well summarize his early goals and his attitude toward the east.

The foreign policy of a folkish State is charged with guaranteeing the existence on this planet of the race embraced by the State, by establishing between the number and growth of the population, on the one hand, and the size and value of the soil and territory, on the other hand, a viable, natural relationship. . . . Only a sufficiently extensive area on this globe guarantees a nation freedom of existence. . . .

Just as our forefathers did not get the land on which we are living today as a gift from Heaven, but had to conquer it by risking their lives . . . only the might of a triumphant sword will in the future assign us territory, and with it life for our nation.

But if we talk about new soil and territory in Europe today, we can think primarily only of *Russia* and its vassal border states. [1]

The question remained whether the responsible leader of a great nation would put such doctrines into practice.

COLLECTIVE SECURITY AND POPULAR FRONTS

Despite the clarity of the Nazi pronouncements on the Soviet Union and communism and the specific actions taken to destroy the Party in Germany, there was no immediate break in relations.

1. Adolf Hitler, *Mein Kampf* (New York: Reynal and Hitchcock, 1939), pp. 935, 949-51.

In fact, in May, 1933, Germany ratified a renewal of the 1926 Treaty of Berlin. In December, 1933 Litvinov declared that the Soviet Union could have friendly relations with capitalist states of all varieties. The Comintern continued to direct its attacks on the socialist parties, and Britain was still regarded as the major leader of the hostile forces. It was obviously difficult for Soviet leaders to adjust to the fact that fascism was more than a decadent form of capitalism and that they were facing a country with potentially expansionist aims in the east. The first great shock to the Soviet government appears to have occurred in January, 1934 when Germany and Poland signed a ten-year non-aggression pact. Although innocuous in its wording, the agreement signified a change of front; Germany and the Soviet Union no longer stood against Poland. Instead Poland and Germany might combine against the communist state. The beginning of 1934 thus saw a moving apart of Berlin and Moscow. By mutual agreement the former military co-operation was ended. German officers and equipment were withdrawn from Soviet territory.

The loss of Germany was serious for Soviet policy. As in the past the country could not remain isolated, particularly in consideration of the hostile nature of the Nazi regime. Within the Soviet Union a shift of emphasis toward patriotism began. Stalin now sought to stand as the representative of Russian national feeling. The size of the army was also increased. Most important the Soviet government next followed in the path of the tsarist regime and looked to Paris, since connections with central Europe had been broken.

France, as we have seen, was the center of her own security system, one based on alliance with Poland and the countries of the Little Entente. In 1934 another group, the Balkan Entente, composed of Yugoslavia, Rumania, Turkey, and Greece, appeared to join this constellation. Formidable as this alignment seemed, it was in fact intrinsically weak. Constituted primarily as leagues of victor states, these combinations directed their attention toward the defeated powers, particularly Austria, Hungary, and Bulgaria. They did not want to tangle with a great nation. With the rise of intensely nationalist and revisionist Germany backed increasingly by Italy, France, too, saw the need of strengthening her alliance system. The little powers were not enough; in the past Britain had failed to back the French position in what Paris considered an adequate manner.

In the face of the new dangers the Franco-Russian rapprochement was relatively swift. In September, 1934 the Soviet Union joined the League of Nations with strong French backing; Germany had withdrawn the previous year. In May, 1935 France and the Soviet Union signed a mutual assistance pact. Two weeks later a similar agreement was concluded between Moscow and the Czechoslovak government. However, the second pact contained the specific provision that neither power needed to aid the other unless France acted first. The treaties were thus tied together, but with the burden of action on Paris.

The Franco-Russian agreement, although significant, was not the equivalent of the alliance of the 1890's. In sharp contrast to the earlier period, no great enthusiasm or public demonstrations accompanied the event. Most significant was the fact that no military conventions were ever concluded and no staff consultations were held. In May Stalin issued a statement approving French rearmament. As a result, the French Communist Party desisted from further opposition to French military preparations, but that was about the extent of co-operation in the military field. The alliance left much to be desired from both sides. The agreement was of no assistance to the Soviet government against Japan. There was also the problem of how it could be carried out. The Soviet Union had no common border with Germany. Soviet armies could not aid France or Czechoslovakia without crossing Polish or Rumanian territory, a problem which was to prove insuperable in later negotiations. Moreover, there was no basic reason for France to support the Soviet communist regime or the Soviet Union to make sacrifices in the interest of the maintenance of the French Empire or the treaty structure of Europe that France favored. Two major French allies, Poland and Rumania, held territory that the Soviet Union regarded as irredenta. Little more than the common fear of the revival of Germany held the two together.

The Nazi danger caused a shift not only in the Soviet relations with the capitalist powers but also in Comintern policy in regard to foreign communist parties. The Soviet Union, in great need of western allies, did not now wish to weaken the governments of these states. With the French Communist Party as the model, a policy was thus adopted which had it been applied earlier in Germany might have prevented the Nazi rise to power. In the spring of 1934 Maurice Thorez, the head of the French Communist Party, was instructed to co-operate with socialist and moderate, centrist parties to defend the French Republic and to resist fascism. This change was clearly enunciated at the seventh and last congress of the Comintern, held in August, 1935. The president was the Bulgarian Communist leader George Dimitrov, who had been one of the accused in the trials connected with the burning of the Reichstag. In the declarations made at the congress, the capitalist states were divided into those who were aggressive and those who were peaceful. Communist parties were instructed to support the peace-loving, bourgeois democracies until conditions were more propitious for a communist victory. With these new directives communist parties were again free to join in alliances with socialists and in organizations against fascism. The popular front policy was carried out in practice in just three places—France, Spain, and China—and only for a limited time. The height was in the second half of 1936. In no place was this policy of co-operation really successful.

The most important front organization was formed in France, where in November, 1935 an alliance was made between the Socialists, the Communists, and the Radical Socialists. They adopted a common program but they conducted separate electoral campaigns. When victory was achieved, a government was formed under the Socialist Leon Blum. The Communists did not join this administration, but they supported its policies. It lasted until 1938 when the coalition fell apart on the Spanish issue.

By 1935, therefore, the Soviet Union had become a member

of the League of Nations, it had a new alliance with France, and the communist parties were instructed to work to support the western capitalist governments. The new Soviet orientation, however, did nothing to halt the advance of the three active powers—Germany, Italy, and Japan. The main burden of meeting this diplomatic challenge fell not on the Soviet Union but on France and, in particular, Britain. The latter was in a difficult situation. The British government found itself the victim of a divided public opinion. Those with liberal views opposed the rearming of the country and "entangling" alliances; the right did not wish a close alignment with the Soviet Union. Yet without adequate arms and allies the western states could not stop the revisionist powers.

The western nations, in particular Britain, were themselves in an ideological dilemma. In seeking to gain their objectives neither Germany nor Italy put forward great programs at once. Germany based her first moves on the right of self-determination, a principle accepted by both British and Soviet opinion. In 1935 Germany had not yet attained its ethnic frontiers. Italy advanced its claims on the right of a great power to colonies. It was very difficult for the greatest colonial power on earth to stand on principle against one nation who had not attained real national unity and another whose colonial ambitions were modest, even in comparison to the gains which France and Britain had amassed in the recent peace treaties. The basically oppressive nature of British and French colonial rule was repeatedly emphasized in Soviet propaganda too.

Western division and frustrations were, of course, of little concern to the Soviet Union. Faced with the hard fact that anticommunist governments that might eventually challenge Soviet control in her own territories were advancing, the Soviet government saw that the victor powers were doing little or nothing to maintain the treaties or to strengthen their own position. From 1935 to 1939 a series of crises passed in swift succession. In all of these the western states retreated with little or no consultation with the Soviet government. The parade of events commenced with the German unilateral denunciation of certain clauses of the Versailles treaty relating to military affairs. In March, 1935 Berlin announced that Germany already had an air force and would introduce conscription. In June, nevertheless, Britain made a naval agreement with Germany in which the latter power agreed to limit its fleet to 35 per cent of the British. In October Italy invaded Ethiopia; in the next months the powerlessness of the League of Nations to deal with aggression was amply demonstrated. In March, 1936, using the excuse that the Franco-Russian alliance was not compatible with Locarno, Germany denounced that agreement and declared that the Rhineland would be remilitarized. This last event had a great effect on the French alliance system. Once the Rhine gateway into Germany was fortified, it would be difficult for France to go to the aid of her eastern allies. In 1929 construction had already begun on the great defensive fortification the Maginot Line. In the next years French money went into this formidable fortress rather than into planes and tanks. This action seemed to indicate that France in a crisis would prefer to sit behind her wall rather than launch an attack on German territory.

The first Nazi moves involved primarily the reversal of what were in fact unequal terms imposed on the defeated by the victor in the Treaty of Versailles, and ones that should have been settled by negotiation earlier. Other German actions, in particular the intervention in the Spanish Civil War and the destruction of Czechoslovakia in 1939, involved other principles. Of these events the Soviet Union was most directly engaged in the Spanish Civil War.

As in France, a Popular Front of left parties was formed in Spain. In February, 1936 it won the elections and organized a government. By July it was faced by a revolt organized in Morocco by Spanish rightist forces. Although the Spanish Communist Party represented but a small proportion of the strength of the Popular Front, the rebels used anticommunist slogans to appeal for support at home and abroad. The government, or Loyalist, forces also sought assistance from outside the country. Both the fascist states and the Soviet Union were quick to respond. Although the Soviet government sent equipment and some advisors, very few Russians arrived. An International Brigade was established, but its ranks were filled mostly by Communists who were not of Soviet nationality.

The entire affair proved to be a disaster for the Popular Front government of Leon Blum. Not wishing to complicate French domestic politics, Blum tried to gain the co-operation of the powers for a policy of strict non-intervention. Although the other states accepted this stand in principle and joined in an international blockade, both the fascist and communist partisans repeatedly violated the agreement. Italy and Germany used Spain to test their weapons. Throughout the crisis the Soviet Union actively backed the republican forces. At Geneva Litvinov consistently supported their position. In 1937, however, aid was gradually tapered off. With no foreign support the Loyalist side was doomed; in March, 1939 General Franco, at the head of the Nationalists, took Madrid.

Meanwhile, in April, 1938, the Blum government fell. It was replaced by a right-center cabinet in which Daladier was premier and George Bonnet foreign minister. With the appointment of this government leadership in European continental affairs passed from France to Britain. There in February, 1938 Lord Halifax replaced Anthony Eden as foreign secretary in the Conservative government headed by Neville Chamberlain. The stage was now set for a new and brief phase in European diplomacy in which the western powers, following a policy of appeasement, attempted to save the peace by their willingness to make reasonable concessions to the revisionist powers as long as such changes were made by regular and legal means.

After 1936 Soviet interest in collective security began to fade. Although rearmament commenced in 1934, a real effort was made after 1936. Between 1937 and June, 1941 the size of the army increased from 590,000 to 4,200,000. The effect on outside opinion of this increase in military strength was largely offset by the negative impression made by the great purges going on at the same time. Starting in 1934 the Communist Party went through a period of great internal convulsion, characterized by the mass arrest and execution of most of the old Bolshevik leaders and others who had been prominent in the government and the Party until then. In August, 1936 a trial of prominent Bolsheviks, including Zinoviev and Kamenev, commenced. For Soviet foreign relations the worst reaction came from the trials of Soviet generals beginning in June, 1937. By the end of this period it has been estimated that about eight million were arrested [2] and hundreds of thousands executed, including Marshal Tukhachevsky and all the former members of Lenin's Politburo but Stalin.

The show trials produced to justify the mass executions caused wonder and perplexity abroad. The accused found themselves charged with impossible crimes, and they all confessed. Members of the Party and the army agreed that they indeed had been plotting with outside powers, usually Germany or Japan, to overthrow the Stalin regime. For the European observer the nature of these trials indicated that either they were an example of the actions of an oppressive and tyrannical regime and the confessions were false, or, even more damaging for the Soviet state, the Communist regime was filled with traitors and opponents of the system. Either way the value of the Soviet Union as an alliance partner declined. Faith in the effectiveness of an army whose officer corps had been largely decimated could not be high.

Meanwhile, the German march forward continued. In March, 1938 Germany took Austria. The French and British governments, although disturbed by the method by which this action was accomplished, did nothing. No consultations were held with the Soviet Union. Since Austria was ethnically German, the *Anschluss* could be justified on the basis of self-determination, but the action had important strategic implications. Czechoslovakia was surrounded and its defenses weakened; the Danube valley was open to Nazi penetration. The eastern European governments now moved closer to Germany. With authoritarian regimes they did not feel politically uncomfortable with the Nazi government. Moreover, the Danubian and Balkan area was linked economically to Germany; this region was simultaneously a market and a source of raw materials for German industry.

2. See Donald W. Treadgold, *Twentieth Century Russia* (Chicago: Rand McNally & Co., 1972), p. 280.

The height of the appeasement policy was reached in the Czech crisis of 1938. After the absorption of Austria, Nazi propaganda next turned to the condition of the three million Germans living in the Sudeten border area of Czechoslovakia. At first the Czech government felt fairly secure because of its mutual assistance treaties with both France and the Soviet Union. However, with Hitler's increasingly belligerent stand the western powers were faced with the possibility that they might indeed have to fight on the issue. Britain was not bound by any treaty. The Czech position was also weakened by the fact that Poland and Hungary supported the German desire to dismember the state. Throughout the crisis the Soviet government advised the Czechs to resist. Assurances were given that Moscow would honor its obligations, which, of course, depended on a prior French action. The problem also remained of how Soviet aid could be given since no common border existed with Czechoslovakia.

The Sudeten German question was decided at the Munich Conference in September, at which Hitler, Mussolini, Chamberlain, and Daladier came to an agreement giving the Sudeten regions to Germany. In later settlements Hungary and Poland also received territory. The Soviet Union was not invited to Munich, nor was it consulted on the final agreement. The conference itself and the apparent front of the western and the fascist powers presented a dangerous diplomatic situation. Relations with the west were bad. The purges were now brought to an end; armaments were again increased.

The Soviet position was considerably eased in the spring of 1939 when Hitler violated both the letter and the spirit of the Munich agreement by marching into Prague and dismembering Czechoslovakia. An independent Slovakia was established; the Czech section, now called Bohemia, became a German protectorate. Hungary annexed the Carpatho-Ukrainian area. At the same time a new German propaganda campaign opened, this time centered on the position of the German minority in Poland and the status of the port of Danzig. These events in central Europe caused an immediate and violent reaction in Britain.

Afraid that Germany now intended to move against Poland, Britain gave that state a territorial guarantee at the end of March. France was already pledged to aid Poland through the mutual assistance pact of 1921. In April the two western powers gave similar assurances to Rumania and Greece; in May Britain signed a treaty with Turkey.

This flurry of diplomatic activity did not compensate for the basic weakness of the French and British position. Should Germany march against Poland, there was in fact very little the western powers could do to assure a Nazi defeat. France had put its efforts into the Maginot Line, not in a striking force. British rearmament had not proceeded far enough. Her air force was sufficient to cover British territory, but not to operate abroad. If Poland was indeed to be defended, the western powers needed the Soviet army. Germany would then be faced with a formidable opposition and the threat of a two front war. Attempts were thus now inaugurated to win Soviet co-operation.

In the same manner that the British and French governments desired an understanding with Moscow, the Soviet government also had reasons to welcome such a connection. Not only had the European states appeared to form a front at Munich, but the three revisionist powers—Germany, Italy, and Japan—had also in the previous years joined in alliances obviously directed against the Soviet Union. In October, 1936 Hitler and Mussolini had formed the so-called Rome-Berlin Axis. In November, 1936 Germany and Japan had signed the Anti-Comintern Pact. This agreement called for co-operation in fighting against world communism. The signatories declared that this alliance was not anti-Soviet, and they used the argument that the Soviet government had repeatedly stated that it was not responsible for the actions of the Comintern. The agreement, however, was only a cover for a secret consultative pact that specifically named the Soviet Union as the opponent. Italy adhered to this alignment in 1937. In May, 1939 Italy and Germany signed a binding military alliance. Although these agreements could operate against France and Britain, their main thrust was anticommunist and anti-Soviet.

From March until August, 1939 the Soviet government therefore carried on negotiations with the western powers. In these talks the Soviet position was in fact strong. The British guarantee to Poland had already given Moscow the assurance that the west would fight if Germany moved eastward. From the western side the negotiations were to prove difficult. The basic problem remained, as before, of exactly how Soviet military aid would be rendered. With no common border with Germany the Soviet Union could only carry out its obligations under any mutual defense arrangement by marching through the Baltic states, Rumania, or Poland. None of these nations wished under any conditions to have Soviet armies on their soil. In fact, if a choice had to be made, the Germans, who did not constitute a threat to their conservative social orders, were probably preferred. The western states were thus faced with the dilemma of finding means to protect small states who did not want to be rescued if the presence of Soviet military forces were involved. These governments correctly foresaw that once in occupation the Soviet Union would re-annex the former tsarist lands—Bessarabia, the Baltic lands, and the Ukrainian and White Russian Polish territories. Communist regimes would also probably be installed.

Under these circumstances negotiations were bound to proceed slowly. At this time, as before the First World War, there was generally a great miscalculation on the relative strength of the different European armies. The Polish army was now rated as an effective fighting instrument—perhaps even equal to the Soviet after the purges. Polish opinion on the question of the transit of Soviet troops thus had to be respected. In August, 1939 a British-French military mission departed by ship for the Soviet Union. By the time it had arrived at its destination, a radical change had occurred in the diplomatic scene.

THE GERMAN ALLIANCE

The Polish sensitivities, of course, caused no anxiety on the German side. After March the Nazi pressure on Poland was intensified. In April Hitler denounced both his non-aggression pact with Poland and the naval agreement with Britain. At the end of March he had decided upon the necessity of a war with Poland; in April a tentative date of September 1 was set. Although the aim of the German leaders was to wage a campaign against Poland alone, preparations had to be made for a larger conflict. Since the experiences of the past had shown the grave danger of a two front war, the obvious course for Nazi policy was to assure that the Soviet Union would not join a western coalition.

After the Munich Pact Soviet-German relations had in fact improved. Distrustful of the west, the Soviet government now moderated its attitude toward Berlin. By mutual consent the two powers toned down their attacks on each other. Negotiations on a trade agreement commenced in May. In that same month Litvinov, who was Jewish, was replaced by Viacheslav M. Molotov, reportedly close to Stalin. The trade delegations met from mid-June to August. As the German date for action against Poland approached, and as the western powers showed no signs of weakening, the German need for a political agreement with the Soviet Union became stronger. On August 19 a trade pact was signed. Then in a dramatic move Hitler got in touch with Stalin; Foreign Minister Joachim von Ribbentrop was sent to Moscow on August 23. There an agreement was signed which, in the published portions, contained the terms of a simple non-aggression treaty. It lacked, however, a clause usual in such cases voiding the document if one party attacked another power. It also was to go into effect at once without formal ratification.

The non-aggression pact signified that the Soviet Union would not join France and Britain in a war for Poland. Equally significant as this assurance were the terms of a secret agreement concluded at the same time. In provisions reminiscent of the Treaty of Tilsit between Napoleon and Alexander I, Germany and the Soviet Union now divided eastern Europe into two spheres of influence. The Soviet government for its share acquired a recognition of its paramount interest in Finland, Estonia, Latvia, eastern Poland, and Bessarabia. Germany was given Lithuania and the rest of Poland. Soviet control was thus to be re-established over the old tsarist possessions, and the basic diplomatic alignment of the nineteenth century, that with Berlin, was restored.

The economic agreements made at this time and later were as important as these political arrangements. In them Germany gained raw materials without which she would have had difficulty waging such an extensive war as this one proved to be. The German purchases included lumber, cotton, feed grain, phosphate, platinum, furs, and petroleum. In return, the Soviet Union received machines, industrial installations, machine tools, and weapons, including airplanes, tank patterns, and patents for war materials. Since German industry was geared for war, it was easier for the Germans to send military equipment despite the fact that the Nazis had no desire to strengthen the military power of the Soviet Union. The economic agreements probably balanced out, with each side making commensurate gains.

The German-Soviet pact was a tremendous shock to France and Britain. Although the action forced a dramatic switch in the position of the world communist parties, there was nothing particularly revolutionary about the agreement when it is considered from the aspects of the interests of the Soviet state. Soviet spokesmen had emphasized in previous periods that regular diplomatic relations were possible with all regimes; in Soviet ideology fascism remained another form of capitalism. Nazi Germany represented a political doctrine of an exclusive racial and national character, but Soviet propaganda had emphasized repeatedly the injustice of French and British control of masses of non-French and non-Anglo-Saxon peoples. On the basis of morality from the Soviet point of view there was thus little to chose between the two camps.

On the practical side the agreement had much to offer. The Soviet Union did not wish a war in 1939, and certainly not one on its own soil. The practical outcome of an alignment with the western powers, given the military situation of the day, would have been the engagement of the Soviet army in a war with Germany to save a Polish state that was no friend of Moscow's. Moreover, the Soviet leaders could never be sure that in case of war the west would not simply remain on the defensive and allow the Soviet and German armies to fight each to the death, thus solving two problems at once. The German pact also gave the Soviet Union territories she wished to control. At this time and later Stalin proved to be personally very conscious of Russian historical claims. Of course, both sides entered into this agreement with few illusions. Neither expected an enduring friendship; the pact met the immediate needs of both powers, nothing more.

After the announcement of the agreement, Britain at once reasserted her intention of standing by the Polish guarantee. On August 24 Britain and Poland signed a treaty of mutual assistance. On September 1 Germany invaded Poland; Britain and France then declared war. The Second World War thus commenced without the participation of the Soviet Union, who now assumed a waiting attitude. Despite the expectation that the Polish army would be able to put up a strong resistance, its main forces were defeated in a week. The Soviet government then moved. On September 17 the Soviet army marched into the area of Poland assigned to it; only feeble opposition was met. The reason for the action was given as the necessity of protecting the Ukrainian and White Russian populations after the collapse of the Polish state. Despite the British guarantee to Poland, this agreement was not applied to the Soviet action.

At the end of September Ribbentrop again flew to Moscow, and a readjustment of the zones was made. Germany gave up Lithuania in return for more Polish territory. The line of the occupation of territories under Soviet control now more closely approximated the ethnic frontier. The Soviet Union acquired about 77,000 square miles of Polish territory with a population of around thirteen million, of whom seven million were Ukrainians and White Russians. To avoid future complications an agreement was made on the exchange of populations. The Germans living in the area were returned to their state, while Ukrainians,

White Russians, and Jews in German-occupied territory were given to the Soviet authorities.

After the occupation of this territory, the Soviet government turned to collecting its other gains in the pact with Germany. Pressure was put on the Baltic states. Although at this time no attempt was made to change the internal regimes, non-aggression treaties were signed giving the Soviet army the right to use certain places as military bases. The first agreement was with Estonia in September; in October Latvia and Lithuania accepted the same conditions. In a redistribution of territory Lithuania was given its ancient capital of Vilna, which Poland had seized in 1920.

Soviet attention was next turned to Finland, but here matters did not proceed smoothly. The Soviet demands included a border readjustment near Leningrad that would have breached Finnish defense lines, territory in the Arctic region, islands in the Gulf of Finland, and control of the port of Hango. Fearing that the acceptance of these conditions would end in the complete surrender of their independence, the Finns chose to resist. War broke out at the end of November. The Soviet government now set up a puppet Finnish regime of Communists residing in the Soviet Union; this body then asked for assistance in freeing their country, and a mutual assistance treaty was arranged. The Finnish War caused consternation in the west. Despite the inability of France and Britain to handle the responsibilities of an enlarged conflict, many pressed for action. The Soviet Union was expelled from the League of Nations. In March, 1940 an Allied expeditionary force was actually being prepared to go to Finland; other plans called for the bombing of the Baku oil fields. Although the Finnish army was able to stop the Soviet attack at first, this small country could not resist indefinitely. In March, 1940 peace was made. The Soviet Union gained its demands; Finland lost about a tenth of her territory and also had to allow Soviet transit rights to Norway and Sweden.

In the winter of 1939/40 there had been a long lull in the action in the west. In April this period of respite was ended. German forces took Denmark and Norway. In Britain Chamberlain left office and Winston Churchill became prime minister at the head of a national government. In May action on the western front commenced. The German army swept through Belgium and Holland, turned the Maginot Line, and defeated the French and British armies. The British were forced to make a hasty retreat through the channel ports. In June France signed an armistice. Meanwhile Italy entered the war.

With Germany in control of France, the Soviet Union moved to collect additional compensation as allowed by the agreement. In June, 1940 complete control was taken of the Baltic states, which now ceased to exist as independent nations. The Red Army entered first Lithuania and then Estonia and Latvia. The old governments were overturned. With Soviet armies in occupation new elections were held for parliaments, which then asked for admission into the Soviet Union. This state was thus enlarged with the addition of the Lithuanian, Latvian, and Estonian Soviet Socialist Republics.

A simultaneous move was made against Rumania. Also in June an ultimatum was sent to Bucharest, which was followed by an occupation not only of Bessarabia but also of Bukovina, which had not been included in the Nazi pact. The Russian action led to a massive partition of Rumanian territory. In August in the Vienna Award, negotiated by Germany and Italy, northern Transylvania was ceded to Hungary. In September southern Dobrudja was given to Bulgaria. Germany and Italy then gave a territorial guarantee to the rest of the country and German troops entered in occupation. This German action added Rumania to Slovakia and Hungary, who were already Axis allies. The further penetration of German power into the Danubian area was not reassuring to Moscow. In June, 1940 Soviet industry went on a war basis with the introduction of the seven-day work week and the eight-hour day.

In the fall of 1940 a new strengthening of the German diplomatic position occurred. In September, Germany, Italy, and Japan concluded a firm military alliance directed against the

United States. The terms of the Tripartite Pact obligated the signatories to aid one another if an additional power became involved in the war in Europe or Asia. It was specifically stated that this provision did not apply to the Soviet Union. Nevertheless, this agreement became the basis of a growing coalition of Axis-associated states. Hungary, Slovakia, and Rumania adhered to it immediately.

In November Molotov paid a visit to Berlin. At this time Ribbentrop suggested that the Soviet Union also join the partnership. Since the Tripartite Pact represented a division of the eastern hemisphere into spheres of influence, the Soviet government was now offered a section of its own in the direction of Iran [3] and India. This area, which would bring the Soviet Union in direct conflict with Britain, was acceptable to the Soviet minister, but the German offer did not include the lands of real interest to the Soviet state. Molotov now asked for what amounted to control over Bulgaria and the Straits. The former main issues in the eastern question thus reappeared; Soviet ambitions now paralleled those of the Russian Panslavs of 1878.

When Molotov returned to Moscow, he composed a list of demands as conditions for the Soviet adherence to the Tripartite Pact. It was quite comprehensive. The Soviet government wished Germany to withdraw the troops she had in Finland. A mutual assistance pact was to be made with Bulgaria and bases were to be acquired on the Straits. The German offer of a sphere in Iran and India was accepted. In addition, Japan was to surrender the coal and oil concessions it had in northern Sakhalin. The German government never replied to this message. In December Hitler decided on Plan Barbarossa, which called for the invasion of the Soviet Union in May, 1941.

Meanwhile, the German armies extended their control in the Balkans. In October, 1940 Italy, without consultation with Berlin, launched an attack on Greece from Albania, who had been occupied in 1939. Contrary to all expectations the Greek army held the Italians back, and soon Mussolini was in the humiliating posi-

3. In March, 1935 the name of Persia was formally changed to Iran.

tion of being forced to ask for assistance. In early 1941 Germany prepared to act. Bulgaria, the object of Soviet designs, joined the Tripartite Pact in March and thereby became an Axis ally. German troops entered the country. In the same month the Yugoslav government also joined the alignment. However, this political surrender to Germany caused a revolt in Belgrade. A new government was established under King Peter. Eight days later, in a surprise diplomatic move, the Soviet government signed an agreement with this regime. Again the German armies marched; on April 6 Yugoslavia was invaded, followed by Greece, Crete, and the Aegean Islands. The German government then concluded a neutrality treaty with Turkey.

Germany was thus in complete control of the Balkans; she had an alliance system that, although ostensibly directed against the United States and Britain, could also be effective against the Soviet Union. In May, in a situation of mounting tension, Stalin assumed from Molotov the position of chairman of the Council of People's Commissars. He was thus in name as well as in fact the leader of the Soviet state. Some diplomatic initiatives were carried out in this period. In the fall of 1940 the Soviet representatives had strongly asserted their desire for a dominant position on the lower Danube. In a conference held in Berlin they demanded that this section of the river be placed under the control of the riparian states. The desire for a sphere including the Straits and Bulgaria and the agreement with Yugoslavia, all actions displeasing to Berlin, have been mentioned. In April, in a move that was extremely upsetting for the German government, Japan and the Soviet Union signed a non-aggression pact. At this time both powers were primarily occupied in areas away from their mutual Siberian frontier. Neither wished a two front war; both wanted their backs secure while they moved in opposite directions.

Throughout this period there was no apparent sign that the Soviet Union expected war with Germany. Although repeated warnings were sent to Moscow from both Soviet and British intelligence, the Russian army was not set to meet a German at-

tack. The Soviet leaders evidently expected the Germans to negotiate further along the lines of the Tripartite Pact conversations.
The Soviet government had scrupulously fulfilled its part of the
Nazi-Soviet pact and had fully lived up to the terms of the
economic agreements even when German deliveries were behind
schedule. Because of the Balkan invasion, the German timetable
was changed from May to June 22, a date closely approximating
that of Napoleon's disastrous adventure in 1812. When the German ambassador officially informed Molotov of the attack, which
had already commenced, the Russian minister protested: "Surely
we have not deserved this." [4]

WAR AND WESTERN ALLIANCE

Faced with the great concentration of German men and matériel,
Stalin chose to meet the attack in the border regions rather than
retreat to better positions. The invading army was therefore able
in the first months of the war to surround and make prisoner
hundreds of thousands of Russian soldiers and to capture great
stores of arms and munitions. The Nazi advance was rapid. By
the first part of December enemy troops surrounded Leningrad
and were in the suburbs of Moscow. Although defeated in the
field, the Soviet government now found two great allies—the
Russian weather and the miscalculations of Hitler and the German
leadership. Winter came early in 1941. Evidently expecting a
quick and overwhelming victory, along the line of previous
events in France, the German soldiers had not been provided with
adequate clothing nor had the mechanized equipment been prepared for a real winter campaign. German activities were thus
halted before Christmas. The Soviet army, experienced in winter
fighting, was able to continue to carry on counter-attacks.

Despite the German failure to win a real victory, in the first
year the Nazi armies were nevertheless able to occupy vast terri-

4. Gustav Hilger and Alfred Meyer, *The Incompatible Allies* (New York:
Macmillan, 1953), p. 336.

tories. The Ukraine, the Baltic lands, Poland, and White Russia were again under foreign occupation. For the next eighteen months the Soviet position was to be difficult in both a military and a political sense. In the winter of 1941/42 the state desperately needed whatever assistance it could gain. Within the country the war was fought on a patriotic basis, as the struggle of the Russian people against a foreign invader. Religious life was revived; revolutionary slogans were moderated. Attacks were no longer directed against the capitalist, colonial powers who were now allies or potential aids.

In the summer of 1941 Britain was the only other power at war with the Axis. Immediately after the attack Churchill sent a message to Stalin pledging support and co-operation. The Soviet Union needed both direct military assistance and supplies, but Britain, hard pressed herself, could send very little in the way of war matériel. The Soviet position was greatly improved when the Japanese attacked Pearl Harbor in December. The subsequent declaration of war on the United States by Germany and Italy brought this great western power directly into the war in both Europe and Asia. Henceforth American assistance through the lease-lend arrangements was to be available to the Soviet Union. This material aid was probably the chief contribution to the Soviet war effort from the west.

Great as the significance of the supplies were, the Soviet leadership was naturally more concerned about receiving direct military help as soon as possible. Throughout the war it remained concerned over the obvious fact that Soviet manpower was bearing the main burden of the fighting and was suffering the real casualties in the conflict. Even in 1941 a second front in France or the Low Countries was desired. In September the request was also made for British troops to be sent either through Archangel or through Iran. Neither Britain nor the United States ever adequately met the Soviet demands on this question. By the time of the Allied landing in Normandy in 1944 the end of the conflict was a foregone conclusion. In August, 1941 Soviet and British troops did co-operate, however, in one action, when they jointly occupied Iran. Thereafter, although both the west and the Soviet government kept in touch, they each conducted the war in their own spheres with little attempt at real co-ordination or co-operative effort. A similar situation existed between Japan and the Axis European powers. In each case the two sides adopted policies in the war to suit their own immediate needs, with less concern about general strategy.

Despite the difficult military situation of 1941 and 1942, political, as apart from military, problems arose almost immediately between the Allies. As could be expected, the Soviet government had no intention of surrendering its gains from the Nazi-Soviet Pact. This determination was bound to cause problems, particularly in regard to Poland. The British government had, after all, gone to war over the question of the independence and integrity of the Polish state. It also recognized the Polish government-in-exile as the legitimate representative of the Polish people. This regime refused to accept the partition of its pre-war lands. The Polish problem was to remain the center of controversy between Moscow and the western capitals throughout the war. Partly because of this territorial issue the entire question of the post-war settlement was left vague as long as the war continued.

Some agreements were nevertheless made at this time. In December, 1941 Britain acceded to the Soviet demand and declared war on Rumania, Hungary, and Finland. In May, 1942 Molotov flew to London, where a twenty-year treaty of alliance was signed, but the Soviet request for a second front was again refused. From London the Soviet minister traveled to Washington, where he appears to have received assurances on the possibility of a second front. Soviet hopes were dampened, however, when Churchill flew to Moscow in August. He informed Stalin that the Allies would invade not the continent but North Africa, an operation which commenced in November.

Although the second front was not opened, in the winter of 1942/43 the Soviet army achieved a military victory that was to be the symbolic turning point of the war. The German army at Stalingrad was encircled and trapped. Hitler's determination that this force make a stand prevented its being withdrawn in time. In February the German Sixth Army surrendered. Thereafter Germany proved unable to mount another offensive of real danger to the Soviet Union. Although two years of fighting were ahead, the possibility had lessened that the Soviet Union would be militarily conquered. The Germans were now fighting with inferiority in both troops and matériel. German military leadership, largely under Hitler's inspiration, also made increasing errors. The attempt was made to hold all the main points in the Soviet Union instead of following a more flexible policy. The Soviet government had met not only the military threat but also the political. Nazi racial and national doctrines made it almost impossible for Germany to use any discontent with communism or resentment of Great Russian domination in the state. The German actions and their ideology appeared to leave the Soviet citizen with no alternative but to fight. At this time also the British were winning battles in Egypt and Libya, and there were Anglo-American victories in Morocco and Algeria.

With the turn of the military tide, the question of the future settlement of Europe became more important. In May, 1943 the Comintern was officially dissolved, but it had long since ceased to fulfill a useful function. In the future Communist political victories, at least in Europe, were to come with the Red Army and not, except in Yugoslavia and Albania, through the actions of local Parties. In the negotiations the Soviet Union had to deal principally with two allies who themselves were not in full agreement on the ultimate aims to be accomplished or the means by which a stable future settlement could be achieved. Of the two, Britain's position was the easier to ascertain. She had gone to war in 1939 on traditional balance-of-power considerations. The aim for the peace would thus logically entail the re-establishment of this condition. She no more desired Russian domination of the entire continent now than she had in 1814. During the war, Churchill, with an eye to the future, had supported the idea of a second front in the Balkan peninsula. The presence of American and British armies there and in the Danube valley would forestall complete Soviet control. As a traditional British statesman Churchill also had no desire to preside over the destruction of the British Empire. In the negotiations the British government was prepared for a realistic discussion of spheres of influence and relative great power strength. This attitude was also approved by the Soviet leaders.

The problem was the United States, a nation that had previously occupied a peripheral position in European diplomacy. She had not been involved regularly in the routine negotiations over major and minor issues that had absorbed the interest and attention of the chancellories; her experience in dealing with major European, particularly east European, problems was limited. Moreover, in this period her government reflected the unique interests and outlook of a state belonging to another hemisphere. Because of the public's basically isolationist outlook, the American aim became the swift military conclusion of the war with less emphasis on the future peace. Much hope was placed on the establishment of an effective world organization after the war; the burden of real leadership and real responsibility could thus be avoided. American statecraft was also burdened with a series of political clichés inherited from a Wilsonian and puritan past, which, if they had ever been truly valid, certainly did not hold in the tough, revolutionary, and violent world of the time. This basic failure to recognize realities during the war made almost inevitable the later strong reaction. During the conflict the American government refused any suggestion of the establishment of spheres of influence, a solution which both the Soviet Union, as shown in the negotiations with Germany, and Britain favored. The right of the Soviet government to keep the gains of the Nazi-Soviet Pact was also not accepted. Even today the United States government still has not recognized the Soviet absorption of the Baltic states. As a result of this determination the peacetime settlement in Europe came to be based on the right of conquest. Where the Soviet armies went, they established their own political system and maintained control. In like manner the western allies decided the fate of the lands they occupied.

The failure of the United States to make adequate provision for the future in its military strategy and in its political decisions during the war was an asset for Soviet diplomacy.

Throughout the war the major problem in Soviet relations with the west was a lack of basic trust. Neither side was ever certain that the other would not make a separate peace. Soviet fears that the western allies would allow the German and Soviet armies to fight each other to the death appeared to find partial justification in the continued postponement of the opening of a second front. The real differences between the Allies continued to be shown best in the Polish question. The Polish government-in-exile was composed of representatives of the major parties of pre-war Poland. It was directly connected with the Polish underground and with the partisan forces of the Home Army. A reflection of past Polish feeling, it was anticommunist and anti-Russian. In April, 1943 the German government announced that it had found the bodies of more than 10,000 Polish officers in the Katyn Forest near Smolensk. The government-in-exile immediately demanded that the International Red Cross investigate the case. The Soviet government reacted violently and broke relations with the Polish organization. Moscow, however, never did account for the approximately 15,000 Polish officers interned in 1939 after the occupation of eastern Poland. The Soviet action greatly complicated the Polish problem for the west, but it left the field free for the Soviet government to form its own regime.

In November-December, 1943 the leaders of the three great Allied powers gathered for the first of three meetings, to be held at Teheran, Yalta, and Potsdam, to discuss war strategy and the future peace. For these nations the year 1943 had been an important one. The victory at Stalingrad had been followed by a successful Soviet blocking of a German summer offensive. The Soviet army now began a great counter-movement, which was to end only in Berlin. The western powers had agreed to a second front in Europe, but, they had, to the Soviet disgust, chosen Italy as their target. The Teheran Conference was preceded by a meeting between Roosevelt and Churchill in Cairo, which was also attended by Chiang Kai-shek, and problems dealing with China and the Pacific war were discussed. Roosevelt and Churchill then joined Stalin in the Iranian capital. At this conference the disagreement between the United States and Britain on many issues was apparent. The American emphasis remained on the military aspects of the war. Convinced that the struggle in the Pacific would be long and difficult, the United States was most eager to gain Soviet participation. As a result, no specific agreements, which might cause disputes, were drawn up for the post-war European political settlement. The Soviet Union did agree to enter the war against Japan after the end of the fighting in Europe. The future of Germany was left very vague, but it was decided that the Soviet Union would keep its eastern Polish territories and that Poland would be indemnified with German lands. It will be noted that Allied pronouncements on self-determination were never applied to the enemy peoples. Agreement was also reached on Yugoslav questions.

Meanwhile, a Czechoslovak as well as a Polish government-in-exile had been established, both of which received western backing. After the invasion of Greece and Yugoslavia, these states also had similar organizations abroad, which were recognized as the legal governments of their countries. Following the German occupation of Yugoslavia, two underground groups came into existence: the Chetniks, under Draža Mihailović, representing the government-in-exile; and the Partisans, under Josip Broz Tito, a Moscow-trained Communist. As a result, a civil war, directed toward the future control of the country, soon began. This conflict paralleled the struggle against the foreign occupation. Since the Partisans proved more effective against the Axis troops, the British in particular were for aiding Tito. This decision was accepted at the Teheran Conference. Stalin showed himself less enthusiastic on the question than did the British. He favored a popular front and not a purely Partisan-dominated government for the future.

In 1944 the Soviet armies entered the Balkans. Although the most direct route to Germany was through Poland, the Soviet military plans, reflecting political objectives, called for a swing southwest and then an advance up the Danube Valley. In August Rumania surrendered; King Michael was not deposed. The country shifted sides and now declared war on Germany. The situation with regard to Bulgaria was a little more complicated, since that state was not at war with the Soviet Union. To simplify matters, the Soviet Union declared war on Bulgaria on September 5, then entered the country, which surrendered on September 9. Soviet armies then entered northern Yugoslavia; Soviet and Partisan units together took Belgrade. The Soviet army then marched on to Hungary, which fell in 1945. Yugoslavia was left in the control of the Partisan army of approximately 800,000 men.

With the exception of Yugoslavia, the states occupied by the Soviet armies were placed under a military administration and not under the control of local Communist groups. Although according to agreements made previously an Allied control commission with western representation was intended to function in each of these states, the Soviet authorities ignored these bodies. Instead they acted to form regimes that they could control. In March, 1945 King Michael was compelled to accept a Communist-dominated cabinet. The government of Bulgaria was entrusted to the Fatherland Front, an organization under Communist control. Thus the situation that Churchill had sought to avoid had arisen; the Soviet Union had predominant military and political power in the Balkans with the exception of Greece. Previously, in a visit to Moscow in October, 1944, Churchill had presented to Stalin the idea of a division of influence in the area between the Soviet Union and the west. At that time the Soviet Union was given 90 per cent control in Rumania, 75 per cent in Bulgaria, and half in Hungary and Yugoslavia; Britain would receive 90 per cent predominance in Greece. Not only was such a division impractical to apply, but also the United States consistently remained opposed to such bargaining. Even in Greece, where a civil war broke out in 1944, the British position was to prove difficult to preserve.

Meanwhile, the Polish situation became more entangled. Having broken with the government-in-exile, the Soviet government established its own Committee of National Liberation under the direction of Boleslaw Bierut. Known as the Lublin Committee, this organization was entrusted with the administration of the Polish lands as they were taken by the Soviet army. Aware of its rapidly deteriorating political position, the London-based government decided to act. Eager to share in the freeing of Poland from German control and conscious of the consequences of a purely Soviet action, in August, 1944 these Polish leaders ordered the Home Army to rise in Warsaw. The Soviet army was then near the city. For three weeks the German army and the Polish partisan forces battled for the Polish capital; the Soviet army remained within easy striking distance, but did not move. The German destruction of the city and suppression of the revolt not only resulted in a loss of prestige for the London regime but deprived it of its military arm in Poland. The Soviet Union was thus faced with no major center of opposition to its takeover of power in the country. In December, 1944 the Lublin Committee declared itself the provisional government of Poland and received Soviet recognition.

The second conference of Allied leaders was held at Yalta in the Crimea in February, 1945. The final defeat of Germany was now a certainty. A second front had been established in Normandy in June, 1944. Thus the necessity had arisen of making some sort of political arrangements for the occupied territories. Although the western governments were still under the illusion that something like the previous governments could be established in eastern Europe, Soviet control was already well entrenched. The major problem thus became Germany. It was decided that German territory would be divided into four zones of occupation with a military commander at the head of each. To co-ordinate this rule an Allied Control Commission was to be established in Berlin. Again it was agreed that Poland would be indemnified from German territory for its losses to the Soviet Union.

This conference also discussed the question of the establishment of a world organization, the future United Nations. Conscious of its weakness in such a body, the Soviet Union first claimed the right to have sixteen delegates, one for each of the Soviet republics, to balance the British Commonwealth nations and the Latin American votes, which were supposed to be under American control. Although the number was reduced to three, the Soviet desire that the right of veto be preserved in the Security Council, the body representing the great powers, was confirmed. In June, 1945 the United Nations was formally established at a conference in San Francisco.

Throughout this period the center of controversy between the Soviet Union, on the one hand, and the United States and Britain, on the other, remained Poland. The western states now stood on the principle that the new regimes in the central European and Balkan states should be democratic and chosen by free elections. In contrast, the Soviet Union wanted them to be "friendly." The point at issue was clearly made by Stalin at the Potsdam Conference of 1945 when he stated that: "A freely elected government in any of these countries would be anti-Soviet, and that we cannot allow." In the preceding years no country had been consistently more anti-Russian than Poland. The fate of this country was to typify that of the states under Soviet occupation. The Soviet and western positions could not be compromised.

At Yalta the powers finally agreed that the Lublin Committee would indeed be the basis of the provisional government, but that representatives of other political parties should be added to it. In theory, free elections were to be held, but the Soviet army remained in control of the country. In June a Provisional Government of National Unity was established; it consisted of fourteen Lublin representatives and seven from outside. The London government-in-exile was ignored. At the Yalta conference the Soviet Union also agreed to sign the Declaration on Liberated Europe, in which the three powers agreed to form "interim governmental authorities broadly representative of all democratic elements in the population and pledged to the earliest possible establishment through free elections of governments responsive to the will of the people." The difference in the definition of the words "democratic" and "will of the people" between the west and Moscow soon became apparent.

Meanwhile, the Soviet and Communist political position in the Balkan governments was strengthened. In Yugoslavia, in contrast to Poland, the government, although in fact in Partisan hands, did contain representatives from the government-in-exile. In Rumania and Bulgaria, formerly enemy nations, the direction was toward a tightening of Communist domination with Communists in control of the ministries of interior and justice. In Rumania, as already mentioned, the Soviet government pressed King Michael into appointing the Soviet candidate to head a coalition government.

In 1945 changes of leadership occurred in both Washington and London. In April Roosevelt died and was replaced by Harry S Truman. The war in Europe now came to a quick finish. Hitler committed suicide in Berlin on April 30; Germany surrendered on May 8. In July and August the final conference of the three Allied powers was held at Potsdam. During this meeting new elections in Britain brought the Labour Party to power, and Clement Attlee replaced Churchill during the deliberations. One outcome of the Potsdam Conference was a clear demonstration of the growing weakness of Britain as a power and the shift of the burden of defending western interests to the United States.

In these negotiations it was finally settled that Poland would cede her eastern lands to the Soviet Union. East Prussia was also partitioned; the Soviet Union took the northern section and Poland took the south along with Danzig. Although in theory the final boundaries were not to be settled until a general peace conference was held, the Soviet government now gave Poland the administration of a large section of German territory, including Silesia, to the line of the Oder-Western Neisse River. This area had formerly contained about nine million Germans. The question of German reparations was also discussed. The Soviets suggested the figure of 20 billion dollars to be paid over a ten-year period, half of which would go to their government. It will be noted that the Soviet proposals for Germany, like those for

Asia, had little resemblance to the Bolshevik program in 1917 for a peace "without annexations and indemnities." The western powers did not accept the reparations figure, but they agreed to the delivery of industrial equipment from Germany as reparations. The German fleet and merchant marine were also divided among the victors. At this time it was assumed that a politically united Germany would eventually sign a peace treaty. Until then the Control Council would administer the country.

At Potsdam the Soviet representatives showed a highly traditional attitude toward Turkey and the Straits. They claimed Kars and Ardahan, which had been returned to Turkish control under Lenin. As in the discussions with the German government in 1940, they asked for a naval base in the Bosphorus and the Dardanelles. Control in Bulgaria had already been established. The western states consented to a revision of the Straits treaties but not to the other demands.

With the war in Europe concluded, preparations were next made to enter the conflict with Japan. At Yalta Soviet participation had been agreed to, but at a high price. The Soviet government now wished to regain what Russia had lost to Japan in 1905 —control of the cities of Dalny and Port Arthur, southern Sakhalin, and a sphere of influence in Korea. Control of the Manchurian railroads and possession of the Kurile Islands were also sought. Under the impression that Soviet assistance was needed against what was believed to be a strong Japanese army in Manchuria, the United States was willing to concede most of these demands, even those that were at the expense of its ally nationalist China. It was agreed that the Soviet Union would enter the war three months after the conclusion of hostilities in Europe.

In the summer of 1945 the war in Japan appeared to be nearing an end despite previous American fears of a long duration. On July 16, the day before the opening of the Potsdam Conference, the United States exploded her first atomic device in New Mexico. During this time the Japanese government had been seeking Soviet assistance in mediating a peace, but the Soviet decision was to enter the conflict, obviously for political objectives. In April the neutrality pact with Japan had been denounced. On August 6 the first bomb was dropped on Hiroshima; on August 8 the Soviet Union declared war on Japan; on August 9 Nagasaki was destroyed; and on August 14 Japan surrendered.

Participation in the last six days of the war in Asia gave the Soviet government the right to claim rewards. The American reaction to Soviet actions here was to prove firmer than in Europe. General Douglas MacArthur, in command of the American forces, made it clear that the United States did not intend to share the control of Japan proper. The Soviet army received the Japanese surrender in Manchuria, Sakhalin, North Korea, and the Kuriles, but not in the main Japanese islands. Henceforth the United States kept clear control of the government of Japan.

THE AMERICAN RIVALRY: DIVIDED WORLD POLITICS

The war ended in Europe and Asia with the three major victors as yet uncommitted on the shape of the peace. The events of the war had obviously shattered the former balance of power on the continent. The roles Germany and France could play in international affairs would not be commensurate with their former positions. One of the most impressive results of the Second World War was to be the collapse of Britain's colonial supremacy and the massive decline in her world position. This situation left the Soviet Union confronted principally by the United States, a nation which after the war possessed enormous military power, a highly developed war industry, the greatest terror weapon ever created, and an enigmatic foreign policy.

Throughout the war the United States had concentrated on the achievement of a military victory by the quickest and least costly means possible. Political considerations remained secondary. The American government had not agreed to Churchill's proposals of a Balkan invasion or to later suggestions that western troops should occupy Vienna, Berlin, and Prague before the Soviet forces arrived. In the Far East a great effort had been made to

CENTRAL AND EASTERN EUROPE AFTER WORLD WAR II

Communist controlled countries
in Eastern Europe

Boundaries of Soviet Union
in 1939

Boundaries of Soviet Union
since 1948

Murmansk

SWEDEN

FINLAND

UNION

NORWAY

OF

Leningrad

SOVIET

ESTONIA

North Sea

LATVIA

Moscow

DENMARK

Baltic Sea

LITHUANIA

SOCIALIST

GREAT
BRITAIN

REPUBLICS

NETHERLANDS

Berlin

Warsaw

BELGIUM

EAST
GERMANY

POLAND

LUXEMBOURG

WEST
GERMANY

CZECHOSLOVAKIA

FRANCE

RUTHENIA

BESSARABIA

AUSTRIA

SWITZERLAND

HUNGARY

RUMANIA

YUGOSLAVIA

Black Sea

ITALY

BULGARIA

Adriatic Sea

ALBANIA

0   300 mi.
0   400 km.

GREECE

TURKEY

assure Soviet participation in the war against Japan. During these years the American position toward Germany and Japan had been, at least in words, tougher and more ideological in content than the Soviet. Unconditional surrender was an American fixation. Great emphasis had been placed on the issuance of lofty declarations such as the Atlantic Charter, with its statement that Britain and the United States "desire to see no territorial changes that do not accord with the freely expressed wishes of the peoples concerned," and the Yalta pronouncement already quoted. More than any other nation the United States placed emphasis on the United Nations and was willing to make political concessions elsewhere to assure Soviet participation in that organization. Immediately after the fighting ended, the United States, the military giant of the time, gave every indication of wishing to disengage from close involvement in European politics and resume her traditional position. The lease-lend assistance was terminated and, under great pressure from the electorate, the government began to withdraw troops from Europe. At the same time real attempts were made to get along with the Soviet Union.

The weakness of all of the other great powers and the attitude of the United States created a political vacuum, not only in Europe but also in Asia, which the Soviet Union proceeded to attempt to fill. In Europe the chief problem for the Soviet government was the political settlement in the Balkans and central Europe, including Germany. In eastern Europe popular front governments had been set up during the Soviet occupation. These coalition regimes made relations with the west smoother and they were also necessary at first. In the interwar and war period the Communist Parties had been eliminated in most of these states. Very few genuine Communists remained to greet the Soviet army. The popular front governments lasted but a short while. In Yugoslavia, Albania, Rumania, and Bulgaria complete Communist domination was established by 1946, in Poland by 1947, and in Czechoslovakia by 1948. The manner in which it was accomplished had a deep effect on the western governments, in particular on the United States, and contributed to the change of American policy.

Although Soviet aims in Germany were never as clear as they were in eastern Europe, the interests of Moscow obviously called either for a united Germany under a Communist or a front government or for the division of the state. According to the wartime agreements, which looked forward to the eventual establishment of a single German government, the control of the German lands lay in the hands of the Allied Control Council, meeting in Berlin and composed of the military commanders of the four zones. This body was assisted by a Coordinating Committee of four deputy commanders and an administrative staff. In the division of the country the Soviet Union received the poorer, predominantly agricultural eastern area. By May, 1946 disagreements over policy had become so acute that the western zones suspended the delivery of industrial goods as reparations.

In conflict with its former allies over general policy and faced with the obvious fact that it could not hope to win a favorable regime in a united Germany, the Soviet Union now turned to establishing a Communist regime in its own sector. Having stripped their zone of supplies and industrial equipment, the Soviet authorities had more difficulty in finding a friendly reception for their political proposals. Moreover, after the years of the Nazi regime, there were very few Communists left. In these years the German Communist Party was headed by Wilhelm Pieck, who had spent the war in Moscow. At first an attempt was made to establish a popular front government. In April, 1946 the Communists and Social Democrats merged to form the Socialist Unity Party under the leadership of Otto Grotewohl and Pieck. Economic and social changes subsequently introduced sharply divided this area of Germany from the western occupied zones.

The first years after the war thus saw the strengthening of Soviet dominance in east Europe and what was to be a lasting division of Germany. In a similar manner the Soviet government moved to improve its position in Iran and the Near East. In these areas also Stalin was to prove a worthy successor to the tsars. It will be remembered that in 1941 Britain and the Soviet Union had agreed to a joint occupation of Iran along the lines of the agreement of 1907. With a predominant position established in the north, the Soviet government had no desire to return to prewar conditions. In an effort to remove these areas from Iranian control, in the winter of 1945/46 it therefore sponsored two new regimes: a government of Azerbaijan under the leadership of a Communist, Jafar Pishevari, and a Kurdish People's Republic. At the same time Soviet support was given in Iran to the Tudeh, or Communist Party. The Soviet Union also sought an oil agreement with the Iranian government. This massive interference caused Iran to appeal to the United Nations in March, 1946, but negotiations between the Iranian and Soviet governments led to a settlement in April. Soviet troops were to be removed from the north in return for an oil agreement, and a degree of autonomy was to be allowed to the Azerbaijan regime. The Soviet forces were evacuated in May. The Iranian government then reasserted its control in the country. The parliament rejected the treaty with Russia, and Iranian forces put down the two separatist regimes and executed their leaders. The Tudeh Party was outlawed.

The Soviet failure in Iran was duplicated in Turkey. Tsarist Russia had failed to become a Mediterranean power largely because of the closure of the Straits. Now, with the weakening of British strength, the Soviet government had the opportunity of moving forward here also. It first sought a trusteeship for the former Italian colony of Libya in order to gain naval bases in the Mediterranean. When this was denied, attention next turned to Turkey, where the Soviets renewed their demand for Kars and Ardahan and a base on the Dardanelles. Again paralleling tsarist policy, they sought a bilateral treaty with the Turkish Republic. Soviet troops were simultaneously concentrated on the Turkish border.

The Soviet pressure on Iran and Turkey coincided with the renewal of the civil war in Greece. Although direct Soviet aid was not given the insurgents there, supplies arrived from Albania, Bulgaria, and Yugoslavia. The possible victory of the rebel forces together with the Russian pressure on Turkey brought into question the problem of the control of the eastern Mediterranean. In this crisis, so reminiscent of the former eastern question, Britain turned to the United States. Despite Britain's predominant role in this area in the past, her power now was not sufficient to maintain her previous position. In response, in March, 1947 President Truman announced that the United States would extend military and economic aid to Greece and Turkey. American ships had already been sent to the Mediterranean, and Greece was granted a loan of 400 million dollars at once. (In the next years American expenditures were increased to the extent that by 1963 the United States had given 3.5 billion dollars to Greece alone.) The civil war ended in 1949. The assistance to Greece and Turkey, the first major American step to counteract what appeared to be a Soviet offensive in Europe and Asia, marked a real change in policy. Truman declared before Congress: "I believe that it must be the policy of the United States to support free peoples who are resisting attempted subjugation by armed minorities or by outside pressures." This statement, the Truman Doctrine, was to initiate a period in diplomatic history when the United States assumed a role of real leadership in the organization of western Europe against further Soviet gains.

As a consequence the Soviet government faced not only an American front in the Near East but also similar firm actions in Europe. In June, 1947 Secretary of State George C. Marshall announced the American willingness to contribute to the economic rehabilitation of Europe. A conference of the European nations was subsequently held in Paris. Molotov, attending as the Soviet representative, denounced the American plan and left the conference, much to the relief of the United States government, which would have faced great difficulties in obtaining from Congress funds for the assistance of communist states. In July the Czechoslovak government attempted to co-operate, but the Soviet government forced it to withdraw. In the following years the Marshall Plan proved amazingly successful. The economic revival and real prosperity of the western nations created a further gap between east and west. The Soviet sphere proved unable to duplicate the economic well-being of western Europe.

The United States also turned to the military organization of the west. In April, 1949 the North Atlantic Treaty was signed by Britain, the United States, France, Belgium, Luxembourg, the

Netherlands, Denmark, Iceland, Norway, Italy, Portugal, and Canada; Greece and Turkey joined in 1952 and West Germany in 1955. A permanent organization, the North Atlantic Treaty Organization, NATO, had offices first in Paris and then in Brussels. This alliance, a mutual defense pact, represented the policy of the containment of Soviet expansion.

Parallel with the economic and military consolidation of the west, the Soviet Union moved to tighten its links with and its control over the east European countries. The basis of a treaty network had already been laid during the war. In December, 1943 a treaty of mutual assistance had been concluded with the Czechoslovak government-in-exile. Agreements were made with Yugoslavia and Poland in April, 1945. In early 1948 a series of bilateral pacts was made between the Soviet Union and Rumania, Hungary, and Bulgaria. To balance the Marshall Plan the Council for Mutual Economic Assistance, COMECON, was established in January, 1949 to co-ordinate the east European economies. This union, which was to develop political problems later, never functioned with complete success. The Soviet Union, unlike the United States, was not prosperous enough to render real aid to the smaller nations.

In addition to these actions, in October, 1947 the Soviet Union sponsored the formation of the Communist Information Bureau, or Cominform. Although this organization was less ambitious in its objectives than the Comintern had been, it too was designed to bring together the communist parties of the world. Its headquarters were first in Belgrade and then in Bucharest. Once again a major propaganda offensive was directed against the west. Communist parties in Europe, in particular the strong French and Italian organizations, were instructed to oppose the Marshall Plan. The Soviet government also actively backed peace movements such as the Stockholm Appeal of 1950 to ban the bomb. Although the Soviet Union acquired nuclear weapons after 1949, it remained militarily far weaker than the United States.

The first major test between the new blocs came over the German question. With the growing division with Moscow and the inability to come to an agreement on Germany, the western powers proceeded to form a government in their own area. In February, 1948 the three zones were joined. The unity of this area and the end of real four-power administration raised the issue of the status of Berlin, which lay in the center of the Soviet zone. This city, like all of Germany, was under four-power administration and divided into separate zones. The Soviet government disliked not only these political changes but also the currency reform introduced at this time, which became the basis for later German prosperity. In June, 1948, in a counter-action, the Soviet authorities closed the routes into West Berlin. This city of two million was to go through the winter without rail or road transportation. The western powers met this challenge not by military action but by the organization of an airlift, which was able to bring in sufficient supplies. In May, 1949 the Soviet government abandoned the action.

With the failure of the Soviet move, the western nations proceeded with the creation of a separate German state. In May, 1949 the Federal Republic of Germany was formed. In elections held in August, 1949 the Communist vote was about 6 per cent. The strongest parties, the basis of the state, were the Social Democrats and the Christian Democrats. The western allies worked closely with the latter party and its head, Konrad Adenauer. The consolidation of the western zones and the erection of the new government with its capital at Bonn forced the Soviet Union to organize its zone more formally. The German Democratic Republic held its first election in October, 1950. A single list of candidates received 99.7 per cent of the votes. Two Germanies had now been set up. In the next years they were to become increasingly divided both in their political alliances and in the character of their internal institutions.

East Europe: Submission and Challenge

Although complete Communist dominance had been achieved in Bulgaria, Rumania, and Yugoslavia by 1946, two states, Poland and Czechoslovakia, retained their coalition governments. In

Poland the chief opposition to Communist control came from the Peasant Party. Its leader, Stanislaw Mikolajczyk, had joined the reorganized Lublin government as vice-premier and minister of agriculture in accordance with the agreements reached at Yalta. In 1947, however, the election was so conducted that the Peasant Party was deprived of its share of the votes. Both Britain and the United States protested that the Yalta arrangements had been violated. Mikolajczyk resigned and fled to London. In 1948 the Communist Party was in complete control in Poland.

Similar events occurred in Czechoslovakia. Of all the east European peoples, the Czechs alone had consistently held pro-Russian feelings throughout the previous century. Romantic Panslavs, they had felt that their Russian brothers would protect them from German domination. In free elections held in May, 1946 the Communists won a plurality of 38 per cent. The president of Czechoslovakia, Edward Beneš, was a firm supporter of close co-operation with Moscow. He had already agreed that a Communist, Klement Gottwald, should be premier, and that the party should also have the vital ministries of defense and interior. The first break in good relations came in 1947 when the Soviet government forbade Czech participation in the Marshall Plan negotiations. A real crisis came in the beginning of 1948. In February twelve non-Communist members of the cabinet resigned in protest over the fact that the ministry of interior was filling the police with Communists. They hoped to force new elections. Instead the Communists took advantage of the situation to take full charge of the government. A Soviet mediator arrived from Moscow, and great pressure was put on Beneš. On February 25 Gottwald chose a cabinet consisting of Communists and some left-wing socialists. Beneš resigned and died soon afterwards; Gottwald then became president.

Until this time the gradual tightening of Soviet control caused no open revolt nor did it lead to foreign intervention. The first rebellion came not from parties organized along western lines but from the strongest communist leader outside of the Soviet Union —Tito. Unlike the heads of the other communist regimes, Tito had won his position by his own efforts and not with the support of the Soviet army. Moreover, during the war he had maintained relations with the western states and he was used to conducting negotiations independently. He also had real popular support within his own country. At first he was in no sense anti-Soviet. On the contrary, he had expected to co-operate with the Soviet Union and he recognized the pre-eminent position of that state in the socialist world. He signed a treaty of friendship in April, 1945. Anti-western, he was particularly angered at the failure to obtain Trieste in the peace settlement with Italy. In 1946 he shot down two American planes that had crossed the Yugoslav boundary, an act which led to the breaking of relations with the United States. In his own government he had rid himself of the coalition cabinet early. In November, 1945 a controlled election gave his slate of candidates 90 per cent of the votes. A new constitution of January, 1946 introduced a communist political system. In the next year the country adopted a five-year plan of economic development on the Soviet model.

As well as being a convinced communist, Tito had wide plans for independent international activities. By this time Yugoslavia had obtained a position of political and economic domination in Albania. The Tirana government was Tito's satellite. In 1947 the Yugoslav leader and George Dimitrov met in Bled, where they decided on a Bulgarian-Yugoslav customs union to serve as a base for a future Balkan union. None of these acts were taken with the express approval of the Soviet Union. In fact, in February, 1948 Bulgarian and Yugoslav representatives were soundly scolded for them. The Yugoslavs were then compelled to sign an agreement that they would consult the Soviet government on all foreign policy decisions. Determined to resist Soviet pressure, Tito called a meeting of the central committee of his party in March, 1948. It was decided that the union with Bulgaria would be abandoned, but that Soviet demands would not be carried out. In reply, Soviet civilian and military advisors were summoned home.

The Yugoslav defection was not easy to meet. The Soviet government hesitated to use military force. Tito had a large army under his personal command that would no doubt fight. The effects in other areas had to be considered also. Instead the attempt was made to put pressure on the country from the outside in the hope that Tito would either surrender or be overthrown. In June, 1948 the Cominform passed a resolution urging the Yugoslav Communists to submit or to replace their leadership. The country was expelled from the organization. In 1949 all the socialist states broke their mutual assistance pacts with Belgrade. At the same time Tito closed his border with Greece and ended his assistance to the rebellion there. In the next years Yugoslavia was to approach the western states. By 1951 economic aid was being received from the United States. In August, 1954 a pact of friendship was signed with two NATO allies, Greece and Turkey. In foreign relations Tito henceforth sought to follow a neutralist course, friendly to communist nations, but not subservient to the Soviet Union.

The Yugoslav action marked not only the departure of a communist state from the Soviet orbit but also a challenge to Soviet doctrinal leadership. Tito now claimed to represent a truer Marxism than did the Soviet party. He introduced the idea of Workers' Councils in the management of factories and he abandoned forced collectivization on the land. Most significant for international communism was his strong support of the idea that each state should follow its own road to socialism.

Tito's resistance had an immediate effect in all the socialist states. Albania, under the leadership of Enver Hoxha, was able to break away from Yugoslav control and join the Soviet camp. In the other countries a purge of the party membership, strongly reminiscent of the events in the Soviet Union in the 1930's, was begun. Everywhere leading Communists fell. Traicho Kostov, the secretary of the Bulgarian Communist Party, Rudolf Slansky, who held a similar position in Czechoslovakia, and Laszlo Rajk in Hungary were all executed. Wladyslaw Gomulka, a leading Polish Communist, first lost his positions in the party and, in 1951, was imprisoned. At the end of 1949 Marshal Konstantin Rokossovsky, a Soviet officer of Polish ancestry, became Polish minister of defense and commander of the armed forces.

EAST ASIA: CHINA POLICY

During the period of Soviet acquisition of pre-eminence in east Europe, great changes were also taking place in Asia: Japan had been defeated, and by 1949 a Communist regime had been established in Peking. The road to power had not been easy. As we have seen, in 1928 the Communist Party had almost been destroyed. The Northern Expedition had left the Kuomintang the strongest force in China with Chiang Kai-shek the outstanding political figure. Although most governments recognized his regime as the legal authority in China, he did not control all of the country. The warlords still ruled over many areas. Kuomintang control was also weak in the countryside. Fearful of a real social revolution the nationalist regime did not acquire a strong peasant rural base. Despite Chiang's position of strength, he had to meet constant political opposition. This civil turmoil, divided political authority, and the subsequent Japanese invasion meant that the Kuomintang, despite its initial idealism under Sun Yat-sen, had little to spare for social measures or reconstruction.

Nor did the shifting Comintern position contribute to tranquility. It will be remembered that after 1928 the Chinese Communist Party was directed to build up its independent power and not co-operate with the nationalists. Like the Kuomintang the Communist Party, too, had its divisions and factions. One group, representing the Central Committee and the Politburo, had its center in Shanghai under the leadership of Li Li-san, whose activities were closely connected with the Comintern and who favored the organization of the Communist proletariat in the large cities and armed uprisings there. Another faction, headed by Mao Tse-tung, relying mainly on peasant support, was in the process of building a rural base on the mountain Chingkangshan in Kiangsi, near the border of Hunan. Differences concerning strategy, general policy, and command existed both within the Politburo and between this organization and the Communists in the country-side. The headquarters in Shanghai suffered heavily from Kuo-mintang suppression. In contrast, Mao Tse-tung's guerilla tactics won victories and gained more territory in Kiangsi province. In an attempt to obtain party unity and to fulfill Comintern direc-tives a Chinese Soviet Republic was proclaimed at Juichin, south-ern Kiangsi, in November, 1931, when the first National Soviet Congress convened in the red capital. Mao was elected chairman of the central executive committee of this regime, but he did not dominate the party organization. His political strength had pre-viously rested on his control of the Chinese Red Army. His hold on the military was reduced at this time.

Although the Soviet government was interested in the fate of the Chinese Communist Party, it was much more concerned over the security of its own Siberian border and the Japanese threat to Manchuria. Care was taken to maintain the tsarist privileges in this area. Near the end of 1928 the warlord in control of Manchuria, Chang Hsueh-liang, known as the Young Marshal, declared his allegiance to the Kuomintang Nanking government. He then attempted to remove Soviet influence from Manchuria. He seized property and officials connected with the Chinese Eastern Rail-road. His action led to an undeclared war with the Soviet Union, who sent in troops in November, 1929. The Chinese Manchurian army was defeated and the former conditions were re-established.

This situation soon changed. In September, 1931 the Japanese army began to occupy Manchuria and in the next year it set up a puppet state, Manchukuo. With its primary interest now in Europe, the Soviet government sought an agreement with Japan. Although it was made clear that predominance in Outer Mongolia would be maintained, the Soviet Union in effect withdrew from Manchuria in 1935 with the sale of the railroad to Japan. In 1932 relations were also renewed with the Kuomintang government. For the next decade, with the rise of Hitler's Germany, Soviet eyes of necessity had to be directed westward. In Asia concern over Japanese actions took precedence over all other matters.

The policy adopted toward both the Kuomintang and Communist Party was thus primarily determined by Soviet security interests. This policy was not of benefit to the Chinese Communists, who once again were almost destroyed.

Chiang Kai-shek was determined to crush the rival political authority in Juichin. After his first efforts failed he hired German experts to replace the Russian military advisors whose services he had enjoyed during the Northern Expedition several years previously. In 1933 the famed strategist Hans von Seeckt, who was well acquainted with the Soviet army, came to assist in the fight against the Communists. From 1930 to 1934 five great campaigns were launched against the Chinese soviet capital. The third was interrupted by the Japanese invasion of Manchuria in 1931 and the attack on Shanghai in 1932. In May, 1933 a truce was signed with Japan, and in the following year the final campaigns could be launched.

The new nationalist assault found the Communist Party again divided. The Politburo remained in opposition to Mao and favored regular and not guerilla warfare. In July, 1934 Mao was punished because he failed to endorse support to a rebellion in Fukien. He and his family were sent to live in Yutu, about sixty miles from Juichin, and were called back only to join in the Long March. Defeated by overwhelming nationalist forces, the remnants of the Red Army and its officials started to move northward in October, 1934. At the beginning about 85,000 soldiers and 15,000 administrative and party officials joined. Of the original number only about 8,000 arrived in northern Shensi in October, 1935, after a circuitous march of 6,000 miles. During this time Mao's leadership became firmly established. At the Tsunyi conference in January, 1935 he was elected chairman of the Politburo. Thereafter he remained in control at the new Communist capital at Yenan, Shensi, but not without challenges to his authority. The northern location had the advantage that it lay closer to Soviet territories and was better located in relation to the Japanese in Manchuria.

The conclusion of the Long March coincided with yet another

change of Soviet policy in China. The great problem facing Moscow then was, of course, Nazi Germany. German and Japanese co-operation was a natural nightmare. In Asia the Soviet Union feared also that the Kuomintang government might come to some sort of arrangement with the Japanese. The nationalists would then be free to deal with their domestic enemy, the Communists, and Japan could turn against the Soviet lands. Throughout this period the Soviet government had a real interest in the continuation of the Sino-Japanese war. To meet these dangers, Comintern policy, which called for united front governments in Europe, now supported similar arrangements in China. In contrast to previous directives strong efforts were to be made to bring the Kuomintang and the Communists back together again. After 1936 Soviet interests called for a union against Japan.

Similar impulses existed in the nationalist camp. Chiang had previously believed that he needed full control over China before he could adequately deal with the external foe. However, in December, 1936 Chiang visited the city of Sian. There he was seized by Chang Hsueh-liang, who although not a Communist had been won over to the popular front policy. The kidnapping of Chiang shocked both the Chinese leaders and the Soviet Union, who did not wish a continuation of the civil war. After two weeks, at Soviet urging, Chiang was freed to return to Nanking. Thereafter a policy of co-operation between the Communists and nationalists slowly evolved. Collaboration was made even more necessary by the renewal of the Japanese attacks. In July, 1937 the undeclared Sino-Japanese War started near Peking and soon spread to Shanghai. In August the Soviet Union made a nonaggresssion pact with the Kuomintang government and promised to send assistance. At the same time the Communists and nationalists ended the civil war and accepted the idea of a united front regime. Meanwhile, the Japanese advances continued; in December, 1937 the nationalist capital, Nanking, fell. The government subsequently moved to remote Chungking in Szechwan province. Soviet aid to Chiang Kai-shek arrived in the next years, including planes with pilots and advisors. The chief Soviet aim remained the weakening of Japan.

In this same period Soviet and Japanese troops waged regular battles on the Manchurian-Siberian border. In the summer of 1938 and May, 1939 engagements of considerable extent, involving tanks and planes, took place. Having been given no previous indication of the Nazi intention, the Japanese were most unpleasantly surprised by the pact of August, 1939. This agreement and the commencement of the war in Europe inaugurated a period in which both Japan and the Soviet Union shared a mutual interest in maintaining calm on the Siberian-Manchurian frontier. Both had primary interests in other directions. An armistice was therefore agreed to in September. In May, 1941, as we have seen, the two powers signed a non-aggression pact.

During the years 1938 to 1941 the Japanese were able to occupy the main Chinese cities and to hold the central lines of communication. They could not, however, control the large rural areas. Although at this time the Kuomintang and the Communist Party were in theory collaborating against the invader, the policy was not very successful. Both sides remained primarily concerned about their relative position in the future and hesitated to throw any real strength against the Japanese. Mao's policy was to direct 80 per cent of his force against the Kuomintang. Repeated incidents occurred between the armies of the two groups. After 1941 co-operation was for all practical purposes ended although negotiations continued. During the war Mao's Red Army was able to extend the area under its control; by 1945 this force numbered about a million regular troops. The Kuomintang had the advantage of being the recognized government of China. It also received extensive aid from the United States. Soviet policy continued to support the co-operation of the two parties and the full use of their resources against Japan. As long as the war continued in Europe, it was to the Soviet interest that Japan remain bogged down in the war in mainland China.

The entrance of the Soviet Union into the war in the Pacific in its last days has been described. Although the Soviet attitude to the Chinese communist movement is not clear, it appears that a quick victory was not expected. At this time, it must be remembered, popular front governments were being supported in east

Europe even where the Soviet army was in full control. At Yalta
the Soviet gains in Asia had been discussed; Chiang did not learn
of these until some months later. The details were negotiated between the Soviet government and Chiang's representatives. In
August, 1945, at the time of the Japanese surrender, an agreement
was signed in which the Soviet Union promised to aid and support Chiang's regime as the legitimate government of China. Although Chinese sovereignty over Manchuria was recognized and
a Soviet military evacuation was promised within three months,
the Soviet government now received concessions that gave it a
predominant influence in the area. It was agreed that joint control
would be exercised over the railroad for thirty years, when it
would revert to China. Dalny was made a free port; Port Arthur
was to be a joint Sino-Soviet base. The Soviet government agreed
to refrain from any activity in Sinkiang; China recognized the
Soviet domination in Outer Mongolia.

Having made this agreement with Chiang, the Soviet Union
next proceeded to assist the Communists in seizing control in
Manchuria. After the armistice there was great competition between the Kuomintang and the Communist Party to acquire the
military equipment left by the Japanese. In Manchuria, occupied
by the Soviet army, the Soviet authorities proceeded to strip the
country of its industrial equipment under the heading of "war
booty." Despite the agreement with the nationalists, the evacuation of the area was delayed until the Communist forces could
take over. However, in other areas, with the active assistance of
the United States and the co-operation of Japan, the Kuomintang
forces were able to assume control. In 1946 it seemed indeed as if
this regime would be able to maintain its position as the recognized government of China. It enjoyed a five-to-one military
superiority.

As we have seen, both Soviet and American policies called for
the formation of a coalition government. Negotiations did take
place toward this goal between the Kuomintang and the Communist Party but with no practical results. Neither side would
surrender real power to the other. There were continual skirm-

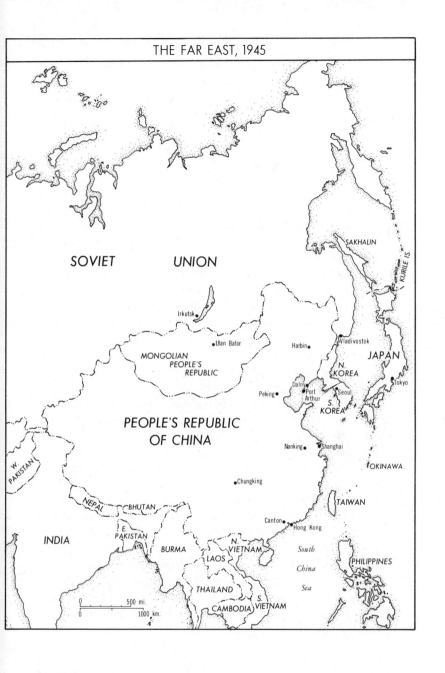

THE FAR EAST, 1945

ishes between the two armies, and large-scale fighting broke out finally in the spring of 1946. At the beginning of the military conflicts Chiang's army was uniformly successful. In March, 1947 the Communist capital of Yenan fell. Thereafter the tide turned. Communist armies now swept through the former nationalist territories. Mukden was taken in November, 1948. Tientsin and Peking fell in January, and Nanking in April, 1949. In December the nationalist government moved to Taiwan (Formosa). In October, 1949 the Chinese People's Republic was formally established.

The Communist victory was a definite defeat for American policy, which had previously called for the support of Chiang's government, but it was not a pure Soviet triumph. Although another communist state now appeared, it owed little to Soviet assistance. Like Tito, Mao had come to power personally and then attained the control of the Chinese mainland through his own efforts. Soviet policy had often been harmful to Chinese Communist interests. Nevertheless, in December, 1949, in his first trip outside of China, Mao went to Moscow, where he stayed for two months. In February, 1950 a series of agreements were reached, including a mutual assistance pact directed against Japan and the United States. The Soviet Union also agreed to modify her position in Manchuria. The railroads and the ports were to come under full Chinese control by 1952. A small 300 million dollar credit was granted to Peking.

The Japanese surrender and the Communist victory did not bring peace to Asia. In June, 1950 war broke out in Korea. At the Cairo and Teheran conferences it had been agreed that Korea would be an independent state, at first under great power trusteeship. As in the case of the European territories, no exact lines of settlement were drawn during the war. At the time of the armistice with Japan, the 38th parallel was set as the line dividing the American and Soviet zones of occupation. As in Germany, the Soviet authorities organized their section according to their own political and economic ideas—the United States did the same. In February, 1946 a provisional North Korean government was established. In September, 1948 it became the Democratic People's

Republic of Korea. In the south the United States supported the right-wing administration of Syngman Rhee. Both sides armed their protégés and then by mid-1949 withdrew their troops. Thereafter, in declarations by high officials, the United States gave the clear impression that it did not consider either Taiwan or Korea areas of vital interest.

On June 25, 1950 the forces of North Korea crossed the boundary into the south. Soviet influence was predominant at the time; the plan of attack must have been known. Apparently an American reaction of real significance was not expected. The Soviet representatives were then boycotting the Security Council meetings at the United Nations in protest against the exclusion of Communist mainland China and the continuation of the membership of the Taiwan nationalist regime. On the day of the invasion the United States called for a special meeting. Two days after the invasion the American Seventh Fleet was sent to patrol between Taiwan and the mainland. The United States was also able to gain United Nations support for South Korea. At first the northern army almost destroyed the South Korean forces. Subsequently, this movement was reversed and American and United Nations troops crossed the 38th parallel. In October, 1950 Chinese troops, designated volunteers, entered the conflict. By summer, 1951 a condition of stalemate existed roughly along the dividing line. After two years of negotiation an agreement was reached restoring in general the previous conditions.

Although the Korean War ended with neither side gaining an advantage, the action had a great effect on world diplomacy. The United States had now entered upon a period of massive rearmament, the level of which was thereafter to be maintained. The Soviet Union also found that it could not block the signature of what was in fact a separate American peace with Japan. Although a general meeting was called in San Francisco in September, 1951, the final terms were not accepted by the Soviet government and its partners. The United States maintained its special close relationship with Japan and its bases there. Thus in Asia the Soviet Union appeared to have gained a firm support in Communist China while the United States found a partner in the neighboring island empire.

THE COLONIAL WORLD

Perhaps the most impressive single result of the Second World War was the collapse of the historic colonial empires of France, Britain, Belgium, and Holland. Although the fall of the British Empire marked the culmination of two centuries of Russian-British rivalry in these areas, the vacuum left by the precipitous departure of the European nations was to create dangers for the Soviet state. The conflicts in Africa and the Near East will be discussed later; this section will concentrate on the fate of southern Asia. In the nineteenth century this area had been a British and French preserve. In 1907 the Russian-British agreement had drawn a boundary that excluded the influence of St. Petersburg from this region. The process by which the colonies broke away commenced during the war when the European powers had to withdraw their forces to meet the more immediate danger in Europe. Wherever Japanese troops were in occupation, they too encouraged anti-European sentiment. After the war the British government, exhausted economically and psychologically, was simply unable to make the effort needed to re-establish its old position. The French and Dutch showed more concern about their former influence, but again they proved powerless against the forces of native nationalism.

The British Empire, of course, involved the greatest extent of territory. The most significant change here was the British withdrawal from India in August, 1947, which was followed by the creation of the two states of India and Pakistan. In 1947 Britain also agreed to Burmese independence, and the Union of Burma was established in January, 1948. A Federation of Malaya came into existence in 1948; it joined the British commonwealth as an independent member in 1957. In the same manner the neighboring Dutch colony of Indonesia broke away in August, 1945. In

December, 1949 the United States of Indonesia was proclaimed under the leadership of Achmed Sukarno.

Perhaps the most complicated situation existed in the French imperial region of Indochina, where unlike the other colonial lands a strong nationalist movement under Communist direction had arisen. Like Mao, the Vietnamese leader Ho Chi Minh had long been active in Communist circles. He had a French education and had been a member of the French Communist Party. Ho had been to Moscow and also had worked with Borodin in China. In 1941 he organized in China the Vietnam Independence League, the Viet Minh. In March, 1945 the Japanese, who were in control of Indochina, promised the country independence. When the French tried to return after the war, they faced the opposition of the Republic of Vietnam, with its center in Hanoi and with Ho as president. Unlike the British, the French government at first did not want to surrender its hold. It preferred to try to join the Vietnamese lands with Laos and Cambodia in a federation associated with France. In 1946 fighting commenced between Ho and the French forces, which consisted chiefly of foreign legion troops. In 1948 a separate south Vietnamese regime was set up in Saigon under Emperor Bao Dai. The French determination to keep Indochina died after the disastrous defeat at Dienbienphu in the spring of 1954.

The fate of Indochina was discussed at conferences held in Geneva from April to July, 1954. China was represented at this meeting by Chou En-lai. The powers settled the Vietnam problem by dividing the state along the 17th parallel, with Ho's regime predominant in the north and the Saigon government in control in the south. Elections were to be held within two years in the entire country. Laos and Cambodia became independent, neutral states and joined the United Nations in 1955.

As can be seen, the Soviet Union played no major role at this time in these areas. Communist policy in southern Asia at first was to co-operate with national liberation movements. After 1947 the emphasis was placed on armed rebellions. A series of small revolts under leftist leadership were thus organized in Burma, India,

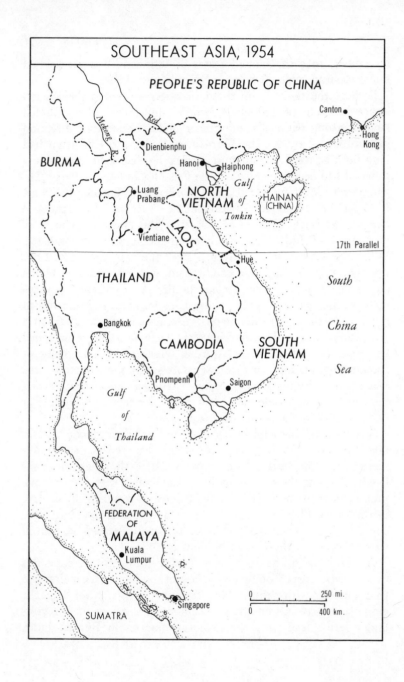

SOUTHEAST ASIA, 1954

PEOPLE'S REPUBLIC OF CHINA

Canton

Hong Kong

Mekong R.

Red R.

BURMA

Dienbienphu

Hanoi

Haiphong

Gulf of Tonkin

HAINAN (CHINA)

Luang Prabang

NORTH VIETNAM

LAOS

Vientiane

17th Parallel

Hue

THAILAND

South

China

Sea

Bangkok

CAMBODIA

SOUTH VIETNAM

Pnompenh

Saigon

Gulf of Thailand

FEDERATION OF MALAYA

Kuala Lumpur

Singapore

SUMATRA

0   250 mi.
0   400 km.

Indonesia, Malaya, and the Philippines; all failed. In the future political alignment India, Burma, Indonesia, Laos, and Cambodia were to be neutral; Thailand, Pakistan, Malaya, and South Vietnam were to ally with the west. North Vietnam remained a Communist center in close relationship with Peking and Moscow. Although under Stalin, Soviet involvement in these areas was limited, this situation was to change radically under his successors.

*   *   *   *   *

On March 5, 1953 Stalin died, after having held the predominant position in the Soviet state since the late 1920's. The length of his term of office rivals that of most of the tsars whose reigns were discussed previously. Like these rulers, his period of power shows certain unique characteristics. During his life and perhaps even more after his death, Stalin was a controversial figure. Many were extremely unsympathetic to him because of the violence of his methods and the intolerance of his views through much of his life. It is difficult to judge him. Adequate material does not exist to tell us exactly what he wanted and how he looked on the world. From the evidence available he appears to have been an unusually tough, realistic, and determined statesman who thought almost solely in terms of power and state interest. He also showed a remarkable awareness of the continuity of Russian policy from tsarist times. All around the map he sought to regain what had been surrendered in the past and to push forward along traditional lines. Like Alexander II and Franz Joseph, he had an almost dynastic concern in acquiring what had previously been lost or in obtaining compensation.

Although the head of a state with a revolutionary ideology, Stalin does not appear in the role of a crusader. He spoke and acted in foreign relations like a Russian patriot despite his own Georgian origins. His doctrinaire communist convictions were reserved for internal policy. He shared none of the idealistic, humanitarian, and cosmopolitan views of many previous socialist leaders. Certainly in his aims after the war we find no trace of the "no annexations and no indemnities" slogan of Lenin's time.

Stalin wanted a great deal of territory and compensation in money and industrial equipment. He took from friend and foe, proletarian and capitalist alike. World communist parties were also expected to serve Russian goals. Comintern directives reflected Soviet internal and foreign policy requirements. Although the doctrine of "proletarian internationalism" had some, if not complete, justification while the Soviet Union remained the single communist state, the same attitude was maintained after the war when this policy was not so clearly needed. This condition underlay the break with Tito. Nevertheless, despite this subordination of ideology to Russian interests, Stalin certainly did much to spread communism. Soviet armies brought this form of government to Poland, Rumania, Bulgaria, Hungary, Czechoslovakia, East Germany, and North Korea; they backed native movements in China and Yugoslavia. Until the later rise of a competitor in Peking, Moscow was the center of world Marxian socialism.

Whether by design or good fortune Stalin's accomplishments are most impressive. In terms of his success in furthering and raising the power of his state he stands pre-eminent among the leaders of the twentieth century. At the end of the 1920's the Soviet Union was a weak state; in the 1950's it was one of two super-powers. A short catalogue of Soviet acquisitions during this period also demonstrates Stalin's abilities not only in recouping the losses of the First World War but also in surpassing the furthest aims of the tsarist period. During and after the Second World War the Soviet Union took Baltic, Polish, Prussian, Rumanian, and Finnish territory in Europe, and southern Sakhalin and the Kirile Islands in the Far East. Unsuccessful attempts were made to control or annex Kars, Ardahan, northern Iran, and Manchuria. In terms of spheres of influence, Rumania, Bulgaria, Hungary, Poland, Czechoslovakia, and the German Democratic Republic were in close association with Moscow; Yugoslavia and Albania, although communist, caused some problems. In the Far East Stalin maintained the tsarist concern with Manchuria and Korea.

By the time of Stalin's death broad lines of international relations had been drawn; with some important modifications these were to last for at least the next twenty years. East Europe was under predominantly Soviet influence; Germany was divided; China had a communist government. The two powers who had emerged from the war as the world's militarily strongest nations, the United States and the Soviet Union, headed two rival military and political blocs. In the next years most of the great international crises were not to center in areas of vital concern to either of these states but in peripheral regions, such as southern Asia, the Near East, and Africa. In these areas their mutual antagonism was played out not directly but through their support of rival forces. The former colonial lands thus assumed a prime importance. In this same period the Soviet government met with increasing problems in its relations with its neighboring communist states.

IX

Khrushchev

Although Nikita S. Khrushchev was the dominant personage of the period from 1953 to 1964, he did not hold real power immediately after the death of Stalin. From 1953 to 1956 three men in particular inherited the top positions in the state—George M. Malenkov as premier, Molotov again foreign minister, and Lavrenty D. Beria in charge of the secret police. Marshal George K. Zhukov, the great hero of the war, also played a major political role. Khrushchev held the important position of party secretary. Of the three at the top Beria was the first to fall. His execution in December, 1953 marks the last occasion of such an action against a Soviet leader. In 1955 a major shift occurred. Malenkov was replaced as premier by Nicholas A. Bulganin, an associate of Khrushchev's, and Zhukov became minister of defense. In this year Khrushchev and Bulganin were recognized as the most important figures in Soviet politics.

Khrushchev came to worldwide attention at the time of the twentieth party congress, held in Moscow in February, 1956. Here, at the first such gathering held since 1939, the doctrine of peaceful coexistence in foreign relations was announced. Especially dramatic was Khrushchev's "secret speech," in which for four hours he denounced Stalin's actions. Although in the next years Khrushchev retained his leading position, he never approached the power held by Stalin. In 1957 an attempt was made to remove him by Malenkov, Molotov, and Lazar M. Kaganovich. Khrushchev successfully met this challenge to his authority, and in 1958 reached the summit of his political power. Like Stalin before him, he now held the posts of premier and first secretary, the top government and party positions.

Khrushchev was the dominant personality of his era, and in many ways, particularly in temperament, was a sharp contrast to Stalin. He was born in Kalinovka in 1894, and joined the party in 1918. From 1938 until 1949 except for a short interval he was mainly involved in party affairs in the Ukraine. He was also concerned with agricultural policy. With only a poor education, he had no experience in foreign countries. Whereas his predecessor had kept to himself, had not traveled, and had shunned public appearances, Khrushchev enjoyed very much being in the center of attention. His period in power was characterized by his worldwide travels, frequent open discussions, and unselfconscious and often undiplomatic utterances. His flamboyant personality and his crude and direct manner made him very popular in his own way. Intensely involved in foreign affairs, he always overshadowed his foreign ministers. Molotov held that office until June, 1956, when he was replaced by Dimitri T. Shepilov, the editor of the party newspaper *Pravda*. He was followed in February, 1957 by Andrei A. Gromyko.

Khrushchev's different style of foreign relations reflected a basic change in the society he represented. By the time he assumed full power in 1956 the Soviet Union had the hydrogen bomb. Being in a relatively secure position, the Soviet government thereafter gave no indication that it had any real fear that the United States, the only state with superior military strength, would launch an unprovoked attack. The nation itself, weary of years of war and tension, needed a respite. No longer truly revolutionary, the Soviet Union was a state dominated by managers, bureaucrats, and technicians. It was not a base from which to launch revolutionary adventures in other countries. Having achieved a maximum territorial extension after the war, the Soviet government had no great foreign policy aims. The need at this time was for a period of stability in international affairs so that prime attention could be directed at internal development. The policy of "peaceful coexistence" with the capitalist world thus reflected the real interests of the Soviet state. That term did not imply that the two systems would remain permanently in a condition of mutual respect and balance. The Marxist idea remained that the victory of socialism was inevitable; as Khrushchev expressed it, "We will bury you." This end was not, however, to be achieved by atomic war. During the Khrushchev period it was felt that the Soviet economic system could indeed equal and then overtake that of the United States. Quite unrealistic targets were set up to achieve this goal in the 1970's.

The new period was reflected in both internal and foreign developments. During the "thaw" more freedom was allowed in literature and in the expression of opinions. The Soviet Union was opened to tourists. Very significant cultural exchange programs were inaugurated with capitalist countries, among them the United States. The Soviet Union now participated in large international bodies such as the World Health Organization and the United Nations Children's Fund (UNICEF). Moves were made to ease tensions with other states, and significant claims were dropped. For instance, Soviet attempts to obtain Kars and Ardahan and a change in the Straits settlement from Turkey were given up; the naval base at Porkkalla was returned to Finland; and in 1955 Port Arthur was given to China. The change of atmosphere was also shown in the signature of the Austrian State Treaty and, especially, in the renewal of good relations with Yugoslavia as demonstrated by Khrushchev's visit to that coun-

try in May and June, 1955. It almost appeared that in Soviet relations with the east European states the concept of separate roads
to socialism would be accepted.

In general, in the field of international relations, the Soviet
Union faced three sets of problems, all connected with developments that had occurred under Stalin in the immediate post-war
period. First, relations with the capitalist powers, primarily with
the United States, had to be adjusted. The issues here involved
chiefly the question of arms limitation and the unsolved problem
of Germany and the status of Berlin. Second, the effect of the
thaw on the east European states and the more general problem
of relations between Moscow and other socialist states had to be
met. The sharp decline in relations with Peking was the most
significant event. Third, the Soviet Union now intensified efforts,
begun before, to influence events in the "third world." More than
in any previous period Soviet diplomats actively entered into
controversies in Africa, the Near East, and Asia which resulted
from the breakup of the western colonial empires. The conflict
with the United States and its alliance system thus extended into
these areas. These three questions will be discussed in sequence.

RELATIONS WITH THE UNITED STATES: EUROPEAN ISSUES

Throughout the Khrushchev period relations with the western
states involved principally negotiations with the United States.
Although Soviet military power did not equal the American until
1969, the country was in a strong position. Moreover, in her
rocket program it appeared that in some areas she had indeed
overtaken the United States. In October and November, 1957
earth satellites were launched. Most spectacular, in April, 1961
the first manned satellite was placed in orbit, an accomplishment
that was most important for Soviet prestige. A state that had
long lagged behind the west in scientific development had now
demonstrated its ability to attain pre-eminence in certain technical fields. Despite its advances in the construction of atomic

weapons and rockets, the Soviet government showed a real respect for the potential danger of such devices. The question of arms limitation joined that of Germany as a major subject of negotiation with the United States.

During this period the Soviet government faced two administrations in Washington; their words were different but their practical actions were very similar. General Dwight D. Eisenhower was president from 1953 to 1961, with John Foster Dulles as secretary of state until 1959, when he was succeeded by Christian Herter. The Republican campaign that brought Eisenhower into office had been conducted on anti-Soviet themes. The Republican platform stated: "The policies we espouse will revive the contagious, liberating influences which are inherent in freedom. They will inevitably set up strains and stresses in the captive world which will make the rulers impotent to continue in their monstrous ways and mark the beginning of the end." [1] Despite such rhetoric and despite talk of a "rollback" of communist influence in Europe and emphasis on nuclear "massive retaliation" in case of war, the Republican administration did not initiate any positive programs to these ends. In 1961 the Democratic victory brought in John F. Kennedy with Dean Rusk in the State Department. A return was made to the idea of containment; conventional warfare received more emphasis than "massive retaliation," but basic American policy did not shift. A high level of armament was maintained and a major effort made to build an arsenal of Intercontinental Ballistic Missiles (ICBMs).

Although both the United States and the Soviet Union wished to avoid a direct conflict, the two powers had great difficulty in conducting successful negotiations. Despite the milder manners of the new regime, the Soviet government maintained most of the objectives and attitudes of Stalin's day. Mutual discussions were hard to arrange and rarely led to real solutions. In the war and the immediate post-war era the United States had hoped that the United Nations would become an effective instrument of inter-

1. Quoted in Robert H. Farrell, *American Diplomacy* (New York: W. W. Norton and Co., 1969), p. 883.

national relations. Not only did that organization prove to be ineffective and cumbersome in operation, but it soon shifted in a direction not entirely pleasing to either the American or the Soviet governments. The Americans in their early enthusiasm had not foreseen that it could become a forum for opinion embarrassing to the United States. As the new states from the old colonial territories joined, their governments showed a tendency to be either neutral or actively hostile toward the former imperial powers, including, of course, the United States. The Soviet Union had similar problems in connection with its actions in east Europe and elsewhere.

Since the United Nations did not work sufficiently well, the chief negotiations were carried on by heads of state and their foreign ministers. Meetings of foreign ministers had been held regularly after 1945, with little success. Conferences between their superiors, called summit meetings, also did not achieve great gains. The first one held after the war met in July, 1955 in Geneva and was attended by Eisenhower, Bulganin, Eden, and Edgar Faure, the French premier. The main subjects discussed were Germany and disarmament. In October and November of that year the foreign ministers of the powers met again. In 1959 Khrushchev visited the United States and talked with Eisenhower at Camp David. Although they made little progress in solving concrete problems, they agreed that another meeting of the leaders of the four powers would be held in Paris in May, 1960.

Immediately before that event was scheduled to take place, the Soviet military shot down an American photo-reconnaissance plane, a U-2. It had been flying at an altitude of 68,000 feet 1,300 miles within the Soviet Union. At first the American government announced that the plane had been lost. When the Soviet reply was received that the pilot and some debris had been recovered, the American government admitted that it was a spy plane, and Eisenhower took full responsibility. This action, which showed the vulnerability of the Soviet air space, provoked a violent reaction from Khrushchev. He demanded an apology, the punishment of those responsible, and the assurance that such action would not take place again. The entire incident resulted in the cancellation of the Paris meeting. In June, 1961 the Soviet premier met with the new president, Kennedy, in Vienna. Again the talks led to no positive result. Khrushchev appeared to have left with a generally negative impression of Kennedy, who for his part felt that the Soviet leader was indeed a man to be feared.

Although no solutions were reached, a further examination of the two major issues discussed in these meetings, arms limitation and Germany, is necessary because they endured as major points at issue between the United States and the Soviet Union. Like the Americans the Soviet government had an intense interest in limiting atomic weapons. Not only were they disproportionately expensive but also their acquisition by certain other nations could be dangerous for Soviet security. Although the Soviet Union at first agreed to aid Chinese atomic research, this attitude changed radically after 1959. Similar fears were felt concerning West German acquisition of these arms. In this sphere also the Soviet Union was at a disadvantage. Although the United States could contemplate the delivery of nuclear weapons to its allies, the Soviet government could not give such arms to its east European partners. In addition to these military considerations, both powers were forced to recognize that the damage done to the atmosphere by nuclear testing was of equal deadly danger to their own populations.

Throughout the negotiations the chief block to a settlement was the Soviet Union's unwillingness to consent to any mutually satisfactory arrangements for ground or air inspection. Nevertheless, some minor advances were made in the field of control of nuclear power. The first steps were taken in 1946 when the United Nations established an Atomic Energy Commission. At this time the United States proposed the creation of an authority that would have the right to inspect plants in all countries. Still without the bomb, the Soviet government refused to accept the plan unless it retained the right to use its veto freely. The United States was also to destroy her bombs before the system went into effect. In the next years the Soviet Union acquired both the atom and hydrogen bombs and proceeded with the construction of increasingly more effective long-range missiles. In 1955 at the Geneva meeting Eisenhower proposed as a method of control an "open skies" agreement for inspection. Refusing to accept this proposal, the Soviet Union in 1957 and 1958 countered with her support of the Rapacki Plan, announced by the Polish foreign minister, for the creation of a zone in central Europe, including the two Germanies, Poland, and Czechoslovakia, from which atomic weapons would be excluded. The Soviet government simultaneously pressed for the departure of American troops from Europe.

The dangers of testing, obvious to both powers, did lead to an advance. In 1961 both the United States and the Soviet Union stopped testing these weapons in the atmosphere. In 1963 the two nations and Britain, who had joined the atomic club in 1952, agreed to ban tests in the atmosphere, in outer space, and under water. A treaty had already been made to cover the Antarctic. The agreement was weakened by the fact that neither France, who successfully detonated a bomb in 1960, nor China, who did the same in 1964, would join the pact. In 1963 the so-called hot line between Washington and Moscow was constructed in an attempt to prevent the launching of a nuclear strike by either power by mistake. Because of the enormous potential danger to all human life the limitation and control of nuclear weapons remained the single major issue in international relations thereafter.

As in the arms discussions, the negotiations over the German question showed the great cleavage between the Soviet and American views. Quite obviously the interest of the Soviet government still demanded either the creation of a unitary state in a form over which it could hope to exercise a predominant influence or the maintenance of the two Germanies. Since it was still clear that the German Communist Party had no chance of winning a free election in the west and that a coalition with the popular Social Democrats was not a practical possibility, the prospect of any advances being made toward German unity was at the best dubious. The Soviet Union, nevertheless, did make some suggestions. Among them was the proposal to set up a Constitutional Council in which there would be equal representation from both German states, even though the population of the west was much larger than that of the east. German unification was also to be allowed but only if the resultant state was demilitarized and neutralized.

Such conditions could not be accepted by the western allies. Since there was no question how the Germans would vote, the position was maintained that a united Germany must be assured free elections. The state was also to be allowed the right to enter any western European combinations. Without German participation the heart would be taken out of any economic or military unions of the area. Because of the basic contradiction in these views on the German question, no agreement could be reached. In 1954 West Germany joined NATO and began to rearm. The German problem was discussed at the Geneva Conference of 1955 again without result. In September, 1955 the West German chancellor, Konrad Adenauer, visited Moscow. Diplomatic relations were established at this time, but concurrently the Soviet Union recognized the German Democratic Republic as a sovereign state.

The Soviet establishment of relations with the Federal Republic and the recognition of the Democratic Republic again brought up the question of the four-power control of Berlin. In November, 1958 Khrushchev declared that unless an agreement were made in six months he would give the administration of the Soviet sector to East Germany along with the control of the access routes to the city. Again no progress was made in the negotiations, but Khrushchev did not carry out his threat. However, in 1961 a dramatic action was taken. Because of its international supervision, Berlin was an easy avenue by which inhabitants of East Germany could leave for the far more prosperous west. By August, 1961 the situation had become serious. Three million persons, out of the East German population of eighteen million, had left the country. In this month, to stop this dangerous flow, which consisted mainly of young people and needed technicians, the Berlin Wall was constructed. It sealed off the eastern sections of the city and effectively halted the mass migration of the German population. Similar structures were built along the entire frontier of the two German states. In June, 1964 the Soviet Union signed a mutual assistance treaty with the Democratic Republic. The Berlin problem was not yet solved, but the Soviet government did not press as hard for the removal of the western governments after the construction of the wall.

Although no German settlement was reached, a treaty dealing with Austria was signed by Great Britain, France, the United States, and the Soviet Union in May, 1955. Since technically Austria was neither an enemy nor an ally, a peace treaty as such could not be negotiated with her. The Austrian State Treaty, as it was called, met a Soviet claim for reparations based on former German assets in the area. It was decided that Austria would pay 150 million dollars in goods over a period of six years, two million dollars in cash, and about a third of her oil production for ten years. By general agreement the state was also neutralized. Although Austria thereafter joined the United Nations, her entrance into the Common Market, the western European economic union created in 1957, was blocked because of Soviet objections that this move would violate her neutrality.

EAST EUROPE

Although the Soviet Union was able to preserve the political *status quo* in western and central Europe, real problems were encountered in her relations with the socialist governments of eastern Europe. Khrushchev's denunciation of Stalin and the lightening of control in the Soviet Union had an immediate reflection in these states. By 1956 many of those who had been executed in the last years of the Stalin period were "posthumously rehabilitated." Thus such names as Laszlo Rajk in Hungary and Traicho Kostov in Bulgaria reappeared on the list of the recognized leaders in the establishment of socialism in these countries. The reconciliation with Tito seemed to assure that the Soviet government now accepted the Yugoslav idea of separate roads to socialism.

For the Soviet Union the relaxation of control offered obvious dangers. Past interference had left feelings of hostility and resentment even among loyal Communists. The push to industrialize had put great pressure on the workers, on whose support the Communist regime was supposed to depend, and also on the rest of the population. The first sign of trouble came soon after the death of Stalin. In June, 1953 German workers in the Soviet sector of Berlin protested against their labor conditions; a strike was called. In answer Soviet troops and tanks were sent in and martial law was declared. Similar actions occurred in other cities and large casualty lists attended the suppression of the movements. Riots also broke out in some Czech cities. Thereafter efforts were made to improve the conditions that had led to the protests.

The first major challenge to Soviet domination came in Poland. In March, 1956 the Soviet-approved first secretary of the Communist Party, Boleslaw Bierut, died. He was replaced by Edward Ochab, who was not a candidate of Moscow. Riots centered in Poznan, resembling those previously seen in Berlin, commenced in June. The protests concerned economic conditions chiefly. The police were unable to handle the riots and the army was called in. The demonstrators who were arrested were given light sentences and attempts were made to meet their grievances with concessions.

The Polish Communist Party now showed that it wished to go further. In October the Central Committee decided to elect a new Politburo. The candidate most favored for the post of first secretary was Wladyslaw Gomulka, who had been imprisoned during the purges of the late forties but had subsequently been released. In August, 1956 he had again joined the party. As the Central Committee met to make these decisions there appeared at the Warsaw airport an impressive Soviet delegation, including

Khrushchev and Molotov and several military representatives. At the same time units of the Red Army were grouped for a possible move on Warsaw.

The meetings between the two sides were stormy. Khrushchev in the end showed himself willing to compromise. Gomulka was elected first secretary and, later, Marshal Rokossovsky, the Soviet citizen who was the Polish defense minister, returned to the Soviet Union. It will be noted that the issue here was purely that of national communism, that is, the right of the Polish Communist Party to control its own internal affairs. The Polish leaders made it plain that they would not disavow the system itself or the association with Moscow. They simply wanted to chose their own officials. Thereafter certain other reforms were initiated. A move to decollectivize the farms was undertaken. More internal freedom, in particular in regard to Catholicism, was also allowed.

The limited challenge to Soviet control was thus successful. Events in Hungary, however, were to proceed in another direction. Here too much was attempted in too short a period. The Hungarian Communist Party was itself severely divided. In 1953, even before Stalin's death, the liberal Imre Nagy had been named premier. In 1955 he was replaced by a candidate identified with the Stalinist position. In 1956 the real changes began. Some political prisoners were released. In July the liberal Ernö Gerö became premier. As can be understood, the Hungarians were deeply affected by the events in Poland, which were watched closely. On October 22, when it appeared that the Polish party had triumphed, a demonstration of university students took place. On the next day similar meetings were held in front of the statues of Petöfi, the national poet, and General Bem, the Polish officer who had fought with the Hungarian revolutionaries in 1849 against the Russian army. A huge crowd then gathered in front of the parliament building. Fighting broke out, and the crowds were able to get weapons from the police and the military. The anger of the demonstrators was turned against the secret police, many of whom were killed.

On October 24 Gerö was replaced by Imre Nagy, who now emerged as the leader of the resistance. Janos Kadar became first secretary of the party. On the same day Soviet troops entered Budapest, only to depart on the 30th. By the end of the month it thus seemed that in Hungary, as in Poland, a national movement would succeed. But the two actions were profoundly different. The Nagy government proceeded to enact measures that openly challenged the Soviet position. The removal of Soviet troops was requested, and the Warsaw Pact, the communist bloc military alliance, was renounced. It soon appeared that the future Hungarian government would be based on a multiparty system, with Communists holding only minor positions in the administration. The challenge was thus to the Soviet Union as a state and to communism as an ideology. On November 4 the Soviet army re-entered Budapest and quickly put down the uprising. About 180,000 Hungarians took the opportunity to cross the open border into Austria. A new government was formed under Kadar.

Imre Nagy soon suffered a hard fate. He first sought refuge at the Yugoslav embassy. Leaving under a safe conduct, he was seized by Soviet officials and executed after a secret trial. Despite this action Tito was unable to react in a positive manner. He reluctantly condoned the use of the Soviet army to save a communist regime, but he specifically blamed the Soviet Union for helping create the conditions in Hungary that produced the revolution. In 1957 and 1958 relations between Belgrade and Moscow declined, but the extreme tension of the Stalin years did not return.

In Rumania, too, there were signs of a growing attitude of independence. Like the Poles and the Hungarians, the Rumanians had a tradition of anti-Russian feeling, arising in part from previous Russian interference in their affairs. Premier Gheorghe Gheorghiu-Dej, although maintaining a Stalinist line internally, moved toward greater independence in regard to Moscow and to wider relations outside the communist bloc. In 1954 and 1955 he made agreements with Yugoslavia, China, and France. In 1958 he secured the removal of Soviet troops from Rumania.

The chief conflicts in Soviet-Rumanian relations were not to be political but economic. The enormous success of the Marshall Plan and the Common Market put pressure on the Soviet Union to show similar advances among the COMECON nations. Quite obviously it would be to the advantage of the entire area if there were a degree of specialization among the members of the bloc. According to the plan Czechoslovakia, East Germany, and Poland were to have the main industry; Rumania and Bulgaria were designated primarily as suppliers of raw materials. Rumania's reaction to what appeared to be a reduction to an inferior status was strong. The specific conflict came over the Rumanian desire to construct a steel mill at Galatz. In this and in other similar issues Rumania continued to oppose hindrances to her industrial development.

Despite these difficulties the only east European nation to move completely away from the Soviet Union at this time was Albania. After the Tito-Stalin break, Soviet aid had been given to this small state. With the death of Stalin and the renewal of fairly cordial relations between Moscow and Belgrade, the Albanian government became concerned lest it again fall under Yugoslav domination. After 1955 assistance was obtained from China; in 1961 relations were broken with the Soviet Union. Henceforth Albania remained a Chinese outpost in the west. Of course, this change of front had no real effect on Soviet power in the Balkans, but the Albanian Communist Party now provided a convenient instrument through which the Chinese could address Europe, a matter of considerable importance once the two largest communist parties quarreled.

CHINA

For the Soviet Union perhaps the most significant development of the Khrushchev era was the break with China. Although the defection of Yugoslavia had caused problems for Stalin, that country was after all not a great power. China, with its vast population and extensive territories, was another matter. After Mao's victory the Soviet government had made an effort to work with and assist the Chinese. Once Khrushchev came to power, the Soviet leadership at times acknowledged the equality of the Soviet Union and China in the communist camp. In October, 1954 Khrushchev visited China, and more favorable economic relations were agreed upon; another Soviet loan was given. Real problems, however, soon arose. The attack on Stalin and "the cult of personality" after 1956 directly affected Mao, who professed to be an admirer and student of Stalin's; to attack his mentor could be regarded as a criticism of the Chinese leader himself. Moreover, in Mao's mind Khrushchev was at most a revolutionary comrade of equal stature. The two states also began to separate on matters of policy. Although China supported Soviet action in regard to Poland and Hungary, great disapproval was expressed over the reconciliation with Tito. After 1957, at a time when the Soviet Union and Yugoslavia had resumed good relations, Peking launched an attack on the Yugoslav leader and his policies. In November, 1957, during his second visit to Moscow, to take part in an international communist conference, Mao's divergence from the Soviet position in many questions was obvious. Nevertheless, in the same year a more favorable economic agreement was negotiated. The Soviet Union also agreed to give assistance in developing nuclear weapons. A sample bomb, regular information, and advisors were promised. Although part of this bargain was fulfilled, by 1959 the increase in tension between the two countries led to the curtailment of Soviet aid in the nuclear field. Thereafter China developed her weapons without Soviet assistance. After the revolution the Chinese government had needed advice, particularly in the industrial and military aspects of its national life. Plans and technical assistance were especially desired. Despite the fact that China could still benefit from aid from Moscow, Mao decided in 1958 that his country could develop alone. More than ten thousand Soviet advisors and technicians in China returned home, taking with them or destroying the blueprints of the industrial plants that had been under construction under their supervision. By 1960 the break between the two states was in the open; in November a conference of eighty communist parties convened to discuss the breach.

As has been shown, with the exception of Yugoslavia, the Soviet Union had succeeded in keeping in its hands the firm leadership of the world communist movement since 1917. As long as she was the single great power with a Marxist system, this effort had not proved too taxing. The appearance of China on the scene introduced another element. Under Mao's direction Chinese communism was to prove decidedly nationalistic. Moreover, after a century of foreign interference, China emerged as a united, independent, and proud power. Even without the doctrinal disputes, it was not likely that this country, with a history far longer and more illustrious than Russia's, would accept Moscow's leadership. At the beginning of 1949 Mao had adopted the "lean to one side" doctrine—that is, when given a choice between imperialism and socialism there was no question which side China would support. Relations with the western powers were also complicated by the problem of Chiang Kai-shek and his regime on Taiwan. However, once Mao's power became consolidated, the Soviet Union found that it had in Peking not a comrade but a rival.

The Chinese government now came to challenge Soviet leadership in both the ideological and the political arena. In regard to doctrine the Chinese Communists claimed that they had adapted Marxist theory to Asia and that they had developed a higher and purer communism. In 1958 the "Great Leap Forward" was inaugurated. Its stated aim was the overleaping of the socialist phase in Marxist development and a direct entrance into the period of communism. In other words, the Chinese intended to outstrip the Soviet Union.

The Chinese leaders also sharply criticized Soviet behavior in international relations. The Soviet government did not wish to bring about a nuclear war or take real chances with world peace. In contrast, the Chinese government favored using communist capabilities in these fields to win definite objectives such as Taiwan. The apparent Chinese willingness to risk nuclear war thoroughly disconcerted the Soviet leaders, as did statements like the one by Chou En-lai that "after the next war there would be 20 million Americans, 5 million Englishmen, 50 million Russians and 300 million Chinese." [2] In the congress of communist parties in Moscow in 1960, China's support of wars, in particular those of national liberation, and her displeasure over the Soviet policy of peaceful coexistence were made plain.

The Chinese challenge to Soviet leadership was most apparent in Asia. Like the Soviet Union, China was intensely interested in the political future of former colonial lands. The Chinese government had the immense advantage that it could place itself at the head of the poor, non-white, Asian socialist parties without embarrassment. As a state with an imperial past and as a white European power, the Soviet Union found itself classed with France, Britain, and the United States as an object of suspicion. In 1955 at Bandung in Indonesia, at a conference of twenty-nine African and Asian countries, the Chinese worked hard to gain recognition for their leadership and to persuade the attending delegates to adopt a neutralist position in the contest between the Soviet bloc and the west.

Like the Soviet government, the Chinese Communists showed a particular interest in those neighboring areas that had once been historically connected with China, in particular Indochina and Korea, which were henceforth to be centers of Chinese activity. India was also to play an important role in the Sino-Soviet struggle. In competition with India for the leadership of Asia, China was engaged in almost continual border disputes with that nation. In 1959 and 1962 Chinese and Indian troops clashed. This conflict put the Soviet Union in the embarrassing position of having to choose between two nations neither of which she wished to antagonize. In the first clash of 1959 Moscow remained neutral; in 1961 and 1962 she sent arms to India but not to China. The Chinese government was able to strike back, at least in the propaganda field, through Albania. For a time the Sino-Soviet argu-

2. See Immanuel C. Y. Hsü, *The Rise of Modern China* (New York: Oxford University Press, 1970), p. 763.

ments were conducted by this means. China would attack Yugo-slavia when the Soviet Union was meant; the latter would de-nounce Albania in words directed to Peking.

In line with its interest in areas once belonging to China and with its anti-imperialist stand, the Chinese government at this time and later put forward claims to lands taken by Russia in the treaties of the nineteenth century. These involved the Ussuri Region and the territory in Sinkiang surrendered in 1881 after the Kuldja dispute. In the face of these Chinese demands and the growing military power of the country, the Soviet Union again saw the necessity of at least considering the possibility of a future two front war. The defeat of Japan and Mao's victory in China had not brought security in Asia.

THIRD WORLD ADVENTURES

Soviet actions in Europe and Asia, as we have seen, paralleled to an extent similar tsarist interests before the First World War. New in Soviet policy was the increased involvement in affairs in southern Asia, Africa, and the Arabian lands. In these areas Soviet policy aimed not so much at setting up communist-dominated re-gimes as in encouraging native governments to join in anti-western, in particular anti-American, blocs, or in maintaining a neutral position. Adhesion to any of the American alliances was vigorously combatted. At this time in Asia and the Near East Moscow faced two alliance systems, both products of the diplo-macy of John Foster Dulles. In the Far East the Southeast Asian Treaty Organization, SEATO, which included the Philippines, Thai-land, Pakistan, New Zealand, Australia, France, Britain, and the United States, was established in September, 1954. The pact was a consultative agreement designed to combat foreign aggression and internal dangers in Southeast Asia. In 1955 the Baghdad Pact was signed by Iraq, Turkey, Britain, Iran, and Pakistan; in 1959 this agreement was replaced by the Central Treaty Organization, CENTO, composed of the same powers without Iraq.

In addition to seeking to compete with this political alignment, the Soviet Union also chose to follow the American example and try to win friends with economic favors. Financial assistance was offered, although usually not in the form of grants, but in loans at low interest rates. She could also offer beneficial barter agreements. Soviet industry could use the raw materials of the former colonial lands and send in return arms as well as manufactured goods.

Unlike tsarist Russia, who had limited her interest in Africa to Egypt, the Soviet Union now attempted to develop relations with the new black African states. Since Russia had never been an imperial power in the area, no residue of resentment existed. Attempts were made to draw close to Ghana, Mali, Guinea, and Tanzania in particular. Some influence was established in Guinea during the regime of Sekou Touré, but in 1961 the Soviet ambassador was expelled for interfering in the state's internal affairs. The deepest involvement was to occur in the troubled and complicated affairs of the Congo, where Soviet support was given to Patrice Lumumba. With his death, the opportunity to aid in the establishment of a sympathetic regime in central Africa disappeared.

Similar efforts were made to find a base of support in the Near East. Since Turkey, Iran, and Pakistan had joined in the western alignment, it was logical for Moscow to seek friends to the south among the Arab states. In this region the Soviet government was able to exploit the tense situation that had developed with the establishment of the state of Israel. At first, support had been given to the Zionist position in line with the initial anti-British policy followed in this region. The Soviet Union agreed to the United Nations 1947 partition of Palestine, and in 1948 recognized the state of Israel. In 1948 and 1949 approval was given to the sale of arms to this government. By 1955, however, Soviet support had shifted to Egypt, then under the control of Gamal Abdul Nasser. Cairo by this time had become a center of Arab nationalism. Because of this attitude Nasser had won the enmity of Britain, France, and the United States. France objected to the aid and encouragement given the Algerian revolution; the United

States resented the fact that Nasser would not join the American alliance system. Closer relations between the Egyptian and Soviet governments offered advantages to both sides. In addition to the political benefits, economic ties would aid both states. Nasser wanted arms, and he could pay for them with cotton and raw materials of use to the Soviet Union.

The Suez crisis of 1956 commenced when the United States withdrew its support from Nasser's project for the construction of a high dam on the Nile at Aswan. Nasser used this occasion to nationalize the Suez Canal Company, stating he would use the profits for the dam. In reply to this move, France, Britain, and Israel joined in a common action. It was decided that Israel would attack in the Sinai Peninsula, then France and Britain would seize the Suez Canal. Britain was also to bomb Egypt. These powers did not notify their ally, the United States, of their intention. On October 29 Israel attacked Egyptian territory and the British bombed Egyptian airfields. Immediate and outraged protests came from the Soviet Union, the United States, and the United Nations. The outcry was so great that the three aggressor nations simply backed down. The entire operation was a great blow to western prestige and a corresponding advantage to the Soviet Union. It will be remembered that in October and early November the Soviet suppression of the Hungarian revolution took place. The western powers' Suez action served to overshadow Soviet moves in east Europe.

After this crisis the Soviet Union maintained its influence with Nasser. It agreed to support the Aswan project and also to send more military equipment. The entire Near East remained in a state of ferment. In 1958 Syria and Egypt joined to form the United Arab Republic. In July, 1958 a military coup against the pro-western government in Iraq succeeded; this state subsequently left the Baghdad Pact. This action so alarmed the western states that Britain landed paratroopers to support the friendly government of Jordan, while the United States Marines occupied Lebanon with the same intention. In the subsequent period the government of Iraq went through several changes, some of which were favorable, and some not, to Soviet interests. It should be noted that although the Nasser regime was co-operating with the Soviet Union and accepting her aid, it was at the same time suppressing local Communist activities. The Arab governments, while welcoming military and economic assistance, steadily resisted Communist control.

In its relations with the states of southern Asia the Soviet Union put the greatest effort in attempting to establish close and friendly relations with India. Although Stalin had no particularly favorable feelings about Gandhi and Nehru, some attempts were made to improve relations after 1949, particularly after the failure of Communist-led revolts in the preceding years. With Stalin's death the Soviet government began the deliberate courting of India. In 1955 Khrushchev and Bulganin paid an extensive visit there. The emphasis was on economic relations since India was officially a neutralist power. Credits were extended and technical assistance offered, in particular in regard to the very well publicized steel plant at Bhilai. Unfortunately for the Soviet Union, a policy of close relations with India involved conflict with two other states. The Sino-Indian tension has already been described. Even more dangerous was the ever-present rivalry between India and Pakistan and their joint claim to the district of Kashmir.

Meanwhile conditions in the former French colony of Indochina remained unstable. In 1954 the Geneva conference had decided that Laos would become an independent neutral state with Prince Souvanna Phouma at its head. Like Vietnam this area had developed a strong Communist movement, the Pathet Lao, which wished a direct share in the government. After 1958 guerilla activity increased. In this conflict, the United States aided the government; the Soviet Union assisted the Pathet Lao. In May, 1961 a cease-fire was negotiated which left the Pathet Lao in control of about half of the country.

In another entirely new aspect of Soviet policy, activities were now undertaken in the Americas. In both the tsarist and the early Soviet periods the western hemisphere had been regarded as an American sphere. The opportunity for a diplomatic offensive there came with the victory of Fidel Castro's forces in Cuba. At first Castro was not a Communist. A simple guerilla fighter, chiefly in opposition to the regime in power in Havana, he finally accepted Marxism and co-operated with the local Communist Party. In January, 1959 he won control over the entire island. His subsequent policy, most important his nationalization of American property, led to actions against Cuba by the United States, which forced Castro to look abroad for support. In February, 1960 the Soviet Union sent a trade delegation under Anastas I. Mikoyan. It agreed to purchase Cuban sugar and to aid in industrialization. Closer relations were established after the U-2 incident of May, 1960.

Meanwhile, Cuban relations with the United States declined even further. In April, 1961, soon after the inauguration of President Kennedy, the disastrous Bay of Pigs operation occurred. The Central Intelligence Agency organized and trained a group of Cuban refugees in Guatemala. About 1,400 of them were landed in Cuba in the expectation that they could lead in a revolt against Castro. The entire operation was a military and political fiasco.

About the middle of 1962 Khrushchev, it appears, decided upon the most adventurous of his policies. In September the Soviet government announced that it was increasing its arms deliveries to Cuba and that this material was of a defensive nature. By the middle of October American air surveillance over Cuba had discovered that launching pads for missiles were under construction. The action was being accomplished in great haste and without adequate camouflage. It was reported that 24 launching pads for medium range missiles (500 to 1,000 miles) and 16 for intermediate range (1,000 to 2,000 miles) were being built. The American reaction was strong. A blockade was immediately established around Cuba to prevent further deliveries. The United States government made it very clear that a missile attack from Cuba would be answered with a similar action against the Soviet Union. Faced with this dangerous situation, the Soviet leadership backed away. Ships bringing more supplies were brought home, and the missile sites were dismantled. A face-saving formula was then found. The Soviet government announced that the missiles had been for the defense of Cuba; since the United States now gave assurances that it would not attack that island, the weapons could be withdrawn. Khrushchev's biggest gamble thus was ended.

*   *   *   *   *

In October, 1964 Khrushchev was removed from office by Party officials who were evidently tired of his methods and manner, what *Pravda* termed his "hare-brained schemes" and his "bragging and bluster." Although the Cuban fiasco undoubtedly hurt, his failures in internal affairs were even more injurious to his position. In retrospect, nevertheless, his period in power had many bright aspects, particularly in comparison with the previous years of war and national disasters. It was a period of détente, particularly in regard to western Europe. Despite the fact that Khrushchev often used harsh words, his actions were usually careful and even conciliatory. The real danger for all nations, then as later, was the launching of a nuclear war between the Soviet Union and the United States. The Soviet government was thoroughly aware of this fact. Little progress was made, but at least negotiations were commenced for the limitation and control of nuclear weapons. When Khrushchev advanced too far in Cuba, he was willing to step down rather than face a possible catastrophic war.

His real problems, of course, were his supposed friends and allies in the socialist bloc. As the other communist regimes consolidated their power within their own states, they had less need of the Soviet Union. National pride made them resent outside interference; they did not wish to follow directives from Moscow once they could stand on their own feet. The question for the Soviet government was how far these nations could be allowed to follow a separate course. Some, like Yugoslavia, Poland, and Albania, simply wanted to run their own communist system; others, like Hungary, had threatened to adopt western forms. In the suppression of the Hungarian revolution the line was drawn on how far a government could go in choosing its own path in political development.

China was another matter. This country was both a great power and a potential nuclear threat. Not only would she not follow the Soviet lead but she also challenged the predominant position of Moscow in the socialist camp. Her militancy and increasing military strength reopened the dangers of the Siberian position. Moreover, unlike any other power, the Chinese government made open claims to Soviet territory along its frontier, especially in Manchuria and Sinkiang. A competing ideological center was also set up. Asia, not Europe, was to be the focus of international rivalry in the next decade. Here the Soviet Union and China, acting sometimes in concert and at other times in opposition, were to have the pleasant experience of seeing their chief opponent, the United States, drawn into a conflict it could not win.

X

Brezhnev

Khrushchev's successors were to be men of an entirely different character and appearance. The new leadership was composed of Leonid I. Brezhnev as first secretary, Alexei N. Kosygin as chairman of the Council of Ministers, and Nicholas V. Podgorny as president of the Presidium of the Supreme Soviet and thus titular head of state. Gromyko remained as foreign minister, a position which he had held since 1957. None of these men came to play the role that Khrushchev did in foreign or domestic politics. Bureaucrats in appearance, gray and colorless in style, they were nevertheless to prove competent and sober guides to their nation. Abandoning adventurous policies, they sought rather the protection of the *status quo* and of the Soviet world position won in the past. In internal policy a similarly conservative course was pursued. There were no more widely heralded attempts to beat the United States in industrial production, and no impressive gains were made in this sphere after 1961. They also had to meet serious difficulties in agriculture. On the cultural front the same controls were maintained with alternating periods of tightening and relaxation.

Brezhnev, the leading figure in the regime, was born in 1906 in Kamenskoe (now Dneprodzerzhinsk), the son of a metal worker. He studied in Kursk and Moscow, and was first an engineer. Later he devoted himself to party work. He served in the army during the Second World War. He was a member of the Central Committee after 1952 and president of the Presidium of the Supreme Soviet from 1960 to 1964. An experienced man, he appears to have been able to work well within the type of collective leadership then instituted. Under his guidance no attempt was made to change the basic lines in foreign policy that had been followed under Khrushchev. The national interests of the state remained the same. The main issues revolved around the problem of adjusting relations with the rival capitalist power, the United States, and the competing socialist state, China. With the first, the policy of peaceful coexistence was continued, but with continual points of friction in Europe and in Asia. Neighboring China was to prove an increasing source of anxiety because of the excesses in her internal development, in particular during the Cultural Revolution. As in previous years the Soviet government was constantly occupied with the adjustment of its relations with the east European states. Problems connected with India and the eastern Mediterranean continued to play a major role in Soviet policy. The dominating concerns, however, remained the questions in dispute with the United States and China.

RELATIONS WITH THE WESTERN POWERS

Despite their ostensible rivalry in world affairs, the United States and the Soviet Union in the 1960's shared many of the same problems. Most obvious was the fact that the two powers alone could no longer so readily decide the fate of the world between them. The Soviet Union was faced with the outright defection of China from its bloc and the continued resistance of some east European governments, while the United States found its western allies increasingly reluctant to follow policies decided in Washington. France, in fact, removed herself from the American orbit and adopted strongly independent policies. The American involvement in Vietnam showed the extreme hesitancy of the western powers, despite the impressive series of American alliances, to provide real support, either moral or material, when one of their members was in difficulty.

Still basic to the relationship between the Soviet Union and the United States was the fact that they were the great nuclear powers and each had the ability to destroy the other many times over. In both states the burden of armament was absorbing a disproportionate share of their national budgets. Since by 1968 the countries had approached parity in land-based intercontinental missiles, the situation should have been favorable for the negotiation of arms limitation. As before, discussions proceeded very slowly. In the previous section we have seen the acceptance in 1963 of the Limited Nuclear Test Ban. In 1967 a similar agreement was reached prohibiting the testing or emplacement of nuclear weapons in space or on bodies such as the moon. In 1970 the Nuclear Non-Proliferation Treaty went into effect; it was aimed at limiting the number of nations possessing nuclear arms. The value of this agreement was lessened by the fact that neither France nor China would sign it. In November, 1969 American and Soviet representatives began the Strategic Arms Limitation Talks, SALT, in Finland. The goal of these negotiations was to limit the further development of intercontinental missiles and also defensive systems. The slow progress of these discussions was paralleled by the rapid development of even more effective missiles. Most important was the American MIRV (multiple independently targeted reentry vehicle), which allowed one missile to carry as many as six nuclear warheads, a weapon that the Soviet Union succeeded in duplicating and testing by the middle of

1973. Arms limitation and control, as well as other matters, were primary items of discussion during the visit of Richard Nixon, who became president in 1969, to Moscow in May, 1972 and Brezhnev's stay in the United States in June, 1973.

Although the United States and the Soviet Union had certain interests in common, the rivalry of the past continued to be played out in the same areas. In Europe the Soviet emphasis remained that of seeking to remove, if possible, the American military presence and to weaken if not destroy such organizations as NATO and the Common Market, which united the west against the Soviet-organized east European states. In the 1960's two major efforts were made by the Warsaw Pact allies to organize Europe on a strictly regional basis, an act that would exclude American but not Soviet participation. The most ambitious plan was issued from a conference of east bloc powers held in July, 1966 in Bucharest. A strongly anti-American program was formulated in the "Declaration on Strengthening Peace and Security in Europe." The dissolution of both the Warsaw Pact and NATO as military organizations was suggested. The European countries were to be brought into a closer relationship and a general European conference was to be held. The purpose of the action was declared to be the protection of the European *status quo*, the reduction of armaments, and the denial of nuclear weapons to West Germany. The proposal also called for the removal of American troops from Europe, which would, of course, have given military hegemony in the area to the Soviet Union. After the invasion of Czechoslovakia in 1968 few western powers were likely to be attracted by such a conception. In June, 1970 at a conference held in Budapest the Warsaw Pact powers made a much more limited proposal. They now suggested holding an all-European conference to discuss common problems, to which the United States and Canada would be invited. The aim was the reduction of foreign forces in Europe, but not the complete elimination of the American presence.

Although such plans, formulated by the socialist states, could not result in a weakening of the NATO alliances, France's policies in this period did. In April, 1959 Charles de Gaulle became premier, and in September president, of the Fifth French Republic. Obviously smarting under wounds to his vanity inflicted by the United States and Britain during the war, de Gaulle now adopted a policy of seeking to restore France to the position of a great power with an independent policy. He also wished France to acquire her own nuclear arsenal, an aim that he attained in 1960, and he did not wish to be a part of any organization in which France could be outvoted by the "Anglo-Saxons." His practical actions took two directions. In 1963 he vetoed the British entry into the Common Market. At the same time he moved against NATO, which he regarded as dominated by the United States. In July, 1963 he removed the French fleet from NATO control; in July, 1966 France withdrew from co-operation in the NATO command. The headquarters was then removed to Brussels. France henceforth also ceased to co-operate with SEATO.

While drawing away from the United States and Britain, de Gaulle sought instead a policy of closer association with continental countries, in particular with West Germany and her chancellor, Konrad Adenauer. In 1963 the two countries signed a Treaty of Cooperation. The policy was of limited success because of German reluctance to break with the Anglo-Saxon states. De Gaulle also sought better relations with the socialist bloc. In 1964 France recognized the new government of China; in 1966 de Gaulle visited Moscow. Kosygin came to Paris in the same year. Despite these moves, no basic change in policy took place. France was now close to West Germany and would not recognize the German Democratic Republic. Although relations with both Peking and Moscow were friendly, no basis existed for a real diplomatic entente.

Although France's division from her western allies was undoubtedly an advantage for the Soviet Union, the situation had certain basic weaknesses. De Gaulle represented the right in French politics; he had no sympathy with the aims or methods of the strong French Communist Party. In 1968 Paris was swept by student riots, but since they were not Communist-led, the French party did not support them. However, when the movement spread to the factories, the circumstances changed. The Communist Party, which was compelled to support the strikes, now attacked de Gaulle. In the next elections the president replied by using anti-Communist themes. French relations with the Soviet Union were also harmed by the strong reaction in France to the invasion of Czechoslovakia, which will be discussed in the next section. Although de Gaulle stood against dominance by the Americans and the British in European affairs, he certainly was not prepared to see the Soviet Union attain a similar position. In 1969 France stayed in the NATO alliance when it was renewed, although she had ceased participation in the joint military command. In April, 1969 de Gaulle was forced to resign and was followed in office by George Pompidou, a Gaullist, who was both right-wing and anti-Communist.

By this time the Soviet attitude toward West Germany had also changed. After Khrushchev's fall, relations with Bonn had been cool. Maintaining this state as a figure of menace to east Europe had propaganda value for Moscow. At first, therefore, the attacks on this government as militaristic, revanchist, and a tool of the United States continued. There were nevertheless strong reasons for modifying this stand, particularly as West Germany emerged in the 1960's as the industrial giant of Europe. The Soviet Union still had to consider the problems of the status of Berlin and the protection of the interests of the German Democratic Republic. At no time in the next years did the Soviet government retreat on the major issues here. Although after 1966 efforts were made to improve relations, the Soviet position on the German question had not been fundamentally modified. It continued to demand that the Oder-Neisse line be recognized as the frontier of Poland, that the boundaries of the German Democratic Republic be accepted, that Bonn surrender its claim to represent all Germans and to be the single legitimate German government, that nuclear weapons be renounced, and that the position be given up that Berlin belonged to West Germany. As will be seen the change in policy came from Bonn and not from Moscow.

The initiative for improved relations with the other socialist states came primarily from the German side. In 1966 a coalition government, with the Christian Democratic Kurt Kiesinger as chancellor and the Social Democrat Willy Brandt as foreign minister, was formed with the express aim of securing a détente with the east, in particular with Poland and East Germany. In January, 1967 ambassadors were exchanged with Rumania, who was also seeking ties outside her bloc. In October, 1969 Brandt became chancellor in a coalition of Social Democrats and Free Democrats with an eastern policy (*Ostpolitik*) as a major part of his political program. In November, 1969 this government signed the Nuclear Non-Proliferation Treaty and thus in effect renounced nuclear weapons, satisfying a major Soviet demand. In December, 1969 serious conversations were begun in Moscow. In February, 1970 the two nations signed a trade and credit agreement. Among other items this pact provided that the Soviet Union would sell natural gas from Siberia to West Germany, who would in turn provide steel pipes to the Soviet Union. The most important agreement was that concluded in August, 1970. In it the parties renounced the use of force to settle their disputes, and the West German government acceded to most of the Soviet desires. West Germany had already given up the acquisition of nuclear weapons. Now she recognized the territorial *status quo*, including the Oder-Neisse line and the boundaries of the German Democratic Republic. In December, 1970 the West German government signed a similar treaty with Poland. Previously, in March, Brandt had met with Willi Stoph, the East German premier, for the first conversations to be held between the heads of the two German states.

Although the terms were negotiated and the documents signed, Brandt did not present the agreement for ratification to the German parliament until an understanding on Berlin had been reached. In 1969 another crisis had occurred when the West German parliament met in Berlin to elect a president. Again the East Germans and the Soviet Union made strong complaints and harrassed land communications. In March, 1970 the four powers once again started negotiations over the status of the city. In

September, 1971 they reached an agreement that was in general favorable to the Soviet position. In return for an assurance that transit traffic would not be interfered with, the powers agreed that Berlin should not be considered a part of West Germany and that international control should be maintained in the city. The Soviet Union was allowed to open a consulate in the western sector. Details of the agreement were to be worked out between officials of the German Democratic Republic and Bonn. In 1972, with this agreement concluded and after a victory in an election campaign in which the eastern policy again played a major role, Brandt presented his treaties for ratification.

East European Intervention

In Soviet relations with east Europe the chief problem was, as previously stated, the degree of divergence that individual states could be allowed in developing their own national programs. The state whose actions most conformed to Soviet wishes remained the German Democratic Republic, whose continued existence was closely linked to Moscow. In international diplomacy the Soviet government endeavored to gain the recognition of this state as a separate and second German government. In Hungary, Bulgaria, Poland, and Yugoslavia relations with the Soviet Union remained as previously. The Kadar regime in Hungary introduced a policy of gradual liberalization that did not challenge the Soviet position. Similarly in Poland, after food riots in some cities in December, 1970, Gomulka was replaced as party secretary by Edward Gierek. Under his direction similar changes were introduced into Poland. Soviet relations with Tito also stayed on an even keel. Despite the increasing national controversy within Yugoslavia, the Soviet government made no overt attempts to interfere. In March, 1973 the Soviet Peace Committee nominated Tito for the Nobel Peace Prize, demonstrating how far Soviet-Yugoslav relations had changed since the Stalin era.

Despite the fairly smooth and uneventful relationship with East

Germany, Poland, Hungary, and Yugoslavia, the Soviet government was to meet difficulties in two other Warsaw Pact states, Rumania and Czechoslovakia. Relations with Bucharest became even more strained. Rumania had resisted economic integration under COMECON, and reacted similarly to Soviet attempts to further strengthen the Warsaw Pact organization. The Rumanian government did not want its forces closely joined into a general east bloc army. It also openly defied the Soviet Union on the ideological front. In April, 1964, in a direct and bold declaration, the Rumanian government stated the right of socialist governments to independent action.

In international diplomacy Rumania's moves made very clear this attitude of nonconformity. She repeatedly took a position in opposition to Moscow. Her attempt to maintain a more independent stand showed most clearly in her relations with West Germany and China. Rumania's diplomatic rapprochement with Bonn in 1967 has already been mentioned, and even more significant were her attempts to maintain a connection with Peking. In fact, in the growing conflict between the two great centers of world communism, the Rumanian government tried to establish itself as a kind of mediator. It played a similar role in regard to attempts by the United States to improve relations with China. Rumania's policy of independence was also shown during the Egyptian-Israeli war of 1967, when she did not break relations with Tel Aviv, and in 1968, when her participation in the invasion of Czechoslovakia was not asked.

In March, 1965, after the death of Gheorghiu-Dej, Nicolae Ceauşescu succeeded as effective head of party and state. Although maintaining an open attitude in international affairs, as we have seen, within the country he maintained firm control. No challenge to the basic principles of communism or to the rule of the party was allowed. There were few signs of the type of liberalization that have been seen at times in other east bloc countries. The Soviet government thus did not have to fear a Rumanian disavowal of the communist political system; the issue was simply how far a socialist country could go in international affairs in diverging from Soviet policies.

The crisis in Czechoslovakia in 1968, like that in Hungary in 1956, involved a different problem. In the east European states the most dramatic developments in the 1960's occurred in Czechoslovakia. After 1966, enthusiastically supported by Czech and Slovak intellectuals, the government had begun a process of destroying the censorship apparatus and other barriers to free expression. The spring of 1968 marked the height of this process. At this time Antonin Novotny, first secretary of the Czechoslovak Party, was replaced by Alexander Dubček. Censorship was abolished and open criticism and discussion allowed. It seemed almost as if the country were about to move to a two-party system.

The developments within Czechoslovakia were watched with keen attention not only by the Soviet Union but also by the other socialist nations. As the Czech state appeared to be undergoing a real internal reform, the other members of the socialist camp consulted. The East Germans and the Poles protested the new developments; the Rumanians and Yugoslavs approved. Clear warnings were sent to Prague. The Soviet Union now found itself challenged not in the international sphere but on the even more vital internal front. A communist regime was in danger of being abolished in a popular and national movement. Should a more democratic system be established in Czechoslovakia, the effects on the other states of the bloc and on the Soviet Union were easy to foretell. Such changes would also affect the Soviet military position. Because of Czechoslovakia's strategic location, her cooperation was needed if the Warsaw Pact were to function properly. If the Czechoslovak government changed too drastically, the country might withdraw from the alignment, as Hungary had sought to do previously.

With these dangers in mind the Soviet government now decided to act, but this time through the Warsaw Pact and not alone as in 1956. On August 21 Soviet troops accompanied by Polish, East German, Hungarian, and Bulgarian, but not Rumanian, forces entered Prague. Although there was no outright resistance, general signs of public hatred showed the Czech reaction. At the same time almost all the top Czech leaders were arrested and flown to Moscow. The Soviet government allowed Dubček to remain at the head of the government, but he had to accept an agreement modifying the internal reforms and he had to allow Soviet troops to remain in occupation. In April, 1969 he was replaced by Gustav Husak; the previous liberal measures had already been reversed.

As in previous crises, the Soviet government felt the need to issue a theoretical explanation for its actions. The declarations made at this time had widespread implications. In September, 1968 Brezhnev asserted that the Soviet Union had the right to intervene whenever a socialist regime was in danger even if such action were not requested. This statement, which became known as the Brezhnev Doctrine, was the most positive declaration yet made of the Soviet Union's insistence on the right to supervise world socialism. The Soviet government would also decide when intervention was necessary, and it would define the terms of the action. This policy involved, of course, the east European countries, but, even more significant at this time, relations with China.

The Chinese Challenge

The break with China, maintained through the Brezhnev period, remained the crucial issue in Soviet relations with her neighboring states. The explosion of China's first atom bomb in October, 1964 coincided with the fall of Khrushchev; in June, 1967 a hydrogen bomb was tested. The Chinese acquisition of nuclear weapons and their increasing improvement changed the main focus of Soviet foreign policy. For the first time in its modern history the Russian state faced a potential military threat along its entire Chinese border. Not only was the Chinese government now a danger in Asia, but its rival ideology and its links with east European opposition to Soviet direction affected European policy as well.

At first relations tended to improve, but only slightly. In November, 1964, when the Chinese premier Chou En-lai visited

Moscow, Brezhnev made it clear that there would be no basic change in Soviet policy. The Soviet leadership evidently expected an improvement from the Chinese side, either through the adoption of other policies or through a change in the regime. Although in the next months statements of mutual denunciation from both sides filled the press and the air, no overt actions occurred until 1966 when the Great Proletarian Cultural Revolution took place. In order to settle differences between his partisans and the party apparatus, Mao moved into an alliance with the army and the revolutionary youth in order to bring down his opposition. The weapon he used was the Red Guard, formed in spring, 1966, primarily from schoolchildren from poor families. The years 1966 and 1967 witnessed a series of violent actions against Mao's opposition and also against foreigners, mainly in Peking. The Soviet Union in particular was an object of attack; Red Guards demonstrated in front of the Soviet embassy in Peking. In 1966 foreign as well as Chinese students in the capital were sent home. At the same time border incidents occurred along the Manchurian frontier. The provocative actions increased the next year. Red Guards and mobs surrounded the Soviet embassy and harassed the Soviet diplomats continually. These events marked the culmination of direct action in regard to Soviet property. Finally the army intervened to restore order in what had become a chaotic situation.

The Cultural Revolution, marked by rioting and disorder on the part of the youth of the Red Guard, including attacks on Soviet individuals and buildings, could certainly not be approved in Moscow, where *hooliganism* was a particularly bad word. Even though the year 1968 marked the end of the Cultural Revolution, relations between China and the Soviet Union were bound to remain tense. The victory by Mao and the army led to a continuation of deep mutual hostility. Chinese policy remained directed against both the Soviet Union and the United States. It was the opposition who had stood for a moderation of actions in regard to Moscow. In 1969 the conflict resulted in repeated border clashes in Manchuria, Mongolia, and Sinkiang. In

March the Chinese engaged a Soviet force on Damansky Island, Heilungkiang Province, in the Ussuri River. Planes and tanks were used, and it is reported that two to three thousand soldiers were engaged on each side. Clashes also occurred on the Sinkiang frontier in the same year. Both sides strengthened their defenses and made preparations for further encounters.

The Sino-Soviet clash was also reflected in Communist Party affairs in this period. At three major Party conferences the Soviet government unsuccessfully sought to form a united front against the Chinese. The twenty-third congress of the Communist Party was held in Moscow in April, 1966. It was attended by representatives from other friendly parties, but not by delegates from Albania, China, Japan, or New Zealand. In a meeting held in Budapest in February, 1968 the Soviet attempt to secure the expulsion and denunciation of China was rejected by thirteen parties. The Rumanian delegation left the conference in protest. In June, 1969 a meeting attended by seventy-five parties similarly failed to give the Soviet Union full support. Fourteen parties refused to sign the final statement; Albania, China, North Korea, North Vietnam, and Yugoslavia did not attend.

In answer to the Soviet diplomatic and party offensive the Chinese government did what it could to hamper Soviet actions around the world. It took positions simply on the basis of whether they harmed or assisted the opponent. Thus in Europe China sought to develop good relations with a western power, France, and she gave verbal support to the concept of the Common Market. In 1972 the Chinese and British raised their representation to the ambassadorial level. On east European questions the Chinese government denounced the Soviet action in Czechoslovakia and gave strong support to Rumanian and Albanian defiance of the Soviet Union. Close relations continued with Albania, and the denunciations of Tito ceased. In June, 1971 Ceauşescu visited Peking; the Yugoslav foreign minister came later that year. Chinese relations with the Soviet friends, Poland and East Germany, remained cold.

Despite the strong animosity shown in the period of the Cultural Revolution and later, the Soviet Union had no desire to come into an open armed conflict with China. In September, 1969, after Ho Chi Minh's funeral, Kosygin stopped in Peking and saw Chou En-lai. Later, negotiations for an improvement of relations commenced. Thereafter the two countries again exchanged ambassadors. A trade agreement was also signed. This change in atmosphere accompanied a general attempt by China to improve her position in international relations and to come into touch with other countries. The armed clashes with the Soviet Union in 1969 had shown the obvious dangers of isolation. In October, 1970 Canada recognized China. Most important, however, was the beginning of serious conversations with the United States.

By the late 1960's the United States, too, largely because of its involvement in Vietnam, came to see the advantages in an end to the enmity with Peking. The chief issue between the states remained the fate of the Chiang Kai-shek government on Taiwan. Peking had hitherto insisted that any government with which it dealt had to sever its ties with the Chiang regime. It also desired entrance into the United Nations and the expulsion of the nationalist delegation; the United States stood against both these objectives. Moreover, just as the Soviet Union sought the removal of American troops from Europe, China had a similar goal in Asia. Large American forces were in Pacific bases and in Vietnam. The massive American intervention in Vietnam, involving half a million men, inevitably played the major role in the conversations that commenced in the late 1960's.

The Chinese-American rapprochement, once begun, proceeded rapidly. In January and February, 1971, ambassadorial talks in Warsaw, which had commenced previously but were then broken, recommenced. In April the Chinese government invited an American Ping-Pong team and then other groups. In July and October presidential assistant Henry Kissinger came to Peking to prepare for a visit by President Nixon. In October the United States agreed to the admission of Communist China into the United Nations, although she opposed the simultaneous ousting of the Taiwan representation. In February, 1972 Nixon went to Peking on a much-publicized visit. Although little of a concrete nature appears to have come from these discussions, the United States did indicate that at some time it would withdraw from Taiwan and, until then, station only a small force on the island. In May, 1973 liaison offices were opened in Peking and Washington as predecessors to the establishment of regular embassies. The significance of the new situation for the Soviet Union was obvious. The Asiatic balance of power was now triangular. No longer did the Soviet Union and China stand together against the United States and her alliance system. New combinations were now possible on individual issues. China, meanwhile, continued to develop her nuclear arsenal and refused to join in talks on limitation; claims on Soviet territory were maintained.

With the improvement of American relations with China, it could be expected that a similar Soviet move toward Japan would take place. Relations with Japan, however, remained bad. In her Far East policy the Soviet Union had long used that state, as it used West Germany in Europe, as a figure of menace with which to threaten others. Since Tokyo was clearly in the American camp, little hope of a real change could be expected. Nor was the Communist Party a major element in Japan's political scene. Some agreements were made concerning airlines and the exploitation of Siberian resources, but no real progress was made toward a true détente.

SOUTHERN ASIA AND THE NEAR EAST

As in Europe and the Far East, the Soviet Union found itself in opposition in southern Asia and the Near East chiefly to China and the United States. In the major disputes that arose in this area the Soviet government was in conflict with China on the question of India and Pakistan and with the United States over Indochina and the Egyptian-Israeli wars of 1967 and 1973. Of these issues, the fate of Indochina dominated American policy in the 1960's. The question absorbed the attention of the Soviet adversary and greatly affected the world diplomatic situation.

In addition to the Geneva accords on Vietnam, similar agreements had been reached in 1962 in regard to Laos. In this area, as in Vietnam, Khrushchev had preferred to remain outside the events; China had been the main communist power involved. The Brezhnev government reversed this policy. In Laos, according to the treaty arrangements, the Communist Pathet Lao was to join the neutralist government of Souvanna Phouma. However, the United States Central Intelligence Agency now supplied the Meo tribesmen, who had a guerilla army which could be used against the Pathet Lao. In a similar manner, American encouragement was given to the removal of the Pathet Lao from the coalition government. Fighting soon resumed with the main effort made in 1963 in the Plain of Jars. North Vietnamese troops were still in the country. In April, 1964 a military coup reduced Souvanna Phouma personally to a figurehead ruler. A new Pathet Lao offensive brought a great part of the country under Communist control. This situation was to aid the North Vietnamese and the Viet Cong in the civil war in their own country.

Meanwhile, the situation had rapidly deteriorated in South Vietnam, where one of the major problems became the establishment of a viable regime that could deal with the Viet Cong, the Communist guerilla army. The Bao Dai regime had been replaced in October, 1955 with one led by Ngo Dinh Diem. In November, 1963 this government fell with the assassination of its leader and his brother. American intervention, which had commenced during the Kennedy administration, was strongly increased once Lyndon Johnson became president. The policy of the United States remained the containment of communism, this time directed against Chinese influence in Asia.

Apparently at first neither the Soviets nor the Chinese expected a massive American reaction to events in Indochina. The growing strength of the Viet Cong and the later obvious involvement of North Vietnamese troops led, however, to a commensurate increase of American activity. After Congress accepted the Gulf of Tonkin resolution in August, 1964, the American position became firmer. On February 6, 1965, Kosygin arrived in Hanoi; on the next day the United States began the heavy bombing of the North. In 1965–66 the American forces numbered 400,000 men; they rose to over half a million in 1967. Unlike the Korean War, in this battle the United States did not have the backing of the United Nations. Only Australia, New Zealand, South Korea, and Thailand contributed a limited number of troops.

The objective of the United States was the protection of the South Vietnamese government and the maintenance of the balance of power in Asia. The conflicting aim of the North Vietnamese was the unification of the state under their direction and the expulsion of the American forces. Soviet and Chinese policy joined in the support of the North, but parted on important details. The Chinese government wished a protracted war and the draining of American strength. It contributed rice and weapons. The Soviet position was more complicated. Under no circumstances did it want a war with the United States over the Vietnam question nor did it wish to see the south Asian balance upset in China's favor. The North Vietnamese regime resembled Tito's in its independence; it could develop close ties with Peking. Moreover, Soviet aid could best be sent on the Chinese railroads. During the Cultural Revolution these supplies had been interrupted. Relations with Vietnam thus were closely connected with the Sino-Soviet controversies. Throughout the war the Soviet government did, however, continue to send modern and sophisticated military equipment.

Despite the American and North Vietnamese intervention in the South, neither side in the civil war was able to win a clear victory. In the spring of 1970 the war widened to Laos and Cambodia. In March, 1970 Prince Sihanouk of Cambodia was overthrown, and he subsequently fled to Peking. A pro-western government under Lon Nol was then established. American troops at the same time invaded but did not occupy a portion of Cambodia used by the Viet Cong and the North Vietnamese. In February, 1971 South Vietnamese troops unsuccessfully attempted an action in Laos. In May, 1968 negotiations had already begun in Paris between American and North Vietnamese representatives. After protracted debates and bitter discussions, these meetings resulted in January and February, 1973 in a cease-fire for both Vietnam and Laos. As a result of the agreements made at this time, the United States withdrew all its forces from Vietnam.

In Indochina the Soviet and Chinese governments had acted in apparent harmony. In India the conflict came into the open. As previously, in the 1960's the two countries fought over control of the Indian Communist groups. In foreign relations they became identified with opposing sides. In 1965 the quarrel between Pakistan and India over Kashmir again erupted into war. Although the Chinese government gave clear support to Pakistan, the Soviet Union attempted to remain neutral. In January, 1966 it then mediated the dispute; a truce was agreed upon and the previous conditions were re-established.

In the next years the Soviet government attempted to improve its relations with Pakistan to prevent an exclusive Chinese influence. Its chief aim was the maintenance of peace in the area. In August, 1971 a twenty-year treaty of friendship was signed with India. By this time another crisis loomed. An uprising in East Pakistan was suppressed with widespread violence and atrocities; millions of refugees subsequently crossed into India. In December, 1971 war broke out again. The Soviet Union now aided India, but China could not be of real assistance to Pakistan. The resultant Indian victory brought about the creation of a new state, Bangladesh, who could be expected to adopt a friendly policy toward Moscow. The conflict also eliminated for the time being the importance of Pakistan as a military ally. Neither China nor the United States could benefit from this situation.

Although in this conflict the Soviet ally won, in Indonesia both Soviet and Chinese interests were injured. Of the countries of southern Asia Indonesia had at first seemed the best candidate for a communist regime. Its Communist Party was second in strength only to that of China. As a result the Soviet government invested heavily in the friendly regime of Achmed Sukarno. To its intense disappointment Sukarno turned to China. In September, 1965, in an attempt to undermine the opposition of the military to his basically inept rule, Sukarno planned a coup with the Communist Party to overthrow his rivals. This action, of which the Chinese government probably had foreknowledge, was a miserable failure. Afterwards Sukarno remained a powerless and virtually imprisoned figurehead. The victorious military regime proceeded to massacre hundreds of thousands of native Communists, many of them ethnically Chinese. The chances thus faded for the establishment of a communist government in this region, whether under Soviet or Chinese influence.

An active Soviet policy continued in the Near East also, along the lines commenced under Khrushchev. The main point of support remained Egypt under the Nasser government. Although this regime was anticommunist, the situation did not cause problems between the states. In 1965 the Egyptian Communist Party dissolved itself; in return in the same period Communists were released from jail. In 1967 the Soviet involvement in Egypt brought the government into another dangerous crisis. During the spring of that year tension had again mounted with regard to Israel. Nasser now asked the United Nations forces stationed in Sinai to withdraw. He then closed the Gulf of Aqaba to Israeli shipping, cutting off Israel's communications with the Red Sea and the Indian Ocean. In June the Israeli army attacked Egypt, Jordan, and Syria. The quick victory that followed in the Six Day War left Israel in possession of the Sinai Peninsula, the Gaza Strip, the city of Jerusalem, lands on the west bank of the Jordan River, and the Golan Heights in Syria.

Despite its close connection with Egypt, the Soviet government could not give assistance. The hot line with the United States was used for the first time. Relations with Israel were broken by the Soviet Union and the east European bloc coun-

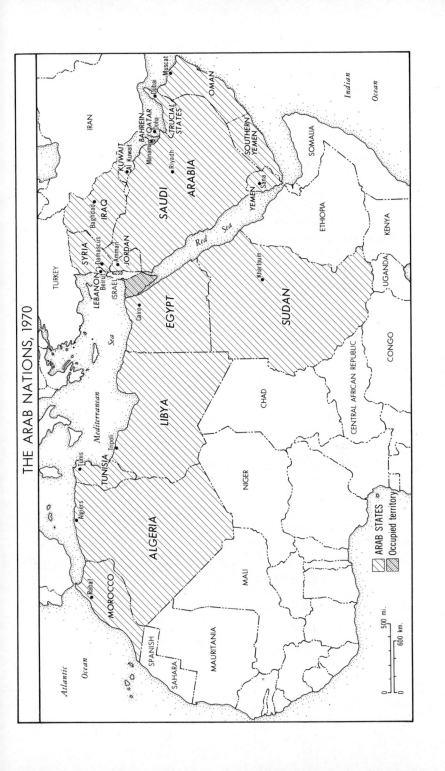

THE ARAB NATIONS, 1970

tries with the exception of Rumania. In the next years, Soviet aid to Egypt continued, but the relationship was not always smooth. In September, 1970 Nasser died; the regime of Anwar Sadat, which followed, was at first friendly. In May, 1971 a fifteen-year Treaty of Friendship was signed, but in the summer of 1972 the Egyptian government asked the Soviet advisors to leave. Relations were not broken, but the ties were less close.

After the Six Day War efforts were continued to secure a peace and a more stable settlement in the area. In November, 1967 the United Nations Security Council adopted the highly ambiguous Resolution 242, which called for Israeli withdrawal from occupied Arab lands and recognition by the Arabian states of Israeli sovereignty "within secure and recognized boundaries." The military buildup in the region continued with both the Soviet Union and the United States providing their sides with increasingly sophisticated weapons. This period also marked the tightening of relations among all the Arab states. In October, 1973 the conflict was renewed with Syrian attacks in the Golan Heights and an Egyptian crossing of the Suez Canal into the Sinai Peninsula. In subsequent counterattacks the Israeli army gained additional Syrian territory and crossed into Egypt. Extensive international intervention resulted in the acceptance by the belligerents of a cease-fire on October 22.

In this crisis neither the Soviet Union nor the United States wished a really dangerous situation to arise. Certain new elements, however, were present in the situation which were of significance for the future. Most obvious was the new-found co-operation among the Arab states not only in the military but also in the economic field. The Arab oil-producing countries, in particular Saudi Arabia under King Faisal, now used their economic power in diplomacy. They announced both cuts in production and a rise in prices, and they linked deliveries to a favorable settlement of the territorial question and the fate of the million and a half Palestinians displaced by the creation and expansion of Israel. Although many countries were affected, Japan with 82 per cent of its oil coming from the Near East, western Europe with 72 per cent, and the United States with a crucial 11 per cent were more drastically damaged than any of the Socialist states. The United States and Holland, the two countries most openly in support of Israel, had a total embargo imposed on them. Peace negotiations to settle the conflict opened in Geneva in December, 1973.

Although the Near East was thus a center of Soviet attention, the Soviet government now, in contrast to the Khrushchev era, attempted no great advances in South America or in sub-Saharan Africa. In the civil war in Nigeria the Soviet Union favored the government forces, while China preferred Biafra, but neither power became really involved. In the Americas the connection with Castro remained, but no enthusiasm was felt for the guerilla-type activities of other South American revolutionaries. The election of the Marxist Salvatore Allende in Chile in September, 1970 and his overthrow by a military coup in September, 1973 were not accompanied by direct Soviet interference.

*   *   *   *   *

Soviet foreign policy in the period after the fall of Khrushchev was not characterized by adventurous policies or new undertakings. The emphasis remained on the maintenance of control over the acquisitions of the past, both in the territorial sense and in the protection of the prime position among the socialist states. Relations with the western European powers were remarkably without incident. The political and military stalemate on the continent continued. The rival military systems remained much as they were despite the increasingly critical attitude showed by some powers toward American policy. West European economic and military unity continued even though de Gaulle attempted to trouble NATO waters. France remained within the alliance, and in 1971 British participation in the Common Market was accepted. Some changes did occur in the relationship of the Soviet Union with West Germany, although they were not of a nature to disturb the balance. In response to German initiatives, the Soviet government did improve its relations with Bonn; in return that regime both renounced nuclear weapons and recognized the boundaries of Poland and the German Democratic Republic. These acts simply confirmed the *status quo* and marked western acceptance of the division of Germany.

The major event in the east bloc was, of course, the occupation of Czechoslovakia by the Warsaw Pact states. This action was designed to protect the Soviet political and military position in the area. As in the case of Hungary in 1956, the Soviet government believed that it could not tolerate the establishment of western forms of representative government within its sphere. The only new element in the affair was the Brezhnev declaration that the Soviet Union had the right to interfere if she considered a socialist regime in danger. Despite the attention given to this pronouncement it was soon made clear that such an intervention would only take place at Soviet convenience. The occupation of Czechoslovakia took place at the time of the height of the Cultural Revolution in China. Although Soviet propaganda ceaselessly denounced Mao's policies as contrary to true Marxist principles, there was no armed intervention in that state. Border clashes of some importance occurred in 1969, but no further moves were made. As in the case of Yugoslavia in 1948, political deviation in the socialist camp was met by attempts to change policy through non-military means.

Throughout the 1960's the most unsettled area of the world was Indochina, a region whose final fate was not clear at the completion of this narrative. In Vietnam it was shown that the greatest military power could not win a clear victory over a national liberation movement backed by a strong native communist regime, which in turn could draw supplies from the Soviet Union and China. In a sense Vietnam suffered the same fate as Spain in the 1930's, when two competing systems tested their military potential. The effects on Soviet policy of the cease-fire in Vietnam and Laos, the new American attempts to approach Peking, and the renewal of the Arab-Israeli military conflict also remain matters for future determination.

Conclusion

ᘒᘒᘒᘒᘒᘒ

Tsarist and Soviet Foreign Policy

In conclusion, it might be well to review the entire span of diplomatic history covered in this survey and to assess the achievements of both the tsarist and the Soviet periods. The purpose of this summary is to account for the undoubted accomplishments of these contrasting regimes and also briefly to compare the advantages enjoyed by each in forwarding the interests of the nation. The emphasis will thus be on the positive aspects of tsarist and Soviet policy; the negative side and the setbacks in foreign relations have been shown in the previous pages.

Viewed in its entirety and not in the light of the final failure in 1917, tsarist diplomacy in the nineteenth century was, under the circumstances, remarkably successful. Not only were the frontiers of the eighteenth century held, but enormous expanses

443

of territory in Asia were added to the empire. At the same time the Russian government played a major role in European affairs, particularly in the Balkans, where the national movements triumphed largely because of Russian aid. Russia's maintenance of her position in Europe and the defense of her extensive frontiers is even more noteworthy when it is remembered how much Russia lagged behind her European competitors in internal development and in those aspects of national life that contribute to military power. In this book less attention has been paid to economic influences on the formulation of foreign policy than to questions of an ideological nature or those pertaining to national interest.

On the wide stage, however, over the entire span of the century between 1814 and 1914 it was indeed the economic development of the Russian nation that determined and limited Russian commitments in foreign policy. Because of the tremendous improvement in the means of transportation and in the weapons of war in the nineteenth century, the military power of a nation became more dependent than before on the technological level and the industrial development of the state. Since the diplomacy of a government depends upon the army that backs it, Russian foreign policy was always strongly influenced by the consciousness of weakness. Although Russian actions as viewed from London appeared aggressive and expansionistic, the responsible Russian statesmen themselves were, in the majority, defense-minded. Their great fear was that a hostile coalition of the powers of the technically superior west would invade their country and destroy their government. These fears were not idle speculation. Western armies entered Russia in 1708, 1812, 1855, and again in 1914, 1918, 1919, 1920, and 1941.

Since Russian policy did not rest on strong foundations, the question naturally arises as to why tsarist Russia was so successful in defending and extending her lands. The answer can perhaps be at least partially found under three general categories: the flexibility of her policy, the division of her potential enemies, and the alliances with Berlin and Vienna. The first consideration, the looseness of policy, is perhaps the most important. Russia had no great ideas on a wide scale; she did not have ambitious plans or grand designs. The conquest of Constantinople most nearly approached such a conception, but certainly Russian national energies were never concentrated on the attainment of this goal. Instead, Russian objectives remained limited and circumscribed. The government seldom sought to continue when faced with formidable obstacles; it concentrated instead on the filling of power vacuums. When strong opposition was encountered, the Russian government either made an agreement or shifted its attention to another place. With three fields—the Far East, Central Asia, and the Balkans—open to their influence, the Russians were able to change to another area when one became closed to them. Russian statesmen usually did not try to knock down stone walls or take perilous risks. In addition, the foreign ministry often failed to control its agents in other countries. Although this situation could be dangerous, it, too, contributed to the flexibility and fluidity of Russian action. When a representative acted against orders but succeeded, the government could accept his gains; when he failed, he could be denounced and his acts disavowed. This method of advance is difficult for other nations to meet since it is hard to determine where a line should be drawn. The British government, in particular, had difficulty countering this slow pressure and basic lack of responsibility in Russian activities in the colonial areas.

The second consideration is the division of the European states and their concentration upon their mutual antagonisms. The powers of Europe remained so involved in asserting their claims against each other that except for a few instances they did not unite against the potentially most powerful state. France and Britain, the western powers, although united by ideology, were divided by their empires and British fear of French continental hegemony. Austria and Prussia, with similar internal systems, were separated over the issue of supremacy in central Europe. When these problems were settled, France and Britain stood against Austria and Germany. Since Russia lacked great plans and after 1814 did not threaten to conquer Europe, there were few bases on which all of the states could join against her. The eastern question alone offered the possibility of supplying such a motive, and the Russian statesmen were well aware of this danger. Therefore, only in the highly unusual circumstances of 1812 did Russia find the continent united against her; and even then, her usual opponent, Britain, at these times stood with her to prevent Europe from falling under the control of a single power.

It is also interesting to note that in the nineteenth century Russia enjoyed a unique advantage among the continental powers in that none of her great neighbors had claims on, or desired parts of, her national territory. In contrast, the other nations—France, Britain, Prussia-Germany, and the Habsburg Empire—all had rich and attractive lands in dispute between them or they quarreled over colonial domains. No major independent state desired a part of Russia; Poland, with enormous historical claims on Russian-held territories, was under foreign domination during this entire period. The Bessarabian question, in dispute between Russia and Rumania, could not influence the policy of the great powers. Moreover, although in comparison with the European powers in general, Russia was a weak and undeveloped state, there was nothing in the Russian lands to attract the booty hunter. Had Russia had the sugar, spice, jewels, or silks of the Orient, she might, because of her military weakness, have fallen victim to imperial movements similar to those that brought about European domination in the Americas, Africa, and the Far East. It was only in the twentieth century that Germany could envisage the Ukraine as a grain-producing dependency and Russia as a source of raw materials in an open colonial relationship with Berlin. Under the National Socialist regime Germany did indeed regard Russia in the same light that the European powers had looked upon their imperial domains in the nineteenth century. Certainly, this attitude toward Russia was at no time apparent in the century between 1814 and 1914.

The third consideration, the policy of alliance with the conservative courts, was as important as the failure of the potential

Russian enemies to combine. For Russia, the principal problem of defense was closely associated with her geography. The center of Russian life and government lay in the general area between St. Petersburg and Moscow, which was not only without natural geographic protection but lay open to invasion from the west through Poland and Germany. In contrast, the peripheral areas of the state were at no time vital to its continued existence. Siberia, Central Asia, the former Polish territories, and even the Ukraine could be sacrificed in time of war; but the existence of Russia itself would be endangered should foreign troops control the crucial area for a protracted period of time. In the peace of 1815 Russia achieved the maximum protection for the center of the state. Poland was in fact under Russian control. Central Europe was split between Prussia, who was a client state, and Austria, who depended upon Russian backing for her domination in Italy and in the Germanic Confederation. The great military threat of the day, France, was defeated and subjected to a military occupation. In the Holy Alliance and the Quadruple Alliance, Russia joined with the powers of Europe to preserve the *status quo*. Although the war combination soon broke, the important association, the alliance with Vienna and Berlin, remained intact for most of the century. When Russia and Austria split over eastern questions, the link with Prussia was always preserved until the dropping of the Reinsurance Treaty by Germany in 1890. The alliance of the three northern courts and the traditional Russian-Prussian link guaranteed the safety of the Russian western border, the most sensitive area of the nation. As long as these agreements held and as long as Prussia herself remained undefeated by another power, Russia was safe from the threat of a direct invasion by a hostile coalition.

The alliance of the conservative powers had the additional advantage for the participants that it formed an ideological unit. The First World War was to justify the belief of the three emperors that their dynasties would stand or fall together. The adoption of the principle of intervention in the affairs of countries threatened by revolution also contributed to the strengthening of the Russian position until the abandonment of the policy after 1856. As long as Russia herself retained a conservative system she had no interest in seeing established on her borders liberal, national states who would offer a threat to her government and to her hold on Poland. Throughout the nineteenth century, to the credit of Russian statesmanship, the relationship between political ideology and foreign policy was recognized: states with similar regimes make the best allies and, conversely, nations with revolutionary governments constitute a danger to their neighbors' internal security. The conservative alliance, thus, shielded Russian autocracy as well as the borders of the state.

During the century Russia made two major efforts to find an alternate combination to that with Berlin and Vienna. The first attempt at an entente with France, in 1856, however, did not signify the dropping of the policy of close collaboration with Prussia. The second, caused by the German refusal to renew the Reinsurance Treaty, resulted in the only lasting major realignment of Russian policy in the century and led to disaster. The formation of the Triple Alliance and the Triple Entente by 1914 signified that Russia no longer had a shield of alliances to cover her western front, but that instead her major national opponent was threatening her at her own front door. The entente also put Russia at the mercy of her allies to an extent not possible in the former arrangement. Britain as an alliance partner would be of little aid in the first period of a war because her strength lay in naval power, and, to use an expression current at the time, the British navy does not run on wheels. Although the French army was indeed strong, it was not equal to Germany's. Moreover, the situation could very easily arise in which the western allies would seek to win the war by sacrificing the Russians. If the western states devoted their efforts to a holding operation on their own territories, the central powers would at some time be forced to invade Russia. The main German efforts would thus be drawn into and consumed on the battlefields of the east. In the two world wars, in which Russia joined with the western powers, this condition did in fact exist. The alliance with Paris and London thus opened the Russian lands to the peril of invasion; the alliance with Berlin and Vienna, in contrast, made such a campaign impossible. The conservative alignment that covered the Russian western frontier for the greater part of the century allowed Russia to move forward on other fronts when the opportunity occurred. In these fields the chief opponent was Britain, and it is the rivalry of these two powers that forms the constant theme of the century. With the possibility of using the center of Europe as a battleground removed, it was very difficult for these two combatants to meet. Britain could not offer dangerous opposition to Russia unless she could obtain a continental ally with an army. The Russian fear of a liberal Prussia in alliance with Britain and supporting the liberation of Poland was, thus, a legitimate concern. Britain could also menace Russia by sailing through the Straits and landing on the Black Sea coast, but the conquest of Moscow from Sebastopol was not a very practical undertaking. An engagement on the Afghan border was similarly difficult. Britain tried to meet the problem by alliance with Japan in Asia and by bolstering Turkey in the Near East, but this policy was not completely successful. Because of the geographic relationship, Russia, with territory on the periphery of the British Empire, was always in a better position to do damage to British interests than her opponent was in to harm her. The relative strength of St. Petersburg explains much of the intense Russophobia that characterized British feeling at various times. Having the unique double standard of the imperial powers, Britain was able to express a great deal of moral indignation over Russian "threats" to India and "aggression" against her overseas possessions. Britain had, of course, no more right in Persia, India, or Afghanistan than did Russia; both had attained their positions by conquest.

Through most of the century the Russo-British antagonism centered at the Straits, where the questions in contest involved not only the control of the waterway but also the domination of the Ottoman government. Russian policy in regard to the Porte followed the pattern adopted in relations with weaker states or those on the verge of dissolution in other areas. Three courses of action were open: Russia could conquer the territory and destroy the regime in power; she could seek to dominate the entire state by control of the government; or she could come to terms with other states and partition the land. These possibilities also held true in Poland, Central Asia, and the Far East. In the nineteenth century, the first alternative, the outright annexation of the Ottoman Empire, was not a practical possibility because the other powers would oppose such a major change in the European balance of power. Undoubtedly the Russian government would have gratefully accepted Constantinople (and the entire empire for that matter) if it had been presented on a platter, but the prize was not worth risking Russia's national existence. The question was repeatedly discussed during the century, but the dangers involved in every instance caused the rejection of the idea. As a result, the remaining two alternatives became the basis of her action. When it was possible for her to dominate in Constantinople, she supported the integrity of the empire. When another power threatened her position, she called for the partition of the empire either on the basis of a division between the great powers or, later, of increased territories and rights for the new Balkan nations.

The significance of the Near East in Russian historical tradition and its effect on policy have also been discussed. It cannot be too strongly emphasized that here considerations that had little to do with Russian national interest had as much influence as those that related to questions of Russian power. Constantinople was not only a strategic piece of real estate but also the former capital of the Byzantine Empire, of which the tsar felt himself the heir, and the religious center for the Orthodox faith. To the hold of historical tradition and faith was later added the additional bond of the brotherhood of the Slavs. These irrational concepts had at all times an immense attraction for the sections of the Russian public that were in a position to influence policy. It was, thus, very difficult for the Russian government to accept compromise solutions in this area.

It has been much debated whether the Russian government

was primarily influenced in its actions in the Balkans by ideological or power considerations. A clear answer is not possible because of the numerous contradictions apparent in the Russian actions. It was undoubtedly through Russian military aid that the small nations were freed from Ottoman control. Although within Russia the government followed a policy of Russification, nationalism was supported abroad even when certain of its principles conflicted with those of Russian autocracy. In return for her assistance Russia received very little. The Balkan peoples themselves were caught between their need for her aid and their dislike of her interference in their affairs. Throughout the century Russian policy wavered between sacrificing Russia's own interests for the Balkan peoples and using these same nations for the attainment of Russian aims. Although the confusion in motivation was always apparent, the Russian government did at all times understand the dangers these issues held for her relations with other powers. It was here that her conservative ally, Austria, could join with her opponent, Britain, to form the base of a dangerous coalition.

In summary, it can therefore be said that in foreign policy the Russian government did attain its major objectives before 1914. Although it was not at all times uniformly successful, the Russian state was adequately defended, and major conflicts, which could involve the existence or the integrity of the empire, were avoided. Russian policy remained responsive and resilient. No attempt was made to inaugurate great programs of conquest; advances were made when the road was clear. The two conflicts Russia lost, the Crimean War and the Russo-Japanese War, were humiliations, but they did not result in a real reduction of national power. Moreover, in foreign affairs Russia learned lessons from her defeats and sought to rectify her mistakes. The nineteenth century thus provided a firm foundation for the further increases in territory and the relative improvement in power status achieved by the Soviet Union by the middle of the twentieth century.

These positive judgments concerning the tsarist period may

also be applied to the Soviet era. It is necessary, however, to make a sharp division between the years 1917 to 1945 and 1945 to the present. For both Europe and the Soviet Union the Second World War marks a far more decisive break in the continuity of diplomatic history than did the earlier conflict. Despite the catastrophic nature of the events of 1914 to 1918 and the subsequent radical political changes in the Russian nation, the European state system continued to function much as it had in the previous centuries. Undoubtedly certain great alterations had occurred in the map of Europe. The Habsburg Empire and the Ottoman Empire disappeared; Germany and the Russian (now the Soviet) state were greatly reduced in power. Nevertheless, France, Britain, Italy, Germany, and to an extent the Soviet Union continued to play the old game of great power politics. Europe remained the center and the pivot of the world. British, French, Dutch, and Belgian colonies spanned its surface. In this constellation of powers the position of the new Soviet regime was at first dangerous. The conclusion of the First World War and the civil conflict left the Russian lands in the weakest condition of any period covered in this discussion. Moreover, the Soviet Union did not participate in any of the great European conferences on the peace arrangements, and it lost great stretches of territory previously under tsarist control. Under these circumstances she could not play a strong and decisive role in international affairs; after 1918 she had to concentrate, as she did after 1856 and 1905, on internal affairs. Despite the hardships of these years, in the 1930's the Soviet Union accomplished a level of industrialization and rearmament adequate to meet the foreign invasion of 1941.

In 1945 the Soviet Union as well as the other powers faced a vastly different situation. The war had shattered the European state system and the bases of past centuries of European diplomacy. The relative strengths of the states had shifted, and the development of nuclear weapons had affected the conduct of war and of international relations. In the sphere of great power diplomacy the Soviet Union had reversed the conditions of 1918 and had again attained the predominant position of 1814. However, in contrast to that period, the Soviet leaders faced no real opposition from within Europe. The most abrupt collapse in power was that now suffered by the British Empire. From a historical point of view one of the victories of the Russian state in the Second World War was the humbling of her great foe of the previous century. French influence, drastically weakened by the humiliating defeat of 1940, could also be discounted. The central European area, too, could offer no resistance to Soviet pre-eminence. The German lands were again divided; no equivalent of Prussia remained. The east European lands were under Soviet military domination.

With the collapse of the western European states a new element entered the European scene. The United States, who emerged from the war as the single greatest military power, took up the role previously played by Britain. She now became the organizer of a coalition to prevent the continent from falling under the domination of one power. The United States assumed the former British position not only in Europe but all around the globe. In almost every area where the tsarist government had formerly met British influence, the Soviet Union now confronted the United States—in Japan, in the buffer zones of Greece, Turkey, Iran, and Pakistan, and in the eastern Mediterranean. The aim of American actions became, like the British before, to maintain a balance and to prevent the extension of Russian influence. In fact, after 1945 the chief areas of conflict were to lie in the former colonial and backward areas, rather than in Europe, where a military and diplomatic balance was soon established. These differences in the nature of the opposition and in the location of the chief points in dispute well illustrate the change in direction after 1945. Whereas Europe and the European powers were the main focus of attention for tsarist Russia, after the Second World War the non-European governments of the United States and China presented the main opposition to Soviet goals. Europe became only one of the areas of Soviet interest.

Of the three elements that characterized tsarist successes, the flexible policies of the government, the division of potential enemies, and the favorable alliance system maintained through most of the nineteenth century, the first two, flexibility of policy and division of opponents, hold for the Soviet period too. Like their predecessors, the Soviet leaders were adept at adjusting their policies to meet the realities of any situation. They, too, concentrated on filling political vacuums; they did not attempt to achieve impossible goals or to risk great dangers. Their acquisition of dominance in eastern Europe came when their armies followed a retreating German power; when they came up against resistance in the west, they stopped. They intervened to put down opposition movements in the weak states of Hungary and Czechoslovakia, but they hesitated to act in Yugoslavia or China, whose governments would have fought. In the most adventurous policy, the emplacement of missiles in Cuba, the Soviet government simply reversed its actions when it became obvious that they were creating a truly dangerous international situation.

The second factor, the division of possible opponents, was certainly of the greatest aid in the first years of the Soviet regime. If Europe had been united between the wars, the Bolshevik revolution would have faced real peril. Instead the continent fell into two camps, divided chiefly by issues arising from the Versailles settlement. In the 1930's the breach continued in the rivalry between the western powers and Germany and Italy. A very difficult situation for the Soviet government did indeed arise in 1940 and 1941. However, despite its impressive victories Nazi Germany could not lead a true European coalition or conquer the Soviet lands with its own forces. The Nazi doctrines carried the seeds of their own destruction. Moreover, once Germany invaded Soviet territory, both Britain and the United States, though they were never in sympathy with Soviet doctrines, nevertheless came to the aid of the Russian state.

After the war, it is true, the world divided into two camps. However, with time the western alliance developed divisions. Even more important, the United States never had either the will or the ambition to launch an offensive action against the Soviet

Union. The nightmare of the nineteenth century, the invasion by a coalition of powers, was not a possibility at this time. Even when a sharp conflict developed with Peking, the Soviet government did not have to worry that the NATO alliance would join with China to attack the common opponent. The divisions between Communist China, the United States, Taiwan, and Japan precluded co-operation in Asia even when all of these states shared the same attitude toward the extension of Soviet power.

Although the Soviet government had the advantage of a divided opposition, it did not share with the tsarist regime the protection of favorable alliance combinations. In fact, Soviet isolation, particularly in the 1920's and 1930's, constituted a major danger in its international position. The two periods of co-operation with Germany, the Rapallo policy and the Nazi-Soviet collaboration from 1939 to 1941, in no sense marked a reconstitution of the former close association between St. Petersburg and Berlin. In the same manner the French alliance of 1934 contrasted sharply with the real partnership of the 1890's. In the post-war period this condition was continued. The Warsaw Pact did not represent a combination of states in any way equivalent to the NATO alliance. The possibility seems slight that any kind of military arrangement will be made with China, the only other great communist power, in the near future.

Despite this negative consideration, the Soviet Union, particularly since the Second World War, has enjoyed two advantages not shared by the tsarist government—a revolutionary ideology and an economic system that can support a high level of armament. In sharp contrast to the previous regime, after 1917 the Soviet state had an exportable doctrine. Tsarist Russia usually supported some form of constitutional government when it had influence in another state. Moreover, the communist system gave the Soviet government instruments of foreign policy not previously available. Parallel with the regular channels of communication with other countries, it could use the party organizations abroad as a means of influencing a wider section of the population than could be reached through normal means. At first, the existence of this revolutionary doctrine and the Comintern was probably a negative factor in Soviet foreign policy; more people were frightened than attracted by the revolutionary side of Soviet activities. After the war, however, it offered many positive advantages. The new socialist states in east Europe, with both regular and party connections to Moscow, were more easily influenced. The existence of large communist parties in France and Italy, despite serious doctrinal disputes, was often a point of support for Soviet policies. In the former colonial areas communist doctrines and the organizational apparatus offered viable political alternatives in backward regions with corrupt governments. Although here the record has not been clear, the advantages over tsarist Russia, which had no similar political program, are obvious.

Not only did the Soviet Union possess a revolutionary doctrine but she never made the mistake of sacrificing state interests to it. After the early failure of the revolution to spread, it is hard to find an instance when the Soviet government subordinated its requirements as a great power to its ideology. Communism served the Soviet Union, not vice versa. In the 1930's Comintern policy called for the subordination of all other considerations to the protection of her position as the only communist government. In the post-war years she attempted to preserve this emphasis. Other socialist regimes were expected to follow the Soviet model and to defer to Soviet advice, even when such action was harmful to their own development. The entire attitude toward ideological deviation served the interest of Soviet state power.

The second advantage, the economic, is of equal significance. Tsarist Russia did not have the economic base for a military system that could compete with the west. By 1914 she was deeply in debt to France for financial and military assistance designed to remedy this weakness. In contrast, the Soviet system and the program of industrialization provided a foundation for the support of large armies and the development of modern, expensive, and highly sophisticated weapons. The economy could support this military emphasis, and the Soviet leadership, like the American, was willing to invest heavily in this sphere.

We have seen the steady progress of Russian national power under both an autocratic tsarist regime and communist rule. Although frequent setbacks were encountered, the state did win control of and subsequently hold a large section of the earth's surface. It also acquired the economic and military capacity to defend this territory. Moreover, by the 1970's many of the national dangers of the past had been dispersed. No continental coalition or great military nation existed in Europe; Asia remained divided. The Soviet Union's chief opponent, the United States, had found its world diplomatic position weakened by the disillusioning conflict in Indochina. In possession of a great buffer zone in eastern and central Europe and equipped with nuclear weapons, the Soviet state enjoyed the most secure position in its history.

¿¿¿¿¿¿

Suggested References

The following list consists of selected books in English that provide further information on the periods of tsarist and Soviet foreign policy discussed in this book. No attempt has been made to assemble a complete bibliography of all the excellent studies available on Russian and general European diplomacy for the period. For further references the reader should consult the two basic bibliographies edited by Paul Horecky, *Basic Russian Publications* (Chicago: University of Chicago Press, 1962) and *Russia and the Soviet Union: A Bibliographic Guide to Western-Language Publications* (Chicago: University of Chicago Press, 1963); and Thomas T. Hammond, editor, *Soviet Foreign Relations and World Communism* (Princeton: Princeton University Press, 1965).

Tsarist Russia

Anderson, M. S. *The Eastern Question*. London: MacMillan, 1966.
Chevigny, Hector. *Russian America: The Great Alaskan Venture, 1741-1867*. New York: Viking Press, 1965.
Churchill, R. P. *The Anglo-Russian Convention of 1907*. Cedar Rapids, Iowa: Torch Press, 1939.
Dallin, David J. *The Rise of Russia in Asia*. New Haven: Yale University Press, 1949.
Florescu, Radu R. W. *The Struggle against Russia in the Roumanian*

Principalities, 1821-1854. Munich: Societas Academica Dacoromana, 1962.

Giers, N. K. *The Education of a Russian Statesman: The Memoirs of N. K. Giers.* Edited by Charles and Barbara Jelavich. Berkeley: University of California Press, 1962.

Gleason, John H. *The Genesis of Russophobia in Great Britain.* Cambridge: Harvard University Press, 1950.

Grimsted, Patricia Kennedy. *The Foreign Ministers of Alexander I, 1801-1825.* Berkeley: University of California Press, 1969.

Helmreich, E. C. *The Diplomacy of the Balkan Wars.* Cambridge: Harvard University Press, 1938.

Henderson, G. B. *Crimean War Diplomacy.* Glasgow: Jackson, 1947.

Hopwood, Derek. *The Russian Presence in Syria and Palestine.* Oxford: Clarendon Press, 1969.

Hsu, Immanuel. *The Ili Crisis.* Oxford: Clarendon Press, 1966.

Jelavich, Barbara. *Russia and the Rumanian National Cause, 1858-1859.* Bloomington: Indiana University Press, 1959.

——. *Russia and the Greek Revolution of 1843.* Munich: Oldenbourg, 1966.

——. *The Ottoman Empire, the Great Powers, and the Straits Question, 1870-1887.* Bloomington: Indiana University Press, 1973.

Jelavich, Charles. *Tsarist Russia and Balkan Nationalism.* Berkeley: University of California Press, 1958.

Kaplan, Herbert H. *Russia and the Outbreak of the Seven Years' War.* Berkeley: University of California Press, 1968.

Kazemzadeh, Firuz. *Russia and Britain in Persia, 1864-1914.* New Haven: Yale University Press, 1968.

Lang, D. M. *The Last Years of the Georgian Monarchy, 1658-1832.* New York: Columbia University Press, 1957.

Langer, William L. *The Franco-Russian Alliance.* Cambridge: Harvard University Press, 1930.

Lederer, Ivo, ed. *Russian Foreign Policy.* New Haven: Yale University Press, 1962.

Leslie, R. F. *Reform and Insurrection in Russian Poland, 1856-65.* London: Athlone Press, 1963.

Lenson, George A. *The Russian Push Toward Japan.* Princeton: Princeton University Press, 1959.

————. *The Russo-Chinese War.* Tallahassee, Fla.: The Diplomatic Press, 1967.

Lobanov-Rostovsky, A. *Russia and Europe, 1789-1825.* Durham, N.C.: Duke University Press, 1947.

————. *Russia and Asia.* Ann Arbor, Mich.: George Wahr, 1951.

————. *Russia and Europe, 1825-1878.* Ann Arbor, Mich.: George Wahr, 1954.

MacKenzie, David. *The Serbs and Russian Panslavism, 1875-1878.* Ithaca: Cornell University Press, 1967.

Madariaga, Isabel de. *Britain, Russia, and the Armed Neutrality of 1780.* New Haven: Yale University Press, 1962.

Malozemoff, A. *Russian Far Eastern Policy, 1881-1904.* Berkeley: University of California Press, 1958.

Medlicott, W. N. *The Congress of Berlin and After.* London: Methuen, 1938.

Mosely, Philip E. *Russian Diplomacy and the Opening of the Eastern Question in 1838 and 1839.* Cambridge: Harvard University Press, 1934.

Mosse, W. E. *The European Powers and the German Question, 1848-1871.* Cambridge: Cambridge University Press, 1958.

————. *The Rise and Fall of the Crimean System, 1855-71.* London: Macmillan, 1963.

Oliva, L. Jay. *Misalliance: A Study of French Policy in Russia during the Seven Years' War.* New York: New York University Press, 1964.

Pavlovich, Stevan K. *Anglo-Russian Rivalry in Serbia, 1837-1839: The Mission of Colonel Hodges.* Hague: Mouton, 1961.

Petrovich, Michael Boro. *The Emergence of Russian Panslavism, 1856-1870.* New York: New York University Press, 1956.

Pierce, Richard A. *Russian Central Asia, 1867-1917.* Berkeley: University of California Press, 1960.

————. *Russia's Hawaiian Adventure, 1815-1817.* Berkeley: University of California Press, 1965.

Puryear, V. *England, Russia and the Straits Question, 1844-1856.* Berkeley: University of California Press, 1931.

————. *Napoleon and the Dardanelles.* Berkeley: University of California Press, 1951.

Romanov, Boris A. *Russia in Manchuria, 1892-1906.* Translated by Susan Wilbur Jones. Ann Arbor, Mich.: J. W. Edwards, 1952.

Rupp, G. *A Wavering Friendship: Russia and Austria, 1876-1878.* Cambridge: Harvard University Press, 1941.

Russian Diplomacy in Eastern Europe. Introduction by Henry Roberts. New York: King's Crown Press, 1963.

Saul, Norman E. *Russia and the Mediterranean.* Chicago: University of Chicago Press, 1970.

Smith, C. Jay. *The Russian Struggle for Power, 1914-1917.* New York: Philosophical Library, 1956.

Stavrou, George Theofanis. *Russian Interests in Palestine, 1882-1914.* Thessaloniki: Institute for Balkan Studies, 1963.

Stojanovic, Mihailo D. *The Great Powers and the Balkans, 1875-1878.* Cambridge: Cambridge University Press, 1939.

Sumner, B. H. *Russia and the Balkans, 1870-1880.* Oxford: Clarendon Press, 1937.

———. *Tsardom and Imperialism in the Far East and Middle East, 1880-1914.* London: Humphrey Milford, n.d.

Temperley, Harold. *The Crimea.* London: Longmans, 1936.

Thaden, Edward C. *Russia and the Balkan Alliance of 1912.* University Park: Pennsylvania State University Press, 1965.

Vucinich, Wayne. *Serbia between East and West.* Stanford: Stanford University Press, 1954.

White, John Albert. *The Diplomacy of the Russo-Japanese War.* Princeton: Princeton University Press, 1964.

Zabriskie, Edward H. *American-Russian Rivalry in the Far East, 1895-1914.* Philadelphia: University of Pennsylvania Press, 1946.

The Soviet Union

Angress, Werner T. *Stillborn Revolution: The Communist Bid for Power in Germany, 1921-1923.* Princeton: Princeton University Press, 1963.

Beloff, Max. *The Foreign Policy of Soviet Russia, 1929-1941.* 2 vols. New York: Oxford University Press, 1949.

Borkenau, Franz. *World Communism: A History of the Communist International.* Ann Arbor: University of Michigan Press, 1962.

Brandt, Conrad. *Stalin's Failure in China, 1924-1927.* Cambridge: Harvard University Press, 1958.

Braunthal, Julius. *History of the International.* 2 vols. New York: Praeger, 1967.

Browder, Robert P. *The Origins of Soviet-American Diplomacy.* Princeton: Princeton University Press, 1953.

Brzezinski, Zbigniew K. *The Soviet Bloc.* Cambridge: Harvard University Press, 1967.

Cattell, David T. *Communism and the Spanish Civil War.* Berkeley: University of California Press, 1955.

———. *Soviet Diplomacy and the Spanish Civil War.* Berkeley: University of California Press, 1957.

Dallin, David J. *Soviet Russia and the Far East.* New Haven: Yale University Press, 1948.

———. *Soviet Foreign Policy after Stalin.* New York: J. B. Lippincott Co., 1961.

Deane, John R. *The Strange Alliance: The Story of Our Efforts at Wartime Cooperation with Russia.* New York: The Viking Press, 1947.

Djilas, Milovan. *Conversations with Stalin.* New York: Harcourt, Brace and World Inc., 1962.

Feis, Herbert. *Churchill, Roosevelt, Stalin.* Princeton: Princeton University Press, 1957.

———. *Between War and Peace: The Potsdam Conference.* Princeton: Princeton University Press, 1960.

Fischer, Louis. *The Soviets in World Affairs, 1917-1929.* 2 vols. Princeton: Princeton University Press, 1951.

———. *Russia's Road from Peace to War: Soviet Foreign Relations, 1917-1941.* New York: Harper and Row, 1969.

Fischer, Ruth. *Stalin and German Communism.* Cambridge: Harvard University Press, 1948.

Freund, Gerald. *Unholy Alliance: Russo-German Relations from the Treaty of Brest-Litovsk to the Treaty of Berlin.* New York: Harcourt, Brace, 1957.

Griffith, William E. *Albania and the Sino-Soviet Rift.* Cambridge: M.I.T. Press, 1963.

———. *The Sino-Soviet Rift.* London: Allen and Unwin, 1964.

Hilger, Gustav, and Meyer, Alfred G. *The Incompatible Allies: A Memoire-History of German-Soviet Relations, 1918-1941.* New York: The Macmillan Company, 1953.

Hinton, Harold C. *China's Turbulent Quest.* Bloomington: Indiana University Press, 1972.

Kennan, George F. *Soviet-American Relations, 1917-1920.* 2 vols. Princeton: Princeton University Press, 1956–1958.

————. *Russia and the West under Lenin and Stalin.* Boston: Little Brown, 1961.

————. *Soviet Foreign Policy.* Princeton: D. Van Nostrand Co., 1960.

LaFeber, Walter. *America, Russia and the Cold War, 1945-1971.* New York: Wiley and Sons, 1972.

Lowenthal, Richard. *World Communism.* New York: Oxford University Press, 1966.

McKenzie, Kermit E. *Comintern and World Revolution, 1928-1943: The Shaping of a Doctrine.* New York: Columbia University Press, 1964.

McNeill, William H. *America, Britain and Russia: Their Cooperation and Conflict, 1941-1946.* New York: Oxford University Press, 1954.

Morris, Bernard S. *International Communism and American Policy.* New York: Atherton Press, 1968.

Pipes, Richard. *The Formation of the Soviet Union: Communism and Nationalism, 1917-1923.* Cambridge: Harvard University Press, 1954.

Rosser, Richard F. *An Introduction to Soviet Foreign Policy.* Englewood Cliffs, N.J.: Prentice-Hall, Inc., 1969.

Rubinstein, Alvin Z. *The Foreign Policy of the Soviet Union.* New York: Random House, 1972.

Seton-Watson, Hugh. *From Lenin to Khrushchev.* New York: Praeger, 1960.

Shulman, Marshall D. *Stalin's Foreign Policy Reappraised.* New York: Atheneum, 1965.

Syrop, Konrad. *Spring in October: The Polish Revolution of 1956.* New York: Praeger, 1958.

Tang, Peter S. H. *Russian and Soviet Policy in Manchuria and Outer Mongolia, 1911-1931.* Durham, N.C.: Duke University Press, 1959.

Thompson, John M. *Russia, Bolshevism, and the Versailles Peace.* Princeton: Princeton University Press, 1966.

Triska, Jan F., and Finley, David D. *Soviet Foreign Policy.* New York: Macmillan, 1968.

Ulam, Adam B. *Tito and the Cominform.* Cambridge: Harvard University Press, 1952.

————. *Expansion and Coexistence: The History of Soviet Foreign Relations, 1917-1967.* New York: Praeger, 1968.

————. *The Rivals: America and Russia since World War II*. New York: Viking, 1971.

Vali, Ferenc A. *Rift and Revolt in Hungary*. Cambridge: Harvard University Press, 1961.

Wandycz, Piotr S. *Soviet-Polish Relations, 1917-1921*. Cambridge: Harvard University Press, 1969.

Warth, Robert D. *The Allies and the Russian Revolution: From the Fall of the Monarchy to the Peace of Brest-Litovsk*. Durham, N.C.: Duke University Press, 1954.

————. *Soviet Russia in World Politics*. New York: Twayne Publishers Inc., 1964.

Weinberg, Gerhard. *Germany and the Soviet Union, 1939-1941*. Leiden: Brill, 1954.

Wesson, Robert G. *Soviet Foreign Policy in Perspective*. Homewood, Ill.: Dorsey Press, 1969.

Wheeler-Bennett, J. W. *The Forgotten Peace: Brest-Litovsk, March, 1918*. New York: Macmillan, 1939.

White, John A. *The Siberian Intervention*. Princeton: Princeton University Press, 1950.

Wolfe, Thomas W. *Soviet Power and Europe, 1945-1970*. Baltimore: Johns Hopkins Press, 1970.

Zagoria, Donald S. *The Sino-Soviet Conflict, 1956-1961*. New York: Atheneum, 1969.

Zeman, Z. A. B. *Prague Spring*. London: Chatto and Windus, 1969.

Zinner, Paul E. *Revolution in Hungary*. New York: Columbia University Press, 1962.

Index